RANDOM
HOUSE
LARGE
PRINT

PLAYING WITH FIRE

PLAYING WITH FIRE

THE 1968 ELECTION
AND THE TRANSFORMATION
OF AMERICAN POLITICS

LAWRENCE O'DONNELL

RANDOM HOUSE
LARGE PRINT

Published in the United States of America by
Random House Large Print in association with Penguin Press,
an imprint of Penguin Random House LLC, New York.

Cover design by Eric White
Cover photograph: Hulton Archive / Stringer / Getty Images

The Library of Congress has established a Cataloging-in-Publication record for this title.

ISBN: 978-0-5254-9883-4

www.randomhouse.com/largeprint

FIRST LARGE PRINT EDITION

Printed in the United States of America

10 9 8 7 6 5 4 3 2 1

This Large Print edition published in accord with the standards of the N.A.V.H.

Photo credits

Insert page 1 (top): Cecil Stoughton/John F. Kennedy Presidential Library and Museum, Boston; 1 (bottom): A. Y. Owen/The LIFE Images Collection/Getty Images; 5 (bottom) (top), 2, 3, 8 (bottom), 16 (bottom): Bettmann/Getty Images; 2 (bottom): Ed Farrand/The Boston Globe/Getty Images; 4: AP Photo/Bob Daugherty; 5 (top): Preservation and Special Collections Department, University Libraries, University of Memphis; 6: Indianapolis Recorder Collection, Indiana Historical Society; 7: AP/Shutterstock/REX; 8 (top), 14, 15 (top), 16 (top): Courtesy of CSU Archives/Everett Collection; 9: Bill Eppridge/The LIFE Picture Collection/Getty Images; 10 (top): Louis Liotta/New York Post Archives/Getty Images; 10 (bottom): Yoichi Okamoto/Lyndon Baines Johnson Library and Museum; 11 (top), 12 (bottom), 13: AP Photos; 11 (bottom): Grey Villet/The LIFE Picture Collection/Getty Images; 12 (top): ABC Photo Archives/Getty Images; 15 (bottom): Courtesy of Kentucky Photo Archive

For Elizabeth

CONTENTS

PLAYING
WITH FIRE

SEIZING THE MOMENT

Richard Nixon was in a makeup chair when he met Roger Ailes. Maybe it was the makeup chair that set Ailes off. He was looking at the man who might have been president now if he had just sat in the makeup chair CBS offered him in Chicago before the first televised presidential debate in American history. Nixon had ignored the network's makeup artist and used a drugstore product called Lazy Shave to cover his heavy five o'clock shadow. Nixon once said, "I can shave within 30 seconds before I go on television and still have a beard." The day after the debate, the **Chicago Daily News** ran the headline WAS NIXON SABOTAGED BY TV MAKEUP ARTISTS? Richard Daley, the all-powerful Democratic mayor of Chicago, said, "My God, they've embalmed him before he even died." Nixon lost the election to John F. Kennedy by two-tenths of 1 percent of the vote, 49.7 percent to 49.5 percent. In an election that close, every mistake matters. A mistake like not getting the makeup right was the kind of thing that infuriated Ailes.

Now, seven years later, Ailes was meeting Nixon for the first time, in the makeup room of **The Mike Douglas Show**. At age twenty-six, Ailes looked like an assistant, but he was the boss, the executive producer of the show. And Nixon was once again a presidential candidate in what was beginning to look like a crowded field coveting the 1968 Republican nomination.

Ailes wanted Nixon to be president, and he knew the most powerful force blocking Nixon's path to the White House was television. To win the White House in the 1960s you had to understand and respect the power of television. Ailes knew that one of Nixon's potential rivals for the Republican nomination understood everything about television: Ronald Reagan, the former film and TV actor. Ailes wondered what Nixon had learned about TV since the makeup disaster of the 1960 campaign.

Sitting in the makeup chair, Nixon offhandedly mentioned to Ailes how silly it felt to try to reach voters by appearing on an afternoon talk show like this one instead of a news show like **Meet the Press**. **The Mike Douglas Show** was targeted at housewives and usually populated by B-list showbiz celebrities. In response, Ailes instantly rattled off a list of every bad move Nixon had ever made on TV. It was a long list. Ailes was a teenager when he had seen some of these things. This was not the way people talked to former vice president Richard Milhous Nixon. There was none of the deference Nixon had been accustomed to for decades. And he loved it.

Nixon made Ailes an offer he couldn't refuse: instead of trying to make Mike Douglas America's biggest afternoon TV star, make Richard Nixon America's next president.

With Ailes on the media team, the Nixon campaign was ready to make the move from being the worst TV campaign to the best. "We're going to build this whole campaign around television," Nixon told his media team. "You boys just tell me what to do and I'll do it."

Roger Ailes's career in Republican politics, which included every day he ran Fox News, turned out to be longer than Richard Nixon's. Ailes became more influential in Republican politics than Nixon ever was. We have reason to wonder who would be president today if Richard Nixon had not provoked Roger Ailes in **The Mike Douglas Show** makeup room. Such are the seeds that were planted in American politics in the 1968 presidential campaign.

"RUN, BOBBY, RUN!"

Bobby was a natural on television. In 1967, he was the only potential presidential candidate who could charm a TV audience just by being himself. All he needed was his smile. Bobby was the Elvis of American politics—the only politician who didn't need a last name to identify him. But his last name was everything.

It was Bobby Kennedy's last name that made every potential candidate fear him. As the field of candidates began to take shape in 1967, every campaign calculation depended on Bobby even when he showed no signs of wanting to run, even when he told people he wasn't going to run.

President Lyndon Baines Johnson feared Bobby to the point of obsession. Johnson thought Bobby was the only one who could do the unthinkable—challenge the incumbent president's grip on the Democratic nomination. Johnson was sure that Bobby was the only Democrat who might dare to run against him. He was wrong.

Nixon feared Bobby, too, as did every Republican planning a campaign. Nixon knew exactly what to fear. He had lost to a Kennedy before. Losing to a Kennedy meant losing to the Kennedy political machine, and it meant losing to the Kennedy style. A political machine can be beaten by a better political machine, though Nixon had never seen a better political machine than the Kennedys'. Kennedy style was something else. Nixon knew there was nothing Ailes could do for his image that could compete with Kennedy style.

Nixon couldn't change his sharply receding hairline. At fifty-four, he was too old to do anything but tamp down his short dark hair as flat as possible on his head. Bobby's hair had grown longer every year of the 1960s; now, at forty-two, he had the shaggiest hair in the United States Senate. His little brother, Ted, was the only other senator with as full a head of hair.

Bobby's hair was beginning to grow over his ears—rock-musician length for the Senate then. And everywhere Bobby spoke outside the Senate chamber, he was treated like a rock star. That's what Nixon and Johnson feared most about Bobby, the way crowds responded to him. They had never seen anything like it in politics. Nixon and Johnson were both old enough to remember the first time anyone saw fans screaming and swooning for Frank Sinatra in the 1940s before, during, and after every song Sinatra sang. America saw an even more intense version of that fan reaction when the Beatles landed in the United States in 1964. And now Nixon and Johnson saw a version of it happening to Bobby.

Everywhere Bobby went, crowds worked themselves into frenzies. When he spoke, he didn't sound like any senator they had heard before. His voice wasn't stiff and self-conscious. His language wasn't stilted or senatorial. What Bobby's audiences believed they were hearing was a man speaking from the heart about the moral issues of the day: racial discrimination, poverty, the increasingly unpopular war in Vietnam. Johnson and Nixon noticed that there was more political calculation in Bobby's speeches than his audiences realized. Bobby never said what he would do about Vietnam. What mattered to his audiences was that he didn't sound like Johnson, who had escalated the war and was drafting hundreds of thousands of young men into the army and sending tens of thousands of them to their deaths for reasons they couldn't understand or accept in a little country they had never read about in history class. Bobby's adoring audiences believed he would never send them or their friends or their brothers or their cousins or sons or grandsons or boyfriends to die in Vietnam. It could happen to anyone in America then. Anyone could lose a loved one in Vietnam. It was a daily fear for almost everyone in the country. Bobby would stop all that. That's what his audiences heard, even if he didn't exactly say it.

Underlying Bobby's speeches was a force we had never seen before in American politics and something we've never seen since, something Shakespearean. When Bobby stepped up to a microphone, no matter how sunny the day, no matter how wide his smile, he was always framed in tragedy, the personal and national tragedy of the assassination of his older brother, the president of the United States, on November 22, 1963, in Dallas.

Bobby's audiences knew his pain because they all

felt their own version of that pain on that horrendous day in 1963 that shook the country to the core. In the Kennedys' hometown of Boston it felt as if the world stopped. I was in Saint Brendan's Elementary School in Boston when the nuns got the news that the president had been killed, the first Catholic president, something the older nuns never expected to see. Now they had outlived the forty-six-year-old Irish Catholic boy who had made them so proud. The Sisters of Saint Joseph were the strongest women I knew, but this was too much for them to bear. They simply couldn't carry on. They closed school early and sent us home. We had never seen them cry before. We were all crying when the nuns got us into our lines to march us out to the sidewalk. Everyone we saw was crying. Every driver stopped at every traffic light. Men carrying tool bags were crying. Men carrying briefcases were crying. Boston cops were crying. Subway cars were filled with people crying who had left work early to go home and cry with their families, and to watch the Kennedy family's ordeal unfold on TV. We watched Bobby holding his brother's widow's hand that night when she arrived back in Washington still wearing her pink blood-stained clothes. We watched him holding her hand at Arlington National Cemetery. Nothing could ever happen in this world to make us forget those images, which were only four years old in 1967, when Bobby's audiences started chanting, "Run, Bobby, Run!"

They would reach their hands up toward the stage. They would try to touch his shoe, the cuff of his pants, anything. When Bobby reached his hand down to them, a thousand hands would fly up toward him. He would shake each one that he could. It was as if he were blessing them, one by one. When they looked up, they weren't just seeing Bobby. They were seeing Jaqueline Kennedy in her bloody clothes. They were seeing Bobby and Teddy Kennedy at their brother's grave site. They were seeing history, painful history. Bobby had a movie star's smile, but when he smiled, his audiences believed they were seeing a grieving man who was somehow strong enough to smile through his pain. Bobby was the only politician whose smile could make people's eyes tear. And with those tears in their eyes, when they looked up at Robert Francis Kennedy, they were always seeing John Fitzgerald Kennedy. For them, justice demanded that RFK take JFK's seat behind the desk in the Oval Office. History demanded it.

No other politician in our history ever had such an advantage. Or such a burden.

Bobby seemed to have softened since the assassination. But most people's political views softened in the 1960s, the decade when even some supporters of racial segregation began to accept the inevitability of racial integration, the decade when gung-ho decorated combat veterans like future senator, presidential candidate, and secretary of state John Kerry returned from war to join Vietnam Veterans Against the War, an organization that began as six Vietnam veterans marching together in a peace demonstration in 1967. By 1967, few people in America held all the same political positions they had held in 1960.

In the 1960s, America was changing utterly, and, to borrow a phrase from William Butler Yeats, "a terrible beauty is born." Yeats was referring to the failed Irish revolution against British colonial rule in 1916. Every revolution has that terrible beauty—the vision and bravery of the revolutionaries, the high-minded commitment to a better future, the one-for-all and all-for-one spirit, the daring acts of heroism, the inspired poetry and music as well as the death, the destruction, the mayhem, and the out-of-control rage. The 1960s had all of that. It was a decade like no other—a high-speed kaleidoscope of the civil rights movement, assassinations, Bob Dylan, the Vietnam War, hippies, America's first real antiwar movement, organic food, the Beatles, massive riots in several cities, the first riots on college campuses, Woodstock, Black Power, countless bombings in the name of the peace movement, Broadway's first naked musical (about hippies), thousands of military funerals for boys who hadn't wanted to go to war, birth control pills, free love, the collapse of dress codes in schools and universities, vegetarian restaurants, young rock stars dying of drug overdoses, fifty thousand deserters from the U.S. military, women's liberation, Muham-

mad Ali on trial for draft evasion, young men fleeing to Canada and Sweden to avoid the draft. When
the 1960s began, parents worried about their kids
maybe drinking too much at the senior prom. By the
end of the decade, parents worried about their kids
getting arrested for possessing marijuana or dying
from a heroin overdose or being killed in Vietnam
for a theory: the "domino theory," that if one country fell to communism, then another one would and
another and another. No one was left unchanged by
the chaos of the 1960s. Among politicians, perhaps
no one was changed more than Bobby Kennedy.

In September 1963, two months before JFK's assassination, Robert Kennedy went to Bismarck,
North Dakota, to speak in his official capacity as attorney general to the National Congress of American
Indians. The attorney general was under no political pressure to make the speech. Nothing was more
ignored in American politics than the concerns of
Native American tribes. JFK had lost North Dakota
to Nixon by a wide margin. The Kennedys had no
political debts to pay there. And there wasn't one
sentence of Bobby's speech that would flip a Nixon
voter in North Dakota. His opening line was "It is
a tragic irony that the American Indian has for so
long been denied a full share of freedom—full citi-
zenship in the greatest free country in the world."
This was radical stuff. By extending the language of
the civil rights movement to the rights of the tribes,

Bobby had added the concerns of the tribes to the liberal list of just causes years before most liberals had given them a thought. He ended the speech by quoting Chief Joseph of the Nez Perce tribe, who in 1877 offered this prayer for the future: "We shall all be alike—brothers of one father and one mother, with one sky above us, and one country around us, and one government for all." Bobby was becoming a liberal inspirational speaker years before most people noticed.

Bobby had made the decision to run only once before, and he made it at the last possible minute. He gave President Johnson his resignation as attorney general in August 1964, nine months after the assassination. He quickly moved to New York and announced his candidacy for the Senate. That was after he initially resisted when some New York Democrats urged him to run, then became indecisive, and finally rushed to New York just in time to be nominated at the state convention on September 1. The Republican incumbent senator accused him of being a carpetbagger because he didn't have an address in New York until days before he was nominated. With his suit coat off, his tie loosened, and his sleeves rolled up as he campaigned on the streets of New York, Bobby smiled through every word of his carpetbagger defense saying: "If the senator of the state of New York is going be selected on who's lived here the longest, then I think people are going

[to] vote for my opponent. If it's going be selected on who's got the best New York accent, then I think I'm probably out too. But I think if it's going be selected on the basis of who can make the best United States senator, I think I'm still in the contest."

Bobby easily won that first campaign, by ten points. But that didn't mean he was eager to gear up for another one just three years later in all fifty states.

"Run, Bobby, Run!"

Bobby was a realist first, a politician second, and a dreamer third. When he heard his audiences urging him to run for president, he knew he was hearing dreamers. Their dream was not so much another Kennedy presidency as it was a restoration of the first Kennedy presidency. They wanted to put their shattered dream back together.

"Run, Bobby, Run!"

Bobby knew what they wanted was impossible, crazy, maybe even political suicide. Running against the incumbent president for the nomination of his own party was madness. Running against Lyndon Johnson for the nomination that he owned was something more than madness. Johnson had been elected in a landslide in 1964, a year after the assassination, and except for his handling of the Vietnam War, he was the most masterful politician and strategist in the presidency since Franklin Delano Roosevelt. Johnson kept getting war strategy wrong and never paused to consider that there might not **be** a right way, that maybe the protesters were right, and the only smart move left was to get out of Vietnam. Johnson was always certain of only one thing about Vietnam: he wasn't going to be the first president of the United States to lose a war. Another president might have faced significant opposition to the war in Congress by 1967, but Democrats controlled Congress and Johnson controlled the Democrats with an iron fist. LBJ was ruthless with political enemies. **Ruthless** is the word people used to describe Bobby when he was protecting his brother on the way to and during the presidency. But you need power to be ruthless and LBJ had all the power in the Democratic Party now. Bobby knew all the levers of power Johnson could use to crush him if he launched a rebellion against the president.

"Run, Bobby, Run!"

No one was demanding that anyone else run. The Republican field of potential candidates was motivated entirely by the egos of the men planning to run. Nixon was likely the front-runner, with three governors circling him: Ronald Reagan, George Romney, and a New York Republican with a spectacular home on Fifth Avenue whose last name was a synonym for massive wealth: Nelson Rockefeller.

Governor Rockefeller had challenged Nixon for the Republican nomination in 1960. He was a billionaire by inheritance, the richest man ever to run for president. He had a messy divorce in 1962 after rather publicly carrying on an affair with a married woman whom he then married in 1963. Three years later, in his successful reelection campaign, Governor Rockefeller greatly expanded the Republican definition of an acceptable marital history. Donald Trump should leave a thank-you note at Nelson Rockefeller's grave in Sleepy Hollow, New York, for paving the way in Republican presidential politics for the rich men of Fifth Avenue with complicated marital histories.

The Republican field was beginning to look like the strongest group of Republican candidates in years. There was no doubt that President Johnson was going to be the Democratic nominee, and as a brilliant manipulator of the powers of incumbency would likely be reelected. Unless . . . unless Bobby ran.

"Run, Bobby, Run!"

Lyndon Johnson and Richard Nixon, the most ruthless Democrat and the most ruthless Republican, feared that dream, as did all the other Republican presidential hopefuls. And Bobby didn't think a dream was enough to run a presidential campaign. Bobby was almost certain that challenging Johnson was hopeless, but it might be the only way to put pressure on the president to de-escalate the Vietnam War. The chants, the dream, the war, and antiwar Democrats privately urging him to do it all contrived to get Bobby thinking about it. It was a rerun of the way he had approached running for the Senate three years earlier. At first he resisted. Then he wavered. Then he resisted again. Then he wavered again. All the while, Johnson and Nixon and the others believed that Bobby held history in his hands.

Bobby did not yet realize that the 1968 presidential election would be about nothing less than life and death. In the nuclear age, all presidential elections were, by implication at least, about life and death because the commander in chief had the power to start World War III in minutes by launching nuclear missiles. But the 1968 election was going to be about the life and death of people we **knew**.

In the spring of 1968, my cousin John T. Corley Jr. graduated from West Point, then visited us in Boston before he shipped out to Vietnam. Johnny was the tallest among us, six feet four inches, a West Point football star. We worried that he would be an easy target in Vietnam. Johnny wasn't worried. He grew up on army bases with his father, a general, and was trained for combat and eager to try to rival his father's World War II and Korean War records, which filled their home with twenty-six awards and decorations, including a record-setting eight Silver Stars. My oldest brother, Michael, showed Johnny his draft notice, which had just arrived in the mail. Michael was worried. He didn't want to go to Vietnam. No one we knew wanted to go except Johnny. He wanted a career in the army like his father, and combat was part of that. Johnny advised Michael that the best

way to avoid Vietnam might be to voluntarily enlist before being drafted because then he might get
a better choice of assignments. Getting drafted was
the fastest route to Vietnam. Michael took Johnny's
advice, enlisted, got easy assignments in the army,
and never left the United States. Johnny arrived in
Vietnam on May 9, 1968. Over the course of that
summer, his letters to Michael began to question the
wisdom of the mission in Vietnam. Johnny earned
a Silver Star in four months, on September 8, 1968,
the day he was killed in action. His funeral was the
first military funeral I attended. Tragedy has many
faces but none quite like a general crying, saluting
his son's coffin. It was just another day in the life
of America in 1968. The presidential election could
end all that if Bobby ran on ending the war in Vietnam and won, as antiwar Democrats were assuring
him he could.

I was in high school in 1968 and I never heard
my brothers and their college-age friends talk about
career planning. They only talked about how to deal
with the draft and Vietnam. There was no long-term
planning, no career hopes and dreams. Life was a
short-term game for many young men in 1968. It
was as if they were prisoners who would only begin
to think about life on the outside when they got outside. Their prison was in their pocket, the draft registration card that controlled their lives and blocked
their hopes and dreams.

The presidential election could end all that. The presidential election was a matter of life and death for real people we all knew. That meant that this time running for president didn't have to be about ego. It meant that running for president couldn't simply be a matter of political calculation. It meant that it wasn't just about what was best for Bobby's future in politics. It was about life and death.

The death Bobby thought about was his own. He worried that announcing his candidacy might tempt an assassin. He knew assassination was driven more by madness than logic, and maybe getting the second Kennedy on his way to the presidency would capture an assassin's twisted imagination. He was the only potential candidate who had to worry about a copycat assassin going for another Kennedy.

And so Bobby's thinking about running was muddled and slow. He was leaning against running most of the time. As he thought about it, Bobby, who had been the manager of his brother's winning presidential campaign, could see every detail of what could go wrong with his own. But he could not yet see what the election was going to be about: life or death.

And so Bobby held history in his hands for so long that someone who **could** see what the election was going to be about decided he couldn't wait any longer and grabbed history out of Bobby's hands, someone no one expected to seize the moment. Until he did.

ONE

DECLARING WAR

Senate hearings are not quite as boring as they look. The senators who listen often learn things they can use in speeches back home to sound as if they know a lot more than they do. There have been precious few moments of drama in the history of Senate hearings—most of that coming in controversial confirmation hearings where lives could be changed by the right or wrong answer. Senators' lives are never changed in hearings—except on August 17, 1967, in the Senate Foreign Relations Committee.

The United States Senate was very slowly catching up to the college campuses that were energizing protests against the Vietnam War. Some senators had begun questioning President Johnson's monarchical approach to Vietnam. Idealistic young Senate staffers with friends and relatives being drafted and sent to Vietnam were becoming increasingly antiwar and wanted to have an effect on policy. A sharp young member of Arkansas senator William Fulbright's staff named Bill Clinton was against the war. Bright and enthusiastic, Clinton frustrated Fulbright, who was chairman of the Senate's Foreign Relations Committee: though Fulbright was Clinton's hero, the younger man loved to argue and could never stop challenging the boss.

Still, a political novice like Clinton and an elder statesman like Fulbright were finding surprising common ground. On the Vietnam War, they were opposing their party's leader, President Johnson.

Senator Eugene McCarthy's eyes were already open. And on this August day in 1967 he was seeing more than he'd seen before. Even McCarthy couldn't know just how thoroughly he was about to change everything, not only in the upcoming election year, but in all of American life. The war in Vietnam was out of control, constitutionally out of control. The Johnson administration had no intention of consulting or listening to Congress about how it was conducting the war.

The witness who was making this painfully clear to the Foreign Relations Committee was Nicholas Katzenbach, whom Democrats like Fulbright and McCarthy always thought of as one of the good guys.

Katzenbach left Princeton in his junior year to join the army after the Japanese attack on Pearl Harbor. His B-25 bomber was shot down over the Mediterranean Sea. He spent two years as a prisoner of war. Afterward, Princeton gave him credits for the five hundred books he'd read in his two years as a POW, and he graduated cum laude with a BA degree. After receiving an LLB from Yale Law School, Katzenbach was a Rhodes Scholar at Balliol College, Oxford. Bobby Kennedy brought him into the Justice Department at the beginning of the Kennedy administration and promoted him to deputy attorney general in 1962. It was in that capacity on June 11, 1963, that Nicholas Katzenbach stepped into history. Alabama's governor, George Wallace, stood at the entrance of the University of Alabama flanked by Alabama state troopers to block the entry of Vivian Malone and James Hood, who, with the backing of a federal court order, would become the first two black students enrolled at the university. With President Kennedy and Attorney General Kennedy monitoring the situation from Washington, Katzenbach marched up the stairs flanked by U.S. marshals, and backed up by the National Guard, to confront Governor Wallace in the doorway of the registration office. It was the most vivid armed confrontation between the North and the South since the Civil War, and the nation watched it unfold on television. After complaining that America was becoming "a military dictatorship" and declaring that his side was "winning," Wallace left the campus, and the University of Alabama enrolled its first black students. Nicholas

Katzenbach became the most famous deputy attorney general in history.

President Johnson appointed Katzenbach attorney general when Kennedy resigned to run for the Senate. In 1966, Johnson moved Katzenbach to undersecretary of state. Katzenbach was a problem solver and Vietnam was Johnson's biggest problem.

Chairman Fulbright pressed Undersecretary Katzenbach on the Johnson administration's legal authority to wage war in Southeast Asia without a congressional declaration of war.

Katzenbach replied that a declaration of war "would not, I think, correctly reflect the very limited objectives of the United States."

Fulbright and McCarthy were studying every word of Katzenbach's answers now. "To 'declare war,'" Katzenbach suggested, was "an outmoded expression."

Fulbright pounced. "You think it is outmoded to declare war?"

"In this kind of a context," said Katzenbach, "I think the expression of 'declaring a war' is one that has become outmoded in the international arena." Eugene McCarthy was silently infuriated.

Katzenbach's argument was that Congress had already authorized everything President Johnson was doing in Vietnam, whether they knew it or not, when they voted for the Gulf of Tonkin Resolution three years earlier.

In early August 1964, the facts in what became known as the Gulf of Tonkin incident appeared clear: two attacks, occurring in rapid succession, that President Johnson said North Vietnam had made on U.S. ships "on the high seas."

The northern part of Vietnam—the part bordering China—was communist. The southern part of the country was anticommunist, a U.S. ally, and North Vietnam wanted to force the whole country into unification under communist rule. With our ally South Vietnam under attack by the North, an insurgent guerrilla force had arisen within South Vietnam itself, the National Liberation Front (NLF), or Vietcong, casting itself as a populist front for throwing off South Vietnam's U.S.-backed military government. The Vietcong were fully supported by North Vietnam. In Washington, the bipartisan consensus was that South Vietnam and the world needed our help in preventing the spread of communism.

In 1964, protests against U.S. military involvement in Vietnam didn't get much attention. In May 1964, twelve young men publicly burned their draft cards in New York City. It was shocking, unmanly behavior to most Americans. And it was highly aberrant, hardly a trend. Few parents were worried that their sons might be the next to burn their draft cards.

So on August 4, 1964, when President Johnson went on live prime-time TV to announce an unprovoked communist attack on two U.S. ships off

Vietnam, people had no reason to doubt anything he said.

Johnson assured the nation that he was prepared to treat any further unprovoked aggression by North Vietnam as a cause for military retaliation, yet he also reiterated his long-standing assurance that he had no desire for a U.S. war in Southeast Asia. Earlier in the year, he'd put it this way: "We are not about to send American boys 9 or 10,000 miles away from home to do what Asian boys ought to be doing for themselves." American involvement in Vietnam meant continuing the Kennedy policy: sending military advisers—at first only hundreds, then thousands— to train South Vietnamese troops.

Now Johnson was telling the nation about an event "on the high seas," as he put it. Any notion that, in response to that event, tens of thousands of young Americans would meet their ends in a far-off jungle would have seemed, to the vast majority of Americans watching the president that night, unthinkable.

Three years later, Gene McCarthy was listening to Nick Katzenbach tell the Senate Foreign Relations Committee that the United States was bogged down in full-scale war in Vietnam thanks to Congress's reaction to the Gulf of Tonkin incident. But disturbing questions had since arisen about what really happened in the Gulf of Tonkin in August 1964.

First, the incident had not begun on the high seas. The president had set the opening of the drama in international waters, as if the United States had been the victim of a vicious sneak attack, without provocation.

But the events had really occurred—not surprisingly, given their name—in the Gulf of Tonkin off the North Vietnamese mainland, in and around that nation's territorial waters. U.S. ships had been patrolling there in a manner that could appear explicitly intended to provoke an attack. In the summer of 1964, Johnson was running for election to the office he had assumed through assassination, and the Republican challenger, Barry Goldwater, labeled Johnson soft on communism and called for increased U.S. military involvement in Southeast Asia. Months before anything happened in the Gulf of Tonkin, the Johnson administration had secretly drafted a congressional resolution for stepping up military action in Vietnam.

Johnson did not tell the American people that the ship that sparked the Tonkin incident, the destroyer USS **Maddox**, was in the Gulf of Tonkin for the express purpose of carrying out electronic surveillance of North Vietnam, part of a covert program, begun under President Kennedy, to intercept North Vietnamese army intelligence and send it, via the Pentagon, to South Vietnamese army forces. That program was coordinated with an even more aggressive covert activity, overseen by the CIA, to direct South Vietnamese and other commando troops in making night raids with high-speed boats on coastal North Vietnam. U.S. air support for both operations was supplied by the carrier **Ticonderoga**, lying in international waters nearby. The United States, that is, was already waging war in Vietnam by August 1964.

The Gulf of Tonkin incident had begun not on August 2, as the president reported, but on the night of July 30, and the first shots had really been fired under U.S. guidance, when two of those CIA-directed South Vietnamese speedboats attacked a North Vietnamese radar station on an island in the gulf. The next day, the destroyer **Maddox** ostentatiously entered the area, and on August 2, three North Vietnamese patrol boats armed with torpedoes approached the **Maddox**, which fired warning shots. The patrol boats fired torpedoes but failed to hit the destroyer, and when the **Maddox** opened fire, the patrol boats retreated. Jets from the nearby **Ticonderoga** also attacked the patrol boats, damaging one and sinking another. There were no U.S. casualties.

That might have been the end of the affair, with nothing serious to report. But President Johnson and the Pentagon escalated. They chose to leave the **Maddox** in the gulf, and to send another destroyer there. On the night of August 3, with the two U.S. destroyers positioned just outside territorial waters, the CIA-directed speedboats again attacked the coast of North Vietnam. In Arlington, Virginia, on

Tuesday morning, August 4, 1964, thirty-five-year-old Daniel Ellsberg was beginning his first day on a new Pentagon job as special assistant to the assistant secretary of the navy. Suddenly Ellsberg found himself confronted by a breathless courier delivering an urgent cable dispatch from the captain of the USS **Maddox** off North Vietnam. According to the captain's cable, both of the American destroyers in the gulf were now under constant, intense torpedo attack by North Vietnamese PT boats. In a series of cable dispatches, the captain continued to narrate events in the gulf: "Torpedoes missed . . ." "Five in the water . . ." "Lucky to have been missed six times . . ." The two U.S. ships were maneuvering and firing, time and again, in rough seas. A major action was clearly under way. In response to this second attack, U.S. planes left the deck of the **Ticonderoga** and fired rockets at North Vietnamese targets, with locations provided by radar from the second U.S. destroyer. The engagement went on for two hours, as Ellsberg took it all in.

Daniel Ellsberg's boss, locked in high-level meetings with Secretary of Defense Robert McNamara, couldn't be interrupted. So throughout the long battle, it was Ellsberg, the special assistant, who kept close track of the entire thing. Ellsberg organized the dispatches into a narrative that his boss could review upon his return.

Finally, quiet from the gulf. The event seemed to be over.

Then a final shocking dispatch arrived from the **Maddox**'s captain, who flatly rescinded all of his earlier dispatches. The entire naval battle had occurred, it turned out, only in the cables. There had been no real engagement. The captain put the error down to freak weather effects on the ship's radar and jumpy officers misreading it. Probably only one torpedo had really been fired. And it missed. And yet that very night, the president went on TV and told the American people that two attacks on U.S. ships had been launched, out of nowhere, by North Vietnam.

After that, Daniel Ellsberg began poking around. Finding out what the Pentagon had really been doing in Vietnam changed the course of his life. He would one day discover proof of what many in the public and Congress had by then long suspected: that without telling the American people or Congress, the United States had been pursuing a wide range of covert military actions in Vietnam since the 1950s. Ellsberg made that story public in 1971 when he leaked what came to be known as the Pentagon Papers to the **New York Times** and the **Washington Post**.

President Johnson had come roaring out of the Gulf of Tonkin incident with a new policy to bring the communist government in North Vietnam's capital,

Hanoi, to the negotiating table by sheer force. Barry Goldwater, calling Lyndon Johnson soft on communism, faded into the background of the '64 presidential campaign. LBJ won the election by the largest popular majority to that point in American history. In 1965, wielding both that electoral mandate and high public approval ratings for his handling of the Gulf of Tonkin incident, Johnson sent the first American ground troops—210,000 of them—to Vietnam. Between 1965 and 1967, that number grew to 485,000. By the summer of 1967, U.S. casualties in Vietnam numbered nearly 11,000.

"Do you think it is outmoded to declare war?"

As Katzenbach smoked cigarette after cigarette in the witness chair, he tried to treat Chairman Fulbright's question as a mere softball. He dissented, the undersecretary explained, from the position that only Congress has the constitutional power to initiate war. He dissented from the notion that the Constitution requires the Senate to play a role in pursuing foreign policy at all. Only a president, Katzenbach argued, is positioned to respond with the necessary speed and decisiveness in emergencies. Because the president would have only minutes to respond to a nuclear attack, declarations of war were no more relevant to modern warfare than letters of marque, quartering troops in homes, and other outmoded ideas included in the Constitution.

Katzenbach admitted that Congress does have a

role in checking the executive in time of war. But regarding Vietnam, that ship had sailed. The senators had been given their chance to check the president. They weren't going to get another one.

In 1964, nearly every member of both houses of Congress voted to pass the Gulf of Tonkin Resolution. Bill Fulbright, Gene McCarthy, and the rest of the Foreign Relations Committee all voted for it. On the Senate floor, there were exactly two dissenters: Senators Ernest Gruening, Democrat of Alaska, and Wayne Morse, Democrat of Oregon. They'd openly expressed doubt about the reality of the second Tonkin attack, and Morse tried and failed to get the **Maddox** logbooks subpoenaed. Dissent only made Morse look paranoid, unpatriotic, soft on communism, possibly a communist sympathizer. Other senators didn't seriously consider supporting him. Wayne Morse's reelection campaign got tougher by the day.

Katzenbach told Fulbright the Gulf of Tonkin Resolution served as "the functional equivalent [of] the constitutional obligation expressed in a provision of the Constitution with respect to declaring war" and "fulfills the obligation of the executive."

Katzenbach had a rhetorical question of his own for the chairman. "Didn't that resolution authorize the President," Katzenbach asked, "to use the armed forces of the United States in any way that was necessary? . . . Didn't it? It seems to me that if your complaint is the drafting of the resolution, it ill becomes—"

Fulbright cut off Katzenbach before the witness could blame Congress for writing the thing.

"That resolution was drafted by the executive and sent up here."

"Mr. Chairman, it wasn't accepted without consideration."

"Yes, it was. Largely without consideration."

"It was explained in the debate," Katzenbach reminded him. He had Fulbright now. "You explained it, Mr. Chairman. As head of this committee."

"But I misinterpreted it."

That's all Fulbright could say.

Gene McCarthy wished there were more to say because he knew they'd all misinterpreted it. The senators had meant to give the president a limited power to cope with the Gulf of Tonkin situation. Under that authorization, President Johnson had pursued all-out war in Vietnam, and Katzenbach was testifying now that the president's power to do so was more or less unlimited. There was nothing left to say, not today, not in this room.

Gene McCarthy rose from his seat. He saw now how the executive branch had set and sprung the trap. Congress had been duped into making the president all-powerful. Some members of Congress had believed the resolution authorized the president only to cope with an immediate threat; some had been sure the resolution was nothing but an election-year ploy to shut Barry Goldwater up and hadn't taken it seriously. It didn't matter. They'd passed it. Now they were living with it. And Americans were dying for it.

In 1965, the president had assured the country that the first ground troops would remain in Vietnam for only six months; in 1967, 485,000 troops were now there indefinitely. Congress had no voice in that escalation. An American president had, in effect, suspended congressional power.

This, McCarthy believed, amounted to nothing less than a brazen assertion of tyranny. The hearing was going on, but Senator McCarthy was moving toward the door. Walking out of a hearing wasn't the kind of move Gene McCarthy was known for. Drama wasn't his thing. That's why Carl Marcy followed McCarthy out into the hall.

Carl Marcy, the committee's veteran chief of staff, was startled by McCarthy's visible upset. This wasn't like Gene. Marcy wanted to know what McCarthy was thinking. In the hall, McCarthy and Marcy ran into Ned Kenworthy, a reporter for the **New York Times**. Kenworthy, too, could tell something was going on. The normally reserved McCarthy was agitated.

"There is no limit to what he says the President can do," McCarthy told Marcy and Kenworthy in the hall. He seemed shaken yet firm.

The Johnson-Katzenbach approach amounted to

dictatorship in foreign policy, McCarthy said. It must not stand. There was only one thing to do.

"Take it to the country," he said. "Someone's going to have to take them on."

Did McCarthy mean the Senate had to keep challenging officials in the Johnson administration?

No. McCarthy meant take on President Johnson himself. Then came the most shocking thing Marcy and Kenworthy had ever heard from a senator.

"If I have to run for president to do it," Gene McCarthy said, "I'm going to do it."

That hearing changed Democratic Party politics forever. It changed the presidential campaign of 1968. It changed the course of the Vietnam War. It changed history.

TWO

"WHY ISN'T HE A PRIEST?"

If I have to run for president . . ."

Senator McCarthy's outburst to Ned Kenworthy and Carl Marcy in the hallway outside the hearing room was off the record, so Kenworthy didn't write it up for the **Times**. McCarthy's thinking about running for president would remain secret for months.

There was no precedent for challenging the president as a "peace" candidate. No major political party had ever fielded a peace candidate. But a "Dump Johnson" movement was gradually developing among liberal Democrats over Vietnam. Former congressional staffer and liberal gadfly Allard Lowenstein had been going around Washington trying to find a candidate willing to challenge Johnson for the nomination as a peace candidate. Bobby Kennedy was his first choice, but Bobby gave him no encouragement.

Everyone knew it was impossible. Everyone except Al Lowenstein and the "Dump Johnson" idealists.

Johnson's policies in Vietnam still appeared popular. Any primary challenger would come off as a communist appeaser; he'd lose his seat; his political career would be over. Running against Lyndon Johnson could only make the challenger a humiliated footnote to the main text of history. This was the conventional wisdom.

Eugene McCarthy was a serious man. In Washington, serious men knew that precedent controls everything. Serious men were not adventurers willing to leap into the unknown. But Gene McCarthy was thinking about running for president. Gene McCarthy of all people. A McCarthy challenge to Johnson for the nomination?

Gene? He was Lyndon's guy. They'd had their differences. McCarthy could be stubborn about his political independence; Johnson could be a bully. Johnson had once berated McCarthy for disloyalty right in front of their wives and other company at a Washington party. The relationship had rough edges, but most political relationships do. Politicians are ego driven, and McCarthy's Minnesota voters and Johnson's Texas voters had put them on opposite sides of some important issues when Johnson was in the Senate.

Still, McCarthy owed much of his career in the Senate to Johnson's patronage. When Johnson had served as Senate majority leader, McCarthy had voted just as Johnson wanted, even to the point of defending corporate interests—like those of the oil industry—seemingly in conflict with McCarthy's social liberalism. Johnson had rewarded McCarthy with plum committee assignments and a friendly ear, at first in the Senate but then, after the JFK assassination, when Johnson became president, in the White House itself.

Until recently, McCarthy had been one of Johnson's more vocal supporters on Vietnam. In 1964, he'd gone on **Face the Nation** to defend U.S. responses in the Gulf of Tonkin incident. "The escalation came from the enemy," McCarthy told reporters without the slightest equivocation.

Insiders saw McCarthy not only as a Johnson ally but also as the most remote of politicians, competent and smart but quiet and unapproachable. Sometimes McCarthy was so aloof that he didn't show up for Senate votes, preferring to read Yeats and other poets in his office. His colleagues sometimes wondered whether that coolness and intellectualism was a cover for laziness.

A passionate run against the popular and politically vicious president of his own party, the man who helped him build his Senate career? No, Gene McCarthy was not on anyone's list of suspects for pulling a move like that.

Abigail McCarthy could have explained a few

things to Washington politicians about their aloof colleague.

She knew that it was really during these past ten years in the Senate that Gene McCarthy had departed from his usual rhythms. The quiescence, the dependence on Johnson's patronage, the apparent laziness—those were the uncharacteristic things. Mercurial decision making had once been Gene McCarthy's best-known style.

Abigail knew her husband as a difficult and unpredictable man. His abrupt and unpredictable choices had already taken the McCarthys on a long, veering, restless, and difficult journey.

IN 1938, WHEN EUGENE McCARTHY, age twenty-two, proposed marriage to Abigail Quigley, also twenty-two, he'd already established himself in their native Minnesota as a mixture of intellectual wunderkind, Roman Catholic visionary, and radical social activist. Gene McCarthy had an abiding belief in the productive virtues of the farming communities that had formed him and high regard for institutions, from the Roman Catholic Church to the Grange, that supported community life across great swaths of the Midwest.

McCarthy became an idealist at a young age. He believed in what he was already calling, by the late 1930s, "distributive justice." Along the lines of Saint Augustine's interpretation of the miracle of the loaves and fishes—"to each his due"—for Gene that kind of justice meant more than equal opportunity. It meant fair economic participation, too. The poverty that began stalking young Gene's small farming town of Watkins in the 1930s inspired his growing vision of justice and good government.

At an aunt's house next door, Gene devoured **The Harvard Classics,** a fifty-one-volume anthology of great works of literature, history, and philosophy by authors from Benjamin Franklin to Homer to Molière and far beyond. It was Lincolnesque: McCarthy would come to know a great deal of Shakespeare by heart many years before he ever saw one of the plays on stage.

To his mother, McCarthy was a priest in the making. But to the Chicago White Sox, Gene McCarthy was a scouting prospect at St. John's University in Minnesota.

HE MET ABIGAIL QUIGLEY when they were both teaching high school in a small town across the border in North Dakota. Abigail had been in line to take over as head of the English department when Eugene McCarthy swept in and was given the position instead. He had more experience. He'd been teaching ever since graduating from St. John's at nineteen. He'd even served as the principal of two schools before arriving at this one. And he was a man.

Stealing her promotion hardly endeared him to Abigail Quigley. But other things did. By then he was tall and lean, his bearing still athletic. Dark eyebrows lent his handsome face intensity; his deep-set eyes were thoughtfully frank, even soulful. A line running down each side of his mouth seemed to reflect mature seriousness. Steeped in classical learning, and drawn to modern poetry, he was still a brilliant provincial with a strong commitment to rural values. When Abigail heard the rumor that Gene never missed morning Mass, she asked, "Why isn't he a priest?" She was a devout Catholic, too, but Abigail would always be skeptical of excess, even in religious devotion.

Abigail soon found that Gene, for all of his intensity, could smile. He could even laugh aloud, especially after getting off a wry crack—sometimes a truly nasty one—at the expense of someone less quick. Gene began driving Abigail around in his '37 Chevy; they were the sharpest-looking couple in that little town on the Dakota plains.

WHEN GENE AND ABIGAIL became engaged to be married, there was no hint of a political career, no way even to imagine such a thing. Their plan was to move back to his hometown of Watkins, buy land, and set up there. Then, on Good Friday 1941, Abigail got the first of many shocks that would mark her life with Gene. He gave his fiancée some difficult news: their engagement was over.

Gene had decided to join the Roman Catholic priesthood instead. This, he'd decided, was the only genuine way to follow his most serious and highest ambitions for good.

McCarthy immediately began his preliminary studies, and in 1943, cut a tonsure in his hair and, as Brother Conan, entered the monastery at St. John's. He suggested that Abigail, in turn, enter a convent.

THREE YEARS LATER, Gene and Abigail were living in St. Paul. They'd been married a little more than a year, and he was teaching sociology at the College of St. Thomas, on the western edge of town, overlooking the Mississippi River. Abigail hadn't joined a convent. She hadn't even considered it. She'd waited, in some turmoil, for Gene to end his fling with the priesthood.

Ending that fling wasn't exactly McCarthy's choice. The monastery gave him the boot. His offenses included sneak-reading theology during Mass, visible boredom with the course of study, and overall spiritual and intellectual pride. His mother was wrong. Gene McCarthy wasn't cut out to be a priest.

He wasn't a soldier, either. Drafted for World War II and then rejected because of bursitis in his feet, McCarthy volunteered instead to serve in the Signal Corps, in Washington, D.C., cracking Japanese code. That first brief stay in the capital awoke no interest in McCarthy in national politics.

Gene and Abigail quickly found balancing the contemplative life with the hard realities of farming an insurmountable challenge. So McCarthy changed course yet again. Now teaching was his vocation. The Catholic academic community of St. Paul and Minneapolis seemed his natural habitat. A certain modest cosmopolitanism suited Abigail and Gene.

In 1946, when McCarthy began dabbling in Minnesota politics, he meant only to extend his teaching life into a sphere that he thought might offer an interesting way of helping improve social conditions and draw on his leadership skills. McCarthy quickly turned out to be a good political organizer— compelling, charismatic, fun. As the McCarthy home became the gathering place for St. Paul's reform-minded political power brokers, Eugene McCarthy learned to pull strings that made things happen. He even held elected office within the regional chapter of Americans for Democratic Action (ADA), the Democratic Party's national organization for selecting and supporting liberal candidates. McCarthy had no plans to hold government office himself. He was sure that his future was in teaching.

McCARTHY'S POLITICAL CAREER STARTED with the statement "I'll run myself if I have to." That's what Gene told his Minnesota political allies in 1947. Abigail was caught off guard by yet another abrupt and passionate decision by Gene to switch their future plans. The political conflict in 1947 was local, but the office at stake was national: the seat for the Fourth Congressional District of Minnesota. Winning the primary would be tough; winning the general election would mean changing everything in the McCarthys' lives overnight. He would have to give up teaching. They would have to move to Washington. One of McCarthy's political pals had encouraged him to run, and Abigail went right over to the man's house and gave him hell. The McCarthys had an infant baby now, Mary. Abigail was happy in St. Paul.

But Gene McCarthy lived in a man's world, competitive, fraternal, rough: the monastery, the locker room, the academic department, and now—suddenly—party politics. He didn't discuss his decisions with Abigail in advance; he just made them and then informed her.

Over and against all of Abigail's concerns, he announced his candidacy for Congress. As a candidate,

McCarthy took up the cause of militant anticommunism. It was not at all strange, in 1948, for a passionate liberal like McCarthy to make a passionate case against communism. In the early 1950s, he would be among the first to call the anticommunist fear mongering and witch-hunting of Republican senator Joseph McCarthy overblown and unnecessary. But American liberalism was entering a new phase in the late 1940s, and in Gene's two political homes, the Democratic-Farmer-Labor Party of Minnesota and Americans for Democratic Action, as in liberal sectors everywhere in the country, a big move was under way to get American Communist Party influences out of the political organizations that had helped build the New Deal and the Fair Deal in the 1930s.

During World War II, a "popular front" alliance had at times prevailed across the liberal spectrum, embracing in American liberalism outright socialists and even Communist Party members. But with the war over, the Soviets expanding into Europe, the rapid development of nuclear weapons, and a cold war between the two superpowers, President Truman's policy was to "contain," as he said, communism around the world.

It was especially important for liberal Democrats like Gene McCarthy to condemn communism, because conservatives had been casting liberal programs like Social Security as tantamount to socialism and even Soviet communism itself. Some conservatives were especially quick to call the big liberal issue of the day, federal support for racial equality, a Soviet-style tyranny. In 1948, the leading Minnesota liberal was U.S. senator Hubert Humphrey, a former pharmacist, political science professor, and mayor of Minneapolis. At the Democratic National Convention that year, Humphrey made a rafters-shaking speech, challenging his party to turn away from its poisonous association with segregation, away from its dependence on racist Southern politicians, snatch the mantle of racial equality from the Republican "party of Lincoln," and take the lead in federally enforcing racial integration. In response, the Southern Democrats staged a walkout of the 1948 convention, founding a third party, the Dixiecrats, and nominating South Carolina governor Strom Thurmond for president. Thurmond was relentless in smearing liberals' efforts for racial integration as creeping communism at home.

Humphrey, with his mix of liberalism on race and anticommunism at home and abroad, was one of Gene McCarthy's sponsors and mentors in Minnesota politics. Humphrey encouraged McCarthy's run, and McCarthy fully subscribed to Humphrey's certainty that it was now critically important for liberals throughout the country to establish in the public mind that there was nothing "soft on communism" about their fervent progressivism. So Gene McCarthy, running for office in 1948 with Humphrey's support, easily blended intense liberalism with fierce anticommunism. And yet McCarthy put the communism problem in his own idiosyncratic way. He had no doubt that communism was a global threat; he firmly defended Truman's containment policy. In the postwar world, the enemy was no longer a flesh-and-blood enemy, Gene McCarthy believed, but an idea, an ideology: totalitarian control.

But communist subversion at home wasn't Gene McCarthy's main concern. For Gene McCarthy the important project was to address the unconscionable economic conditions that had made communism attractive to so many poor and working Americans during the Depression, when communists had rallied support among downtrodden people by brandishing the popular-front idea that, as the American Communist Party put it, "Communism is 100% Americanism." Only the social programs of the New Deal, Gene McCarthy believed, had fended off a communist influence in American life. The falsity of communism would be revealed, McCarthy believed, only if what he called social justice prevailed in America.

With McCarthy working as an organizer, Minnesota's liberal anticommunist coalition had achieved triumphant success in throwing out communist-leaning operatives from liberal organizations. Then the liberal coalition began splintering, over what McCarthy saw as American anti-intellectualism. On one side: organized labor, the traditional backbone of Democratic Party political power in Minnesota. On the other: young, well-educated, moderately affluent, academic liberal intellectuals from St. Paul, people like Gene and Abigail McCarthy. The labor side was sure that nominating a Democratic congressional candidate from the effete intellectual side of the anticommunist coalition could only spell disaster in the general election.

McCarthy won the Democratic primary by the narrowest of margins, then trounced his Republican opponent in November. Gene McCarthy was hooked. Anything but a reluctant campaigner, Gene "loved the business from the start," a friend said later.

Abigail hated the idea of moving the family back and forth between the capital and St. Paul, but she had no choice. No one who had heard Gene McCarthy say "if I have to run myself" the first time would have been surprised to hear him say it again twenty years later.

THREE

SLEEPY HOLLOW

Gene McCarthy served ten years in the House before making his move for the Senate. For Democrats, 1958 was a very good year in the midterm election, and McCarthy was swept to victory. His new boss was Lyndon Johnson, the Senate majority leader.

While he was only eight years older than McCarthy, Johnson seemed a man of an earlier time and a different place. He'd begun as a national politician in prewar Washington. The terrifying global concerns of the nuclear age would have been unimaginable in Johnson's early career as a Southern populist New Dealer. He grew up in the hardscrabble central-Texas hill country, near Austin. A rambling, nonstop talker, Johnson's spiel was thick with deliberately crude, rib-digging, often outright racist Southernisms, delivered in an accent that made him sound older than he was and more rural. On the stump, he was a bombastic speechmaker, practiced in the arts of small-town Texas barnstorming, glad-handing, baby kissing. Up close, when Johnson wanted you to do something, his shambling, nearly shapeless figure and big inelegant face—small mouth, flapping ears, prominent nose—leaned into you, literally and figuratively. Hands jammed in his pockets, he'd get his face millimeters from yours. You could smell his breath. His shoulder grab could wither a less powerful man, yet he could wheedle and whine and plead, too, and if you outranked him, Johnson would court you relentlessly.

Having entered the Senate in 1948, the same year McCarthy entered the House, Johnson's rise in the leadership was fast. In 1951, his energy was rewarded with his election as his party's majority whip. When General Dwight D. Eisenhower won the White House for the Republicans in 1952, Republicans were swept into power with him, capturing the majority of the Senate. With the loss of some senior members, Johnson became, at the age of forty-five, the most junior minority leader ever. Then, in 1954, with the return of a Democrat majority, Lyndon Johnson was the majority leader. By the time Gene McCarthy took his Senate seat four years later, Johnson had built a reputation as the ultimate political deal maker, a man who could steer bipartisan legislation through Congress. His biographer, Robert Caro, called LBJ the "Master of the Senate," but his command was based less on dominance than on a relentless search for compromise.

The new liberals coming into the Senate majority in 1958 weren't interested in compromise. They wanted social progress. Their leader could expect trouble from his junior senators, but that's not what he got from Gene McCarthy. In helping stabilize Johnson's role, McCarthy gained a leg up in the power politics of the Senate.

Lyndon Johnson's Senate was a far simpler legislative body than it became in the last decades of the twentieth century. Senate procedure was simpler. Legislating was child's play compared to what it became in the 1970s, when suddenly Congress started counting the money. In LBJ's Senate no one asked, "How much does it cost?" And if that question somehow came up, Johnson could just make up a number. No one really knew. Johnson never had to worry about how to pay for a highway or a post office he'd promised a senator. He never had to take away a highway or post office from another senator to pay for the promise he'd just made. The Senate Budget Committee did not exist until 1975, and with it came budget bills more complex than any document Johnson ever saw as a senator or president. Johnson never had to master the parliamentary intricacies of the budget rules. He never had to muster the 60 votes to override a budget point of order. He never had to worry about "extraneous" matters being removed from budget reconciliation bills. LBJ could attach a minimum wage increase to a tax bill or to any legislation, something that became virtually impossible in 1975. The job of majority leader in Lyndon Johnson's Senate was like flying a single-engine aircraft in good weather. Twenty years later it was like flying a jumbo jet in the rain. Now it's like flying a jumbo jet low on fuel in a hurricane.

The personal lives of senators in Johnson's Senate were actually personal. Private. They didn't have to reveal anything about what they did off the Senate floor. No one ever saw their tax returns. There was no such thing as financial disclosure. They could engage in all sorts of income-producing activity outside of the Senate, including sweetheart business deals that no one ever had to know about. Campaign fund-raising and spending was not policed in Johnson's Senate. The Federal Election Commission was created to monitor campaign finances fifteen years after Johnson left the Senate. And, luckily for Johnson, the Senate Ethics Committee was created five years after he left.

As a congressman in the 1930s and 1940s, Johnson had begun building a fortune, with his wife, Lady Bird, when she purchased Texas radio station KTBC. Johnson owned a half share, but there was supposedly no conflict of interest because the business was in Lady Bird's name. Leaning on key officials of the Federal Communications Commission (FCC) and trading congressional votes for FCC favors, Johnson made all the regulations that normally limited stations' reach and power evaporate for Lady Bird's station.

Soon KTBC dominated all other players, reaching sixty-eight Texas counties. When Johnson pressured CBS's president, William Paley, to make the station a CBS affiliate, the Johnsons were on their way to becoming millionaires. Everything worked together: LBJ's political clout helped the radio business; radio dominance helped LBJ's political campaigns. When the FCC announced that it would allow a TV station in Austin, Texas, no one but Lady Bird Johnson even bothered to file an application for what everyone knew was a gold mine.

Johnson picked up the nickname "Landslide Lyndon" for his 1948 victory in the Democratic primary for the Senate, which he won by a mere 87 votes. That primary was a runoff, and Johnson's opponent, Coke Stevenson, was declared the winner at first. Then came late tallies from one of the most corrupt counties in Texas, reflecting a thoroughly organized effort, throughout many counties, headed by Johnson's campaign manager (and future Texas governor), John Connally, to falsify hundreds—some claimed thousands—of ballots, with friendly judges certifying them. One tally was hand-altered, gaining Johnson 200 votes simply by replacing the 7 in 765 with a 9.

Coke Stevenson took the matter to the federal district court with the clock ticking for issuing the official ballot for the general election. Just before dawn, his people awakened a U.S. district court judge vacationing in his sister's lake cabin. Stevenson got a preliminary injunction to keep Johnson's name off the general-election ballot while the primary results were being assessed. Johnson, growing desperate, hired a friend, Washington lawyer Abe Fortas, to seek a stay of the injunction from the U.S. Supreme Court. Somehow Fortas got the case on the Court's docket in Washington—despite its having no history of decisions from lower courts—and achieved an in-chambers hearing, alone, with Justice Hugo Black, another friend of Johnson's.

Black issued a last-minute stay order. It didn't even have a case number. It made Lyndon Johnson the only name on the Texas Democratic Party ballot for U.S. Senate.

Texas was a one-party state. The Democrats owned it. Winning the Democratic primary meant winning the election. The general election wasn't close.

JOHNSON SURPRISED EVERYONE by giving freshman McCarthy a seat on the prestigious Senate Finance Committee. Johnson decided to get some of the incoming liberals lined up behind him by handing out good assignments. As Johnson saw it, McCarthy was the kind of guy he preferred to have "inside the tent pissing out" instead of the alternative. Johnson told McCarthy that senior colleagues were enraged at being bypassed in favor of the liberal freshman from Minnesota. Johnson now considered McCarthy deeply in his debt. Then Johnson loaded up the debt. Again passing over senior members, he appointed McCarthy chairman of a committee to investigate unemployment in the recession, and to propose a better plan than President Eisenhower's. As the decade ended, Eugene McCarthy, under Lyndon Johnson's wing, seemed well on his way to becoming a major player in the U.S. Senate.

Gene McCarthy's aloofness began to overtake him in 1963 after the assassination of President Kennedy. He struggled to understand what the assassination had done to the country and to him. In a TV interview he said:

> To try and embellish it and make it more clear to people is a task that should be left to the poets—and to those poets who have enough restraint not to touch it for ten, fifteen, or twenty years. . . .
>
> It would be my hope that . . . this might have some kind of purifying and redemptive influence, not just on the United States, where we are concerned about hate and suspicion

and doubt and all of the forces of unreason,
but it might also have an influence for good
on the entire world.

McCarthy's shock and grief was real, but his private truth was that he had never respected his former Senate colleague Jack Kennedy, whom he'd always regarded as a bit of a lightweight playboy.

In the speculation and ramp-up to the 1960 election, nothing had galled McCarthy more than the idea that John Kennedy, of all people, might become the first Catholic president. He objected to the famously wealthy Kennedy lifestyle representing Roman Catholicism in America. "Any way you measure it," he told the Massachusetts congressman Tip O'Neill, a Kennedy ally, "I'm a better man than John Kennedy. I'm smarter, I'm a better orator. . . . I'm a better Catholic. Of course I don't have a rich father." As Hubert Humphrey and Jack Kennedy approached the starting gate for the race for the Democratic nomination, **Time** quoted McCarthy as saying, "I'm twice as liberal as Hubert Humphrey . . . and twice as Catholic as Jack Kennedy."

At the 1960 Democratic convention, McCarthy blocked an effort to support JFK in the Minnesota delegation. When nominating Adlai Stevenson, a fellow intellectual, at that convention, McCarthy gave perhaps the most passionate and compelling speech he'd ever given. Investing Stevenson with the language of the biblical prophet Jeremiah, McCarthy delivered this sermon:

> I say to you the political prophets have prophesied falsely in these eight years. And the high priests of government have ruled by that false prophecy. And the people seemed to have loved it so. But there was one man—there was one man who did not prophesy falsely . . .

In a dig at what sometimes seemed the rawness of Kennedy's ambition, McCarthy praised Stevenson for not seeking power:

> He did not seek power for himself in 1952. He did not seek power in 1956. He is not seeking it for himself today . . . history does not prove that power is always well used by those who seek it.

At that line the Stevenson supporters cheered mightily.

McCarthy's secret that night was that Lyndon Johnson had given McCarthy permission to nominate Stevenson. Johnson, confident Stevenson wouldn't make it, still hoped for the nomination himself and was eager to make support for JFK look weak.

In the end, the only real effect of McCarthy's open disdain for Kennedy was to send his Senate career into a tailspin. In January 1961, JFK became the youngest president in history, and he took McCarthy's Senate patron, Lyndon Johnson, into the White House with him as vice president. Gene McCarthy would have no part in the great American adventure of the Kennedy White House.

McCarthy grew listless. He did so little work that Humphrey's staff started calling McCarthy's office Sleepy Hollow. Nobody could count on him for a vote. He began missing hearings, preferring to write poems in his office or to gab mean-spiritedly with colleagues in the Assembly Restaurant on Capitol Hill. During Finance Committee meetings, McCarthy made calls to friends, just to chat. He quit the ADA, the organization he'd helped reform in the 1940s. He was often out of town now, making speeches— uninspiring but well paid—on the liberal lecture circuit. By early 1963, friends had managed to make some headway in reconciling President Kennedy to McCarthy, but McCarthy kept hanging out in the Senate press gallery entertaining reporters with new jokes about Kennedy's "New Frontier" theme.

McCarthy was even becoming less respected back home in Minnesota. His reelection to the Senate in 1964 was beginning to look dicey.

THE ASSASSINATION OF JFK had the unsettling effect of reviving McCarthy's political career.

In the eerie shadow of that violent transfer of power, Lyndon Johnson and Gene McCarthy found themselves resuming their clumsy dance. All of a sudden, McCarthy's patron was president of the United States, and LBJ was already holding auditions for a running mate in the 1964 election.

Johnson liked drama. His favorite drama involved the public display of dominating other men.

When it came to the VP choice for 1964, the strategy was to balance Johnson's down-home Texas conservatism with well-educated, Northern liberalism. That description fit Minnesota's junior senator, Eugene McCarthy, nicely, but it also fit Minnesota's senior senator, Hubert Humphrey. LBJ's plan was to pit the two Minnesota liberals against each other for the running-mate spot.

Tension between two senators from the same state is inevitable. They or their staffs fight for credit for federal government treats delivered to the state. Johnson knew this. And he knew that every year that tension gets thicker. He knew that his vice presidential auditions would push that tension to the breaking point.

McCarthy thought his chances of being chosen for running mate were good. With Johnson in the White House, his career had regained energy. There were private dinners in the president's quarters with Abigail and Lady Bird. The men discussed backchannel tactics for keeping Democrats on the Finance Committee in line behind LBJ's policies; they planned McCarthy's attack on Johnson's Republican challenger Barry Goldwater. McCarthy was running for reelection to the Senate. When LBJ made an appearance at a McCarthy campaign dinner, McCarthy's hope of being named the running mate soared.

McCarthy could get no reassurance from Johnson. Neither could Humphrey. In fact, as the 1964 convention in Atlantic City drew near, LBJ grew more and more coy.

What Johnson demanded from a running mate was a flat-out loyalty oath. McCarthy was too independent to swear absolute fealty, but he was pretty sure his main competitor, Humphrey, would have no such reservations. As the convention ramped up, McCarthy got excited and at the last minute, he told Abigail to come to Atlantic City and bring the four children. The kids were gathered from their summer camps and hastily dressed in new clothes. When the big McCarthy family strolled the Atlantic City boardwalk, news photographers snapped pictures of the children of the man who might well be the next vice president.

There was no suspense about Johnson's becoming the nominee. At the convention there was to be a memorial film about JFK, and Bobby Kennedy was scheduled to give a speech introducing that segment: Johnson feared being overshadowed by the Kennedy mystique living and dead. He wanted to keep the real attention on himself by amping up suspense over his choice of running mate. One of his ploys was to insist that McCarthy and Humphrey go on **Meet the Press** together to discuss the campaign, knowing they would be asked about their interest in the VP nomination. Embarrassed, McCarthy had no choice but to comply.

On **Meet the Press**, they were each questioned alone. McCarthy went first. Lawrence Spivak said, "You have written a great deal on democracy in your various books. Everyone seems to be agreed that the President of the United States should pick his running mate, who may be the next President. Why should one man, rather than the Convention itself, in your judgment, be allowed to select the man who may be the next President of the United States?"

McCarthy's answer was everything LBJ wanted to hear:

"I don't believe that under all circumstances this would be the position of the party people, but I think in this instance it reflects a confidence in President Johnson and a realization that in making his choice he will make the choice which will reflect the overall interests of the party and his good judgment, in which we have confidence, with reference to the kind of man whom he would want to serve with him in the office of Vice President."

With a smile, **Newsweek**'s Ben Bradlee asked,

"Senator, about this Vice Presidency, do you know anything that we don't?"

"I don't know what you know," replied McCarthy. "I know very little about it. It may be that you know more than I do."

When it was Humphrey's turn, **Time**'s John Steele asked, "Senator, you did have an hour with the President alone this week?"

"Oh yes," replied Humphrey.

"Twice?" said Steele.

"I said 'Oh yes.' "

"Did the matter of the Vice Presidency come up?"

"No it did not. My colleague, Senator McCarthy, and I have had much the same experience. The President has not discussed with me the matter of the Vice Presidency. He has had an opportunity to discuss—I have had an opportunity to discuss with him legislative problems and some of the problems that relate to our party in general, but not the Vice Presidency."

NBC's Ray Scherer asked Humphrey, "On the more personal aspect of things, what kind of loyalty, what kind of man would make the ideal Vice President for a strong personality like Mr. Johnson?"

"The President himself has outlined what he considers to be the qualification for a Vice President," said Humphrey. "One of you good newsmen said to me one time, 'Don't you believe those qualifications are the standards for a saint?' and I said, 'If that is the case, then I have to withdraw, because I can't qualify under that.'"

Despite growing disgust with LBJ's audition process, McCarthy still wanted to believe he had a shot, but Adlai Stevenson, meeting Gene and Abigail for breakfast in Atlantic City, seemed doleful, and others started shaking their heads in sympathy. Abigail had spent sixteen years as a congressional wife. She'd become a shrewd political analyst. She sounded out Lindy Boggs, the wife of Louisiana congressman and Democratic power broker Hale Boggs. The Boggses had long been intimate with the Johnsons. Lindy let Abigail know Gene's chances were not good.

The convention was drawing to an end without a breath of clarity from Johnson about his running mate. It seemed the president planned to reveal his choice to the two hopefuls at the same moment he revealed it to the nation: his plan was to stand on the convention rostrum before a packed house full of delegates, and the American public watching on TV, with Humphrey and McCarthy standing on either side of the incumbent. There they would await his verdict, in suspense, like Miss America contestants.

"Sadistic son of a bitch," said McCarthy.

And so it was, as he'd done before and as he'd do again, that Gene McCarthy made a sudden and unpredictable move that a more careful politician, such as Hubert Humphrey, could easily resist. At the last minute, McCarthy wrote Johnson a telegram withdrawing his name from consideration for the vice presidency. He told his aides to send the telegram to Johnson's people. Once the Johnson camp had time to absorb it, McCarthy said, the aides should release the news to the press.

Abigail made a move of her own. Overriding Gene's orders for the first time, she privately told the aides to release the telegram to the press simultaneously with delivery to Johnson's people. She knew Gene. She knew Johnson. If there was any room to move, Johnson would reel her husband back into his game. Doing it Abigail's way, there could be no going back.

She was right. Johnson aides, receiving the cable, begged McCarthy's people not to send it to Johnson or release it to the press, but now it was too late. The aides, trembling at the prospect, had no choice but to let LBJ know that McCarthy was withdrawing, that the press already knew about it, that the president had been upstaged by Eugene McCarthy. Of all people.

Johnson went into what witnesses described as a towering rage. McCarthy had seized control of the whole convention drama. It was McCarthy, the junior senator from Minnesota, not the president, who made the choice for vice president. Political observers who discovered only in 1968 that Gene McCarthy had a flair for the dramatic had not been paying close enough attention.

The confetti and balloons fell, the bands played,

the delegates pumped their signs. McCarthy nursed his anger. He felt stabbed in the back by his two patrons and mentors, Humphrey and Johnson. Johnson, meanwhile, demanded McCarthy demonstrate at least some modicum of unity and loyalty: McCarthy must give the nominating speech for Humphrey's candidacy for vice president. McCarthy complied, and in contrast to his solemn, heartfelt speech for Stevenson four years earlier, this one was, in the words of the **Washington Post**, "barely perfunctory." It scarcely mattered. Johnson and Humphrey won by a landslide. On Inauguration Day 1965, they already looked unbeatable for reelection in 1968. No other Democrat could think about running for president until 1972.

FOUR

"A HARD AND HARSH MORAL JUDGMENT"

The pace of change in American politics and American culture between Lyndon Johnson's landslide victory over Barry Goldwater in November 1964 and the opening rounds of the presidential primary campaigning only three years later, in the fall of 1967, was faster than Americans had ever seen before. The counterculture explosion of protest, irreverence, generational mistrust, iconoclasm, rebellion, and all the various forms of radical experimentation—sexual, musical, communal, psychotropic—began polarizing the nation on questions of basic American values. That explosion's flashpoint was Lyndon Johnson's war in Vietnam.

At the end of 1964, the singular importance of Vietnam was not yet obvious. Race and civil rights were the most explosive issues of the day, and for good reason. Having defeated Goldwater with a mandate, Johnson was launching the innovative federal antipoverty programs he called the Great Society, and early in his administration, he changed his old Southern approach to race. There were huge risks involved. George Wallace, the segregationist governor of Alabama, had entered the Democratic presidential primaries in 1964 on the strength of opposition to LBJ's civil rights plans, and he'd gained surprising ground in Wisconsin, Indiana, and Maryland. During the campaign, the president had nevertheless signed the first of the famous civil rights acts. After the election, he signed the Voting Rights Act of 1965. At the risk of the loss of Democratic power in what had been "the solid South," Johnson did what Hubert Humphrey had demanded back in 1948: he made the Democratic Party the leader on racial equality.

Meanwhile, a series of landmark federal court cases supporting equality for African Americans was shaking up not only unabashed racists but also some traditionalists who liked to see themselves as reasonably moderate. The famous **Brown v. Board of Education** decision by the Supreme Court in 1954 had struck down state laws segregating schools, and segregationists were still pushing back against it. Race matters took on a more intimate form, shocking to many, in the case of **Loving v. Virginia**, filed in federal court by Mildred and Richard Loving, an African American woman and a white man. They were charged with the crime of interracial marriage—"cohabiting as man and wife against the peace and dignity of the Commonwealth"—under Virginia's 1924 Racial Integrity Act. The Lovings were forced to move to Washington, D.C., and in 1964 they filed suit in federal court to have the state charge vacated on constitutional grounds.

That the Lovings' lawsuit, and not the law itself, sent shock waves through much of the country was an indicator of the extent of American racism in 1964. The case would move toward a unanimous ruling in favor of the Lovings in the U.S. Supreme Court in 1967. (The Loving case was cited as precedent when the Supreme Court extended marital voting rights to same sex couples in 2015, an unimaginable outcome in 1967.)

In 1965, Yale dropped its dress code. Jackets and ties were suddenly not mandatory. Two years later, much of the campus looked like Woodstock was going to look in 1969. As the American body count in Vietnam went up, opposition to the war went up with it. Opposition to the war increasingly meant opposition to the establishment in all things from neckties to draft cards. By 1967, a coalescence of liberal movements occurred on the Vietnam War. At its emotional center was hatred for Lyndon Johnson.

In 1967, Dr. Martin Luther King Jr., America's greatest civil rights leader, having long maintained a strained silence on the subject, spoke against the war in Vietnam. The New Left organization Students for a Democratic Society (SDS), organized by Tom Hayden and others throughout college campuses, made opposition to the war its centerpiece. The war was on television every day, invading the American living room, where generational arguments began flaring.

The president of the United States was suddenly a figure of disdain and mockery: "Hey! Hey! LBJ!" the protesters chanted. "How many kids did you kill today!" Music became even louder and more aggressively electrified with woozy lyrics about revolution and free love. Bob Dylan, having begun as a folk singer in the 1930s Woody Guthrie vein, now fronted an amplified band and sang elusive, unsettling, even apocalyptic lyrics. An alien exotic bohemia in political opposition to, it seemed, America itself had somehow zoomed in out of somewhere and invaded suburbia.

The faraway war was everywhere in American life all the time. Everyone was affected by the same fear: Who would be next? The war was dividing the home front in ways never before imagined.

Gene McCarthy's evolution on Vietnam occurred spasmodically during those dizzying twenty-four months from 1965 to 1967. McCarthy had long supported, without any serious doubt, the U.S. policy of containing communism. McCarthy unflinchingly supported President Kennedy in tripling aid and sending the 16,000 advisers to South Vietnam. The Kennedy approach to covert action did inspire McCarthy to some new thinking, however. To McCarthy, the failure in 1961 of exiled Cuban partisans to invade Cuba with secret U.S. support at the Bay of Pigs seemed to point to a rise in presidential deceit and adventurism.

Power must have moral limits. Might it be possible, McCarthy began considering, that the American fight against the spread of the dehumanizing Soviet gulag, ethically correct in its origin, could lead the United States into arrogance, hubris, secrecy, paranoia, and self-destructive quagmires?

When an opening occurred on the Foreign Relations Committee in April 1965, McCarthy grabbed the seat. He began following William Fulbright's turn against the war. That, of course, meant a turn against their own party's president. The dissenting senators were not outspoken at first, at least in public. This was a mild patriotic dissent, within a supposedly unified party, within a country where most college students wouldn't dream of violating the dress code, never mind taking over a building or rioting.

By January 1966, U.S. casualties in Vietnam neared 2,000. Protests by antiwar students were gaining traction. Mary McCarthy, Gene and Abigail's daughter, now a senior in high school, was already committed to ending the war. Mary was pushing her parents to live up to their religious and ethical commitments and help end the war. Parents of students like Mary were the first parents to turn against the war.

In hopes of getting North Vietnam to the negotiating table, Johnson had suspended the bombing of North Vietnam for the 1965 Christmas holidays. On January 27, 1966, McCarthy and fourteen other senators took the shocking step of sending the president an open letter urging him to continue the bombing suspension. It was nothing but a suggestion to hold off, at least for a time, on further bombing, in no way a push for anything like U.S. withdrawal from Vietnam. But sending a letter inviting public response was shockingly unprofessional to LBJ. Opposing Johnson was one thing, surprising him was worse. Anything he perceived as disloyalty sent him into an altered state. Now he feared his own party was turning against him.

Stopping the bombing, not total withdrawal, was becoming the middle-of-the-road position on the war, but McCarthy was beginning to cross a line. He was getting out from under Johnson. He was coming to believe, for one thing, that the Vietcong should be included in peace negotiations. The conflict within South Vietnam was starting to look more like a civil war than outside communist aggression. The United States might really be propping up a decadent military dictatorship in South Vietnam in order to fend off communism. What if the entire anticommunist consensus of the past twenty years had been misguided? If so, then America would need what McCarthy was coming to think of as a New Politics.

THEN, ON JANUARY 31, 1967, a group called the National Emergency Committee of Clergy and Laymen Concerned About Vietnam (CALCAV) gathered in D.C. for two days of lobbying and prayer. This CALCAV meeting was nothing like the full-scale antiwar demonstrations that would soon be jamming the Mall. Still, CALCAV held the first large-scale action in Washington to protest Johnson's Vietnam policy and propose quick ways to peace. Twenty-four hundred people attended. These were McCarthy's people. And they had some news for him.

Many prominent Catholics, especially the intellectuals, McCarthy's old friends, were bucking the church establishment by joining CALCAV. Martin Luther King Jr. was a member. Protestants like Richard Niebuhr, Catholics like Daniel Berrigan, and Jews like Abraham Heschel came to the Washington convention. They were demanding a halt to what they called the immorally disproportionate bombing of North Vietnam. They wanted Vietcong insurgents admitted to the peace talks. They challenged the longstanding notion that in the service of combating communism, any and all violence employed by the United States was justified. These people of

faith spoke McCarthy's language of ethics, morality, and justice. On the first day of the gathering, a
huge group of demonstrators walked en masse to the
Capitol to meet with their legislators.

Senator McCarthy was startled to find his office
suddenly crowded with Minnesota constituents of
various religions. They weren't there to bond with
him, or to thank him for his efforts to date against
the war, or to gently persuade him to do more. For the
first time, they were yelling at him—all of them—
and the cacophony in the office grew outrageous, like
a football rally. Some were actually berating McCarthy in full-throated screams. These sounds had never
before been heard in the Senate office building.

McCarthy was stunned. These weren't scruffy students. These were grown-up, middle-class, church-
going Minnesotans, and they were wild in their fury
at Gene. It seemed that while Senators McCarthy,
Fulbright, George McGovern, and others in Congress had been moving at their deliberate legislators'
pace toward a new position on Vietnam, ordinary
people, outraged by the bombing and terrified by the
draft, had sped far ahead of them. These people were
here to tell their senator to his face and at high volume that horrific violence was being committed by
the U.S. government, and North Vietnamese babies
were being killed, and American boys were being
drafted to die for no reason while their senators were
attending hearings and making speeches and doing

nothing decisive in the face of this unspeakable immorality.

For a Catholic like Gene McCarthy, such passivity represented not only a political disgrace but a profound and unacceptable moral and spiritual failing. Senator McCarthy had no good answer for his constituents that day.

THE NEXT DAY, FEBRUARY 1, all of the CALCAV demonstrators crowded into the New York Avenue Presbyterian Church near the White House for their convention's closing session. Senator Wayne Morse, who had voted against the Gulf of Tonkin Resolution and was solidly opposed to the war, addressed the crowd, condemning Johnson's policy. He got huge ovations. So did Senator Ernest Gruening, the only other senator who opposed the Gulf of Tonkin Resolution.

(Wayne Morse would reap no reward back home in Oregon for his political bravery. He was already in trouble for reelection in 1968 because of his opposition to the war. Morse's political plight was a cautionary tale for any other senator contemplating opposition to it. For being right on the Gulf of Tonkin Resolution and the war, Wayne Morse lost his reelection to Republican Bob Packwood in 1968.)

After the heroes in that church spoke—Wayne Morse and Ernest Gruening—Eugene McCarthy rose to speak. McCarthy made what he saw as his first complete break with Lyndon Johnson on Vietnam. Speaking the language of faith, he told the cheering crowd that politics do not escape God's purview. The U.S. position in Vietnam was overdue, he said, for "a hard and harsh moral judgment." Americans must stop assuming that morality "stops at the doors of the Central Intelligence Agency." McCarthy closed by quoting some warnings from the historian Arnold Toynbee: "War posthumously avenges the dead on the survivors." Reporters for the **New York Times** and the **Washington Post**, among others, played down the significance of the speech—the **Times** reported only that the senator "commended the religious leaders for underscoring the 'moral dilemma' of the war"—as did the big columnists, while heartland papers with Washington bureaus—the **Des Moines Register**, McCarthy's hometown **Minneapolis Tribune**, the **Shreveport Times**, and others—ran with it, quoting in particular Senator McCarthy's "a hard and harsh moral judgment" line. McCarthy was a story again, back in touch with his vocation: a politician with the heart of a priest and the head of a professor.

The next day, President Johnson gave a press conference. When the reporters barraged him with questions about achieving peace in Vietnam, Johnson said he saw no serious efforts on the part of the enemy to come to any diplomatic agreement for peace. Reflecting on the frustrations of his job, Johnson said, "I go to bed every night feeling that I have failed that day because I could not end the conflict in Vietnam. I do have disappointments and moments of distress, as I think every President has had."

He added, "But I am not complaining."

AS GENE McCARTHY LEFT the New York Avenue Presbyterian Church that winter day, he knew he had finally taken a stand, but he didn't know what for. He did not yet know how to end the war in Vietnam. It was six months later when he heard the testimony of Nicholas Katzenbach and he saw the way. The only way.

To do it, he had to be willing to bring down both of his patrons and mentors at the same time—the president and the vice president of the United States. Once he saw it as a moral decision, Gene McCarthy had no choice.

FIVE

DUMP JOHNSON

There was only one Democrat who could beat President Johnson, and then beat any Republican, and Allard Lowenstein knew who it was. That's why he wouldn't give up trying to persuade Bobby Kennedy to run.

Al Lowenstein was the only person in Washington who could embrace a crazy idea and still be taken seriously by some members of Congress: the liberal members. Lowenstein was a 1954 graduate of Yale Law School. He joined Hubert Humphrey's Senate staff as a foreign policy assistant, and in 1959, he went to South Africa and collected evidence of the human rights abuses of the South African government, which he published in a book. He persuaded Eleanor Roosevelt to write the introduction to that book. In 1964, he went to Mississippi to participate in Freedom Summer to expand black voter registration.

Lowenstein knew everyone in liberal politics and more than a few Republicans. He was a mentor and an inspiration to younger Democrats who would become Washington power brokers—Bill and Hillary Clinton, Congressman Barney Frank, Clinton aide Harold Ickes, and the former White House counsel to President Obama, Greg Craig. He took in the spectacle of the 1964 Republican convention with his friend Donald Rumsfeld. In 1966, Lowenstein helped Bobby Kennedy write an extraordinary speech that the senator delivered in South Africa at the University of Cape Town. Here is the first paragraph:

> I came here because of my deep interest and affection for a land settled by the Dutch in the mid-seventeenth century, then taken over by the British, and at last independent; a land in which the native inhabitants were at first subdued, but relations with whom remain a problem to this day; a land which defined itself on a hostile frontier; a land which has tamed rich natural resources through the energetic application of modern technology; a land which once imported slaves, and now must struggle to wipe out the last traces of that former bond-

age. I refer, of course, to the United States of America.

Two months before Bobby delivered that speech, Al Lowenstein told **Village Voice** columnist Jack Newfield, "I'm going to be spending the rest of the year organizing a movement to dump Johnson." That was in April 1966. By the end of that year of organizing "Dump Johnson," he was just getting started. He still needed a credible candidate to run against the president of the United States for the Democratic nomination.

Al Lowenstein had no time for, and was not particularly good at, small talk. He was a thirty-eight-year-old nerd in rumpled suits with thinning hair and thick eyeglasses who roamed the halls of Congress looking for a presidential candidate to do the impossible. He was, by all appearances, a man obsessed.

The immediate goal was to end the Vietnam War by denying Lyndon Johnson reelection. And there was a larger goal, too. Working with Curtis Gans— Lowenstein's opposite number, a patient analyst of electoral statistics—Lowenstein believed the Dump Johnson movement might not only deny a second term to Lyndon Johnson, but also begin changing American politics for good.

Lowenstein and Gans weren't New Left radicals. They weren't hippies, and they weren't kids. Lowenstein was known to Democratic politicians in Washington and all over the country: mayors, governors, state legislators and their staffs. Curtis Gans was a thirty-year-old who was quietly and steadily immersed in the study of voter-turnout patterns in the United States. Gans grew up in Manhattan and was a member of Students for a Democratic Society. He worked as a reporter for the United Press International wire service, then worked on liberal Democratic campaigns.

Lowenstein was at the center of the rift developing between liberalism and radicalism in 1966. The National Student Association (NSA) was founded in 1947, in part with CIA money, as the anticommunist liberal umbrella for college student governments. NSA served as the major organizing platform for mobilizing liberal campaigns among young people, and in August 1966, when it held its annual meeting, the organization split into two camps: liberal and radical.

The liberals, rallying behind Lowenstein, believed real change could be brought about only by working within existing institutions. The radicals, by contrast, behind David Harris of Stanford, believed the Vietnam War had made things so dire that direct action and civil disobedience were the only effective courses of action. At the meeting, Harris called the Lowenstein liberals who wanted to work through the system "good Germans." Lowenstein shot back that David Harris's lying down in front of a troop train would do nothing, but that organizing a hundred student-body presidents to do the same would have an impact. NSA adopted Lowenstein's position and had him draft a calm, closely reasoned letter from NSA to LBJ, questioning his policy in Vietnam. The letter made the **New York Times** front page.

Dean Rusk, LBJ's secretary of state, agreed to meet with the campus student-body presidents to discuss Vietnam policy. Favoring U.S. nuclear buildup for deterrence, Rusk was famous for having raised the fearsome idea that by the year 2000, there would be a billion Chinese ready to roll over the free world. Now one of the student-body presidents asked him to consider what might happen when both the United States and the USSR, escalating the nuclear standoff, started dropping hydrogen bombs. Rusk exhaled cigarette smoke. "Well, somebody's going to get hurt," he explained to the kids.

If it was a joke, it fell flat. In the chilling silence that followed, many students who had never imagined opposing a president, or an American war, found themselves transformed into antiwar activists. The establishment—Dean Rusk, the war cabinet, the compliant Congress— was doing the Left's work for it, pushing new converts toward David Harris and the now radical SDS, toward what Lowenstein saw as self-defeating radicalism and away from pragmatic politics. Dump Johnson was meant to corral all that political energy.

Lowenstein faced opposition not only from his left but also from mainstream liberalism. While to SDS he seemed the classic middle-of-the-road bourgeois liberal, in his other political home, Americans for Democratic Action, Lowenstein seemed a wild-eyed insurrectionist. ADA had no use for any talk of dumping an incumbent Democratic president.

ADA was the organization that set the liberal agendas and supported liberal Democratic candidates. Hubert Humphrey and Eugene McCarthy had helped reform ADA's Minnesota chapter in the late 1940s. One of the ADA's leaders was now the vice president of the United States. While President Johnson wasn't in every way an ADA-certified liberal, he seemed to many in the organization a far better bet for preserving and even extending the New Deal's liberal advances than anyone the Republicans were likely to nominate for president. Johnson had been moving forward vigorously on Great Society programs and civil rights. The ADA's idea was to hold on to the executive branch, not shake things up.

So to the big labor leaders on the national board of ADA, Dump Johnson made Allard Lowenstein look just like one of those kids burning their draft cards far away from professional American politics. At thirty-eight, Lowenstein was the ADA board's youngest member, and to the old labor lions he represented a dangerous shift in values and strategy. Liberalism, they believed, was about economics and class fairness, not a single issue like ending a war, especially a war against communism in Asia. The unions had purged communists from their ranks long ago. They associated labor's successes during and after World War II with freedom from the socialistic climate of early union organizing. Many leaders were not only die-hard anticommunists but also military veterans, proud of their records and eager to support U.S. troops in the field. When Vice President Humphrey himself had addressed both the general ADA meeting and the organization's leadership cadre regarding Vietnam, he had passionately made the classic liberal argument in favor of continuing the war. The United States must contain communism in Southeast Asia, Humphrey told those powerful labor liberals, or, like Prime Minister Chamberlain after giving up Czechoslovakia to Hitler in 1938, be disdained by history as an ineffectual appeaser. That was a powerful argument to Humphrey's ADA, the organization whose support Al Lowenstein would need most.

Fortunately for Lowenstein, some of the intellectual leaders of ADA had come to oppose the war in Vietnam and its exponent in chief, Lyndon Johnson, as much as the kids at the protests did. Two of them had never trusted Johnson, personally or politically: Arthur M. Schlesinger Jr., a JFK intimate and Harvard historian, and John Kenneth Galbraith, JFK's ambassador to India and a Harvard economist.

When Humphrey came to the ADA national leadership and cast holding the line against communism in Southeast Asia as a Munich moment, Arthur Schlesinger, who had worked in the White House when LBJ was vice president, said, "Hubert, that's shit, and you know it."

Still, Schlesinger and Galbraith could not see any way to overthrow an incumbent Democratic president. Lowenstein's friend Barney Frank, a twenty-nine-year-old Massachusetts activist, found himself questioning Lowenstein's political judgment. Even the antiwar contingent within ADA couldn't get behind dumping Johnson.

So Allard Lowenstein took the Dump Johnson movement out of ADA. Within the liberal system, that counted as a radical move, but the organization, Lowenstein decided, was obviously out of touch. It was time for real change, within the system, and Lowenstein was going to have to try to dump Johnson without the support of the most important national organization in liberal politics.

By the fall of 1967, Dump Johnson had caught fire. The phrase had taken on a life of its own, a new kind of political mantra. Lowenstein's Dump Johnson movement had become a public phenomenon.

Political slogans had usually taken cheery, vacuous form: Eisenhower's "I Like Ike," Stevenson's "Madly for Adlai," Kennedy's "Let's Back Jack," Johnson's "All the Way with LBJ." "Dump Johnson," referring at once to an inside-the-party lobbying effort and an outside antiwar protest movement, was so clear, personal, rude, and defiant that it became the rallying cry for student and other organizations that were against traditional political institutions. An insider's phrase sounded like a revolution.

Lowenstein didn't want a revolution. He wanted enlightened liberal members of Congress and he wanted an enlightened liberal president to end the war. He wanted Bobby.

In Lowenstein's movement, system politics remained the order of the day. At first he had no money: he worked from his apartment and in one of his father's New York restaurants, calling everyone he knew in reform Democratic clubs and equally young antiwar organizations to plead for funds and support. He called in favors and offered inspiration. Soon Gans and he, still with very little budget, had formed campus groups across the country, deploying volunteers to knock on doors with Gans assessing the data they collected on voters. Lowenstein and Gans crisscrossed the country, Gans working the phones from hotel rooms and supporters' homes, Lowenstein making fiery speeches in student unions and church basements. At the microphone, the nerd became one of the most inspiring liberal preachers of the day. State legislators and other lower-profile politicians from New York to the Midwest to California started coming on board. Many of them would be Democratic convention delegates. But delegates at a presidential nominating convention need a candidate.

Many within the Dump Johnson crowd thought a candidate would serve only as a strong protest against escalating the war. Johnson would win the nomination but be chastened along the way and at least stop escalating the war. Nobody thought a protest candidate could actually beat Johnson.

Lowenstein saw it differently. Johnson could be beaten, he insisted. Even better, the ideal insurgent candidate wouldn't split but would unify the Democratic Party and then galvanize the whole country. That candidate was obviously Bobby Kennedy. Lowenstein's now massive, electrified Dump Johnson movement was either a Kennedy presidential campaign or it was just a mirage. Without Bobby, Al Lowenstein had nothing.

SIX

THE GENERAL

Al Lowenstein's friend at the **Village Voice**, Jack Newfield, was an activist columnist. He did not just report on antiwar protests, he participated in them. By April 1967, Newfield had decided "Johnson had to be defeated for reelection." He picked up vague suggestions here and there about a third-party ticket of Martin Luther King Jr. for president and pediatrician–turned–peace activist Benjamin Spock for vice president. Later, he described the dark days of 1967 on college campuses this way: "I spoke at a few campuses in the spring and watched the violence and fury against the war mount, turning English majors into guerrilla fantasists. Several thousand white, middle-class college students, with successful careers already tracked inside the system, burned their draft cards, risking five years in jail. Other thousands became men without countries by exiling themselves to Canada to avoid the rising draft calls. Despairing of changing the world, more and more students were turning to new chemicals to shut out the world, and change the universe inside their heads. And within the deepest coils of the New Left, kids talked of sabotage and assassination."

In April 1967, Newfield wrote the definitive Dump Johnson column: "I voted for him in 1964 and now I don't believe a word he says," Newfield began. "I am too old to defy the draft," he wrote, "so I will withhold twenty percent of my taxes." A rumor later spread through college campuses that the federal telephone service tax was somehow used to directly support the war. So college students started paying their phone bills minus the tax. For most of them, the back taxes caught up with them when they graduated and tried to obtain phone service in their new apartments. Such was the range of protest during the war. Newfield ended his Dump Johnson piece with this: "At Auschwitz a child who knew he was about to die screamed at a German guard, 'You won't be forgiven anything.' This is my saying the same thing to Lyndon Johnson. He is not my President. This is not my war."

In the middle of that column, Newfield offered a strategic insight that no politician believed: "My perception of LBJ is that, like Sonny Liston, he is a bully with a quitter's heart, that he will not run if he thinks he cannot win."

In 1962, Sonny Liston was a boxer on the rise, hoping to get a shot at the heavyweight champion of the world, Floyd Patterson. Patterson was everyone's idea of a true champion. He won a gold medal at the Olympics when he was seventeen, and at twenty-one, he was the youngest heavyweight champion in history. In 1962, he visited the White House, and in a private chat with the president, JFK urged Patterson not to fight Sonny Liston, who had learned how to box in prison when he was sentenced to five years for armed robbery. Liston was boxing in prison when Patterson was boxing at the Olympics. JFK thought that Floyd Patterson was an ideal heavyweight champ and an invaluable asset to the civil rights movement and that Sonny Liston was the opposite. Patterson had insisted that promoters desegregate seating at his matches. Liston was rumored to be managed by mobsters. The president of the NAACP, Percy Sutton, said, "Patterson represents us better than Liston ever could or would." JFK might also have been worried about how hard Liston could punch. Liston was knocking out everyone in his path. Patterson was a talented, determined fighter. Liston was a fearsome, menacing fighter. Patterson told JFK, "I'm sorry, Mr. President, the title is not worth anything if the best fighters can't have a shot at it. And Liston deserves a shot." Years later, Patterson said that by the time he stepped into the ring, he was made to feel as if a loss would doom the civil rights movement.

Sonny Liston won the title in what politics would call a landslide by knocking out Floyd Patterson in the first round. In a rematch, Patterson stayed on his feet longer— by exactly four seconds—when Liston again knocked him out in the first round. Liston couldn't find challengers after that. Finally in 1964 another Olympic gold medalist named Cassius Clay stepped into the ring with Liston. The odds were eight to one in Liston's favor. Betting on the match was disappointingly low for the criminals who ran the gambling rackets then because no one wanted to bet on Cassius Clay, even with a possible return of $8 for every dollar bet on Clay. Liston could not be beaten. When Clay survived the first round, the world was shocked. By the sixth round, Liston seemed sluggish. When the bell sounded for the start of the seventh round, Liston didn't move. He sat on the stool in his corner and quit. And the world was stunned. Two weeks later, the new heavyweight champ changed his name to Muhammad Ali. Jack Newfield could see LBJ as Liston, but no politician who had ever dealt with LBJ could see him that way. And there was still no political Muhammad Ali in sight.

Newfield covered Bobby's New York Senate campaign in 1964. Two years later, Senator Kennedy watched Newfield on TV discussing his latest book, **A Prophetic Minority**, about the civil rights and antiwar movements. Bobby invited him to lunch. That lunch sparked Newfield's next book, a biography titled **RFK**. Later, Newfield said, "Kennedy was the first national politician I had met who had human reactions. He wasn't plastic. He wasn't programmed. He could get angry or be funny and yet always be himself. He was a complicated person with a rich enough character for a whole book." Newfield wanted RFK to run for president. The question was when, 1968 or 1972?

The Kennedy loyalists Arthur Schlesinger and John Kenneth Galbraith saw it the same way: not should Bobby run, but when should Bobby run? Speechwriter Ted Sorensen, whom President Kennedy once called his "intellectual blood bank," along with everyone else in the RFK circle, including his senior staff, all lived with the vision of seeing Bobby inaugurated. Their only question was when.

Meanwhile, they watched Bobby change. Sometimes he actually wore love beads around his neck. He listened to Bob Dylan albums. He hung out at the pop artist Andy Warhol's fabled Factory, home of downtown New York City decadence and cool. When Bobby went to Hollywood, he stayed with the old-fashioned crooner and TV star Andy Williams. The RFK stereo blasted Broadway more than folk rock. To the true believers on the staff, that meant Bobby crossed cultural and generational lines like no one else, at once an explorer and a unifier unafraid of new ideas. There was no question for the staff that RFK would run for president. And there was no question that he would win. But only RFK himself could answer the biggest question: When?

Bobby grew up weak and klutzy, unfocused academically, always worrying about something. Tense and thin-skinned, easy and fun to upset, shirt untucked, hair uncombed, Bobby was always a bit of a mess. His hard-edged father, Joseph P. Kennedy Sr., called him "the runt." Joe Kennedy's attention and expectations were focused on his two older sons, Jack and Joe Jr. Bobby's older brothers seemed of another generation. Jack was eight years older than Bobby. Joe was ten years older. Joe and Jack were tall, athletic, and confident, dazzling in their accomplishments. Unless they were mocking little Bobby, they never paid attention to him. Bobby couldn't impress Joe at all, or even get his attention other than the occasional snide remark. Jack could be nicer, now and then, with a roughly humorous, semidespairing affection for this nervous, scrawny, too-serious little kid.

Bobby was his mother's pet, open and charming with her, and nice and polite to others, the nicest of them all. Bob took up Rose's intense religiosity early on. An altar boy, he learned all he could about serving Mass and the theology of Roman Catholicism. He seemed filled with a devoutness unusual in a small boy. This mixture of seriousness, fragility, and religiosity endeared him to Rose. If there was to be a priest in the family—and in an Irish family of this size it was expected—it would be Bobby.

He was, Rose told him outright, her favorite. That only made his father and big brothers and sisters see Bobby as more of a sap.

Joe and Jack were competitive and rough. Bobby wanted so badly to be a part of that roughhouse, but there was no place for him there. Hoping to toughen him up, the family got Bobby boxing lessons. No good: he seemed to lack the killer instinct. At his schools—he went to a lot of them, from Portsmouth Priory, a Catholic boarding school, to Milton Academy and others—he was passive intellectually, mediocre athletically, isolated socially.

Bobby's tension and isolation were only highlighted by the peripatetic, gregarious Kennedy lifestyle. Joseph Patrick Kennedy Sr. was a big player at the highest levels of business and politics, with a web of connections from the Irish American political machine that had formed him in East Boston, to steel mills and shipyards he owned and managed; from the Chicago Merchandise Mart, the country's biggest office building, which he owned, to the distilleries in Scotland that made the oceans of liquor he distributed; from Hollywood, where he had a longstanding affair with the screen star Gloria Swanson, to the nation's capital, where he served as Security and Exchange Commission chairman, to London, where he served as U.S. ambassador. At Kennedy homes in Boston, suburban New York, Cape Cod, Palm Beach, and the Court of St. James's, on vacations in the Alps and the Caribbean, Bobby remained odd boy out in the turbulent, competitively busy cluster of Joe's kids. That cluster grew to nine in 1935, with the birth of baby Teddy.

Rose badgered her bewildered, scrawny favorite to get involved in the dances and tennis matches and races in which most of her children excelled. Kennedys were charged not merely with enjoying but also with dominating every kind of activity. In the overprivileged world of pedigreed Protestant Harvard families they had invaded, they weren't to hang back, or even fit in, but to prove themselves superior. They must win. That's how Kennedys had fun.

Bobby had no interest in all that. As he moped about in his slovenly clothes, Jack thought he captured his mood with the nickname "Black Robert."

Bobby longed to show, to really feel, the courage and decisiveness that seemed so natural in Jack and Joe. He tried too hard. At the top of a ski slope he nervously weighed his options longer than anyone else, then abruptly hurled himself down the steepest part, far more challenging than he could handle, flailing all the way to the bottom, more reckless than brave. These spasms of over-the-top bravado gained him no sibling respect. The others only shook their heads and marveled at the awkward, embarrassing strangeness of their little brother.

His older brothers' future triumphs were easy for little Bobby to envision. Their father lived for that future. Joseph Kennedy's biggest plans rode on his oldest son, Joe Jr. His father wasn't the only one with high expectations for Joe Jr. John Fitzgerald, known as Honey Fitz, was mayor of Boston. When his daughter Rose gave birth to Joseph P. Kennedy Jr., he announced, "He is going to be the President of the United States."

TO ANYONE NOT RELATED to Joe Kennedy Jr., Honey Fitz's prediction was as likely as the grand-father of a black baby born in 1961 predicting the child would be president when black people were still fighting for the right to vote. Irish Catholics had much less discrimination to overcome than African Americans, but when Joe Jr. was born in 1915, America was still forty-five years away from accepting a Catholic president, and most Catholics believed it would take much longer than that.

At the rowdy, jousting family dinners where their father quizzed and challenged Joe on political questions, Jack served as sparring partner to the champ. The father set his elder sons against each other and refereed debate with gusto. It was all part of the grooming. Given Jack's own talents, it started to seem that maybe a Joe Jr. presidency would launch the Kennedys as a dynasty to rival and surpass the Adamses and the Roosevelt cousins. Little Teddy was growing up handsome, pugnacious, athletic. He, too, might be presidential timber. They would have to find something else for Bobby.

In 1942, Joe and Jack Kennedy went off to serve in World War II. Bobby didn't. Left behind in the Navy Reserve, Bobby brooded. His father had arranged it: with his two oldest sons risking their lives, Joe Sr. had no choice but to keep Bobby in reserve, a weak backup plan. Bobby had no way to refuse. He read the letters that came from abroad from Joe and Jack telling him of their brave and manly struggles. They ribbed him for an easy life stateside. Stuck in training camp in Maine, Bobby felt, he said, like some kind of draft dodger. "Me being my usual moody self," he wrote a friend, "I get very sad at times." He was missing what he thought was his best chance of showing courage. Bobby wanted his chance at war.

Twenty years later, when Robert F. Kennedy was nominated and confirmed as his brother's U.S. attorney general, much had changed, both within Bobby and outside him. And much had not. Perhaps the most important transformation that Bobby underwent in those decades was in his father's estimation of him. How their father ranked the Kennedy brothers had long defined them not only in his eyes but also in their own.

That change in Bobby's status was a function of painful necessity. In 1944, Joe Jr. volunteered for a secret combat mission. The mission was part of Operation Aphrodite, a combined U.S. Army Air Forces and U.S. Navy project to crash unmanned bombers full of explosives, controlled via radio, onto enemy targets and blow them to smithereens, a kind of secret robot kamikaze. Though unmanned, Operation Aphrodite bombers needed human piloting in order to get into the air and on their paths, and Joe was in the first pair of pilots to make the attempt. A two-man crew would fly to an altitude of two thousand feet, fire up the radio control, wait while the craft made its first remote-controlled turn, pull a pin to arm the explosives, radio a confirmation code back to base, and about five minutes or so later, when the plane flew over a predetermined spot, bail out and open their parachutes. The aircraft would continue and crash itself on its target. A 1940s version of drones.

No one had done it yet when Joe and his copilot took off from the Royal Air Force's Fersfield airfield in England on the evening of August 12, 1944, loaded up with about twenty-one thousand pounds of explosives, headed for northern France to knock out German cannons that were capable of firing

V-3 missiles at England. At first everything went as planned. With the plane under remote control, Joe gave the code over the radio. Two minutes later, with the pilots still on board, the entire payload detonated. It blasted the plane out of the sky. Fire and debris rained on the coastal English countryside.

Joseph P. Kennedy Jr. was dead, his courage immortalized. For a time, his father was unable to function. Then he did the only thing he could think of to carry on: he changed the lineup.

Everybody moved up one. Joe Jr. had been planning to run for Congress from the Massachusetts Eleventh Congressional District in 1946; now Jack would run for that seat. The incumbent, and legendary, James Michael Curley was urged by Joe Sr.— and funded by him—to run for mayor of Boston. With Jack heading to Congress and then the Senate, Bobby was to follow along in line. Bobby was being encouraged now, not spurned. With that, new strengths began to show themselves. New weaknesses, too.

Having graduated from the University of Virginia law school, Bobby followed Jack to Washington, D.C., in 1951, moving his family to a house in the wealthy Georgetown neighborhood and taking a job in the Justice Department. He had married Ethel Skakel a year earlier. The first of their eleven children was also born in 1951. In 1952, Bobby managed his first political campaign—Jack's election to the Senate—and it was a success. Jack still razzed Bob, called him Black Robert, complained about his irritating intensity, mocked his messy hair, humiliated him before others. And yet the brothers were beginning to form a team.

After Jack Kennedy's Senate election, Bobby became perhaps the best-known Senate committee lawyer. He had a rough start. In December 1952, he began work as assistant counsel for his father's friend Senator Joseph McCarthy in the Senate's subcommittee on investigations, seeking communist spies and subversives. Joe McCarthy's top staffer was the attorney Roy Cohn, famous for aiding in convicting Julius and Ethel Rosenberg of espionage; the Rosenbergs were now awaiting execution. Bobby couldn't stand working with Roy Cohn, and he quit after six months. Eighteen months later, the Senate voted overwhelmingly to censure Joe McCarthy for the dishonest tactics used in his so-called investigations, many of which were conceived and executed by Roy Cohn. "McCarthyism" became the one-word description of those tactics. Boston lawyer Joseph Welch became the most quoted Senate witness of the decade when, staring down Joe McCarthy, he said, "Until this moment, Senator, I think I never really gauged your cruelty or your recklessness. . . . Have you no sense of decency, sir, at long last? Have you left no sense of decency?" Joe McCarthy's ten years in the Senate ended with his dying as an alcoholic at age forty-eight. Roy Cohn returned to New York City, where he eventually became Donald Trump's legal adviser and mentor. Bobby's six months with Joe McCarthy were not enough to leave his career permanently stained by McCarthyism, which would have left him with no political career in the 1960s. Bobby soon found another job in the Senate as minority counsel, and in 1955, with the Democrats back in the majority, he became majority counsel and enjoyed great visibility.

Robert Kennedy first became nationally known in 1957 as chief counsel to the Senate Select Committee on Improper Activities in Labor and Management, known as the rackets committee, investigating corrupt practices in choosing leaders of big unions, especially the Teamsters. JFK was on the committee, but as counsel, Bobby was taking full charge of the investigations, running hearings, scheduling testimony, cross-examining witnesses. That's where Bobby quickly gained a reputation for toughness, even ruthlessness, with some signs of the old trying-too-hard.

Bobby finally had his own arena now, a place to display fearlessness. These men he hounded and humiliated in public were dangerous, violent, and cunning. The committee room seethed with hatred. Off-mike, Bobby spat fighting words at Teamsters president Jimmy Hoffa: "You're full of shit, you're full of shit."

This one-man crusade to force evildoers to break down in front of him and confess their many crimes posed the Kennedy family some problems. Jack Kennedy's career—and the careers of the entire Democratic Party—depended on support from labor. Exposing criminality and violence in the Teamsters risked making other key labor leaders distinctly uncomfortable. The Kennedys were close to Walter Reuther, head of the United Auto Workers (UAW). Certain politicians saw pure hypocrisy in Bobby's attacking Hoffa. They accused Bobby of diverting attention from corruption in Walter Reuther's UAW. "The Kennedy boys," the Republican senator Barry Goldwater of Arizona told reporters, were using a Senate committee to serve private ends.

Jack Kennedy's career was supposed to come first, but Bobby now was often center stage. As a committee member, Jack often sat at the dais immediately to Bobby's left while his little brother did battle with witnesses. Newsreels caught Jack in a circle of senators gathered equally around the committee's counsel, making Bobby, not Jack, the center of attention.

All of that bothered their father. But worst of all, for him, was the irony in Bobby's probing the closely guarded secrets of gangsters and labor racketeers. Bobby knew that for decades his father's wealth and success had often been imputed to associations with organized crime. Was the Kennedy children's luxurious lifestyle—the sailing and the skiing and the prep schooling and the romps on sunny lawns at Hyannis Port—dependent on black-market thuggery and corruption? Nothing had ever been proved against Joseph Kennedy, but right or wrong, it was widely assumed that he was a bit shady.

Joseph Kennedy decided to put a halt to Bobby's crusade. With the clan gathered in Hyannis Port for Christmas in 1956, even as new rounds of committee investigations were gearing up, the father ordered his son to stop. The whole thing was dangerous to Jack's shot at the presidency. This ill-conceived crusade was bound to anger the unions, annoy old friends, and ruin everything the family had been working for. It was time for Bobby to take a big step back.

Bobby refused.

This display of defiance was almost impossible for Joseph Kennedy to process. Joe Jr. had never defied his father. Jack could be truculent, but nothing like this. Bobby was different.

As the angry Christmastime at Hyannis Port wore on, and Bobby and his father kept arguing, Joseph Kennedy saw that he had a new and unforeseen problem. Bobby was in outright defiance of the overarching, long-range Kennedy political strategy they had all agreed on. Joe called in William O. Douglas, the Supreme Court justice, to act as a go-between—a political intervention that would be inconceivable for a Supreme Court justice today. Bobby told Douglas he didn't believe he was risking Jack's presidential ambitions with these investigations, but if that really was a risk, he was willing to take it. He was doing the right thing.

His rectitude was certain. The family loner had his own project now. He was thirty-one years old. He wasn't afraid of Jimmy Hoffa, he wasn't afraid of the Italian Mob, and he wasn't afraid of Joseph P. Kennedy.

Bobby won. He beat his father at his own game, and as a result, Joseph Kennedy changed his family's story. Of all his sons, he now began saying with pride, the really tough one is Bobby. Jack was the idealist, the intellectual, the visionary, the knight errant. Bobby was the pit bull, enforcing loyalty. The father now saw the two brothers as a perfect team.

Reality was more complicated, at times precisely the reverse. Jack Kennedy was consistently and ruthlessly tough. He made decisions and stuck with them and remained willing to disable anyone who got in his way. Bobby did, of course, demand loyalty to the Kennedy operation, on his own and Jack's behalf, yet he still veered between hyperbolic ruthlessness and aggression and the old moody, brooding sensitivities and vulnerability. Jack still thought Black Robert lacked a key sense of proportion and a sense of humor.

Still, in Jack Kennedy's 1960 presidential campaign, the brothers' tight teamwork cemented itself. Because of his fussy execution of every last detail,

Bobby became Jack's sole indispensable man. It was understood from the beginning that Bobby would be Jack's campaign manager, but Jack didn't understand until partway through that grueling, chaotic struggle to defeat the incumbent vice president, Richard Nixon, just how much Bobby was able to do. In this new, high-stakes arena, with all of the Kennedy ambition on the line at last, the younger man's most evident talent came to the fore—sleepless attention to everything and everyone, all at once, a superhuman ability to absorb all the chaos and remain undefeated.

Bobby learned the real techniques of electoral politics. He knocked already weakened primary opponents to the floor by spreading money around and floating questionable accusations at key moments. In the West Virginia primary, Bobby and his father gave Franklin D. Roosevelt Jr. documents purporting to show that JFK's opponent Hubert Humphrey had dodged the draft in World War II. Roosevelt took the job of making the implication public. Humphrey had made repeated efforts to enlist; he'd been rejected for a double hernia, color blindness, and calcification of the lungs, but the rumors lingered. Suitcases of cash, sent by his father and dispensed on the ground in West Virginia by RFK himself, bought the votes that ended the cash-strapped Hubert Humphrey's bid for the nomination in 1960.

Then, at the Democratic convention that year,

Lyndon Johnson made a belated "stop Kennedy" move, hoping to sweep in and steal Jack's nomination. To that end, Johnson leaked the news that JFK suffered from Addison's disease. The story was true. But Bobby had a phony medical report cooked up to deny it and personally presented the report to reporters. LBJ also told reporters that Joe Kennedy had appeased the Nazis when he was ambassador to Great Britain. Bobby now felt an intense personal enmity toward Johnson. For LBJ, the feeling was mutual and permanent.

In response to Johnson's Addison's disease attack, Bobby Kennedy promised Johnson's top aide, Bobby Baker, "You'll get yours." The last thing he could have envisioned at that moment was Jack Kennedy's offering Lyndon the running-mate spot.

The morning after his victory at the convention, JFK went to LBJ and offered to make him the running mate. The idea had been around for months because LBJ would, of course, help JFK in the South. But Bobby was telling reporters point-blank that Johnson wasn't even remotely in contention for the job. Bobby thought labor leaders wouldn't support Johnson for VP. Bobby was sure Jack was offering Johnson the spot only as a formality, that the majority leader of the Senate would never give up that power to become subordinate to JFK. Wrong.

LBJ accepted JFK's offer. Jack tried to explain to Bobby that now there was little they could do, but

Bobby went to LBJ's hotel room to try to turn this ship around by offering Johnson the chairmanship of the Democratic Party instead. Bobby blamed resistance to Johnson's candidacy on labor and Northern leaders. Johnson listened and simply said that if Jack Kennedy would have him, "I'll join him." Bobby's trick didn't work. Outfoxing Lyndon Johnson wasn't that easy.

The general election came down to the wire—two-tenths of 1 percent of the vote gave Jack Kennedy the presidency. Without Bobby, JFK knew he probably would have come in second. No longer the runt who would never amount to anything, Bobby had become the Kennedy family's ultimate go-to guy: enforcer, counselor, caretaker, fixer, protector. Jack—President Kennedy now—took to calling Bobby "General," the direct address form for attorney general. Now as president and attorney general, the brothers made their father's and their grandfather's dream come true.

Just before publicly announcing that he was going to nominate his brother as attorney general, Jack discussed with Bobby how they would present it to the awaiting reporters. Then Jack said, "So that's it, General. Let's grab our balls and go."

But first, Jack added, Bobby should comb his hair.

SEVEN

"WE WILL NEVER BE YOUNG AGAIN"

I t was unusually warm for a late-November Friday in Washington, and the attorney general was poolside at his home, Hickory Hill, in a working lunch with the U.S. attorney from New York, Robert Morgenthau, when at about 1:45 p.m. he was called to the phone. It was the FBI director, J. Edgar Hoover. Right away Bobby knew something bad had happened. Hoover never called him at home.

In the flattest, most unemotional way possible, Hoover said, "The President has been shot."

Bobby asked if it was serious.

Hoover said he thought so, and that he would call back with further news, and hung up.

Bobby had his hand over his mouth and his face turned away when Ethel came to him. She embraced him. Bobby didn't speak.

When at last he tried, his sentences were short, as if

each word were a struggle. "Jack's been shot." Then: "It may be fatal."

Almost immediately, out of his shocked, choked silence, Bobby started doing a lot of talking. In the next forty-five minutes at Hickory Hill, still not knowing his brother's fate, Bobby used the phones to circle the wagons.

Keeper of the president's secrets, steward of his reputation, Bobby, wearing sunglasses to hide the horror that was only just beginning to overcome him, did what he always did for President Kennedy. He started getting things done.

He called McGeorge Bundy, the national security adviser. He told Bundy to change the locks on JFK's White House files: the most important stuff was to be moved immediately to the national security office and put under guard. He called the Secret Service. They were to uninstall the secret Oval Office and Cabinet Room tape recorders.

At 2:30 p.m., Hoover called Bobby back.

"The President is dead."

Eight minutes later, the CBS anchorman Walter Cronkite announced that news to the nation.

Who did it? As the awful day wore on, that became Bobby Kennedy's only question. Somehow his horror and overwhelming grief focused, in those early hours, on a desperate need to know.

The CIA. That was Bobby's first thought. He called John McCone, director of the CIA, and asked him to come over, right away. McCone arrived minutes later. Bobby wasted no time. He put the question directly to McCone. McCone was startled. Though he was director, he felt there were things about CIA activities that Bobby knew more about than he did. RFK had been deeply involved in covert activities, among them assassination attempts on Fidel Castro. Many in the CIA hated JFK; among other things there were rumors that he'd been planning to restructure the agency, dissipating its power. McCone was Roman Catholic. These two grieving men shared a language of faith, and they fell back on it now. The CIA director swore to Bobby Kennedy by everything they both held sacred, in fear of eternal damnation, that the CIA was innocent of the death of President Kennedy. Bobby believed him.

Certain Cubans were also on Bobby's list. There were Fidel Castro and his operators in Havana, of course. They had reason enough to kill JFK. JFK's operatives had tried to kill Castro. But there were also the anti-Castro Cuban exiles in the United States. They felt betrayed by JFK's withdrawal from the Bay of Pigs operation. A U.S. warship that the exiles had expected to support the invasion of Cuba had pulled out, leaving them stranded. And the FBI had received intelligence of threats against the president from exiled Cuban freedom fighters.

It was late afternoon now, and the Kennedy children were coming home from school. Bobby spent time hugging and comforting them. The radio reported the arrest in Dallas of Lee Harvey Oswald. Early news on Oswald placed him with Cuban exiles who had been plotting against Castro in New Orleans.

Kennedy called Enrique Williams. Bobby was close to Williams, a leader of the Cuban exiles still hoping to invade Cuba and oust Castro. Williams was in D.C. that day, meeting at the Old Ebbitt Grill with his exile compadres. On the phone with Williams, Bobby was accusatory.

"One of your guys did it," he told Williams.

Williams denied all knowledge. Bobby hung up. The list was so long, so bewildering. There were Mafia kingpins with reasons to have JFK killed. Sam Giancana, the Chicago mobster, had shared a girlfriend with JFK. Bobby himself, as attorney general, had drawn Giancana's and others' ire by aggressive investigation into their activities. To Giancana's face, Bobby had compared the mobster's laugh to the sound of a little girl.

There was big labor, hardly above committing murder, often indistinguishable from the racketeers that Bobby had spent so much time harassing and prosecuting. Jimmy Hoffa, the leader of the Teamsters, was on Bobby's suspect list that afternoon. But so was the Soviet regime. So was Lyndon Johnson. Any and all of them could sound plausible enough to keep the world guessing for the rest of the century.

Hundreds of books would be written about what was driving Bobby Kennedy crazy that afternoon. Who killed JFK?

The day was ending. Bobby had to meet the plane bringing Jack's body to Washington. He had to stand by Jackie Kennedy, the sister-in-law whom Bobby, nearly alone of JFK's relatives, adored. He had to face up to the secondary horror of Lyndon Johnson being sworn in as JFK's successor.

As he steeled himself to make the trip to the airport, Bobby's focus on finding out who killed his brother, relentless all that awful afternoon, finally broke. That's when the real pain began kicking in.

There was a moment in the White House late that day that captured what everyone in the Kennedy circle was feeling. Mary McGrory, a columnist close to the Kennedys, said through her tears, "We'll never laugh again."

Daniel Patrick Moynihan, then an assistant secretary of labor, said, "Heavens, Mary, we'll laugh again. It's just that we will never be young again."

In the months that followed President Kennedy's assassination, it was as if Bobby still tried to cling to him. He wore Jack's blue overcoat. He wore Jack's tux. He couldn't fill those garments. He was swimming in them. He took trip after trip to Arlington Cemetery with Jackie, sometimes late at night. They would kneel and pray at Jack's grave site. Bobby couldn't eat, couldn't sleep. He looked almost no one in the eye. He winced persistently as if in chronic physical pain. Bobby fell into despair. The toll his pain took on him was horribly evident to everyone who knew him.

Despite the insomnia, the wincing, the wasting away before everyone's eyes, Bobby was busy serving as his stunned family's patriarch. Courage, which Bobby believed Jack had shown at every moment, that's what Bobby had to find now. He didn't even have his father to lean on. Late in 1961, Joseph Kennedy had suffered a stroke that left him mentally aware but nearly unable to speak.

So it was Bobby, on that first afternoon, who called his mother and told her she'd lost another son. Bobby sent Ted to Hyannis Port to tell the stricken father, face-to-face, that Jack was gone. It was Bobby who met Air Force One that horrible evening, rushed into the cabin, ignoring Johnson—already sworn in, already the president—and pulled Jackie into an embrace of mutual devastation. Bobby then tried to cover his anguish as Jackie, in the car from the airport to Bethesda Naval Hospital, confided every grisly detail of that awful moment of impact in the open car in Dealey Plaza, the bullet entering Jack's head, the blood splattering on her pink suit. The dried blood was still there.

It was Bobby who on Jackie's behalf took over every detail of the lying in state at the Capitol Rotunda and the public and private funeral arrangements. With

Jackie, he felt he had to look at Jack's face in the open casket; it had remained closed for the public. Much funeral socializing had to be done the night before the service and then the night after it. Family and old friends and allies mobbed into rooms at the White House. Lyndon Johnson was even then in the process of taking over, but Jackie and her children still lived there. When the guests had left and the White House rooms fell silent, Bobby and Jackie drove alone to the grave. They knelt and prayed.

Bobby was still attorney general. But not really. He always referred to Jack as "the President." Bobby almost always referred to LBJ only as "Johnson," or "that man."

In his pain and horror and loss, feeling every day the sting of having to report to his enemy instead of to his brother, Bobby began to see Johnson as worse than simply a crude man and a bad president. Johnson became, in Bobby's eyes, a monstrous, demonic force of sheer evil. The assassination changed nothing about LBJ's attitude toward Bobby. Johnson called him "the little shitass."

At LBJ's first cabinet meeting, where the new president hoped to count on their full support, Bobby showed up late, making an entrance that drew the cabinet to its feet in respect for his loss. Johnson took that move as a calculated insult. He didn't rise. Bobby took that move as a calculated insult.

When Lee Harvey Oswald was killed by Jack Ruby

in Dallas on national TV only days after the JFK assassination, LBJ called Bobby into the Oval Office and tasked him with getting to the bottom of it. "You've got to do something," the new president harangued his attorney general. "It's giving the United States a bad name in the rest of the world!" Bobby didn't do much about the Ruby matter. Stunned with grief, he couldn't focus on anything but the enormity of LBJ's giving him condescending orders days after Jack's death.

When, in early 1964, Johnson got wind of an effort by one of Bobby's top staffers to get RFK's name into the New Hampshire primary as LBJ's running mate, the president called Bobby into the Oval Office and demanded he get the staffer fired from the Democratic National Committee. Bobby began to protest that JFK had originally hired the man. But Johnson cut him off.

"President Kennedy isn't the president anymore," LBJ told him. "I am." Bobby walked out.

He knew that Johnson lived in fear of a rumor: that in the 1964 primaries, and at the convention, Democratic delegates might draft RFK as the vice presidential nominee. It satisfied Bobby to imagine Johnson staying up at night over that prospect. Indeed, the whole time Johnson played Eugene McCarthy and Hubert Humphrey against each other that hot summer, all the way to the convention in Atlantic City, LBJ was really watching his back for a surprise attack from Bobby. Johnson even came to believe that Kennedy was behind an uprising of African American civil rights activists, the Mississippi Freedom Democratic Party, on the convention floor. Johnson got J. Edgar Hoover to bug the attorney general's office to find out what was brewing. It was in part because he was so distracted checking up on VP rumors about Bobby that LBJ saw no hint of Gene McCarthy's sudden decision to withdraw from vice presidential consideration. When McCarthy sent that infuriating telegram, LBJ was blindsided because he had his eye on Bobby.

Johnson's final frustration at the 1964 convention was all about Bobby Kennedy. On the convention's last night, the Democrats showed a short film honoring JFK. Bobby was scheduled to make a short speech before the film.

As he came to the podium, the hall went wild. The applause and cheering went on and on. It wouldn't stop. Television commentators were speechless. No one had ever seen anything like it. Bobby didn't even try to speak. He waited, looking bashful. When he tried to speak, the applause and cheers got louder. Twenty-two minutes. The longest ovation anyone there had ever seen. Bobby knew it wasn't for him. It was for the assassinated president who should have been there running for his second term.

Bobby quoted from **Romeo and Juliet**. "When he shall die, take him and cut him out into stars and he shall make the face of heaven so fine that all the world will be in love with night and pay no worship to the garish sun."

Then Bobby promised his party he was looking not only to the past but to the future. The place exploded again. It was the most moving moment ever seen on an American political stage.

It was the rawness of the emotion, the intimacy of reverential love, and Bobby's open, nearly shy reading of Shakespeare that made his speech the glory of the convention.

Was LBJ "the garish sun," unworthy of worship when compared to "the face of heaven"? Even someone less paranoid than Johnson might have taken that moment as a declaration of war.

The truth of what Johnson just saw was not something he could comprehend or imagine. It was not the clever trick of a speechwriter trying to poke an opponent. No political speechwriter in 1964 would want their man invoking Juliet's blend of female passion, worship, and yearning.

Adding the Juliet passage was not Bobby's idea. It was Jackie's. She had read the speech in draft and at the last minute added the passage. The grieving widow put a female voice in Bobby Kennedy's beatification of Jack Kennedy. She gave Bobby the words that would mythologize Jack and Bobby at the same time.

Jackie's contribution of the Juliet passage wasn't an

isolated incident. Bobby and Jackie had committed themselves to building a permanent American memory of what they saw as JFK's special greatness. It was a closely held program. The closeness took Bobby away from Ethel and naturally triggered rumors.

No one would ever know exactly what went on between Bobby and Jackie in those struggling years, but the bereaved widow and the wounded brother did come to share a deep faith in the idea that JFK's presidency had been America's great chance, tragically cut short, for a new national flowering, a national redemption, solving the deepest problems confronting not only the nation but also humanity itself. That vision of a lost chance for transcendence clicked with the American public. It helped Robert Kennedy out of his emotional paralysis.

Jackie and Bobby were trying to preserve the high-minded side of the Kennedy presidency. But down in the engine room of the Kennedy presidency, where Bobby was so often, things were different. If Jack Kennedy had made it to the 1964 convention to be renominated, Bobby might have had as many enemies in that convention hall as friends.

"Plausible deniability" had been the catchphrase and the technique for all of Bobby's secret efforts during Jack's administration: at all costs, keep the president free of any direct accountability for the dirty tricks and complicated internecine wars that were often part and parcel of American executive-branch ambitions. It was Bobby Kennedy who signed off on J. Edgar Hoover's plan to start wiretapping Martin Luther King Jr., ostensibly to determine whether King was under Soviet communist influence. After RFK left the Justice Department, the bugging revealed details of King's sexual encounters, which Hoover used to anonymously threaten Dr. King.

It was the same Bobby Kennedy who most angered white supremacists throughout the South when, in 1962, he negotiated—at first through back-channel intermediaries, and then personally—with Mississippi governor Ross Barnett to allow the enrollment of the African American student James Meredith at the University of Mississippi. Meredith had sued in federal court for admission and the Supreme Court had found in his favor. In this case, plausible deniability meant Bobby and the governor agreed that they had no agreement about Meredith's enrollment. On September 29, when Meredith arrived on campus to enroll, with 500 federal marshals for protection, along with Assistant Attorney General Nicholas Katzenbach, white students rioted. Bobby had Jack call out the National Guard. A well-organized, well-armed student militia fired on the Guard, and in the shoot-out Katzenbach, held down under fire and on the phone with RFK, requested federal troops, and Bobby sent in the army. By the time order was restored, 160 marshals had been wounded, a French reporter had been killed, and "Bobby" was a term of sneering hatred among segregationists.

Black activists, too, had reason to see the Kennedy administration as ruthless and duplicitous. As attorney general, Bobby felt compelled to protect the Freedom Riders of 1964 as well as Meredith, but he believed they were causing these problems by moving too fast. He wanted the respect of civil rights leaders. He wanted them to see him as a liberal on civil rights, but he found their demands too much, too soon.

RFK invited the young black novelist and intellectual James Baldwin to bring a group of black intellectuals and activists to a discussion at Joseph Kennedy's huge apartment on Central Park South in Manhattan. That meeting, held on May 24, 1963, didn't go as Bobby had hoped. When he told the group that federal lawyers were doing a good job in the South, the group laughed openly in his face. Then, with Bobby sputtering in bewilderment, one of the young attendees told the attorney general that as a black man, he would never fight on behalf of the United States against Cuba. This was unthinkable—just the kind of communist-inspired thinking, as far as Bobby was concerned, that the Kennedys had feared was influencing the civil rights movement.

Irish Americans, too, had faced prejudice, Bobby told the group, and now there was an Irish Catholic in the White House. Maybe in another generation, there would be a black president. That was too much for Baldwin. "You know, I have to tell you," he said, "your grandfather came over here from Ireland just a generation or so ago, and your brother is president. My ancestors came over here a couple of hundred years ago on a slave ship, and you have the right, only through race and color, to tell me when I can participate in this government."

Bobby was disturbed both by Baldwin's ideas and by his apparent homosexuality. He sensed in that room a barely veiled threat. If enormous progress was not made, right away, on civil rights, there would be violence. After the meeting, Bobby asked Hoover to start FBI files on all of the attendees.

Bobby gave Hoover, during the JFK administration, a general approval for keeping FBI wiretaps on suspected mobsters, especially on his old nemesis Sam Giancana. Meanwhile, Bobby was constantly fending off Hoover's implications of what the director might reveal from those wiretaps about Bobby and JFK themselves. Bobby mocked such threats, but like presidents and attorneys general before and after them, the Kennedys feared Hoover. At the same time, Bobby was desperately trying to keep secret from the FBI, and from the general public, his multiple overlapping efforts, in collaboration with the CIA, to overthrow Castro in Cuba. RFK pursued covert operations not only against Cuba but also, excited by the growing appeal of "counterinsurgency" in fighting communism, elsewhere in the world. He brought his friend William Parker, the chief of the Los Angeles Police Department, to training sessions with security forces of Latin American and Asian dictatorships. Parker had transformed his department into a military-style, highly mobile response force—he called it the "thin blue line"—with cops off the walking beat and riding in cars. Parker was among the pioneers of the preemptive policing technique known as stop and frisk. RFK thought communist uprisings might be prevented by employing Parker's tactics, and he pushed nervous State Department officials to supply foreign governments with advanced police equipment for cracking down.

Sometimes bureaucrats wouldn't go along with his more exotic ideas, so Bobby ran covert operations himself. Schooled in the clandestine, he set up what spies call cutouts: go-betweens whose activities on his behalf could supposedly never be traced to the administration, or even directly to the CIA. The cutouts got arms and money to forces that it was U.S. diplomatic policy not to deal with. In Mozambique, Bobby secretly helped out the liberation front against the U.S. ally Portugal. In Vietnam, he tried to push the Pentagon—in this case, the CIA was dragging its heels—to get serious about covert operations against the communist North. In Cuba, while plausible deniability and cutouts ensured that evidence would remain incomplete, historians would consider it likely that Robert Kennedy approved at least some of eight miserably failed CIA efforts to assassinate Fidel Castro.

Some of those efforts employed Sam Giancana and other mobsters, even as Bobby and the FBI were aggressively investigating them. The streams did cross: Hoover found out about the CIA's attempts on Castro's life; CIA agents blamed one of Bobby's favorite cutouts, Robert Maheu, for blowing the game. Giancana had been given the distinct impression that working with the CIA might now get him out from under relentless judicial scrutiny directed by RFK. When that didn't happen, Giancana became enraged by a sense of betrayal.

So it was through this maze of covert and overt projects that Bobby Kennedy had busily made himself conspicuously open to hatred and revenge. After JFK's assassination, everywhere Bobby looked, he could see himself as a possible cause of his brother's murder. So he stopped looking. In stark contrast to that energetic, nearly crazed investigation he undertook on the afternoon of November 22, 1963, Bobby became unable to cope with any questions about who might have killed JFK. He tried to ignore the commission headed by Chief Justice Earl Warren that was investigating the assassination for Congress. No one had a better sense than Bobby of the secrets that might have sparked an assassination attempt on the president. Some thought RFK must also have at least countenanced the CIA-involved assassination of Rafael Trujillo of the Dominican Republic. No one was less available for questioning by the commission than Bobby. Yes, he was still grieving, but there were too many tangled linkages he might be asked to unravel.

Finally, prodded personally by Chief Justice Warren, Bobby wrote a pro forma, legalistic note—as if he really were only the attorney general—indicating that the files of the Justice Department contained no evidence of conspiracy in the assassination.

The relentless day-to-day realpolitik of the Kennedy administration died with Jack. In partnership with Jackie, Bobby was transforming the Kennedy reality into the Kennedy myth. In that process, he was transforming himself as well. At the 1964 convention, Democrats saw the beginnings of a new Bobby Kennedy. Bashful, pained, yet tentatively hopeful, he recited Juliet's lines as a humble yet worthy heir apparent to the slain hero. This was the Robert Kennedy that, three years later, Al Lowenstein believed could dump Johnson.

EIGHT

OLD POLITICS

There were many good reasons for Robert Kennedy not to take on LBJ in a primary run in 1968. Some of Bobby's most experienced advisers were sure that challenging LBJ wasn't just a bad idea but a dangerous and crazy one. They hoped to squash it as quickly as possible. But there were others in the RFK camp who had become fervent in their certainty that this was Bobby's year. To them, 1968 was a historic opportunity to heal a nation wounded by war, riots, and rage. Bobby must not miss his moment in history.

For Bobby himself, still often indecisive, the question was becoming impossible. The summer and fall of 1967 turned into slow-drip torture.

On the one hand, it was crazy political suicide. On the other, Bobby himself, with his Juliet speech at the last convention, had stimulated the demand for a new Kennedy candidacy. When he made that speech, the earliest he could have hoped to return to a convention stage to accept a nomination was 1972. Now, with liberal sentiment rising against Johnson over Vietnam, it seemed to many of Bobby's supporters that 1968 would be a far, far better time to run, not just to make good on the promise of a restored Kennedy presidency, but to stop an immoral war.

The crowds coming out to cheer for Bobby in his 1964 New York Senate campaign were the most excited people New York politics had ever seen. There was a wild feeling of expectancy. That is when Bobby first saw those hands reaching out to shake his hand or just touch him. When he toured the country that fall in support of other candidates, he drew huge crowds everywhere he went. In LBJ's Austin, Texas, Bobby's crowd was full of impoverished farmworkers who were beginning to be organized nationally by the charismatic labor leaders Cesar Chavez and Dolores Huerta. The farmworkers chanted, "Viva, Kennedy!"

As a senator, RFK made his great cause ameliorating poverty. His strongest efforts focused on New York City, but his profile on the issue was national. In Senator Kennedy's hands, the Bedford-Stuyvesant neighborhood in Brooklyn became a highly visible test case for new ideas about antipoverty legislation. Years of New York City ghettoization caused by the racist lending policies of banks, racial discrimination by landlords like Donald Trump's father, fears and fantasies of white residents, and deliberately discriminatory housing policies had left Bed-Stuy with all the deprivations and hopelessness of race-based urban poverty, the North's form of segregation. Bobby began to sound nearly revolutionary on the problem of race and poverty in urban America. Two years after RFK was offended by James Baldwin's dissent, the philosophical space between Bobby and Baldwin was closing. Bobby argued against complacent liberal conventional wisdom and against LBJ's comparatively tepid antipoverty efforts. Problems for black Americans were growing worse, not getting better. Bobby brought passion and immediacy to his speeches on the issue.

Senator Kennedy walked the neglected, littered streets of Bed-Stuy and sat down and listened to the confrontational demands of community leaders. In a Senate hearing in March 1966, RFK took up the farmworkers' cause, supporting a strike led by Chavez and Huerta and chastising a California sheriff who had sent in police against peaceful picketers.

In the summer of 1966, after years of urban neglect and abuse took their toll, rioting erupted in cities around the country. Bobby decided to launch a comprehensive test plan of urban renewal for Bedford-Stuyvesant: the idea was to use government power to address everything—jobs, housing, education, and violence—at once. It was ambitious, and Bobby admitted it might not all work because some of it was experimental. Bobby knew he was not a Brooklyn senator, he was a United States senator. Everything he was pushing in New York City he hoped would go national. And everything Senator Kennedy did or said got national attention.

In a Bobby crowd, a woman told Jack Newfield, "I can't hear a word he's saying, but I agree with him."

Bobby helped create the public fervency around him. He fed it. But he did not know what to do with it. Not now. Sometimes, when pressed for definite assurance that he'd run in 1972, Bobby would go all "Black Robert" on the questioner: "I don't even know if I'll be alive in 1972. Fate is so fickle." No one knew better than Bobby how a happy day full of cheering, loving crowds could go bad in a second.

In 1967, with Lowenstein's Dump Johnson effort gathering speed, the press had picked up with gusto on this dramatic possibility: a history-making primary run by the Kennedy heir apparent against his own party's incumbent, President Johnson. This drew the attention of more than just the political news media.

Pulitzer Prize–winning author and essayist Norman Mailer had called JFK an existentialist hero but had often derided Bobby in print as a mix of Kennedy bravado and prep-school arrogance. Now Mailer had a new vision. He rewrote Bobby as a compassionate man, schooled by suffering, maybe the last hope for resisting the dark rise of the American war-mongering right wing that Mailer saw coming.

Some in the press kept writing reminders of the old Bobby. They scrutinized the organizer and enforcer of the JFK presidency. **Ruthless** was the word they always used. Bobby was learning to hate hearing it. In June 1967, as primary speculation mounted, Bobby appeared with the journalist Roger Mudd on a TV special. Mudd asked him to explain the feeling among some in politics and the public that "there's always an ulterior motive in what you do." Bobby could find nothing to say about the old Bobby.

"I don't know," he told Mudd. "I don't know . . . I don't know . . . I don't know . . . I don't know."

Mudd prompted him: "The McCarthy thing, and the Hoffa thing, and the '60 campaign."

"I suppose," Bobby replied, "I have been in positions which—" He stopped himself. "But I don't know exactly," he said. "I don't know."

In the RFK inner circle, only Bobby was indecisive. Everyone else in his camp was absolutely sure about exactly what Bobby should do. They just disagreed with one another.

The Kennedy Senate staff trended young, intensely idealistic, and closely connected to the youth movement that was challenging everything in establishment politics, with the war in Vietnam at the top of their list. Adam Walinsky, a key speechwriter, was twenty-eight. He wore boots and loud, "mod" shirts.

Men's hair length advertised their distance from the establishment. Walinsky's hair covered his ears, radical for Senate staff. He tried mightily to persuade RFK to oppose the war in Vietnam. He was unafraid of arguing with the boss, and the senator seemed to listen especially closely to him. As the Dump Johnson movement gained steam, Bobby never forgot that the day he was sworn in as a senator in January 1965, he found a note on his office desk from Walinsky saying simply, "Lyndon Johnson is a lame duck president."

Jeff Greenfield was only twenty-three. He'd been working on a book about rock and roll when he joined the staff. As a speechwriter, Greenfield was especially well tuned to Bobby's sometimes oddball speech patterns. He played guitar and sang civil rights songs, and he was as intense as Walinsky in his opposition to the Vietnam War.

Some of the senior staffers joined the young in encouraging Bobby to challenge Johnson. Frank Mankiewicz and Tom Dolan were tough, experienced aides who were Bobby's age. Tom Dolan, usually a careful speaker, despised Johnson and told Bobby that "anything that hurts him is good for America." Press Secretary Frank Mankiewicz was witty and irreverent, with a strong background in journalism. He had grown staunchly opposed to the war and wanted to see Johnson stopped.

On the Senate staff the two generations were more

or less agreed. They shared the enthusiasm that Walinsky had expressed during the 1964 Senate campaign when he saw the excitement in the crowds: "To hell with '68. Let's go **now!**"

Some older advisers in the Kennedy camp felt differently. Despite Arthur Schlesinger's growing hatred of the war in Vietnam, within ADA it was Schlesinger who had been cautioning Allard Lowenstein against trying to unseat a Democratic president. Schlesinger, a Kennedy loyalist, tried to find more moderate measures Senator Kennedy might use to restrain Johnson on the war while avoiding dangerous party division.

Also urging Bobby to wait was Pierre Salinger, White House press secretary to both JFK and LBJ, now a successful businessman. Salinger was dedicated to RFK's future, but he felt 1968 was not the year.

At the top of the old JFK team was Ted Sorensen. He'd been many things to President Kennedy: special counsel, adviser, speechwriter. Sorensen was now an adviser to General Motors. Bobby listened to Walinsky and the gung-ho Senate staffers, but he'd more or less grown up listening to Ted Sorensen, and Sorensen was adamant. This idea of challenging Johnson, Sorensen told Bobby, was dead wrong.

Bobby's younger and now only brother, Senator Ted Kennedy, was against running in 1968. In those days much of the Kennedy world did not take Teddy very seriously. But Bobby did. Teddy was a two-year veteran of the Senate when Bobby arrived there. Teddy was already more of a Senate political operator than Bobby would ever be. Teddy Kennedy coached and prodded his brother to be more of a clubhouse guy, better informed on procedures and rules and constituent issues. Bobby knew Teddy had things to teach him.

The Kennedy old guard's arguments against trying to unseat Johnson were solid. Bobby was a near lock for 1972 already. Why rock the boat? Party power brokers never liked insurgencies. Why alienate them now? Richard Daley, the mayor of Chicago, perhaps the most powerful kingmaker in Democratic politics, expressed no interest in an RFK insurgency against LBJ. Running for president without Daley was a fool's errand. Dividing the Democratic Party would only give aid and comfort to the Republicans. Richard Nixon, George Romney, and Nelson Rockefeller were the kind of Republicans who could exploit a divided Democratic Party in a general election. A divided Democratic Party might collapse in November. The RFK-versus-LBJ feud was an open secret and source of fascination for the press. Any move by Bobby to take on Johnson could look like nothing more than a personal vendetta. That would play into the "ruthless" thing, the "ulterior motive" thing. Bobby had to erase those labels in time for 1972. Bobby still divided public opinion. Those who liked him loved him. Those who didn't like him could be intense about it, too. Throwing the cards in the air in 1968 and hoping for the best wouldn't show Kennedy courage; it would show Kennedy impulsiveness, immaturity, emotionalism. That's how Ted Sorensen saw it. So Bobby remained undecided. And he remained undecided on the issue that was the driving force to dump Johnson: the Vietnam War.

Senator Kennedy's little-noticed actual position on Vietnam was to support President Johnson. Bobby was characteristically cautious on issues on which political strength had long been defined: war, and especially war on communism. RFK was there at the creation of the Vietnam War. In the Kennedy administration, no one had been more excited by the techniques and theories of guerrilla counterinsurgency than RFK. He had since moved on, but it wasn't easy for him to publicly foreswear everything Jack and he had done.

The peace movement wasn't really Bobby's style. The protests were becoming more rowdy and audacious. That disturbed him, and he said so publicly. Privately, he was becoming ever more certain that the war was a foreign policy disaster, but he still couldn't bring himself to call it an "immoral war," which the antiwar crowd called it.

In February 1967, Bobby was on a European trip when he met in Paris with a French diplomat. Soon a cable arrived at the State Department stating that the diplomat had told Kennedy that North Vietnam would ask for peace talks if LBJ would halt the bombing without placing any conditions on North Vietnam. The cable got leaked to **Newsweek**, and Johnson was furious at the story's implication that while LBJ did nothing, Kennedy was traveling the globe seeking peace. Johnson was sure Bobby had leaked the story. The president summoned Senator Kennedy to the Oval Office.

In the Oval Office, with Nick Katzenbach and National Security Adviser Walt Rostow attending, the president complained about the leak. Bobby denied leaking the story and noted that the cable came from Johnson's (and Katzenbach's) State Department. That infuriated Johnson. He knew there were lots of Kennedy holdovers in his State Department eager to leak to Bobby. Johnson went from lecture to rant in seconds—talk of unconditional bombing halts takes the pressure off the enemy and stops progress toward peace. If Bobby didn't stay out of his way on Vietnam, Johnson said, "I'll destroy you and all your dove friends." Johnson yelled, "You'll be dead politically in six months!" Rostow was startled. Katzenbach thought the president was totally out of control.

Bobby kept his cool. He suggested Johnson stop bombing and seek a negotiated solution to the war.

"Not a chance in hell!" said Johnson. Talk of negotiation was encouraging the enemy and only extending the war.

Bobby walked out. Johnson seemed to him mentally unstable. Now it seemed irresponsible to allow that man to continue to hold the office.

"How can we possibly survive five more years of Lyndon Johnson?" Bobby put it to Arthur Schlesinger. "Five more years of a crazy man?"

On March 2, 1967, RFK gave a speech on the Senate floor openly questioning Johnson's Vietnam policy and offering a three-point plan for bringing the war against communism to a favorable conclusion. Unconditional withdrawal was not in the Kennedy plan. He called for a bombing halt; oversight by an international agency, with multinational troops eventually replacing U.S. troops; and then free elections in South Vietnam. What passed for daring on the Senate floor in those days would have got Bobby booed off the stage on a college campus. Adam Walinsky's original, far more radical draft had gone through more than ten revisions, with input from, among others, Arthur Schlesinger, as well as Henry Kissinger, then a Harvard foreign policy professor, anticommunist hawk, and consultant to politicians of both parties. Bobby had been penciling in revisions the night before. Walinsky thought the speech got so watered down that it made no real case at all. But there was a unique element to the speech that other Senate speeches on Vietnam didn't include. Senator Kennedy took some personal responsibility for the conflict in Vietnam.

In what would become known as the long, hot

summer, now Newark and Detroit were hit especially hard with many days of rioting in both cities. Twenty-six died in Newark, forty-three in Detroit. To war protesters, Johnson's militarized response to unrest at home looked identical to the way he conducted the Vietnam War.

To Bobby Kennedy, too, poverty at home and the out-of-control war in Southeast Asia were coming together. The president had been working against RFK's antipoverty legislation. Increased war spending seemed to track with decreasing efforts to help those at home. "He's through with domestic problems, and with the cities," Bobby told allies about Johnson. Another reason to run?

Bobby's indecision about running inevitably became public. Rumors flew. Early reports in the spring of '67, after his three-point plan for Vietnam, had Bobby absolutely planning to run. Others had him swearing he wouldn't. Then RFK published a book titled **To Seek a Newer World**. Politicians publish books like that when they're planning to run for president. **To Seek a Newer World** promoted a national and global revival but stopped far short of revolution. This wouldn't be a new world. It would be a newer one. It wasn't necessarily to be gained— only sought. Campaign books like this one were not meant to be read beyond the title. The political press regarded **To Seek a Newer World** as the first draft of Bobby's bumper sticker.

In the inner circle, the "Run, Bobby, Run!" faction had the most important cheerleaders of all, the two people whose permission Bobby would need. Ethel Kennedy, Bobby's wife, wanted him to run in '68. Nobody hated Johnson more than Ethel. She called him Huckleberry Capone. Jackie Kennedy hoped Bobby would run, too.

It was on a plane, in August 1967, that for the first time Al Lowenstein hinted to Bobby, as broadly as possible, that he hoped he would run as the Dump Johnson candidate. They were bound for San Francisco. Lowenstein, in coach, was going to meet with a chapter of the Conference of Concerned Democrats, a younger organization he helped form, more radical than the creaky ADA, which Lowenstein had largely given up on. Lowenstein's new group was organizing a peace rally. Bobby was in first class, with staff, on his way to make a speech. Frank Mankiewicz gave up his seat next to the senator so Lowenstein could plop down there and bend Bobby's ear. Mankiewicz knew what Bobby was going to hear and he wanted him to hear it.

Bobby had first met Lowenstein in 1966 at a Veterans Administration hospital in Queens; Lowenstein trailed behind as the senator spoke to men wounded in Vietnam. There was something in the way RFK touched those men that made Lowenstein see him as a national healer. At that moment, Lowenstein became what he called a "zealous" supporter.

Knowing that Lowenstein had written about conditions in southwest Africa and South Africa, Bobby
asked Lowenstein to draft the speech he delivered in
Cape Town, which became as critical of the United
States as it was of South Africa and as hopeful for
both. Lowenstein's sharp, hard-driving, peripatetic
liberalism opened a world Bobby was drawn to,
wanted to understand, maybe even be part of, maybe
lead. But the extremes that Lowenstein's young followers were flirting with concerned Bobby. Lowenstein reassured him. Lowenstein wanted to build a
responsible movement and marginalize the crazies.

On the plane, Lowenstein laid out a plan for seiz-
ing the nomination from the seemingly unbeatable
Johnson. It all had to do with the early primaries,
where Johnson could be expected not to compete directly. Lowenstein admitted that he had much more
organizing to do and he was sure this was not the
time to ask Bobby directly to run, not in their first
conversation about 1968. Still, Lowenstein's enthusiasm was infectious for a man who had already been
mulling it over in an anguish of indecision, while
Johnson, Nixon, and the rest each believed he held
history in his hands. Lowenstein could not resist
framing it as a joke to which Bobby obviously did
not have to reply. He told Bobby, "If you want to
run, we'll let you." Bobby laughed.

When RFK and Lowenstein got off the plane,
reporters mobbed Bobby and asked him what he

thought of the peace movement in California. The answer was classic Bobby, summer of '67. "That's a matter for the people of California to decide for themselves," he said. Bobby's answer could not possibly have been more cautious. Lowenstein's friends were disappointed with that statement, but Lowenstein, the eternal optimist, the Bobby fan, took it the other way. Bobby Kennedy had declined to criticize the antiwar movement.

A month later, Lowenstein got his second chance with Bobby. In late September 1967, with Bobby paralyzed between the Adam Walinsky "run now" position and the Ted Sorensen "run in '72" position, the annual national ADA board meeting was convening in Washington. Liberals from all over the country flew in. The crowded conference was abuzz with talk of Johnson, Kennedy, and what the coming year might hold. Lowenstein was invited to dinner at Bobby's house two nights running. The first night, the whole Kennedy crowd was there. Richard Goodwin had arrived—the former JFK and LBJ speechwriter, at once politically savvy and idealistic, had influenced Lowenstein's Dump Johnson thinking. Goodwin had now published an op-ed under a pseudonym in the **New York Times** making the Dump Johnson case from a pragmatic political point of view. Johnson would not, Goodwin believed, have the guts to withstand a challenge by RFK. This was a version of Jack Newfield's Sonny Liston theory of

LBJ. Goodwin worked for Johnson and had come to believe the president's fear of defeat was so great that he would end the war, or even withdraw from the campaign, before engaging with Bobby.

At the dinner, Goodwin said of Johnson what Bobby had already thought: the president had literally gone around the bend. He was psycho. By now, Arthur Schlesinger seemed to be leaning Goodwin's and Lowenstein's way.

The next night, again at the Kennedys' house, the whole quandary came to a head. The evening became a kind of impromptu freewheeling debate on Bobby's prospects and strategy. The group was small this time. The most strident advocates of each position—run now versus wait till '72—were not invited. Ted Sorensen and Adam Walinsky were not there. Lowenstein knew this was his moment. He had to give it everything he had.

The Bobby who welcomed his guests that night was a new Bobby, a transformed man. He wore bright green pants and a string of beads. His hair was now down to his earlobes. This was Bobby the charismatic reformer, the man who connected his own pain to that of others, New York City's urban poor and California farmworkers alike, the U.S. soldiers and their families and the shattered people of Vietnam.

Bobby missed Jack's wisdom and guidance. He clung to it any way he could. Only days after Jack's death, Bobby came across a fragment of the president's notes from what turned out to be his final cabinet meeting. On that paper, JFK had written and circled the word **poverty** more than once. Bobby had the note framed and hung it in his office. JFK did make poverty in America a key part of his political agenda, but Bobby seemed to think that Jack was telling him, from the grave, what to do about Watts, Cesar Chavez, Bed-Stuy. And maybe Vietnam.

The bead-wearing Bobby had also become something of an intellectual. He had always been engaged in cultivating appropriate interests and reading history. He was forever asking deep questions—naive and charming—and seeking recommendations and insights from famous academics and writers. Under Jackie Kennedy's tutelage, he devoured poetry and philosophy. He met with poets ranging from the Soviet dissident Andrei Voznesensky to the American counterculturist Allen Ginsberg. Ginsberg chanted "Hare Krishna" for the bemused senator. He met with Harvard professor and poet Robert Lowell, an antiwar activist. He read the work of existentialist authors like Albert Camus and the nineteenth-century American transcendentalist Ralph Waldo Emerson, as well as Sophocles and Winston Churchill. After Jack's death, he searched for meaning beyond that offered by the Catholic Church. He knew he had to run for the presidency. He also knew that when he ran, he would be running for himself, for Jack, for the Kennedys, and for the realization of the nation's best hopes.

Jack Kennedy had never carried a burden that size. Jack was pressured to run for himself, for his father, for the Kennedys, for Irish Catholics. That was enough pressure. Expectations of Bobby now included wholesale national redemption. That was Bobby's burden alone.

Lowenstein was sitting on the floor that night at Hickory Hill, legs crossed, looking like the perennial student in stocking feet. On his side in the debate was Jack Newfield, who was tracking Bobby's every move for the RFK biography he was writing. On the run-in-1972 side were Arthur Schlesinger—wavering already—and James Loeb, a former JFK ambassador. Bobby, lounging on a sofa, asked them to argue the case in front of him.

It wasn't really a debate. It was Al Lowenstein talking and everybody else responding. Finally Schlesinger proposed a solution that, he said, the ADA would support. Instead of a run against Johnson, which would split the party, how about getting a plank for peace in the platform for the Democratic National Convention?

Bobby had been silent on the sofa. Now he spoke.

"You're a historian, Arthur," he said. "When was the last time millions of people rallied behind a plank?"

That gave Lowenstein hope. "I think Al may be

right," Bobby went on. "I think Johnson might quit the night before the convention opens. I think he's a coward." Lowenstein's spirits soared, then Bobby restated all of the two Teds'—Sorensen and Kennedy—perfectly good reasons not to make a primary challenge: splitting the party, no help from Mayor Daley, the inescapable appearance of a petty vendetta. Bobby decided running now made no sense. He would wait until 1972. He did not mention Lowenstein's reason for running, the life or death reason—stopping the war in Vietnam. Lowenstein was crushed. He put his shoes on. He rose from the floor.

"You understand, of course," he told Bobby, "that there are those of us who think the honor and direction of the country are at stake."

On the way out, Al Lowenstein had one more thing to tell Bobby, the man whom he had dreamed would be his knight-errant: "We're going to do it without you, and that's too bad. Because you could have become President of the United States."

Al Lowenstein discovered Bobby Kennedy was a mere mortal, not a knight, and that Camelot wasn't real.

NINE

"A DECENT INTERVAL"

Of course Al Lowenstein had a backup list of potential candidates to dump Johnson, but they had all rebuffed him. Lowenstein was hurt. He was concerned Bobby could have won not only the primary, but the presidency itself. He didn't have that kind of confidence in anyone else on his backup list. Still, Lowenstein had the discipline to keep his real goal in mind: ending the war in Vietnam.

Lowenstein and Gans were successfully organizing a mass referendum against the war via Democratic Party electoral structures. In the Wisconsin primary, voters were to be allowed to vote a simple no. Enough no votes for Johnson, organized by Lowenstein's youth movement, might encourage candidates to jump into the race for the Democratic nomination. Maybe even Bobby.

Senator Fulbright was now antiwar, so Lowenstein

had written to him—never mind that the Arkansan was also a segregationist—but Fulbright had no interest. There was Senator George McGovern of South Dakota, a true liberal, and now fervently antiwar. McGovern was especially appealing for Lowenstein because his vision didn't stop with classic postwar liberalism, or even with the new "dove" twist that liberalism had been taking. McGovern was the only senator who enthusiastically shared Lowenstein's vision for thorough reform of the entire United States political system. But nationally George McGovern was an unknown, and in South Dakota, Senator McGovern was facing a stiff reelection battle. This was no time for George McGovern to risk his career running for president against Johnson.

There was retired lieutenant general James Gavin, whom JFK had appointed ambassador to France because of Gavin's working relationship with French president Charles de Gaulle, who was a general during World War II. Bobby himself had once suggested that Lowenstein should approach Gavin in his search for a candidate. Jim Gavin was adopted when he was two years old from the Convent of Mercy orphanage in Brooklyn. Thirty-five years later, he became the youngest major general to command an army division in World War II. After the war, he became the youngest lieutenant general. As a paratroop commander, "Jumpin' Jim" had become famous for leading combat jumps with his men. He integrated the all-black 555th Parachute Infantry Battalion into the 82nd Airborne Division. In 1967, General Gavin went to Vietnam hoping to offer helpful tactical suggestions. When he returned, he shocked LBJ and the country by announcing, "We are in a tragedy."

When Lowenstein approached Jim Gavin, Gavin was also being approached as a candidate by some antiwar Republicans. He never gave Lowenstein or the Republicans the slightest encouragement.

George McGovern suggested Lee Metcalf and Eugene McCarthy to Lowenstein. Senator Metcalf was not up for reelection that year in Montana. McCarthy wasn't either. Both were now officially doves on the war. George McGovern thought Metcalf, a complete unknown nationally, was slightly more likely to say yes. McGovern believed McCarthy would feel like he had more to lose—his political future in national politics.

Metcalf dismissed Lowenstein's idea out of hand. An unknown senator from Montana taking on the head of his party, the president of the United States? Insane. Lee Metcalf and the rest were teaching Lowenstein that it is not true that every senator looks in the mirror and sees the next president of the United States. Most don't. Most see someone who will be lucky to hold on to the job he has.

Mary McCarthy, Gene McCarthy's daughter, had started trying to stop the war in high school. By 1967, Mary was a junior at Radcliffe, the women's college partnered with Harvard but not yet fully integrated into the university. Mary McCarthy admired Allard Lowenstein. Curtis Gans began talking to Mary about her father. There was hope.

In August 1967, Gerry Hill, Lowenstein's antiwar ally in California, invited Bobby Kennedy, George McGovern, Gene McCarthy, and others to come to Los Angeles to discuss running against Johnson in the California primary. Only McCarthy wrote back to say he'd be visiting the state in October. Gerry Hill immediately alerted Lowenstein and Gans.

Lowenstein and Gans had a big national Dump Johnson meeting coming up in November in Chicago. This was the first gathering of the Conference of Concerned Democrats (CCD), the organization the two men helped found as an insurgent antiwar alternative to ADA. With Bobby out, they needed a potential candidate to rally their crowd. Lowenstein was not excited about Gene McCarthy. Senator McCarthy had finally come out strongly against the war, but his Senate career was built on support from LBJ, who had come so close to choosing McCarthy as his vice president. Gans thought McCarthy was worth asking, and he pressed Lowenstein to make direct contact with the senator—talking with his daughter wasn't going to get them a candidate. To pursue Gene McCarthy, they postponed the CCD conference by two weeks.

Then, on August 17, Nick Katzenbach provoked

Gene McCarthy to blurt out that he would run against Johnson if he had to.

If he had to.

Gene McCarthy's goal was in sync with Al Lowenstein's. Suddenly energized by the moral, religious, and political imperatives of his younger days, McCarthy wanted to turn the upcoming Democratic primaries into a national referendum on the war in Vietnam. That might push Johnson out altogether, but, more realistically, it would force the president to submit to public opinion, to follow the rules regarding separation of powers in American government, to stop carrying out an immoral war with secretive tactics, and to get the United States out of Southeast Asia. Those goals were ambitious enough. Never mind actually beating the president of the United States for the nomination of his party.

For McCarthy there was only one candidate for challenging Johnson, the only candidate Johnson feared—Bobby Kennedy. McCarthy saw what Bobby was doing to shape his image and fuel enthusiasm. McCarthy understood the unique power of Kennedy charisma, especially since the assassination. It had to be Bobby.

In a first vague talk with Lowenstein, back in the spring, McCarthy had suggested that Lowenstein should get his friend Bobby to run. McCarthy's second choice was George McGovern. Lowenstein's possible candidates kept volunteering one another.

No one would step up. That's when Lowenstein had given up on McCarthy.

But now, in October 1967, out of other options, Lowenstein tried McCarthy again. Lowenstein flew to Los Angeles to attend the meeting McCarthy had agreed to have. On October 20, breakfast was served in McCarthy's hotel suite for Lowenstein, Gerry Hill, the CCD West leader, and McCarthy's top Senate staffer, Jerry Eller.

McCarthy seemed his usual diffident self. Lowenstein launched into his spiel, giving McCarthy his strongest pitch for the feasibility of beating Johnson in the primaries. Lowenstein emphasized the strength and commitment of the national movement he and Gans had built on the campuses and the crying need to bring those kids along in Democratic Party liberal politics, not lose their idealism to New Left radicals and counterculture dropouts.

That was the visionary, generational, hopeful part of the pitch. Lowenstein also used Gans's electoral analysis to explain the pragmatic approach to dumping Johnson. It required laserlike focus on certain primaries beginning with New Hampshire. He assured McCarthy that he was already building an organization to bring out the antiwar voters in the key primary states. McCarthy listened, made some jokes, and asked tough questions. "Where's labor on this thing?" was the hardest to answer. "Do you have any money?" was not easy, either.

The meeting went on for more than an hour. McCarthy also thought Lowenstein was wrong to see New Hampshire as a good battleground for an insurgent. Lowenstein's hopes dimmed. Then McCarthy asked, "How do you think we'd do in Wisconsin?"

We?

McCarthy smiled. "You fellows have been talking about three or four names," he said. "I guess you can cut it down to one." He said it with characteristic calmness. Gene McCarthy was in.

Abigail McCarthy was not. At age fifty-two her husband was embarking on a terribly dangerous course. While Gene assured her, with characteristic bravado, that his decision to run against Lyndon Johnson need not affect her and the rest of the family, Abigail knew better.

Abigail McCarthy always loved fall in Washington the best. A new school year full of new possibilities. Not this fall, not the fall of 1967. This year Abigail saw only new problems.

Abigail knew Lyndon Johnson all too well. Any deviation from total loyalty was always met with swift and harsh reprisal, and no one had ever done anything like this to Johnson before. To Johnson this would be the ultimate betrayal, the worst of LBJ's career. The president remained overwhelmingly powerful in Washington, not only politically but also in the social networks of the city. The McCarthys would be ostracized. Gene would be cut out of the

Senate club. He would be the outcast in the Senate cloakroom.

And there was Minnesota. If Eugene McCarthy became a laughingstock in Washington, he would face a grueling reelection battle with no support from the party.

Abigail knew, too, that once he was in it, her husband would pull no punches. His hatred of Johnson would become visible to the public. His sarcasm would know no bounds.

On October 21, antiwar protesters converged on Washington for the first truly mass antiwar demonstration in the nation's capital. The edgy tone set by the rally that day excited some and unsettled others, both within and outside the peace movement. Abigail McCarthy found herself among the unsettled.

Early reports had it that a few hundred thousand protesters might arrive. The police presence was massive. This would not be a genteel, responsible gathering like the Clergy and Laymen Concerned About Vietnam conference of a year earlier. "Confront the War Makers" was the demonstrators' slogan. The youth counterculture turned out, along with the peaceniks, in what formed a new combination of protest, party, revolution, civil disobedience, and utopian campout. The event had been orchestrated by a coalition of groups spanning the entire antiwar culture. Loosely calling itself the National Mobilization Committee to End the War in Vietnam, it was commonly known as MOBE. The key words were **mobilization** and **end**. MOBE was not going to listen to a three-point plan like Bobby Kennedy's. Nothing less than a definitive and absolute end to the war in Vietnam was acceptable.

David Dellinger was MOBE's main coordinator. Dellinger was not one of the kids. He was Gene McCarthy's age, fifty-two, a lifelong pacifist. During World War II, when nothing like the antiwar fervor of the 1960s could have been imagined, David Dellinger refused to serve in the military and was imprisoned. He had a history in radical pacifism like no one else in the anti-Vietnam movement. By 1967, Dave Dellinger's time had finally come.

Dellinger coordinated the October 21 march with a man of a totally different stripe, twenty-nine-year-old Jerry Rubin, whose activism was born in the Berkeley Free Speech movement of 1964. Rubin dropped out of Berkeley then and had been making trouble for establishments ever since. Rubin's radical style seemed frivolous compared to Dellinger's. Jerry Rubin mixed stunts, costumes, nudity, drugs, music, and jokes. Rubin concocted a theatrical potion intended to turn on the kids and build a movement based in part on the purely oppositional moods of adolescence itself. Working with the activist Abbie Hoffman, the critic Paul Krassner, the poet Ed Sanders, and others, Jerry Rubin gained publicity for what was not yet called performance art, under the name of a parody political organization, the Youth International Party, with the nickname "Yippies."

Jerry Rubin's philosophy would be summed up in his 1970 book title: **Do It!** Abbie Hoffman's 1968 book was **Revolution for the Hell of It**. Unlike the confrontational yet intellectually sober SDS activist Tom Hayden, Rubin and his Yippies looked like a traveling carnival, driven by impulse. And they looked like they were having fun.

Dellinger's decision to coordinate with Rubin was a stroke of genius for turnout and attention. About a hundred thousand people came to Washington on October 16, 1967. That was a shockingly high number. Both the mood and the events of the day drew the fascinated attention of the nation. This wasn't just a demonstration against a war but a cultural explosion in opposition to American social norms. Norman Mailer came, as did Robert Lowell and Allen Ginsberg, to behold a culture in transition.

The day was about youth in all its recklessness and passion, and Dave Dellinger was wise enough to envision attracting and unleashing that energy in service to ending the war. The day before the main event, a few hundred people marched peaceably to the Justice Department and tried to hand in a thousand young men's draft cards collected from all over the country. Officials declined to accept the cards.

The protesters put them on a table and left. It was a federal crime not to carry your draft card, but there were no arrests of those protesters.

The next day crowds gathered on the Mall at the Lincoln Memorial, where Martin Luther King Jr. had delivered his famous "I Have a Dream" speech in 1963. Dellinger told the crowds along the Reflecting Pool that the time had come to move from protest to nonviolent resistance. Dr. Benjamin Spock, author of the famous baby-care book these kids had been reared on, told them that President Johnson had betrayed the country.

Then about fifty thousand people started marching to the Pentagon. Dellinger had wanted protest to take a new form, to merge with resistance and "confront the war makers," so he planned a second rally at the Pentagon, where war was really made. The crowd flowed across the Memorial Bridge and arrived at a parking lot where the rally was supposed to occur. Nearby, the Yippies were doing their thing, and that was drawing much of the press attention.

Abbie Hoffman was leading a small group in an effort to "exorcise" the evil from the Pentagon. The evil would be exorcised by forming circles around the Pentagon. They tried to encircle the entire building. Their plan was to chant until the building levitated. In midair, it would then turn orange, Hoffman predicted. And then the evil spirits would leave, and the war would end. It was all about turning the mighty

Pentagon into their toy and showing the Defense Department the respect that it deserved. None.

Meanwhile, a few thousand of Dellinger's people headed for the entrance to the Pentagon building, where more than 2,500 U.S. marshals formed a heavily armed barricade. Demonstrators stepped over the ropes meant to keep them away from the building. They were arrested, as they had planned to be. A few hundred kids ran forward. Some got into the building through an unguarded door and were quickly tossed down the steps. Other kids rushed forward and took rifle butts to their skulls.

More than five hundred arrestees were jailed overnight. Many of the other kids spent the night outside the Pentagon. All night, they cajoled and taunted and tried to seduce and recruit the young soldiers. Norman Mailer spent a night in jail with the kids, scribbling notes for what would become his Pulitzer Prize–winning nonfiction book **The Armies of the Night.**

All publicity, good and bad, was fuel for the antiwar movement. The crowds kept getting bigger. With the antiwar movement shifting from protest to resistance, Dellinger and Rubin began looking ahead to the Democratic National Convention scheduled for Chicago in August.

Mary McCarthy had come home to Washington from Radcliffe for Dellinger and Rubin's October demonstration. Abigail found Mary's friends hard to talk to. As playful as the kids behaved—pretending to levitate the Pentagon, putting flowers in soldiers' rifle barrels, turning Winston Churchill's famous wartime V-for-victory hand gesture into a peace sign—they also had a tone of inflexible rectitude that Abigail found disturbing. Her daughter was in the thick of it all.

Later that fall, Abigail was on the phone with Mary when she opened up about her concerns for her husband.

"I know that somebody has to challenge the president," she told Mary. "Something must be done. But does your father have to be the one to do it?"

"Mother," said Mary, "that is the most immoral thing you've ever said!"

After Gene McCarthy's meeting with Lowenstein in California, George McGovern ran into McCarthy in the Senate chamber and said, "I sent some people up to talk to you, Gene, about running against Johnson."

"Yeah," Gene said, "I talked to them. Thanks for sending them. I think I may do it."

McGovern could hardly believe what he was hearing. He called Arthur Schlesinger and told him McCarthy was going to enter the primaries against Johnson. Schlesinger, too, was amazed. Schlesinger's view of Gene McCarthy was not unusual for a Kennedy man: McCarthy was a weak senator, passive, even a cynic. Another Kennedy man, Pierre Salinger, attended a party in California given by the state Democratic chairman for Gene McCarthy. McCarthy's talk sounded like a campaign speech. Salinger ribbed him afterward. "Gene, what day are you announcing?"

"What day would you suggest?" said McCarthy.

Salinger, also amazed, called Bobby. "We've got our candidate," Salinger said.

Bobby asked who it was, and when Salinger told him, Bobby said, "You're kidding."

Before formally announcing his candidacy, McCarthy made the rounds that fall testing the waters with the Dump Johnson crowd. The number one question on his mind was, what was Bobby Kennedy really planning to do?

No one was less convinced than Gene McCarthy by the new Bobby. To McCarthy, the word for Bobby was still **ruthless**. He saw RFK as insincere, calculating, self-involved, and morally and psychologically weak. It would be just like a Kennedy, McCarthy thought, to take a wait-and-see attitude about entering the race. It would be just like a Kennedy to use McCarthy as a stalking horse to probe Johnson's weakness and then, if things went well for McCarthy, jump in himself.

McCarthy still believed Bobby would be the better candidate. McCarthy had always said so. So even as McCarthy toured the country, and even as he began rousing youthful enthusiasm, he began wavering, right on the brink of making a formal announcement of his candidacy.

McCarthy called Martin Luther King Jr. to let him know he might announce his candidacy soon. McCarthy asked King for as much public support as the great civil rights leader could give. King had only recently made the Vietnam War a central issue. With so much of the fighting and dying in Vietnam being left to poor and black young men, McCarthy and King saw natural common cause between the civil rights movement and the antiwar movement. King expressed support during the call for McCarthy's run against Johnson, but King also felt it important to keep that support private. He was still trying to nudge Johnson on civil rights. Abigail McCarthy had lunch with Coretta Scott King, Martin's wife, at the Church Women United conference in Atlanta in November. The organization was ecumenical and dedicated to social justice. At its conferences Abigail and Coretta had become close. Coretta made a rare confidante of Abigail. Mrs. King badly wanted to be at the organizational forefront of Dr. King's latest effort: the Poor People's Campaign, which would go beyond civil rights, bringing all races together in a struggle against economic inequality. Her husband, however, was insisting she stay focused on raising their children. Abigail and Coretta had formed a bond as Christians, as women, and as loyal spouses to public, self-assured, and sometimes difficult men.

At lunch in November, Abigail could tell that Dr. King hadn't mentioned Gene's call to Coretta.

McCarthy began to worry he was being set up by Bobby. In November 1967, within weeks of promising Lowenstein he would run, McCarthy's promise started crumbling. McCarthy told the **New York Times** that a primary challenge was "only a possibility." He told the **Minneapolis Star** he hadn't made up his mind. Lowenstein was getting worried about McCarthy.

Thus began a series of indirect communications—tense, vague, and inconclusive—between McCarthy and Kennedy on the question of whether Bobby was still considering running. The outcome of these oddball negotiations would have a profound effect on the later stage of the campaign.

One intermediary was Mary McGrory. "The queen of the Washington press corps," as **Time** dubbed her, McGrory was a veteran, much-admired liberal journalist, having begun at the **Boston Herald** and spent the past twenty years at the **Washington Star**. She was close to the McCarthys, Abigail in particular, and to the Kennedys. She tried to serve as go-between.

"Well, tell him that if I run," Gene blithely told McGrory one night, "I only want one term. He can have a free run in '72." The presumptuousness of the idea appalled McGrory. She knew Bobby would react the same way. She refused to deliver the message.

Mary McGrory did set up a face-to-face meeting between the two men, hoping they would form an alliance. She got Bobby to carve out a full hour to discuss with Gene the opportunities and risks in each of the primaries. Bobby was a winning presidential campaign manager. He knew a lot about presidential primaries. He had some thoughts about how McCarthy ought to play them. The RFK staff even put together lists of the key people to talk to in the key states.

McCarthy arrived late and said virtually nothing. The only thing he told Bobby was "I'm not worried that I'm a stalking horse for you." Then, after seven minutes, McCarthy left.

McGrory was crestfallen by McCarthy's rudeness. Some further back-and-forth ensued, also inconclusive. McCarthy sent this message to RFK via Joseph Kraft, a columnist and former JFK speechwriter: all McCarthy hoped was that Bobby wouldn't "throw stones on the track while I'm running out there."

Bobby told Kraft he wouldn't throw stones but "tell him not to run a one-issue campaign."

Then McCarthy heard from two men he was surprised to hear from: the Kennedys' most prominent intellectual, John Kenneth Galbraith, and Joseph Rauh, the prominent labor lawyer and liberal activist. Antiwar moderates in the ADA, Galbraith and Rauh had begun 1967 by questioning the entire Dump Johnson concept. Now they were thinking they might have blown it. With a Dump Johnson candidacy almost under way with Gene McCarthy, Galbraith and Rauh feared that if McCarthy backed out now, someone else might step forward, someone too radical, too New Left. That would turn the movement against LBJ into a left-wing, almost third-party campaign. It would boost LBJ's credibility with mainstream Democrats. The Vietnam issue wouldn't present a threatening challenge to Johnson with a candidate like that. Now they needed McCarthy to run.

Galbraith and Rauh met with McCarthy. They pledged their support for his candidacy. They urged him to make the announcement. Galbraith was among the Kennedy men McCarthy respected the most—the intellectuals. And he knew Galbraith was a loyal member of the Kennedy inner circle. If Galbraith was urging McCarthy to run, that could only mean Bobby told them he wasn't running.

Snow was falling in Washington on the last day of November when Senator Eugene McCarthy called a press conference in the Senate Caucus Room, the biggest, most majestic room in the Senate office building. When the reporters gathered, they heard the strangest campaign announcement they had ever heard.

McCarthy read from notes and without any visible emotion. "I am concerned that the administration seems to have set no limit to the price it is willing to pay for a military victory." To the disappointment of the "Peace now!" chanters at demonstrations, he said, "I am not for peace at any price." He said he wanted "an honorable, rational, and political solution to this war."

Here is how he announced what he was about to do: "I intend to enter the Democratic primaries in four states: Wisconsin, Oregon, California and Nebraska. The decision with reference to Massachusetts, and also New Hampshire, will be made within the next two or three weeks." That was it. He did not say, I intend to run for president. He did not even say, I intend to run for the Democratic nomination. Just, I intend to run in four, maybe six states. What did that mean? Was this a real campaign? There was no hint to reporters in that room assigned to the McCarthy "campaign" that they were in for something exciting, something historic.

McCarthy said he hoped putting the war on the ballot this way would "alleviate at least in some degree of this sense of political helplessness and restore to many people a belief in the processes of American politics and of American government."

McCarthy said he had "waited a decent interval" to see whether others would take on "this challenge which I am making." When a reporter asked whether he would step aside if Bobby Kennedy chose to run, McCarthy said he would have been glad if Bobby had chosen to run. "If he had," said McCarthy, "there'd have been no need for me to do anything."

TEN

PEACE WITH HONOR

All of Lyndon Johnson's advisers saw this Gene McCarthy thing as a tempest in a teapot. Poll numbers showed the president trouncing McCarthy. Johnson knew McCarthy had been angered by the vice presidential competition with Humphrey in 1964. Johnson was never going to forget how McCarthy blindsided him by publicly withdrawing from VP consideration. Johnson gave up on McCarthy then.

The McCarthy challenge did not scare Lyndon Johnson.

Bobby. That's who Johnson worried about. Always. "The Bobby problem" dominated conversation in the White House. Johnson railed against RFK, tried to predict his next moves, laid traps, polled scenarios, and employed eternal vigilance. Bobby was the real threat to Johnson because if Bobby ran, Bobby could win.

Johnson's advisers began to think that if Bobby was considering making a primary challenge, then McCarthy wouldn't have announced. Maybe Johnson could relax about having to fend off the real threat from within his own party. Johnson wasn't so sure. Bobby was such a manipulator, and McCarthy wasn't sharp enough to anticipate Bobby's chess moves. Bobby must be playing him. There was no reason to count Bobby out. Jack Kennedy had struck Johnson as nice enough, overly relaxed, unthreatening. Bobby seemed like nothing but dead-eyed calculation, and Johnson always recognized menace directed straight at him personally. Bobby just didn't like him.

Johnson was accustomed to being disliked. The segregationists hated him for his civil rights legislation, the civil rights activists were never satisfied, the Black Power crowd insulted him, the right-wingers called him a socialist, the anticommunists called him an appeaser, the doves called him a warmonger, the Fulbright antiwar senators called him a tyrant. Some of his opponents were in two of those camps at once: Arkansas's Fulbright was both an antiwar senator and a segregationist.

None of that bothered Johnson more than watching Bobby Kennedy become the great national hero to the peaceniks. This irony of Robert Kennedy the reborn dove was just too much for Johnson. He knew that Bobby had been more eager than anyone else in the JFK cabinet for covert action against the communists in Vietnam. In 1964, Bobby called for victory in Vietnam. Now Bobby was harassing Johnson with bombing-halt ideas, making speeches proposing three-point plans, and pandering to the Left.

Johnson wondered obsessively about what could account, again and again, for Bobby's transformation from combating anticommunism—he'd always been too eager, Johnson thought, to make displays of toughness and courage—to this waffling flirtation with the peaceniks? Johnson was never going to see it as an honest evolution in Bobby's thinking.

"Hey! Hey! LBJ!" one chant ran. "How many kids did you kill today?" They'd been chanting that just this October, when thousands of kids, clearly under communist direction as far as Johnson could tell, came to Washington and turned the capital into a zoo. One protest sign read "LBJ: pull out like your father should have." Another read "Where's Lee Harvey Oswald now that we really need him?"

Marches like that, he believed, could only give North Vietnam the impression that the United States was too internally divided to win a war. So in preparation for the October protest, Johnson had created a cabinet task force to suppress the protesters. Defense Secretary Robert McNamara, Nick Katzenbach, Attorney General Ramsey Clark, and Interior

Secretary Stewart Udall set up a central command post to cover all matters, from pressuring bus companies to deny the protesters transportation to deploying troops. Johnson's special assistant Joe Califano made sure the government would supply the march with no electricity, speaker stands, water, toilets, or first aid.

By the time Gene McCarthy announced his primary challenge, Johnson's health was not what it should have been as a reelection campaign approached. He had been hospitalized twice in 1965, once for chest pains, once to remove his gall bladder. People thought he'd had a heart attack, so he lifted his shirt to show reporters exactly where his gall bladder surgery scar was. The media saw the lifted shirt as the crudest moment in the modern presidency. It would not be outdone until Donald Trump moved into the White House.

Lyndon Johnson's health was a more serious issue than anyone outside of his family realized. During the campaign of 1968, he would turn sixty, the same age at which his father died from a second heart attack. LBJ was going to feel lucky if he outlived his father, and he never expected to outlive him by much. Lady Bird saw the toll the job was taking on her husband—awake in the middle of the night studying bombing maps, feeling the relentless hatred hurled at him in slogans and signs by war protesters, pushing his heavy legislative agenda, an open revolt in his party led by a formerly loyal senator he had almost made his VP, and all the while carrying the nuclear codes in his pocket. Lady Bird worried about how much of this he could take physically. She didn't want him to run for reelection. She knew he was secretly thinking of dropping out.

Johnson's single most important guiding principle was that he would not be the first American president to lose a war.

Since 1965, LBJ's war policy had involved a ground war in the South with massive bombing, including the incendiary chemical napalm to literally burn the Vietcong. The bombing campaign reached beyond North and South Vietnam to enemy supply routes and safe havens in parts of Laos and Cambodia. The main enemy supply route into South Vietnam was what the American military called the Ho Chi Minh Trail. The trail ran through some of the most challenging terrain in Southeast Asia. Its creation and maintenance represented a triumph of technical engineering, involving five bases serving Soviet and Chinese trucks moving hundreds of tons of supplies. The bases were in turn served by a maze of narrow foot and bicycle paths, hard to see under jungle cover. The system enabled big trucks to travel the entire length of the trail without emerging from that natural canopy.

In 1967, with Johnson's reelection approaching, his war strategy was changing. His new policy in Vietnam used a surprising word that his reelection team would like: **withdrawal**.

It was only a label. LBJ was not about to withdraw American troops from Vietnam. Just the opposite. He had been pushing, nagging, bullying, and browbeating Secretary of Defense Robert McNamara, a holdover from the JFK administration, and the commander in Vietnam, General William Westmoreland, to step up the bombing and to put more troops on the ground. LBJ had to end the war, he knew that, but ending the war had to come only on his terms.

To get North Vietnam to agree to those terms he was going to have to bomb them and burn them into submission. And if they didn't submit? The North Vietnamese had been fighting nonstop for twenty-two years, first to overthrow French colonial rule. What if they did not submit to American bombs? Johnson had no plan B.

Johnson needed to be in a position to declare victory before getting out of Vietnam. North Vietnam must submit to a negotiated peace with the United States, agree to take no military advantage of any halt in bombing during peace talks, and emerge from peace talks with South Vietnam still a noncommunist state. A victory like that would prove that Johnson had been right all along in carrying out the war. The line against communist aggression in Southeast Asia would hold.

As images of civilian victims of bombings and

napalm filled the news media, favoring a halt in the bombing had become the middle-of-the-road political position on the war. By stepping up the bombing, Johnson was at risk of losing the political middle ground. LBJ could never understand why it wasn't obvious to everyone that peace required not less bombing but more bombing. "Withdrawal" required not only more bombing but also gearing up the South Vietnamese Army of the Republic of Viet Nam (ARVN) and getting it on its feet to defend itself without U.S. support. That meant sending more, not fewer, U.S. troops for training and support, while also continuing aggressive combat operations against the Viet-cong in South Vietnam. LBJ's "withdrawal" meant more bombs and more troops to force North Vietnam to accept his terms for peace.

LBJ thought he was middle of the road on Vietnam. The right wing wanted to "bomb them back to the Stone Age." They accused Johnson of creating a "stalemate" in Vietnam, a humiliating military standoff with no foreseeable chance of success. Johnson's right-wing critics did not understand that to avoid risk of war with China and the Soviet Union, his bombing had to be restricted to highly specific targets. There were Chinese railroads running through Vietnam; there were Russian ships off its shores. Bombing the North took meticulous planning. LBJ constantly pored over those maps himself.

Richard Nixon's revived political career was based

in large part on criticizing Johnson for weakness in Vietnam. All we needed to win, Nixon said in 1964, was "the will to win." After LBJ in effect followed Nixon's advice and escalated the war, Nixon took to bemoaning the war in a more general way, playing to its increasing unpopularity.

Everyone knew that on Vietnam, what LBJ most wanted to hear was good news. There was a price to delivering bad news. Bad news always incited LBJ to further demands on Vietnam delivered with tirades of abuse. And so the Vietnam news LBJ got was always better than the truth.

On an early November trip to Vietnam, Vice President Humphrey cabled this: "We are winning. Steady progress is everywhere evident. . . . What we are doing here is right . . . we have no choice but to persevere and see it through to success." Secretary of State Rusk told the president that recent elections in South Vietnam were clean, which they never were, and thanks to the election of President Nguyen Van Thieu, Hanoi would soon be asking for peace talks without conditions. When General Westmoreland found significant discrepancies between predictions of enemy troop strength and actual enemy troop strength, he did not feel compelled to rush that crucial information to Johnson's attention.

One member of the cabinet was losing his ability to maintain a positive attitude about progress in Vietnam: the man who knew the most, Secretary of

Defense Robert S. McNamara. As McNamara's confidence collapsed, Johnson began to think the secretary was having a breakdown.

McNamara served in World War II in the statistical control office of the Army Air Forces. Viewing warfare as a matter of technological rationalism, he analyzed and devised innovative ways to enhance the effectiveness of B-52 bombing campaigns. He went to the Ford Motor Company in 1946 as one of its famous managerial "whiz kids," and rose quickly to be the company's first president from outside the Ford family. JFK quickly came to regard his defense secretary as the star of his cabinet. McNamara tried to design efficient means for suppressing communism around the world by obstructing those wars of "national liberation" supported by China and the Soviet Union in places like Vietnam.

As in all of his previous projects, from the air force to Ford, McNamara swore by data as the key to efficiency and effectiveness. For JFK, he pioneered efforts like the Five Year Defense Plan (FYDP): tables projecting forces, costs, and manpower in categories like general purpose forces, strategic forces, intelligence and communications, airlift and sealift, National Guard and reserve, research and development, central supply and maintenance, training and medical. In Vietnam, he calculated totals of crop destruction to be achieved by pouring flaming napalm down on villages. He used defoliants like Agent Orange to make jungle environments less friendly to guerrilla forces. **Escalation** was a McNamara term—technical, bloodless. What it meant was using B-52s to carpet-bomb the Mekong Delta, one of the most densely populated areas in the world. This was all done unemotionally in the name of efficiently bringing North Vietnam to its knees. McNamara was using every tool he had short of nuclear weapons. He saw no reason why it wouldn't work. But it didn't work. And by late 1967, McNamara knew it. This war, McNamara was concluding with horror, was unwinnable. And if the war was unwinnable, then it was also immoral, because the United States had been sending American troops into harm's way to be wounded and killed for nothing. McNamara was secretly thinking what every war protester was saying: it was an unwinnable, immoral war with our soldiers dying for nothing. LBJ's defense secretary was not having a nervous breakdown. He was having, quite literally, an awakening. Robert McNamara was having sleepless nights.

In late August 1967, Secretary McNamara admitted to a Senate subcommittee that LBJ's strategy could not work. He said North Vietnam "cannot be bombed to the negotiating table." He added, "Bombing the ports and mining the harbors would not be an effective means of stopping the infiltration of supplies into South Vietnam." Johnson called McNamara into the Oval Office and yelled at him for three hours. Success in Vietnam was becoming more elusive as Johnson was becoming even more eager to believe that success was within his grasp— just in time for the reelection.

Johnson had only one thing he wanted McNamara to do: win. The secretary's phone would ring at 3:00 a.m. It would be Johnson saying, "Tell me how I can hit them in the nuts, Bob!"

On November 21, 1967, General Westmoreland told the National Press Club that he was absolutely certain that "whereas in 1965, the enemy was winning, today he is certainly losing." And on November 29, the day before Eugene McCarthy's announcement of his primary challenge to LBJ, Westmoreland gave an interview to **Time**. Asked whether the Vietcong and North Vietnam would make a concerted attack on U.S. troops, he replied, "I hope they do try something, because we are looking for a fight."

Both U.S. and South Vietnamese intelligence suggested that a major counteroffensive from the North was being planned. In October 1967, more than double the average number of trucks were heading south on the Ho Chi Minh Trail. By November, that number had more than doubled again. It looked as if this effort might begin sometime around the beginning of the Vietnamese New Year in January, during the celebration called Tet.

For Johnson, the intelligence came as excellent news. He believed a North Vietnamese offensive would bring everything to a head. By handing a crushing defeat to North Vietnam in combat, he would force them to the peace table in a state of weakness. He could dictate terms that fit his formula for "peace with honor." And LBJ could declare victory. His reelection just might be another landslide.

ELEVEN

PETER THE HERMIT

I n the final month of 1967, Eugene McCarthy's astonishingly unlikely primary campaign against President Johnson started its engines. It was still not really a presidential campaign, just a seemingly polite challenge to a heavily favored president in four primaries, which did not even include the first and therefore most prominent one, New Hampshire.

Four days after McCarthy announced his candidacy, the CCD, Lowenstein and Gans's Dump Johnson organization, held its national meeting in Chicago. Lowenstein had delayed the national meeting in the hope of having a candidate to present to the group. And now, finally, he had one.

Lowenstein's new problem was that his national meeting venue suddenly wasn't big enough. Four thousand people crowded into the Chicago Hilton ballroom. Two thousand more stood outside on the street. This would be the first antiwar presidential candidate's first major speech of the campaign. No one seemed to have noticed that Gene McCarthy had not committed to a full-scale campaign to dump Johnson and seize the nomination.

McCarthy was late. He stayed in his hotel suite working on the speech. The crowd was getting restive, so Lowenstein took the stage himself. "I'm going to give you a little pep talk," Lowenstein told the crowd. In his suite, McCarthy looked up in surprise at the closed-circuit TV covering the event. At the podium, Lowenstein launched into one of his most passionate tirades. The crowd got wildly pumped up. Every time Lowenstein mentioned Johnson's name, the crowd howled. McCarthy was shocked. This was as far as you could get from the tone of his announcement in the Senate Caucus Room and what he intended to be the tone of his challenge to Johnson. It was to be about the policy, not the man. McCarthy would adhere to the polite protocols of Senate debate. Now in the first big event of the McCarthy campaign, Al Lowenstein was ruining everything. Furious, McCarthy yelled, "Let's go!" at his Senate staffer Jerry Eller and the two ran through the hotel to the ballroom.

In the ballroom, McCarthy had to wait for Lowenstein to finish. Future senator and presidential candidate Gary Hart, a top Lowenstein operative, knew right away he had a problem. McCarthy was obviously upset with Lowenstein, but this was turning into one of Lowenstein's most inspiring speeches for Lowenstein's fans. Gary Hart could tell Lowenstein was nowhere near stopping. Lowenstein kept taking the crowd higher and higher. "Get this straight!" Lowenstein yelled about LBJ, "If a man cheats you once, shame on him! But if he cheats you twice, shame on you!" Curtis Gans could see the problem. Lowenstein had made all this happen. He'd created the CCD. He'd created the candidate he was about to introduce to them. It had all seemed hopeless for so long and he'd finally done it. And what he was talking about, what this candidacy was going to be about, was nothing less than a matter of life and death. Adrenalized with triumph, Lowenstein was turning it into **his** moment.

McCarthy started kicking a paper cup against the wall in frustration. Gans began pushing his way to the stage, yelling, "Someone get him to stop it, for Christ's sake!" When Gans reached the stage, he yelled right at Lowenstein, "Stop it!" Lowenstein waved his notes at Gans. "There's only a little bit left," he said.

When McCarthy finally took the stage, he was greeted with the wildest applause of his career. Then he began reading his speech. The audience went quiet listening to McCarthy with bated breath. They knew this was a historic moment—the major party antiwar candidate for president was delivering his first major speech. What he was saying, they began realizing, was something about the Punic wars of the Roman republic. Then he was saying something about the Dreyfus affair in turn-of-the-century France. Excitement turned to silence in the audience. This was beginning to feel like history class. McCarthy was looking more like one of their professors than a gutsy, defiant candidate ready to take on the establishment. When McCarthy's slow roundabout route arrived at "Finally, the war is no longer morally justified," the audience dutifully rose to their feet, but they seemed more bewildered than aroused. The Dump Johnson movement had just heard their candidate's first speech, and he never mentioned Lyndon Johnson.

McCarthy then declined to go outside and rally the thousands of kids waiting on the street who couldn't hear the speech. He also decided not to visit the many state CCD caucuses that wanted to see him. He told staffers he would never again follow Al Lowenstein on a stage.

That speech set the McCarthy tone. As the campaign proceeded, McCarthy remained diffident. He made few appearances. He struck reporters as having been pressed into service, a figurehead for an idea, not a passionate leader. The campaign felt colorless. There wasn't much for a reporter to cover.

Part of the problem was the awkward dissonance between Al Lowenstein and Gene McCarthy. They had not really known each other very well; now they didn't like each other. Lowenstein was unrepentant about his speech. He said he had only been trying to hold the crowd because McCarthy was late. To McCarthy, Lowenstein was a young hothead. To Lowenstein, McCarthy wasn't his first choice anyway. McCarthy cooled off a hot crowd. Bobby would have known what to do.

That tension only increased when McCarthy appointed a campaign manager. Lowenstein had assumed he would get the job. On December 12, McCarthy appointed Blair Clark.

Ledyard Blair Clark was a rich New Yorker who appeared to be the personification of the establishment. At boarding school he befriended poet Robert Lowell. At Harvard he became fast friends with his classmate John F. Kennedy. He was editor and president of the school newspaper, the **Harvard Crimson**. He used an inheritance from his grandmother to create a successful New Hampshire newspaper where he hired a young reporter named Benjamin Bradlee, another Harvard friend. Ben Bradlee went on to become the legendary editor of **Newsweek** and the **Washington Post**. As president of CBS News, Blair Clark hired Walter Cronkite, Dan Rather, Mike Wallace, and Morley Safer. Cronkite described him as "a scholar and a gentleman." What he was not was a political strategist. Gene McCarthy hired a presidential campaign manager who had never managed a campaign.

McCarthy and Clark had known each other for only two years, having met at a Washington dinner party. Clark was a Kennedy man, but he never held an official position in Washington. He turned down JFK's offer of an ambassadorship to remain at CBS News, which he left in 1964. Clark was in London when McCarthy announced his campaign. Clark dashed off a letter of support and encouragement to McCarthy. Mary McGrory convinced Clark that he should see McCarthy's first big speech, so Clark flew from London to Chicago for Lowenstein's Conference of Concerned Democrats event. He saw a campaign that needed a steady hand and a candidate who needed to find his comfort zone quickly.

Blair Clark went to Washington to set up a real campaign headquarters. He took two rooms of the Carroll Arms Hotel. He had a candidate so above it all that his whereabouts were hard to know at any given moment. Because few people knew where the campaign office was, Abigail McCarthy found her home invaded by would-be volunteers with nothing to do.

Only Curtis Gans seemed to Clark to have any idea what he was doing, so Clark did some quick hiring. He went young: Sam Brown, twenty-three, to organize campuses; Seymour Hersh, twenty-nine, press secretary; Peter Barnes, twenty-five, researcher-writer. Clark's focus was on building organizations on the ground in the states holding the four primaries where McCarthy said he would challenge Johnson: Wisconsin, Massachusetts, Oregon, and California. There was substantial antiwar enthusiasm in each of those states.

The campaign needed money, but the candidate found fund-raising distasteful. That was not an uncommon feeling among senators of that era, when Senate campaigns cost tens of thousands or hundreds of thousands of dollars instead of the millions and tens of millions they cost now. It was a mark of distinction in Gene McCarthy's Senate to disdain fund-raising. The intellectuals and statesmen of the Senate felt sullied by it. Only the hacks embraced it. Senators like McCarthy were never envious of Lyndon Johnson's fund-raising prowess. They were, as a matter of ethics and personal dignity, above it all. At an upscale New York fund-raising event, McCarthy came in, shook some hands, and headed for the bar. Letters with checks and offers of financing poured into the office, and no one answered them. Lowenstein finally did get some student volunteers working on that.

No one was better at dulling the excitement of the McCarthy campaign than Gene McCarthy. When he arrived to make a speech to thousands of students in New Bedford, Massachusetts, they gave him a standing ovation. When he left the stage, they didn't move. Clark started to feel that his candidate was deliberately running an anticampaign. Clark said that

McCarthy refused to rely on real organization and wandered aimlessly around the country "like Peter the Hermit." Before the Roman Catholic Church was ready to dispatch the first organized crusade to the Holy Land, some of the faithful got impatient and set out for Jerusalem on their own. They were led by Peter the Hermit in what came to be known as the People's Crusade. Peter began marching with forty thousand people in April 1096. By the time he reached Constantinople in July, he had lost ten thousand followers. Some returned home. Some starved to death. Some were captured and sold into slavery. With his crusade stalled, Peter made several side trips in search of support and supplies. In the end, the People's Crusade never made it to the Holy Land. Gene McCarthy making it to the Democratic convention in Chicago wasn't looking any easier.

McCarthy was not fully embraced by the Left. Some radicals condemned McCarthy as a phony or a secret front for Bobby or even for LBJ himself. Senator McCarthy was part of the system and therefore part of the problem. The radical magazine **Ramparts** accused McCarthy of actively seeking to destroy the peace movement. On the liberal establishment side, John Kenneth Galbraith was hearing from some within ADA that McCarthy was so weak he was making Johnson look good. The ADA could never support him. Jack Newfield urged Bobby to run and was over the moon about McCarthy's announcement in November. In January, Newfield wrote that the candidate was "vain and lazy." And then there was always the wistful longing for Bobby. And Gene McCarthy knew it. The McCarthy insurgency was beginning the election year totally stalled.

GENERAL WESTMORELAND had plenty of intelligence on the attack the North Vietnamese were planning for January. At age fifty-four, "Westy" was a modern general for 1968. Not only did he have combat experience in World War II, but he took a management course at Harvard Business School, exactly the kind of the thing that impressed his boss, the secretary of defense. "The best we have," Robert McNamara had told Johnson, "without question."

Without question, too, was Westmoreland's certainty of ultimate U.S. victory in Vietnam. Everything the general knew about warfare told him that both the North Vietnamese army and the Vietcong would be finally defeated by a committed war of attrition involving artillery and airpower, and by drawing the enemy into pitched battle.

It was therefore with high anticipation that on December 20, 1967, from his headquarters at Tan Son Nhut Air Base, just outside Saigon, General Westmoreland cabled Washington to say that the Vietcong and the North Vietnamese were soon "to undertake an intensified countrywide effort, perhaps a maximum effort, over a relatively short period of time." This would bring the enemy into exactly the kind of conventional battle that both Westmoreland and LBJ believed the United States would readily win. That belief was grounded in part on Westmoreland's confidence in the growing success of U.S. operations to date. Westmoreland publicly reported that 68 percent of South Vietnamese people were under the control of the government in Saigon; only 17 percent were Vietcong. "The Viet-cong has been defeated," one of Westmoreland's field force commanders told the press. "He can't get food and he can't recruit."

Westmoreland believed he was ready for anything the North threw at him. Westmoreland had 331,000 U.S. Army troops and 78,000 U.S. Marines deployed in Vietnam, plus the First Australian Task Force, a Royal Thai army regiment, and two South Korean infantry divisions and a Republic of Korea marine brigade, as well as 350,000 regulars in the South Vietnamese armed forces supported by 300,000 regional and local militias. Westmoreland was so sure that this upcoming attack would be quickly dealt with that he didn't tell his officers much about the intelligence he was getting.

IT WAS CLEAR TO Blair Clark that the McCarthy campaign needed to do something big and unexpected, and they needed to do it fast. He decided he had to get his candidate in direct combat with LBJ as soon as possible. That meant running in New Hampshire. Everyone knew running in New Hampshire was risky. That's why McCarthy didn't want to run there. He wanted his neighboring state of Wisconsin to be his first test of strength against Johnson. Risky is what Clark liked about New Hampshire. He knew how his friends in the news media would react. He knew they would be bored by the predictable move—Wisconsin—and McCarthy had already bored them enough. New Hampshire was bold. Brave. That is what the media would call it. But Clark knew New Hampshire better than McCarthy and the national press. He used to run a newspaper there. He knew running in New Hampshire was not as bold and brave as it looked.

Polls gave McCarthy no more than 10 percent of the New Hampshire vote. The state's Democratic governor, John King, told McCarthy he would get wiped out there. Bobby Kennedy had advised McCarthy to run in New Hampshire. That was almost reason enough for McCarthy not to.

Nixon beat JFK in New Hampshire in 1960. Being from a neighboring state didn't help Jack Kennedy with New Hampshire's conservative voters. Wisconsin was a more liberal state. McCarthy believed he knew how to appeal to Wisconsin voters. New Hampshire was not the place to launch an antiwar campaign. He thought getting wiped out in his first state would kill his campaign. Two New Hampshire activists, David Hoeh and future congressman Gerry Studds, went to Chicago for McCarthy's first big speech to the CCD. They liked what they saw. They believed McCarthy's calm, sober, mordantly witty style, so disappointing to the CCD kids, would be an asset in New England. They offered themselves to the McCarthy campaign that day in Chicago. Studds and Hoeh were not hippies. They were both thirty-year-old teachers. They knew the mood of the young people in their state. Hoeh's wife was number four on the state's Democratic committee. They agreed that McCarthy would not do well in northern New Hampshire, but the southern part of the state was coming to resemble liberal Boston suburbs in recent years. And most of the state's population was in southern New Hampshire now.

Blair Clark got McCarthy to reluctantly agree to have a look around the state. He agreed to give the Sidore Lecture in Manchester, New Hampshire, on December 14. Studds and Hoeh delivered a full house of fourteen hundred people who left their homes on a frigid night to hear Eugene McCarthy speak. McCarthy did his usual thing, beating an eager audience into stupefaction. Later that night, meeting with about sixty mid-level Democrats at an organizer's home, McCarthy was asked if he should take a poll before challenging the president.

"No, I don't think so," McCarthy replied. "I think it would be very discouraging."

In the car on the way to the airport, Hoeh's heart sunk. **New York Times** reporter David Halberstam was riding along interviewing McCarthy for an article. McCarthy told Halberstam that he planned to stay out of the New Hampshire primary.

If McCarthy had said that on the radio, Studds and Hoeh's New Hampshire organization would have collapsed at that moment. But there was one thin ray of hope. The Halberstam article wasn't for the next day's paper. He was working on a longer profile that wouldn't go to print for a few months.

Studds and Hoeh briefed Blair Clark on every detail of their New Hampshire plan for the McCarthy campaign. Just before Christmas, Clark joined McCarthy on the train from Washington to New York and pushed the Studds and Hoeh New Hampshire plan hard. Clark said McCarthy was getting nowhere and had to do something dramatic. Every apparent disadvantage of New Hampshire was really an advantage. The image of the conservative state's governor predicting under five thousand votes for McCarthy meant any vote greater than that could be spun as an upset victory. The press would think taking the risk was daring, maybe even brave, but Clark stressed another word—McCarthy's preferred self-image—**serious**. The press would think he was serious if he did battle in New Hampshire. Clark told McCarthy that Studds and Hoeh had heard that the state party hierarchy was panicking over the possibility of a McCarthy run in New Hampshire. That meant the party bosses feared voter flight from LBJ. Clark described Studds and Hoeh's well-oiled machine, ninety student volunteers in every city just waiting for McCarthy to say yes. Studds and Hoeh had put together a twelve-day, highly detailed campaign schedule that would get the candidate in front of three quarters of the primary vote for just the right amount of time in each city and town. All the work was done in New Hampshire. All Studds and Hoeh needed was McCarthy's name on the ballot.

On the train, McCarthy took it all in and said very little. Clark knew he had done all he could. It was McCarthy's decision to make now.

Studds and Hoeh kept telling the New Hampshire press and the young eager volunteers that McCarthy was moving toward making a run there. Privately, though, they had given up.

THE NORTH VIETNAMESE MILITARY buildup continued while being closely observed by U.S. intelligence. Something close to eighty thousand tons of supplies and 200,000 troops moved down the Ho Chi Minh Trail. The Vietcong received new AK-47 assault rifles and B-40 rocket-propelled grenade launchers, far more powerful material than anything the South Vietnamese army had.

The North Vietnamese had also begun carrying out attacks on South Vietnamese troops near remote borders. A battle broke out between a North Vietnamese regiment and U.S. Special Forces at a remote outpost on the Cambodian border. It went on for ten days and cost 800 North Vietnamese soldiers their lives.

U.S. intelligence just could not get a handle on these border outbreaks. They were unrelated to the military buildup the United States was monitoring. They were far from the cities in the South that the United States knew the North wanted to attack. Why would North Vietnam waste men and materiel in big actions like this, unprovoked, so far from the urban centers? In engagements like that, U.S. artillery and airpower were always bound to succeed in the end. Westmoreland just had to redeploy his forces away from the coastal lowlands and cities and out to the borders. Which he did. Westmoreland saw no risk in leaving the cities weakly defended because the North was incapable of mounting a meaningful offensive there anyway. That's what all his training and experience told him.

ON JANUARY 2, Blair Clark called Studds and Hoeh and told them he was getting the next flight to

Manchester, New Hampshire. They would meet that night, and their meeting would have to be kept secret. They met at the Wayfarer Inn for dinner. Clark had a message to deliver to Studds and Hoeh directly from McCarthy that would change their lives: prepare the troops; within forty-eight hours Senator McCarthy would announce he was running against President Johnson in the New Hampshire primary. As Gerry Studds and David Hoeh sat there in a mix of disbelief and joy listening to Clark, they were interrupted. Hoeh was called to the phone. It was McCarthy. He told Hoeh he would be running in New Hampshire, and they could tell the press in the morning. When Hoeh went back to the table and told Clark that McCarthy had just called him to say he was running and they could tell the press tomorrow, Clark was just stunned. And irritated. Why did McCarthy make him fly here for a secret meeting to tell Studds and Hoeh what he was going to tell them in a phone call? At the same time! By now Blair Clark knew the answer. It was classic Gene McCarthy.

TWELVE

"CLEAN FOR GENE"

I n 1968, fewer than a third of U.S. states held presidential primary elections. That's not because the primary system was new. It was in decline. Primaries began as the idea of the early twentieth-century political reformers. Wisconsin held the first primary election in 1905. By 1920, about half of the states were holding primaries. Before that, party bosses got together in the fabled smoke-filled rooms to select nominees based on considerations kept hidden from the electorate. Because the nominees weren't democratically selected, reformers asked, how could presidents be said to be democratically elected? Hence primaries. State delegates would still choose the nominee at conventions, but primary elections would guide, and sometimes bind, delegates in that choice.

As the system developed in practice, not everything went according to the reformers' hopes. The states that did not hold primaries still sent delegations to conventions with unclear mandates. Each party in each state played by different rules in interpreting primary results. The complexity of those rules was poorly understood by the voters the system was designed to empower.

By 1968, primaries still did provide some candidates with committed convention delegates from some states, but mainly they offered candidates cards to play when the convention's backroom dealings began. A strong showing in key primaries could gain a candidate the commitment of unbound delegates from states that didn't have primaries. Strength in primaries demonstrated the potential for getting people's votes in the general election. Dominating multiple primaries demonstrated a record of appealing to majorities.

In 1968, 1,312 was the magic number for Democrats. The party's presidential nominee needed 1,312 delegate votes at the national convention in Chicago. There was no way to get even half of those votes through the primary system, which consisted of only fourteen elections, scheduled between March and July. Most of the delegates were not bound to support the candidate who won the states' primaries. With a ruthless incumbent president, a consummate political infighter and deal maker as head of the party, and well-organized state organizations in thrall to the national committee, the nomination seemed a foregone conclusion. The president was expected to dominate the primaries even without deigning to run in them. LBJ's refusal to even place his name on a primary ballot would send the message that he already had the nomination locked. No need to trudge through the snows of New Hampshire and Wisconsin to cast a vote that wouldn't matter. Taking no chances, local party organizations would send out fleets of write-in voters for LBJ and he would win the primary vote seemingly by popular demand. There was nothing wrong with that plan. Nothing. Unless everything Lyndon Johnson and party professionals knew about politics was suddenly going to change in 1968. If it was, they would be the last to know.

Al Lowenstein, Gerry Studds, and David Hoeh saw something in the primary system that no one else did. Political systems are usually designed by office-holding incumbents to protect incumbents. Congressional districts are gerrymandered by the parties to protect incumbents. Though the primary system was created by reformers, it was owned and operated by incumbents who set up what economists would call barriers to entry to the marketplace. Everything about the primary system—including a state's decision not to have a primary—was designed as a barrier to entry to the political marketplace. Lowenstein, Studds, and Hoeh saw the holes in those barriers.

They thought the primary system inadvertently offered an insurgent a chance precisely because of some of the bizarre state-by-state complexities.

Studds and Hoeh's study of how convention delegates were awarded based on the results of the New Hampshire primary convinced them that they had a good chance of getting McCarthy more delegates than his election day vote total would deserve. More study found more ways to manipulate the rules in McCarthy's favor in New Hampshire and other states. But the single most important strategic insight that Lowenstein, Studds, and Hoeh had was the new paradigm they applied to the concept of winning. They believed there was a way to win without getting the most votes. They imported the paradigm from sports betting where you could win even if you bet on the losing team as long as the losing team didn't lose by as much as it was expected to. If McCarthy was expected to get only 10 percent of the vote and he won 15 percent, then the McCarthy campaign could celebrate their surprising "win." They would just have to persuade the political media, who would in turn persuade voters in the next primary states to see Gene McCarthy as a winner even if he finished in second place. At this point, Studds and Hoeh told Blair Clark, anything better than crashing and burning in New Hampshire might be spun as an attention-getting victory that would help turn out volunteers, press, and funding for the next states.

And so in New Hampshire in 1968, the expectations game was born in American politics.

Studds and Hoeh had exactly $400 in the bank. When they announced McCarthy's candidacy to the two major papers, the **New Hampshire Union Leader** and the **Concord Monitor**, the papers declined to run big stories. Studds and Hoeh rented a former electrical-supply warehouse on Main Street in Concord and began signing up the local student volunteers. In the absence of any press coverage or money, the students were going to have to make this thing happen. Studds and Hoeh themselves held full-time jobs and were running the campaign part time. It wasn't until January 25, three weeks after the New Hampshire announcement, that Eugene McCarthy himself finally showed up in the state.

Abigail McCarthy arrived earlier. Abigail had been managing what she called the Attic Group, antiwar women, mostly homemakers, who met on the third floor of the McCarthys' house in Georgetown. They instantly proved more efficient and focused than the national campaign staff in organizing for New Hampshire. Abigail and her Attic Group of female volunteers connected with the idealistic, unpaid part-timers in New Hampshire before the so-called professional campaign staff in Washington did.

The campaign staff's hotel room offices in Washington, D.C., became too small, but no one in Washington wanted to rent space to someone challenging the president. They finally found office space at Seventeenth and H Street, a block from the White House. The candidate never went there. Blair Clark was rarely there because he was already concentrating on the biggest delegate prize: the California primary. With the campaign manager on the road, there was no organizational structure at the campaign office. When Curtis Gans began calling Abigail to ask about possible campaign contributors, she didn't know who he was. Most of the other campaign office staffers were unknown to Abigail, and they seemed less than interested in New Hampshire. Only national volunteer coordinator Arleen Hynes, whom the McCarthys had known for decades in Minnesota, seemed to take a strong interest in communicating with the fledgling organizations in the states.

Abigail realized that to make anything happen in New Hampshire, she had to ignore the office staff and use the dedication and energy of her Attic Group. One member, a biographer and mystery writer named Pat McGerr, researched New Hampshire in detail—primary law, numbers of registered voters, movers and shakers. Pat and Abigail used all that to create a mimeographed pamphlet for New Hampshire volunteers. Days later, Pat went to the campaign office to ask if they had any research on New Hampshire.

"Yes," said Sy Hersh, "we do have research on the primary states." He handed Pat her own mimeographed pamphlet. No one in the office knew where they had gotten it.

Arleen Hynes gave Abigail a list of people to see in New Hampshire, so Abigail packed up the kids for a ski weekend in the state. Mary McCarthy was one of the Boston area college kids who went north that weekend to help the McCarthy campaign.

Abigail met up with Mary and they began meeting the people on Arleen's list while the younger McCarthy kids were skiing. Abigail established coordination between the New Hampshire campaign office in Concord and the Washington headquarters. The Attic Group wrote literally thousands of personal, individualized letters to influential people in New Hampshire, hand addressed and signed by the specific letter writer herself. That was unusual. People in New Hampshire began to pay attention.

Gene McCarthy finally made his first campaign visit to the state. Gerry Studds and David Hoeh thought it would make for a powerful image to have the candidate make his first primary speech where JFK had done so eight years earlier outside the Nashua City Hall. There was a bust of Kennedy there and McCarthy stood beside it, visibly unhappy. The speech was characteristically dull. Then McCarthy went to a shopping center to shake hands. Most people there had never heard of him.

Now that Abigail had everyone working hard, the commitment of the candidate himself remained an open question. Gene McCarthy planned to spend only about ten days in New Hampshire before the election on March 12.

ON JANUARY 30, thirty-five battalions of Vietcong hit six separate points in Saigon, including the U.S. embassy compound. They found both South Vietnamese and U.S. forces totally unprepared because their attention, manpower, and matériel had been directed at countering those bewildering attacks in remote border locations. Suddenly the diversionary purpose of those strikes became clear: to leave the U.S. and South Vietnamese forces out of place when the North launched the Tet Offensive.

Suddenly American TV screens and front pages exploded with horrific images. TV coverage showed surprised-looking American soldiers running to get into position within the embassy compound walls. South Vietnam's ancient capital city of Hue was the scene of weeks of house-to-house fighting. Photos from Hue showed bodies of U.S. Marines, soldiers, and civilians stacked in piles.

The Tet Offensive hit thirty-six provincial capitals including Saigon, which had never been attacked before. One CBS reporter said that now there was nowhere to hide.

The first polls showed the American public reacting to Tet with increased support for intensifying warfare in Vietnam. At the end of January, new majorities supported more bombing of the North and expanding action on the ground. That was only the "rally effect" typical after a surprise attack. Johnson worked the effect as hard as he could. He held a top secret meeting with four senators and three congressmen and warned them that enemy agents were working within the United States "to destroy confidence in your leaders and in the South Vietnamese government. I ask you," he went on, "to measure your statements before you make them. The greatest source of Communist propaganda statements is our own statements." He also urged Westmoreland by cable to show nothing but staunch confidence during his daily briefings. On February 8, Johnson told Westmoreland, "The United States government is not prepared to accept a defeat in Vietnam. In summary, if you need more troops, ask for them."

In the first week of February at about 4:30 in the morning, a Vietcong captain named Nguyen Van Lem led an attack on a South Vietnamese armor camp in a suburb of Saigon. Lem captured a South Vietnamese lieutenant colonel and his family, including his eighty-year-old mother, and demanded the colonel show the Vietcong how to drive the tanks stationed at the camp. The colonel refused. Lem executed him and his family, along with many others in the camp. Thirty-four dead civilians were dumped into a mass grave.

Lem himself was soon captured near that grave by Saigon police. The police were under the command of General Nguyen Ngọc Loan, the South Vietnamese National Police chief. Loan himself had witnessed Lem executing the colonel and his family. When Lem was brought before Loan in handcuffs, the prisoner told Loan he was proud of killing all thirty-four civilians. General Loan responded by raising his .38 special Smith & Wesson revolver and shooting Lem in the head.

Almost as the bullet passed through Lem's head, Loan's shot became world famous. AP photographer Eddie Adams's photo showed Lem, who looks like a civilian in a plaid shirt, with his hands tied behind his back as Loan, in uniform, fires his handgun inches away from Lem's head. The photo ran in papers all over the world. No one knew the backstory. Americans who had been uneasily supporting Johnson's Vietnam policy found themselves shocked and disgusted by what appeared to be a barbaric execution. Still, Lyndon Johnson thought victory in the war would win him the election, secure his legacy, and make the world safer.

IN FEBRUARY, the McCarthy campaign, still listless, began experiencing internal conflicts. Curtis Gans went to Concord and decided right away that he didn't like how the Studds and Hoeh operation there was working. Too many kids, said Gans, not enough grown-ups. This wasn't supposed to be a hippie, countercultural rebellion.

Studds and Hoeh disagreed. First, the local students were all they had, and the young were the center and the energy of the peace movement—and McCarthy was the peace movement's candidate. Still, all Gans could imagine was old-time New Hampshire Democrats recoiling from a children's crusade of raggedy youth.

Sy Hersh got along okay with the Concord office from his spot in the D.C. campaign office; his problem was with McCarthy's Senate staff, especially Jerry Eller. The Senate staffers were older; they'd known McCarthy for decades in some cases; and they didn't enjoy the newcomers' demands for face time with the candidate, who to Senate staffers was also a working senator. Hersh saw Jerry Eller as unbearably picayune and proprietary about scheduling. One day Hersh introduced Eller to some reporters as "the man who's been helping the Senator on and off with his coat for twenty years." Abigail McCarthy tried to get the warring factions working together.

Her brother Stephen Quigley, a former comptroller of Minnesota, had been deputized to work with the Washington office to keep spending under control.

There were four big players in the McCarthy campaign in New Hampshire: Blair Clark, the campaign manager; Arnold Hiatt, a Boston shoe company owner; Martin Peretz, a young scholar at Harvard; and Howard Stein, president of the Dreyfus Fund. Stein was the biggest donor. When Abigail first heard of Stein, word had it that Stein had raised several million dollars, and because he was paying for all the advertising, he brought in his own ad people. Rumors flew that Stein was scheming to take over from Clark as campaign manager. But the McCarthy campaign was being shaped less by internal tensions and factions than by events on the other side of the world.

THE FIRST WAVE OF the Tet Offensive was complete in March 1967. Another phase would be launched later in the spring, another in the fall. In the end, about 5,000 South Vietnamese soldiers and 4,000 U.S. soldiers were killed in Tet. North Vietnam and the Vietcong lost nearly 60,000 soldiers. Tet was technically a military victory for U.S. forces. The North failed to achieve their military objectives.

Westmoreland was accurate in saying the enemy was being driven back. But this was the enemy the American people had been told was incapable of such an attack. This enemy had planned and executed a fully orchestrated surprise attack against the U.S. military, killed 4,000 Americans, and put the cities of South Vietnam in chaos. It seemed clear now that the North Vietnamese and the Vietcong were undaunted, highly organized, and committed—and might well strike again at any time.

The North and the Vietcong had undermined their enemy's will to go on fighting. Not their military enemy, not the U.S. and South Vietnamese forces, not the commander in chief of U.S. forces, but the enemy in whose name the war was being fought: the American people. LBJ's polling bump collapsed. In February, the president's approval rating fell to 41 percent, with 47 percent disapproval. Public confidence in the war in Vietnam was at 35 percent. Lyndon Johnson slept almost not at all during Tet, constantly looking for new ways to win.

Tet sent thousands of kids unexpectedly flooding into New Hampshire in February to work for Eugene McCarthy. Curtis Gans thought there were too many students already, but they were almost all local. Suddenly there were five thousand students, working weekends throughout the state, plus two thousand new full-time volunteers. Gans was wrong about the kids. They brought the campaign to life.

The Tet Offensive accelerated hatred of the war to critical mass with lightning speed on college campuses. LBJ's "withdrawal" policy of intensifying warfare to bring the North to the negotiating table seemed more hopeless than ever. Then Johnson announced a new strategy: escalating the war. Having prompted Westmoreland to ask for them, Johnson promised to send 10,500 more troops to Vietnam.

Johnson also planned to extend tours of duty and call up the reserves. Maybe the time had come to ask Congress for a full declaration of war. Johnson was sure he needed to set an even more aggressive course for victory.

The Joint Chiefs of Staff seized on Johnson's idea of calling up the reserves. They thought that would make an enormous difference. They asked the president to call up 200,000 men. Half would go to Vietnam, the other half to other trouble spots.

It was as if Lyndon Johnson and the Joint Chiefs were working as recruiting agents for the McCarthy campaign. College students poured into New Hampshire from all over the country. Curtis Gans worried about the image of out-of-state hippies representing the McCarthy campaign, so the volunteers' motto became "Clean for Gene." My older brother Kevin was a junior at Suffolk College in Boston then. When I saw him shaving off his beard, he said he had to get "clean for Gene" before heading up to New Hampshire for the weekend.

McCarthy had the largest number of campaign volunteers New Hampshire had ever seen. Students traded in their hippie overalls for neckties, blazers, and neat shirts, and they rang the doorbells of half the households in the state. They created mailing lists of ninety thousand registered Democrats and a hundred thousand independents. Forty Yale students created McCarthy pamphlets in French and went door-to-door in the French section of Berlin.

"My campaign may not be organized at the top," McCarthy told a reporter, "but certainly it is tightly organized at the bottom."

The "Clean for Gene" kids not only woke up New Hampshire for the McCarthy campaign, they woke up the candidate. They made Gene McCarthy come alive. He started really campaigning. It seemed he finally felt understood.

The students never seemed confused by McCarthy. His professorial style was familiar to them. When he spoke, they heard courage without bravado, wisdom without pontification or condescension, moral clarity without absolutism. McCarthy wanted to encourage their intelligence and creativity. He wanted to help them resist the lure of the new radicalism. They believed Gene McCarthy could save their country and save their lives. In a time of dire generational strife, he was a good father.

It wasn't just kids who began responding to McCarthy. New Hampshire voters of all ages did, too, not only in the more sophisticated precincts but in the all-important factories and working-class social clubs and small-business organizations. McCarthy refused to criticize Johnson personally. He did not call the war immoral. He would not allow Howard Stein's advertising team to mention burning babies in Vietnam. McCarthy wanted his campaign's rhetoric to be controlled, calm, and serious. He talked directly to people about Johnson's failed policy, now so painfully evidenced by Tet. He asked ordinary people to think about it. He seemed to be certain that if asked to think, they would. Agree or disagree with him, no Democratic voter who saw Gene McCarthy in New Hampshire thought of him as a radical, a revolutionary, or anti-American. He was in a Canadian border state with the kind of people he grew up with. He understood them and he believed they understood him. McCarthy's slogan was "New Hampshire can bring America back to its senses."

The Democratic machine in New Hampshire unwittingly helped McCarthy. LBJ's strategy had always been not to campaign in New Hampshire but to rely on write-in votes organized by the state machine. There had not been a shadow of a doubt that the approach would work. Governor John King was sincere when he'd predicted a disastrous showing for McCarthy. Not only the governor but the Democratic U.S. senator and other leading Democrats in New Hampshire were all Johnson men. All they had to do was deliver the write-in votes on election day, so they sent out something called a pledge card. The voter was to tear off one perforated section and keep it as a reminder to vote. The other two sections were to be filled out and returned to the local Democratic Party office. One section pledged the voter to write in Johnson's name; that would be kept in the local office. The other section would be sent to the White House. In exchange for this pledge, a free picture of LBJ and Lady Bird would be mailed to the voter.

Many New Hampshire voters were startled by this ploy. Some were truly scandalized. This was almost a parody of crude, old-fashioned political machine strong-arming. McCarthy's campaign seized on the pledge card and the local outrage it stirred. "Whatever happened to the secret ballot?" read a McCarthy poster, featuring a blown-up picture of the pledge card. McCarthy told his crowds that he saw the pledge cards as a test of New Hampshire's famous independent spirit. They loved it.

If Johnson's people in New Hampshire were listening to the popular protest songs of the day, they would have heard what they were beginning to feel in Stephen Stills's lyrics: "There's something happening here but what it is ain't exactly clear." McCarthy seemed to be gaining momentum and they felt powerless to understand it, let alone stop it. "What can you do," complained Governor King to one of his aides. "It's all these kids." Johnson's people had presumed victory. They had not prepared for a fight.

Back in December, Studds and Hoeh had insisted that anything better than the local machine's prediction of 10 percent for McCarthy might be spun as a kind of victory. By the first week of March, they were pretty sure they were going to do better than that.

Johnson's people were polling obsessively and they raised their predictions, saying McCarthy couldn't get more than 25 percent. Five days before the primary, one of the Johnson operatives looked at their polls and raised that prediction again: it would be a disgrace for McCarthy if he got less than 40 percent. Everyone in the McCarthy campaign and the press assumed the Johnson spinners were picking a number far bigger than they thought McCarthy could really get.

The Democratic machine placed a full-page newspaper ad announcing that "the Communists in Vietnam are watching the New Hampshire primary." New Hampshire's Democratic senator Thomas McIntyre called McCarthy "a friend of draft-dodgers and deserters." Radio ads said McCarthy was urging surrender in Vietnam.

Euphoric. Much to her surprise, that is the word Abigail used to describe her husband in the last few days of the New Hampshire campaign. The upswell of support and love from the most reflective, intelligent, and dedicated segment of the younger generation was redeeming the very idea of liberalism itself, of America itself, and, Abigail knew, of Gene himself. In the Katzenbach hearing, McCarthy heard something terrifyingly stirring—genuine tyranny in America. Now he heard something else—a roar against tyranny. That roar came straight out of the heart and soul of the American people, and the hope and inspiration it gave McCarthy changed him. He looked and felt like a winner.

On election day, March 12, snow fell heavily. At Johnson headquarters in Manchester, the machine politicians steeled themselves and started blaming the snow in advance. At McCarthy's election night headquarters at the Wayfarer Inn, three hundred volunteers packed into the room to watch the returns. Around the state and around the country, people were watching with an excitement never seen before on a primary night. Studds and Hoeh were at the Wayfarer with Curtis Gans and Lowenstein.

As midnight approached, McCarthy was way ahead of expectations with 42 percent of the vote, and hundreds of first-time campaign volunteers at the Wayfarer were cheering each gain.

In Washington that night, Lyndon Johnson gave a speech at the Veterans of Foreign Wars dinner. His speechwriters kept him covered with a joke about the primary written and delivered before anyone knew the final results. Johnson quipped, "I think New Hampshire is the only place where a candidate can claim 20 percent is a landslide, 40 percent is a mandate and 60 percent is unanimous." His audience loved it.

All I remember from that night was hearing my older brothers yelling that McCarthy had won. I wasn't yet a newspaper reader so I didn't see the next day's headlines, which were all variations on the

New York Times headline: SENATOR EXCEEDS TOP
PRIMARY PREDICTIONS IN PEACE CAMPAIGN. It was
decades later that I learned LBJ had received more
votes that night, 49 percent to McCarthy's 42 percent. That was the night that LBJ could finally see
how completely upside down his world was. Everyone thought the guy who came in second "won" the
New Hampshire primary. If image was becoming
reality in Vietnam and in the presidential campaign,
then LBJ was in worse trouble than he thought.

In the way that mattered most, Gene McCarthy did win the New Hampshire primary. Because
Gerry Studds and David Hoeh outsmarted the political machine in the way they'd filed their slate of
possible delegates, when all the primary votes were
counted, McCarthy won twenty delegates and LBJ
won only four. McCarthy was officially ahead of the
president in the earned delegate count for the convention in Chicago.

Gene McCarthy made history that night in New
Hampshire. He vindicated the reformers' vision of
the primary system. He challenged the powerful
incumbent president of his own party and "won."
He put war and peace on the ballot, life and death,
and he won. The insurgent won, and that changed
Democratic Party politics forever. Every presidential
nominating season since then, the Democrats have
gone looking for the inspiring insurgent on the Left
who will re-create the feeling of New Hampshire in

1968. The crowd at the Wayfarer was ecstatic when McCarthy got up to speak. Al Lowenstein stood behind him as the audience in front of them chanted, "Chicago!" The Chicago convention was five months away, but to them that felt like tomorrow. "Chicago!" "People have remarked that this campaign has brought young people back into the system. But it's the other way round," McCarthy said. "The young people have brought the country back into the system!"

THIRTEEN

THE NEW NIXON

echnically, the biggest winner in New Hampshire that night was Richard Nixon, who won the Republican presidential primary with 78 percent of the vote. But Nixon was running unopposed at that point, so there was no suspense or excitement on the Republican side, and with Gene McCarthy making history that night, Richard Nixon's political resurrection went largely unnoticed. Nixon was as unlikely a New Hampshire primary winner as McCarthy because the only thing worse than being an unknown in presidential politics is being a known loser. Nixon's road to victory in New Hampshire was almost as improbable as McCarthy's.

We can only wonder what Richard Nixon's place in political history would be if he had gone to Harvard. What kind of person would he have become? It's reasonable to imagine that he probably would not have spent his life in deep personal resentment of what he saw as the Northern establishment: the intellectuals, the Jews, the Harvard men, the Kennedys. Perhaps having some of those Harvard men as roommates for four years might have humanized them for Nixon. Perhaps a Jewish roommate would have tamed his anti-Semitism. Nixon was accepted at Harvard College and offered a partial scholarship, but his family still couldn't afford it and needed him at home. So Nixon went to a local school on a full scholarship, Whittier College, twenty miles southeast of Los Angeles.

Nixon grew up just south of Whittier in Yorba Linda in a family of Quakers—no alcohol, no dancing. Like Bobby Kennedy, Nixon was surrounded by brothers in his childhood, and he knew the pain of losing two brothers. There were five Nixon brothers, Richard second in the birth order. When the Nixon farm failed, Nixon's father ran a gas station and store in Whittier. It was barely profitable. The Nixons lived the life of the working poor in the 1920s, which only worsened in the Great Depression of the 1930s, when Richard went to college.

Nixon was twelve years old when he watched his little brother Arthur waste away and die of tuberculosis at age seven in 1925. He cried for weeks after Arthur died. Nixon was at Whittier College when his older brother, Harold, died, also of tuberculosis, at age twenty-three in 1933.

Nixon became an academic star at Whittier High School, but finding time to study wasn't easy. Every day before school, Nixon drove the family truck to Los Angeles, bought produce, then set it up for display at the family store.

From Whittier College, Nixon won a full scholarship to law school at Duke, where he had a reputation for putting in superhuman hours of nonstop studying and graduated third in his class. He practiced law back in Whittier and married Pat Ryan there.

After the Japanese bombing of Pearl Harbor, the Nixons then moved to Washington when Richard Nixon was offered a job as a lawyer in the wartime Office of Price Administration, overseeing rationing and regulating prices. Four months later, Nixon enlisted in the navy, despite being entitled as a birthright Quaker to an automatic exemption, completed officer candidate school with flying colors, and rose to lieutenant in charge of an air transport unit at Guadalcanal, not engaging directly in combat yet taking bombing several times by the Japanese. He received a letter of commendation and rose to lieutenant commander before resigning his commission to run for Congress.

NIXON DEFEATED his hometown congressman, a popular five-term incumbent, by doing the kind of thing that earned him the nickname "Tricky Dick."

He willfully and repeatedly confused the similar sounding names of two groups—one that endorsed his opponent and another that endorsed no one but was widely believed to have some communists in its membership. Nixon captured little attention during his first term in Congress, but after his reelection in 1948, the year Gene McCarthy was elected to the House, Nixon rocketed to national fame by once again exploiting the fear of communists in America.

Nixon was an eager member of the House Un-American Activities Committee, searching for communists operating inside the U.S. government. When Alger Hiss, a State Department official in Franklin Roosevelt's administration, appeared before the committee, Nixon tripped him up to the point where Hiss was eventually charged with and convicted of perjury without having been proved to be a communist. The massive publicity around the Hiss case was exactly what Nixon needed to move up from the House to the Senate.

In 1944, Helen Gahagan Douglas became the first Democratic woman elected to the House from California. She left a successful career as an actress to enter politics. She and her husband, Melvyn Douglas, a prominent actor, had become close friends of the Roosevelts, President Franklin and First Lady Eleanor. Mrs. Roosevelt became Helen Douglas's political mentor. Lyndon Johnson immediately took her under his protective wing when she entered the

House. Her ensuing affair with LBJ became an open secret in the House. In 1950, Helen Gahagan Douglas won a hard-fought race for the California Democratic nomination to run for the Senate. Her Republican opponent welcomed her into the general election campaign by accusing her of being a communist sympathizer and calling her "the Pink Lady."

Douglas was stunned.

By the time she woke up to the fact that Nixon was smarter and more ruthless than she had imagined, she could only resort to comparing his "big lies" to those of Hitler and Stalin. That sounded like an overblown effort at catch-up defamation. She called him "Tricky Dick." The name would stick, but the race had become about Nixon. He could turn on a dime from heedless accusation to sheer sanctimony. "Truth is not a smear," he solemnly intoned.

Nixon won with 59 percent of the vote. "I personally believe," Helen Gahagan Douglas said in 1973, "that Richard Nixon might well have won that campaign even without the campaign of character assassination and misrepresentation of my record, without smearing himself."

In Washington, no one was on a faster track than Richard Nixon. Two years after winning his Senate seat, General Dwight Eisenhower chose Senator Nixon as his vice presidential running mate. The Democratic presidential nominee was the liberal Adlai Stevenson. While Eisenhower took the high road, Nixon would be perfect for attacking Stevenson as soft on communism.

But suddenly the attacker was under attack, and Eisenhower considered dropping Nixon from the ticket.

Democrats accused Nixon of drawing on a "secret political fund" for personal expenses. The fund had been established after Nixon's Senate race in 1950 with contributions from big business. Nixon decided to make a bold move unprecedented in American politics. He scheduled a television appearance starring himself. Seated at a desk in an empty theater, he made his case to the entire country at once, speaking directly to the camera. He reviewed his personal finances in detail. He talked about the $80-a-month apartment the Nixons had rented in Alexandria while saving for a home. He discussed their mortgages, loans from their parents, a two-year-old Oldsmobile, even the household furniture. He said that Pat owned no mink coat but only a respectable Republican cloth coat and that he always told her she looked great in anything.

Adlai Stevenson, Eisenhower's rival, was a rich man, but Nixon wasn't a rich man, he reminded his viewers, and by the way, Stevenson, too, had a fund. The only ethical way for a nonrich man to make political speeches and campaign for office, Nixon said, was to raise funds from supporters. He even presented an audit performed by Price, Waterhouse & Co.

and a legal opinion stating that he had done nothing wrong. Just as he seemed to be finished, Nixon said there was one more thing he had better reveal or "they'll probably be saying this about me too." He told the story of the little black-and-white spotted cocker spaniel puppy that a supporter had sent to the Nixon family. Nixon said his daughter Tricia named the dog Checkers and the kids loved that dog. And no matter what anyone said, Nixon told his viewers, speaking just as a dad: "We're gonna keep it."

Nixon ended the speech by asking viewers to wire and write the Republican National Committee to say whether Nixon should be removed from the ticket or not. Nixon had tried to get Ike to commit to making a decision about the ticket upon the broadcast's conclusion. Eisenhower had been vague. "Well, General, you know how it is," Nixon said, "there comes a time when you have to shit or get off the pot." The Checkers speech was an overwhelming success; Eisenhower kept him on the ticket.

Nixon's adroit use of television in 1952 was well ahead of its time. The columnist Walter Lippmann worried about what it meant for the future of politics. He privately called the speech "the most demeaning experience my country has ever had to bear." Lippmann wrote that Nixon's choosing to appeal to the entire country via television had ushered in a new era of electronic mob rule.

In the liberal circles of both parties, "the Checkers speech" quickly became all you needed to say to summarize the character and career of Richard Nixon: a three-word eye roll. In 1952, Eisenhower won in a landslide: 442 electoral votes to 89. In six quick years, Richard Nixon had gone from small-town lawyer to vice president of the United States.

Nixon's 1960 presidential campaign had two big problems: Dwight Eisenhower and Jack Kennedy. President Eisenhower was never proud of his vice president and was occasionally embarrassed by him. In 1956, he had again briefly considered switching running mates. Eisenhower was publicly reluctant to endorse Nixon and when he finally did, it was obviously halfhearted. Jack Kennedy was an opponent unlike any Nixon had ever faced. "The Pink Lady" stuff couldn't work on a war hero.

Lieutenant (junior grade) John Kennedy had used his father's influence to enlist in the Navy Reserve after being medically rejected by the army because of his chronic back pain and weakness. In the South Pacific, he took command of **PT-109,** an eighty-foot, high-speed, wooden torpedo boat designed for stealth attacks on large Japanese warships. After just over three months in combat, Kennedy's boat was sunk by a Japanese destroyer in the middle of the night. Kennedy and ten survivors swam more than three miles to a tiny deserted island. One crew member was too badly injured to swim. Kennedy grabbed the strap of the man's life jacket, clenched it between his teeth and towed his mate the three and a half miles to shore. Kennedy then swam alone to another island in search of food and water. He then led his men to that island, where coconuts kept them alive until they were rescued. It was the stuff of World War II movies. In the third year of the Kennedy presidency, it was made into a movie titled **PT-109**—Hollywood's gift to the JFK reelection campaign that never was.

Nixon couldn't play the class resentment card that he had used so often against the elites. JFK was the definition of elite. He was the rich man's son. But he'd used his father's connections to get into combat, not to avoid it. And he'd saved his men's lives. In post–World War II America, war heroes ranked above movie stars and professional athletes in terms of the awe Americans reserved for them.

Senator John F. Kennedy was as staunchly anticommunist as everyone else in the Senate in the 1950s, but he didn't pander to anticommunist fears the way Nixon did. Nixon had never run a campaign where he did not accuse his opponent of being soft on communism. His favorite tactic was useless against JFK.

The life of a losing presidential candidate after the general election is difficult. On a Wednesday in November, they wake up to a world of bad choices. The senators can stay in the Senate, as John McCain and John Kerry did. But most of them aren't senators. Most of them are forced to mourn the death of their political careers. And what is a politician without a political future? Nixon could not kick the habit. He made the rarest choice for presidential campaign losers: he ran for a lesser office. And exactly two years after losing the presidency, he lost again. In 1962, governor of California was Nixon's new, lower target. When he lost that race, he finally ended his political career in a burst of public bitterness unlike anything yet seen on American television.

Nixon had earned his bitterness in 1960. Without Texas and Illinois, JFK would have lost to Nixon. Kennedy won Texas by only two points with a Texas running mate famous in the political world for having won his first Senate race by getting away with election fraud. In Illinois on election night, Nixon won 92 out of 101 counties, essentially all but Chicago. It looked so bad for Kennedy that his brother-in-law Sargent Shriver, Kennedy's Illinois campaign manager, went to bed depressed at what he assumed was a loss. Chicago mayor Richard Daley, a Kennedy ally, was always expected to deliver the city. It was never clear how much of that was due to the Daley machine's ability to turn out the vote and how much to its ability to manufacture votes. On election night, Chicago vote totals were not being reported.

The Chicago vote would not be reported until the next morning, long after the rest of the state's votes had already been counted. Sargent Shriver was awakened by a knock on his door and a shout, "Sarge, the votes from Illinois have completely changed."

Chicago delivered just enough votes to win the state for Kennedy by 0.18 percent of the vote. The state's popular Republican senator, Everett Dirksen, told Nixon the election had been stolen and with it the presidency. Republicans urged Nixon to fight, to demand a recount in Illinois, but Nixon declined. He thought Mayor Daley would be just as able to steal a recount if he was able to steal the election. And Nixon feared a sore loser image. He gracefully conceded defeat the day after the election.

Two years later, the day after losing the governor's race in California, Nixon had no strength left to contain his bitterness. His final comments to the gathered media were extemporaneous. Nothing had been written. He was going to leave it to his press secretary to publicly bring the Nixon campaign to a close. Then Nixon spontaneously and angrily decided to have the last word. He entered the room, elbowed his press secretary aside, and said, "Now that all the members of the press are so delighted that I have lost, I'd like to make a statement of my own." No one hated the press as much as Nixon. No one. He complained about their coverage of the campaign, and he reached back before that campaign: "For sixteen years since the Hiss case, you've had a lot of fun, a lot of fun. You've had an opportunity to attack me." He offered a suggestion: "Just put one reporter on the campaign who will report what the candidate says now and then." And there was the line that instantly took its place in political history: "Just think how much you're going to be missing. You don't have Nixon to kick around anymore because, gentlemen, this is my last press conference." It is the only time in American history that the whole country seemed to have instantly memorized and couldn't stop quoting a line from a concession speech in a governor's race. "You don't have Nixon to kick around anymore." No one who heard Richard Nixon say that ever forgot it, and that included the voters who made him the winner of the New Hampshire primary six years later.

No one in the television age had ever quit politics as definitively and as bitterly as Nixon did the day after losing the governor's race. No one was going to miss him, not the press, certainly not the Democrats, and not the Republicans other than former Nixon staff. He had publicly flamed out as a nasty and bitter two-time loser who had not won an election on his own since 1950.

Nixon soon realized that there was only one problem for the Republican Party trying to find a leader in the post-Nixon world of 1963. They didn't really have anyone who could take his place. Nixon came within a hair—or a few boxes of stolen ballots—of beating JFK, the Democrats' golden boy. Republicans had no one else they could point to who could have done that well. So in 1963, as the Kennedys began planning for the next year's reelection campaign, Nixon began thinking about it, too.

Nixon knew he needed to change his image, especially after ABC broadcast a special called **The Political Obituary of Richard Nixon**. He was going to have to be reborn. He decided the perfect place for a Californian to do that was New York City. Joining a Los Angeles law firm was the obvious choice after losing the governor's race, but Nixon decided to move to New York and join the prestigious corporate law firm of Mudge, Stern, Baldwin, & Todd. Nixon had resented and battled the Eastern establishment long enough. It was time to join them.

The Nixons moved into a Fifth Avenue apartment in a building with unfortunate memories for Nixon thanks to the penthouse occupant: the billionaire Republican governor of New York, Nelson Aldrich Rockefeller.

In 1960, just before the Republican National Convention, Nixon had met with the ever imperious Governor Rockefeller at his penthouse apartment. It was like nothing Nixon had ever seen: a gigantic multistory apartment decorated to resemble Versailles. It was covered in art, including works by Leger, Matisse, and other modernist masters.

Rockefeller was implicitly threatening to withhold liberal Republican support for Nixon's nomination, possibly even from Nixon's run in November. Rockefeller made some disparaging remarks about Nixon to the press. The platform was important in 1960, something worth fighting over. It would tell the public what the presidential nominee and the party stood for. Rockefeller gave Nixon the details after dinner of what he wanted in the platform. Nixon sat at Rockefeller's desk, while Rockefeller sprawled on a bed. Three hours later, with the young, liberal Republican strategist Charles Percy joining by phone, they arrived at a platform that put Nixon in a bind.

Rockefeller was liberal on racial integration and social programs. On the cold war he was militant, aggressive, even paranoid. He'd had a deluxe bunker built below the governor's mansion in Albany in case of nuclear attack. So one price of Rockefeller's support would be an agreement to boost America's nuclear-weapons capacity of every kind, strategic and tactical, to degrees that the Eisenhower administration had long resisted as hysterical, dangerous, and expensive. Agreeing to such a buildup would put Nixon at odds with Eisenhower.

Rockefeller demanded that Nixon agree to massive federal planning for farm programs, environmental conservation, racial integration, and health insurance. That put Nixon at odds not only with the conservative Barry Goldwater crowd but also with more centrist conservatives.

When this platform, known as the Fifth Avenue Treaty, was released, Senator Goldwater called it a Munich. Goldwater went as far as he safely could toward calling Richard Nixon a liar. Racist white Southerners objected. They had been looking since

1948 to the Republican Party for possible protection from civil rights legislation. Nixon got the word that Eisenhower was outraged about the nuclear buildup and threatening to withhold an endorsement of Nixon. That could end it all for Nixon's candidacy. And the press called the treaty a display of Rockefeller's dominance over a servile Nixon.

Nixon looked at it differently. He knew he had to give Rocky enough, but Nixon couldn't realistically run against Eisenhower's record as a foreign policy moderate. Nixon decided to embrace Rocky's domestic platform on civil rights—face down the wrath of the Goldwater people—while rejecting Rockefeller's exaggerated talk about a "missile gap" with the Soviets and promote a reinvigorated version of the judicious foreign policy that Eisenhower laid out when warning against the rise of what he was the first to call "the military-industrial complex." Nixon knew that would anger both the Goldwater people and the Rocky-Percy liberal Republicans in one blow. Yet Nixon saw no better choice.

In the end, the Nixon compromise platform passed. Eisenhower endorsed Nixon. Rockefeller grudgingly supported the nomination. The right wing's threat to draft Barry Goldwater failed. At the convention, Senator Goldwater released his delegates to Nixon and made a riveting speech laying out the right wing's philosophy yet urging solidarity with Nixon.

Now rich enough to live in Rockefeller's building, Nixon dined at the "21" Club and Delmonico's, played golf in Westchester County, and served on boards. He presented his daughter Julie at a debutante ball. Nixon got to know William Paley, the head of CBS. He vacationed in Florida in Key Biscayne, fishing and drinking with his banker friend Charles "Bebe" Rebozo, whom Nixon had grown close to since meeting him in 1950. Rebozo was one of Nixon's closest confidants.

In 1967, a merger brought the star bond lawyer John Mitchell to Nixon's law firm; Mitchell would soon become not only Nixon's campaign manager but also a sort of all-around right hand.

Nixon started building a political organization at his law firm, beginning with senior partner Leonard Garment, who was ten years younger. Richard Nixon and Leonard Garment were a highly unlikely alliance. Garment was unlike anyone Nixon had ever really known for the simple reason that he was Jewish and from Brooklyn. Garment thought Nixon was, as he put it, about 20 percent anti-Semitic. Nixon made negative remarks about Jews without a second thought. Garment voted for JFK in 1960. But now he began finding Nixon fascinating. When Nixon talked to Garment about political philosophy, he emphasized the Quaker angle. Garment saw Nixon as a centrist.

Nixon's longtime secretary Rose Mary Woods maintained Nixon's huge Rolodex, which Nixon used to work the phones all day. He stayed in constant touch with hundreds of political people through- out the country. Leonard Garment was intrigued by Nixon's immense political knowledge. And Garment was bored with practicing law.

Garment soon realized that Nixon never really thought about anything but party politics. His heart and soul were still fully in the game, and there was still opportunity. The man counted out—by himself!—in 1962 was still a name at the beginning of 1964. Garment and Nixon began having conver- sations about the presidential possibilities.

To Nixon, one of the appealing things about Gar- ment and the Mudge law firm crowd was their lack of experience in politics. They had no idea how tough and disappointing the political process could be. As lawyers, they were hard-nosed. As political opera- tives they were fresh, unjaded, imaginative. Nixon blamed his 1960 defeat partly on being saddled with old-time party operators. Jack Kennedy had put to- gether a youthful, creative crew.

In the 1962 California race, Nixon appointed some key younger staff. The ad man and staunch Repub- lican Bob Haldeman, that campaign's manager, had been promoted from doing advance work for the 1960 presidential campaign. Nixon wanted to stick with Haldeman, but if there was going to be a New Nixon, he needed some New York people, too.

With Nixon having taken himself out of contention after the California campaign, Arizona's Senator Barry Goldwater was considered the front-runner for the 1964 Republican presidential nomination. At first, all polls had showed JFK beating Goldwater soundly. But when Kennedy began pushing a new civil rights bill, Goldwater and Nixon saw new opportunity. Now the South was facing a serious civil rights bill from a Democratic president. The South might finally start listening to Republicans. A backlash forming against civil rights in the working-class North might also be an opening for Republicans. Barry Goldwater's opposition to the civil rights bill began attracting those voters' attention.

On the advice of one of his legal advisers, future chief justice William Rehnquist, Goldwater framed his opposition to the civil rights bill not in pro-segregation terms but on states' rights grounds. And Goldwater objected to federal civil rights enforcement as top-down-planning authoritarianism, with its shades of socialism and even Soviet-style communism. Goldwater linked the two critical issues of the day—racial integration and the cold war—and shaped a right-wing response to both at once. It worked: in the fall of 1963, an AP poll showed that 85 percent of Republicans saw Goldwater as the strongest candidate for their party.

Then the assassination of President Kennedy changed everything. Nixon believed the postassassination national mood doomed Goldwater. He would be seen as too intemperate, too risky to a country that was crying out for stability. Nixon was convinced that with Goldwater as the Republican nominee, the country would vote overwhelmingly for the new incumbent, Lyndon Johnson. The trick was to position himself exactly in the party's center.

As the 1964 primary season began, Boston's Henry Cabot Lodge Jr. was the favorite of the liberal side of the Republican Party. Lodge was the Republican Senate incumbent whom Congressman John F. Kennedy defeated in 1952 in his move up to the Senate. President Eisenhower chose Lodge as his ambassador to the United Nations. Nixon chose Lodge as his vice presidential running mate in 1960. President Kennedy then asked his former rival to serve in the vitally important position of ambassador to South Vietnam. Lodge was still serving in South Vietnam as the New Hampshire primary approached. He did nothing to discourage talk of a write-in campaign. Nelson Rockefeller was the other likely candidate on the liberal side of the party. On the conservative side, Senator Barry Goldwater was increasingly militaristic—not willing to rule out the use of nuclear weapons in Vietnam—and seemed eager to dismantle the New Deal safety net of Social Security and welfare and to oppose federal efforts to end racial segregation.

To establish a center, Nixon began spinning in all directions. Only days after the Kennedy assassination, he began making inquiries in New Hampshire regarding the primary, suggesting he might make an active run, but he did not formally enter the primary. Soon Nixon was making speeches to excite the Goldwater crowd, condemning economic planning as contrary to liberty and calling for victory in Vietnam. To the moderates, Nixon played up his White House experience and establishment credibility.

In New Hampshire, Ambassador Henry Cabot Lodge Jr. won with 36 percent as a write-in candidate. Goldwater got 22 percent. Nixon ran third at 17 percent. Goldwater won Oregon. Nixon finished fourth in Oregon despite having set up a secret boiler-room call center to manufacture a groundswell upset. When Goldwater won California, Nixon announced his support for the presumptive nominee. A week later, Nixon made a speech implying that he was the only Republican who could give Johnson a run for his money. Then he publicly called a Goldwater nomination a disaster for the party. After meeting with Republican governors working on a stop-Goldwater effort, Nixon hoped they would draft him as a candidate. They didn't. Nixon then called the GOP chair Bill Miller and asked if he could introduce Goldwater at the national convention. Many observers saw this behavior as the wild flailings of a confused has-been. It wasn't.

The Cow Palace in San Francisco saw, in 1964, the ugliest Republican convention in memory. At the podium, Nelson Rockefeller denounced Goldwater extremism and was booed, hissed, and jeered off the stage.

The last Republican nominee, Richard Nixon, had the honor of introducing Barry Goldwater as the new Republican nominee. Meanwhile, Bob Haldeman waited in a hotel room ready to start a draft-Nixon movement on the floor if they saw an opening.

After Goldwater was nominated, Richard Nixon became the best-known, most fully committed supporter of the man he believed had no chance of winning. Nixon spoke on Goldwater's behalf more than 150 times and campaigned ceaselessly for every other Republican candidate he could think of. Nixon was right about Goldwater. He carried only six states. Goldwater had aroused his base and alienated everyone else by saying "extremism in the defense of liberty is no vice." After election day, Barry Goldwater couldn't get invited to speak at traditional party events.

After LBJ crushed Goldwater, the Republican Party was lost, splintered, terrified, angry, and even, some thought, in danger of dissolution. Eisenhower and Nixon met with Goldwater a month after the election in a New York hotel and demanded a total revamp of the national committee. Goldwater's right-wing chairman was out; the moderate Ray Bliss was in. Interviewed by the **New York Times**, Nixon said that both the right and liberal wings of the party deserved a voice. "The center must lead," Nixon intoned.

But no one was left in the center. Except Nixon. Holding the center now meant spinning in any direction at any moment. Watching all this from his front row seat at Nixon's law firm, Len Garment was amazed by Nixon's political shrewdness. In speaking to liberals, Nixon didn't call for throwing out Great Society and New Deal programs, only for restraining them in the interests of both liberty and efficiency. When speaking to conservatives, Nixon railed against the evils of government planning. Mainstream party officials saw Nixon as the only man who campaigned loyally for the party and for Goldwater. In 1965, the New Nixon was born—Nixon the uniter, the centrist, all things to all Republicans.

At Nixon's law firm Christmas party in 1966, Leonard Garment saw John Mitchell, pipe clenched, as usual, in his teeth, heading for the men's room. Garment followed him in.

"Say, John," Garment said, "how would you feel about managing a presidential campaign?"

Mitchell eyeballed him. "Are you out of your fucking mind, Garment?"

So John Mitchell was in. The gruff, laconic, confident New York lawyer brought to the Nixon campaign a broad set of political connections to money and government. John Mitchell had pioneered a new kind of tax-free municipal bond. It enabled governments to finance projects without raising taxes. Legal language crafted by Mitchell boosted investor confidence by obligating the state or municipality issuing the bond not only to make payments on it but also to appropriate funds to honor the bonds in the event of default. These bonds were called "moral obligation bonds" because the obligation to appropriate money to pay them was moral, not legal. Mitchell's innovation was a bit of a mirage, but it energized the municipal bond business and made him a recognized expert.

John Mitchell had never run a campaign, but he seemed to be just what Nixon was looking for. Mitchell was the kind of man who took care of things. Nixon quickly came to trust Mitchell's operational sense. Nixon placed all management in Mitchell's hands.

The campaign that John Mitchell was taking over in the early days of 1967 had really begun a year earlier. After the Goldwater failure placed Nixon at the party's center, Nixon began developing his new claim to being the only viable national Republican. The strategy in 1966 was to position Nixon as the chief national antagonist of President Johnson. The midterm election season gave him the opportunity. Nixon was asked to speak at about a thousand events every month and accepted dozens of invitations in support of GOP candidates all over the country. Nixon always accepted the right invitations. He chose events held in those districts where the Democratic incumbent had won in 1964 largely thanks to the JFK assassination—places where voters had traditionally voted Republican before that. Nixon was betting these districts would return a GOP candidate to office in 1966. Now Republican voters were objecting to social disorder associated with civil rights and brewing dissatisfaction with Vietnam. At each event, Nixon would give a press conference, without notes, and then make a speech in support of the candidate before enthusiastic crowds, also without notes. Suddenly the stiff candidate who had lost two elections in a row looked relaxed and confident.

To clearly establish himself as LBJ's chief antagonist, Nixon knew he needed to goad Johnson into going head-to-head with him on Vietnam, which was going to take some luck. The war had become Johnson's weakest point, and the antiwar movement was becoming a major national story. Ronald Reagan had begun slamming the Johnson administration for military weakness against communism. But Nixon didn't want to attack Johnson. He wanted Johnson to attack him. Johnson could ignore Reagan as a far-right nut, but Nixon thought it would be far more difficult to ignore a former vice president reborn as the voice of centrist reason constantly weighing in with gravitas on the many challenges facing the United States in Southeast Asia.

Nixon began all remarks on Vietnam by professing support for the president, then offered Johnson advice on how to handle the war. The tone was calm, but everything Nixon said was calculated to send Johnson over the edge and bring him out to fight. At first, Johnson wouldn't bite. Nixon tried everything. He used his status as a former vice president to travel independently to South Vietnam and confer with officials there. When he returned, he said that with the way Johnson was handling the war, it might take twenty years to end it. Whenever Johnson escalated the war, Nixon advised even further escalation. Whenever Johnson seemed to hold firm against peace negotiation, Nixon advised peace negotiations. Whenever Johnson seemed hopeful about negotiations, Nixon expressed concern that hope for negotiations was naive.

As the antiwar protests rose to a pitch of passionate outrage, Nixon found the domestic theme he knew he could exploit: lawlessness in the streets. All Johnson's fault. Nixon knew the only thing that could happen in Vietnam that would be bad for his campaign—the only thing he couldn't exploit—would be the end of the war.

In October 1966, right before the midterm elections, LBJ announced a trip to Asia. The president would confer with Asian leaders about peace in Vietnam and then meet in Manila with the South Vietnamese prime minister and others. Nixon had to counter fast. He had already called for an all-Asia peace conference. That had been another way of harassing Johnson, but now the president was actually doing it. The announcement of the scheduled conference seemed designed to take wind out of Nixon's sails and help Democrats in the midterms.

Nixon did his best to undermine public confidence in Johnson's Asia conference. "Is this a quest for peace or a quest for votes?" he asked rhetorically. Finally, that did get to Johnson. On October 12, speaking at Rodney Square in Wilmington, Delaware, the president went off script and gave the nation a dire warning: a Republican victory on election day "might cause the nation to falter and fall back and fail in Vietnam."

This was the chance Nixon had been waiting for. He issued a statement demanding an apology for the president's "vicious, unwarranted, and partisan assault." Nixon noted that it was Democrats—Fulbright, McCarthy, and others—who were calling for "peace at any price," thus "giving heart to Hanoi." Nixon said, "He is the first president in history who has failed to unite his own party in a time of war."

During the final weeks of the 1966 midterm campaigns, LBJ went to Asia, as planned, and the Nixon camp grew tense. If the president scored a victory for peace, the midterms might swing Johnson's way.

During the midterm campaign, Nixon's team was growing. Len Garment brought in William Safire, a public relations man. It was in the team discussions of how to burnish the Nixon image that the words **New Nixon** were first used. The law firm's executive assistant Patrick Buchanan was hired full time by the Nixon group to do opposition research and write op-ed pieces and speeches. Pat Buchanan was a twenty-nine-year-old Goldwater campaign veteran; Nixon wanted him there in part to balance Garment's moderation and speechwriter Ray Price's liberalism. With a great-grandfather who had fought in the Confederate army, Buchanan attended meetings of the Sons of Confederate Veterans and was more strident than Northeastern conservatives on protest demonstrations and the nonviolent civil rights movement of Martin Luther King. Pat Buchanan regarded Dr. King as "one of the most divisive men in contemporary history." Buchanan was the exception in Nixon's growing organization. Nixon wanted to know what his young right-winger was thinking, but Nixon did not want to run a Goldwater-style insurgency.

Nixon also hired Alan Greenspan, future chairman of the Federal Reserve. Greenspan was in the grip of the philosopher Ayn Rand's ideas about the redemptive graces of pure free markets. Much of Nixon's support came from traditionally conservative corporate types, including Elmer Bobst of Warner-Lambert Pharmaceutical Co. Dewitt Wallace and his wife, Lila, the founders of **Reader's Digest**, were also key financial backers. Nixon's Key Biscayne confidant Bebe Rebozo was always an important source of funds. The corporate backers were all establishment Republicans, not right-wingers like Buchanan or economic fantasizers of pure markets like Greenspan was then. Elmer Bobst shared a comfortable anti-Semitism with Nixon filled with certitude that they believed was earned through experience. Years later, Bobst wrote a letter to Nixon saying, "Jews have troubled the world from the very beginning. If this beloved country of ours ever falls apart, the blame rightly should be attributed to the malicious action of Jews in complete control of our communications."

Many of the corporate backers had turned against the Vietnam War. Elmer Bobst told Nixon that the war couldn't be won. To Bobst, the only solution was immediate withdrawal. But while Nixon privately agreed that the war couldn't be won, he knew the war was working for him.

With President Johnson's Asian peace conference under way and election day approaching, Nixon was flying around to campaign events. He told audiences that if the war wasn't resolved by 1968, the president would be courting World War III. In the same breath, he told them that any hasty effort to make peace would give communism a deadly advantage. What was Nixon actually advising? It didn't matter: it was all anti-Johnson now, and Bill Safire and the rest of the speech-writing team exercised extreme discipline. The approved phrase wasn't "win the war" but "end the war."

When Johnson returned from the peace conference in Manila, Nixon was in Boise, Idaho, having barely slept; now he gathered the core team to prepare for whatever Johnson might announce. If there had been any big breakthrough for peace, they would need a quick strategic response. When Nixon got off his next flight in New Jersey, he got the news. It came from Safire in Manhattan. There was a declaration of peace. It was signed by the leaders of seven Asian nations. Johnson had just released a detailed statement with a communique between the president of the United States and Prime Minister Ky of South Vietnam. The bottom line: if North Vietnam would withdraw forces northward, and cease infiltration of South Vietnam, the United States and its allies would withdraw troops from Vietnam within six months.

Even if North Vietnam eventually rejected the offer, coming at the last minute before election day, it would give the Democrats something to run on: a peace plan negotiated by the president, just what the Nixon team had been afraid of.

Under intense time pressure now, Safire began studying the text of the communique. He sought something in it, anything, to spin for Nixon. Safire got Len Garment to drive him to Nixon's hotel in New Jersey. Safire had typed up a mass of notes, and with great excitement he and Garment pitched their idea to Nixon. Johnson's plan could be described, Safire said, as an agreement for mutual withdrawal.

That, in turn, could be described as a form of surrender.

Nixon loved it. Safire was proposing that Nixon
quickly put out an open letter criticizing the communique. Nixon had a better idea.

First, he told Garment and Safire, slow down. This
was a time for New Nixon gravitas. At a bigger meeting back at the law firm, the team worked up something called "An Appraisal of Manila." Buchanan
announced to the press that Nixon would have a
major statement on the Thursday before election
day. Nixon wanted coverage for his statement on the
front page of the **New York Times**, something he
would have no idea how to orchestrate if he were still
living in California. Nixon's decision to live inside
the Eastern establishment payed off perfectly on this
one. Nixon got Safire to persuade his friend at the
Times, Harrison Salisbury, to run the statement.

On November 4, on the front page, the most important newspaper in the country carried Richard
Nixon's characterization of Johnson's policy as "mutual withdrawal" and his prediction: "Communist
victory would most certainly be the result."

It worked. Lyndon Johnson did exactly what Nixon
had wanted for so long. In a morning press conference
in the East Room, the president began by answering
questions, but he ended by unwinding a long tirade
against one man: Richard Nixon. Johnson called
Nixon a man who was playing politics with the lives

of troops in Vietnam. LBJ ridiculed the Old Nixon, the loser: "He made a temporary stand in California, you remember what action the people took out there. Then he crossed the country to New York. . . . Now he is talking about a conference that he obviously is not well-prepared on. . . . Mr. Nixon doesn't serve his country well. . . ."

"He hit us!" Pat Buchanan whooped with glee when he told Nixon the news. The **Times** headline quoted Johnson: DOES NOT "SERVE COUNTRY WELL."

The president himself had made the midterm campaign about Richard Nixon. Now Nixon could respond directly without losing credibility as a statesman. And he could up the ante. In a series of TV-talk appearances, Nixon accused Johnson of trying to stifle loyal dissent. He said LBJ had "broken the bipartisan line on Vietnam policy."

The Sunday before election day, the Republican Party bought a half hour of TV time to allow Nixon to answer Johnson. Nixon looked into the camera as if talking to Johnson. "I respect you," he said, "and my respect has not changed because of the personal attack you made on me." Nixon added sympathetically that the president must be very, very tired.

Two days later, the Republicans gained forty-seven seats in the House. Even the man who had beaten Nixon in the governor's race two years earlier, Pat Brown, was beaten by Republican actor-turned-politician Ronald Reagan. The Democrats still controlled Congress and the White House, but Nixon believed he was loosening their grip. The 1966 mid-term election ended with Nixon exactly where he wanted to be: alone in the center of the Republican Party.

The only 1968 presidential campaign team with less experience than Nixon's was Gene McCarthy's. Nixon knew he needed more political experience so he turned to Maurice Stans, an investment banker who was budget director in the Eisenhower administration. Stans had served as finance chair for Nixon's gubernatorial campaign. With Stans on board, the campaign would not have to worry about money.

John Mitchell's approach to managing the campaign was cold-bloodedly anti-ideology—all business, with a relentless focus on political gain, not political passion. Mitchell's top aide was Kevin Phillips, a young political strategist with a new theory. Based on close studies of popular-vote and electoral-college politics and shifting demographics, Phillips believed that despite the crushing defeat of 1964, the Republicans were in a strong position to form an electoral majority that might last for decades. The ad man Bob Haldeman, whom Nixon had used in 1960 and 1962, came in as chief of staff. Haldeman was all business, too. He had worked as manager of the Los Angeles office of J. Walter Thompson and had the knack of charming their most difficult clients while keeping employees intimidated into working long hours. He was on the Nixon campaign to serve as all-around enforcer. Haldeman showed no patience for mistakes. He controlled scheduling and moving the candidate around, spending every waking hour of every day with Nixon and limiting access to him.

Haldeman brought in John Ehrlichman. Nixon had used Ehrlichman before, under cover in the 1960 presidential primaries. The Nixon campaign had sent John to get a job as a driver in Nelson Rockefeller's 1960 campaign and report back anything he might learn. Haldeman and Ehrlichman were fellow UCLA graduates and fellow Christian Scientists who never drank alcohol. Ehrlichman was notably unafraid of Nixon. The candidate, like most of his New York law cohort, enjoyed stiff drinks. Ehrlichman demanded that the candidate stay sober at all times during the campaign.

Together these men began crafting the New Nixon. This Nixon was to be no firebrand. He wasn't going into outright battle with the Eastern snobs or the press or even, at first, the war-protesting kids and black activists. The New Nixon had a confident, relaxed, statesmanlike maturity. He seemed steady and well rested. He would not be rushing into a TV debate harried and exhausted. That was the Old Nixon. The New Nixon was never going to seem to be trying too hard.

The New Nixon even had a sense of humor. The campaign brought in Paul Keyes, who had written for the comedian and talk-show host Jack Paar and had served as a producer of NBC's revolutionary sketch-comedy TV show **Rowan & Martin's Laugh-In**. Keyes wrote jokes for Nixon and was amazed at the increasing smoothness of Nixon's delivery.

When Nixon announced his campaign for the presidency on February 2, 1968, at the Holiday Inn in Manchester, New Hampshire, he brushed away his biggest liability with a joke. Nixon was indelibly etched in the public mind as the two-time loser who bitterly quit politics on live TV. Nixon looked out at the reporters gathered before him in New Hampshire that day and said, "Ladies and gentlemen, as we start this campaign, there's one thing we should say at the outset. This is not my last press conference."

And so the New Nixon campaign began with a miracle. Richard Nixon got a laugh.

FOURTEEN

"NIXON'S THE ONE"

The press and the pollsters were not convinced that the New Nixon was the Republican Party's only viable option for president in 1968. Important segments of the Republican Party didn't think Nixon was their man. The GOP wanted desperately to recover from Goldwater's defeat in '64, the worst of the twentieth century. Nixon might cast himself as the party unifier, but he hadn't won an election on his own in eighteen years. Nixon knew he needed impressive, decisive wins in the early primaries to silence all doubters.

"Nixon's the One." That was the slogan for 1968. It summed up the candidate's entire rationale in three words. Like it or not, Nixon is inevitable.

Nixon didn't announce in New Hampshire until February—the last possible moment before the filing deadline. That same day, New Hampshire households received letters informing them that Nixon was running. That afternoon, he gave the press conference where he surprised everyone by joking about his last losing campaign and getting a laugh. That evening he made his first big speech. Between press conference and speech, Nixon rested. That was one part of the new strategy: the candidate wasn't to go bounding about snowy New Hampshire pressing the flesh. He wasn't to go to New Hampshire much at all. "You can't handshake your way out of the kinds of problems we have today," his campaign literature explained.

The Nixon campaign had a new plan for reaching the voters, thanks to the brash young Roger Ailes. His idea was to have Nixon appear to connect directly and personally with the ordinary New Hampshire voters whom he was in reality avoiding. Ailes would make a TV show about meeting and impressing citizens.

Working with Ailes, Nixon's media director, Frank Shakespeare, formerly a CBS executive, reviewed and critiqued a full seven hours of Richard M. Nixon on TV over the years. They saw that Nixon came off well—relaxed, genuine, human—when he was talking to people one-on-one in impromptu, informal settings. In prepared speeches, he seemed ponderous and stiff. So why not put Nixon in impromptu, informal settings that they could totally control and film?

For New Hampshire, Ailes's idea was to have the

team interview and select the right kind of locals, get them into a small-town public space, and place security guards at the entrance to keep out the press if they found out about it. Then with cameras rolling, the locals would ask Nixon their questions and he would answer. Ailes and Shakespeare would then take the raw footage into an editing room and with input from Garment and others cut together the most favorable bits of Nixon for a spot to be aired on TV. Such ads are now a staple of political campaigns. They were invented by Roger Ailes in New Hampshire in 1968.

It was Bob Haldeman, in constant contact with the candidate and controlling his schedule, who made sure Ailes got enough candidate time to make his idea work. The reporters in New Hampshire trying to cover Nixon found the candidate almost never available, and impossible to talk to even on the rare occasions when he did appear in public. Naturally, the reporters began howling at Haldeman about Nixon hiding from them, holding fake meetings with New Hampshire citizens instead of taking press questions. Roger Ailes, expecting just this, had a solution. Give them access. Tell the reporters that when the Q&A sessions were being shot, they could watch on a monitor in another room. Afterward they could conduct interviews with the locals. The reporters accepted that.

The Nixon TV ads aired in targeted markets, reaching key New Hampshire voters with a flawless imitation of a meet-and-greet campaign. It looked more like news coverage than an ad.

THE FIRST PERSON WHO looked like he could stop Nixon was the Republican governor of Michigan, George Romney. Early polls had given George Romney a significant edge—39 to 31 over Nixon for the Republican nomination and 54 to 46 over President Johnson in the general election.

In 1968, George Romney was trying to do for Mormons what JFK had done for Catholics eight years earlier: become the first successful Mormon candidate for president. Romney was born in Mexico, where his family had fled to avoid prosecution for polygamy in the United States. Romney's parents were not polygamous, but his grandparents were. In 1910, his family fled the Mexican Revolution, leaving everything behind in Mexico, and moved from town to town in the United States, settling in Salt Lake City. The Romneys hit hard times, and in the Depression it got worse. But George was a bright, hardworking student. He had preached his faith on an upturned crate at Speaker's Corner in London's Hyde Park. As difficult as politics could be, it was never as difficult as trying to convert Londoners to Mormonism.

George Romney set himself the goal of marrying his high school sweetheart, Lenore LaFount. Lenore was also from a Salt Lake Mormon family. She fin-

ished high school in three years and when her father was appointed by President Coolidge to the
newly created Federal Radio Commission, her family moved to Washington. Lenore graduated from
George Washington University, again in only three
years. She and George wrote constantly while he was
in Britain. When his missionary work ended, George
showed up in Washington. He had saved enough
money to attend George Washington University with
Lenore, but Lenore was ready to move to New York
to pursue her dream of acting. She studied the Stan-
islavski acting technique at the American Laboratory
Theatre, working on Shakespeare, Ibsen, and Che-
khov. Romney went to George Washington at night
and worked as a stenographer during the day. He
took the train up to New York to see Lenore almost
every weekend. When MGM offered Lenore a con-
tract, she was off to Hollywood. Romney wrangled
a training sales job with the Los Angeles branch of
the Alcoa Aluminum Company. Because he worried
about Lenore hanging around leading men, Romney
picked her up from work at MGM every day. His
five-year-old Oldsmobile had one operating gear:
third. He would park on a hill, walk down to the
studio, escort Lenore out to the curb, go get in the
car, and roll downhill in neutral before popping it in
gear to jump-start it. He slowed down just enough
that she could jump in beside him.

Lenore got bit parts and met stars like Clark Gable,

but her Mormon devoutness recoiled from much of what she saw in Hollywood. She knew George would never fit in there. She chose George over Hollywood.

In 1935, Lenore Romney was back in Washington, a stay-at-home mother of one child with more to come. Lenore's father was guiding George's early career in Washington. Alcoa sent him to work as a lobbyist in the aluminum industry's Aluminum Wares Association. He joined the National Press Club and the Congressional Country Club. In 1939, when the American Automobile Manufacturers Association, the main trade organization for the booming auto industry, opened in Detroit, Romney was asked to take charge. The Romneys moved to Michigan and soon bought a house in Palmer Woods, developed in the 1920s as a fantasia of mighty elms and set-back Tudor revival mansions near the Detroit Golf Club. By the time America entered the Second World War, George Romney was well on his way to becoming one of the chief spokesmen not only for the American automobile business but also for America's rapidly growing car culture.

Before moving to Detroit, Romney had never known any black people, but after World War II, he saw the racial segregation built into the Northern housing boom. Beginning in the 1940s, Romney became an ardent champion of civil rights.

When Lenore was told she might not survive another pregnancy, she insisted on trying, and in 1947, after spending a full month lying on her back in a hospital room, she delivered her miracle baby, Mitt.

In 1954, George Romney became president of American Motors Corporation, where he revived the struggling automaker with innovative management techniques. In 1962, Romney found himself at a crossroads, with a major life decision to make: Should he enter politics or continue his career as an auto executive? Romney stopped his life for a day to pray and fast. Then he resigned from AMC and ran for governor of Michigan and won.

Martin Luther King Jr. led a march in Detroit when Governor Romney declared Freedom Day in Michigan. Romney supported the 1964 civil rights bill. When Senator Barry Goldwater refused to support the bill, Romney refused to support Goldwater for president even after Goldwater won the Republican nomination.

George Romney started his presidential campaign in 1967, but his announcement was planned for the traditional announcement season in the campaign year. Romney visited New Hampshire and Wisconsin again and again, shaking hand after hand, knocking on doors, even drawing prospective voters into long bear hugs. "My name is George Romney," he would tell whoever answered a door. "I hope you will support me." Romney would stand there and talk to that voter for as long as it took. Where Nixon and his team were on the way to inventing the television campaign of the future, Romney was campaigning the old-fashioned way. But there was a brand-new data-driven approach to Romney's old-fashioned knocking on doors. His Michigan campaign team had worked up a computer system—they called it an electronic data process—to survey voting histories and census data for every person in every county in Michigan. Now they scaled that system up to a national level, running big, whirring punch-card machines day and night to pick neighborhoods and even exact addresses where Romney would benefit the most by turning up at voters' doors. Romney was the first to move corporate information systems into campaign use.

The best news for Romney's campaign was that Nelson Rockefeller, who, in 1967, was widely viewed as the most powerful player in the Republican Party, seemed to want Romney to run. It was in relationship to Nelson Rockefeller—endlessly gregarious, endlessly enthusiastic, endlessly unclear about his own presidential ambitions—that Romney began to find his campaign at once ushered toward success and strangely, infuriatingly, bewilderingly undermined.

ROCKEFELLER, SIXTY-TWO, WAS BORN a year later than Romney into the richest family in America. Rockefeller's great-grandfather, William

Rockefeller, was a traveling salesman and con man selling elixirs to cure everything. Bill Rockefeller once said of his sons, "I cheat my boys every chance I get. I want to make 'em sharp." His son John was very, very sharp. John D. Rockefeller graduated from Cleveland's first public high school, took a ten-week course in accounting, and then went on to become the richest man in the world, controlling 90 percent of the oil supply in America through his company, Standard Oil. His grandson Nelson did a tour of duty in Rockefeller family businesses, which had branched out to banking, before accepting a series of presidential appointments in Franklin Roosevelt's State Department. The Truman administration and the Eisenhower administration also found spots for Nelson Rockefeller. For Eisenhower he served as special assistant to the president for foreign affairs and was in the thick of cold war strategy. This was all a preamble to his inevitable political career. In 1958, Nelson Rockefeller easily defeated incumbent Democrat Averell Harriman for governor of New York.

Rockefeller began eyeballing the presidency in 1960 and again in 1964, but he was never able to make up his mind to go all in. Flamboyantly optimistic, Rockefeller outlasted a scandal when he left his first wife to marry Happy Murphy, who was recently the wife of a friend of his. The real scandal for the press was that Happy had given up custody of her children to her enraged former husband in order to obtain the divorce that allowed her to marry Rockefeller—deeply shocking stuff in those days. Still, Rockefeller won reelection to the governorship and continued to be the Republican Party's leading "big government" liberal.

Rockefeller transformed the State University of New York into the biggest higher-education system in the country. He created the biggest wilderness park east of the Mississippi in the Adirondack Mountains. He took over New York City's mass transit system, merging it with suburban commuter rails to create one of the biggest transportation systems in the world. He created financing incentives for low-income housing. He gave New York the country's biggest Medicaid program.

George Romney and Nelson Rockefeller both focused on racial discrimination. Rockefeller wanted to outlaw all discrimination in housing based on race. The Federal Housing Authority (FHA) was giving out federal loans and subsidies to developers willing to build in the cities. In New York City, developers like Donald Trump's father, Fred Trump, knew how to work that system. Through political connections, Fred Trump benefited from preferential treatment in gaining millions in federal dollars. Then he built low-income housing and discriminated by race in renting those apartments. Rockefeller saw that black citizens who qualified for low- and middle-income home-buying programs found they couldn't buy in white neighborhoods. Restrictive racial covenants were common in FHA projects. There was rank discrimination in lending. Blockbusting—scaring white homeowners with the prospect of having black neighbors and lower property values—sent whites running from urban neighborhoods. The ultimate effect was to transfer what was becoming the stable source of new, middle-class wealth in the postwar era, ownership of homes with rising values, to whites and away from blacks, with consequences in wealth inequality that would cripple African American opportunity for generations.

Rockefeller pressured the legislature not only to outlaw blockbusting but also to ban racial discrimination in selling and renting housing. During Rockefeller's governorship the number of blacks and Latinos in state government jobs increased by 50 percent. In 1958, when first running for governor, Rockefeller appeared with Martin Luther King Jr. and Jackie Robinson at a rally for integrating schools. In 1960, when King was arrested, Rockefeller spoke in a church in Brooklyn on behalf of Dr. King. In 1962, he offered King help in creating a New York office of the Southern Christian Leadership Conference. King said that if the South had governors like Rockefeller, racial inequality would be solved in a matter of months.

As the 1968 presidential campaign approached, the only thing that didn't make sense in Nelson Rockefeller's political career was why the most famous governor in America wasn't running for president. Why was he backing a more obscure liberal Republican governor? Or was he? Rocky's ambivalence about his presidential ambitions was notable enough to have become, as early as 1960, a subject of discussion in the press, a concern to his party, and a source of voters' ambivalence about him. After acting as if he might make a strong run in 1960, he bowed out early when Nixon got ahead in the polls, using his leverage instead to summon Nixon to the penthouse and force the Fifth Avenue Treaty on him. In 1964, after vacillating publicly, he entered the primaries as the front-runner, but the divorce scandal and his unpopular new wife were too recent. When Happy Rockefeller gave birth to their first child during the campaign, Rockefeller lost the California primary.

Rockefeller gave Romney all of his own top advisers, including the foreign policy expert Henry Kissinger, the director of the Harvard Defense Studies Program. Rockefeller made a deal with the governor of Pennsylvania, Raymond Shafer, pledging New York and Pennsylvania delegates at the convention as a package for Romney. Rockefeller sidelined New York's liberal Republican senator Jacob Javits's hopes of becoming the first Jewish presidential nominee. Rockefeller suggested that Javits might make a good vice presidential running mate on a Romney ticket. Romney actually tried to come up with a cogent Vietnam policy to contrast with Johnson's. He traveled to Vietnam in 1965 in hopes of boosting his non-existent foreign policy credibility. Romney took the official tour and came home to tell the press that he believed the U.S. role in Vietnam there was "morally right and necessary." The American effort in Southeast Asia, he said, "had probably reversed a shift in the balance of power greater than if Hitler had conquered Europe." By spring of 1967, Romney was in a quandary over the war. When reporters asked Romney about the war, he said he was still thinking about it. Romney wondered aloud whether the war was really winnable. In April, he decided to address the Vietnam issue head-on. Romney's speechwriters came up with a draft that was dovish. He sent it to his sponsor Nelson Rockefeller for vetting.

On Vietnam, Rockefeller's liberal anticommunism put him closer to Johnson's position. In the music room at the Rockefeller estate on the Hudson River, Rockefeller and Kissinger went over the Romney speech and together they converted it to a militantly anticommunist call for stepping up the bombing campaign. Romney was irritated. He cut half of what Rocky and Kissinger had put in the speech. That left Romney with a middle-of-the-road speech with peace as the goal and national honor as the key.

LBJ's staff studied the speech and noticed that there wasn't really much room between Romney's position on Vietnam and the president's. So Johnson didn't attack the speech, he praised it. That instantly nullified Romney as an opposition leader on foreign policy. In the polls, Romney abruptly lost his lead over LBJ. The winner in that exchange between Romney and Johnson was Nixon. LBJ knew that hurting Romney was good for Nixon. Johnson feared a run against the likable Romney. Johnson was sure he could beat the unlikable Nixon.

The worst day of the Romney campaign was August 31, 1967. He arrived for a taping of a TV talk show in Detroit. The show's host was Lou Gordon, an old Romney friend. Gordon's new show was being picked up in markets beyond the Midwest. One of the new markets for Gordon's show was Boston, which reached voters in southern New Hampshire. The program was scheduled to be aired a few weeks after the taping.

Romney arrived late for the taping. He had spent the morning in campaign meetings. Then he made a visit to the Michigan State Fair, where one of his grandchildren had gone missing. The schedule froze while state police found the kid riding a Ferris wheel. The governor then raced to the Detroit TV studio and arrived just in time to fall into the guest chair as Gordon began peppering him with questions about Vietnam.

Gordon asked Romney why his position on Vietnam had changed since his trip to Vietnam, when he was prowar. Romney said that the hawkish position he took just after returning from Vietnam had been a result of the "greatest brainwashing that anybody can get when you go over to Vietnam." He said, "Since returning from Vietnam, I've gone into the history of Vietnam. . . . And as a result I have changed my mind. I no longer believe it was necessary for us to get into Vietnam."

It was only a few days later when Lou Gordon was reading the transcript of the taping that the "brainwashing" remark stood out. He thought a major presidential candidate accusing generals and diplomats in South Vietnam of brainwashing visiting politicians was a story. He called the **New York Times** bureau chief in Detroit, who filed a story that made small mention of the "brainwashing" far down in the text. The **Times** editors found the "brainwashing," and on September 5, the **Times** ran the headline ROMNEY ASSERTS HE UNDERWENT "BRAINWASHING" ON VIETNAM TRIP.

The three networks' nightly news shows picked up the story. All three networks got in touch with Lou Gordon, who supplied the video to all of them. Romney tried to defend himself. He said the clip was taken out of context. That went against the strong advice of all his advisers. They wanted the story to die. The candidate kept bringing it back to life. Every time he explained, the clip ran again.

Henry Kissinger exited the Romney campaign in disgust over the "brainwashing" comment. John Bailey, the Democratic national chairman, said that

Romney had insulted General Westmoreland and Ambassador Lodge. Secretary of Defense McNamara said Romney was incapable of seeing the truth before his eyes. His local newspaper, the **Detroit News**, called for Romney to withdraw his candidacy. **Time** magazine ran a cover featuring Nelson Rockefeller and California governor Ronald Reagan as the only viable GOP alternatives to Nixon. A Gallup poll showed that a Rockefeller-Reagan ticket would beat a Johnson-Humphrey ticket by fourteen points.

In October, the National Governors Association Conference was held on a nine-day cruise from New York to the Virgin Islands and back. Romney met with Rockefeller. Journalist Theodore White later reported that in their sit-downs in Rockefeller's stateroom, Romney pleaded with Rockefeller to run in order to stop Nixon, and let Romney step aside. In a contradictory description of those meetings by Rockefeller biographer Richard Norton Smith, Romney pleaded with Rockefeller to make it clear to the public that there was no possibility of a Rockefeller run, that Romney still had Rocky's full support. After the cruise, Rockefeller did go on a publicity blitz to deny he had any intention of entering the race. He demanded his New Hampshire supporters stop campaigning for him. He denied holding out any hope for a draft. In denying hope for a draft, Rocky was raising the possibility of a draft. To Romney, Rockefeller seemed to be maintaining attention on his possible candidacy while appearing reluctant to run. Lenore Romney had no doubt that Rockefeller was deliberately undermining George so that Rocky would be liberal Republicans' only hope for stopping Nixon.

With George Wallace riling crowds with fears of increasing lawlessness, Nixon began running as a law-and-order candidate. George Romney took a different view of the crime problem. During the five-day riot in Detroit in 1967, Romney called in the National Guard, but he also supported formation of the New Detroit Committee, the first official investigation in the nation to determine causes of urban violence. For Romney, the Mormon ethicist and hands-on governor, the solution to rising crime wasn't a hard crackdown. Any real solution would have to be based on understanding what was causing the rise in crime. If the nation could rediscover its ethical purpose, the crime problem might begin to be solved. In New Hampshire, Romney billboards went up, saying "The way to stop crime is to stop moral decay." Reporters put Romney on the defensive about the billboards, observing that they sounded like a nineteenth-century message with no practical anticrime proposal. Romney now had a muddled message on the two top issues of the campaign, Vietnam and crime.

Thirteen days before the New Hampshire primary,

Romney held a major campaign meeting in Washington with his team. The situation in New Hampshire looked grim. Later states didn't look much better. At 4:00 p.m. in a packed press conference at the Washington Hilton, Romney announced his withdrawal from the race for the Republican presidential nomination. In a brief speech, he thanked Rockefeller for his support and said the Republican governors must get together behind one candidate. Romney would support whoever that turned out to be. Then he left the podium without taking any questions.

Lenore Romney was in southern Wisconsin on a campaign trip. She watched George's announcement on TV in private. When she came out to speak to the press, the reporters noted signs of dried tears. "The country was asking for a straight arrow," Lenore said. "They get him, and they don't understand what they have."

George Romney got zero percent of the vote in the New Hampshire primary. Nelson Rockefeller, the write-in candidate who didn't campaign, came in second at 11 percent. Richard Nixon's 79 percent win went largely unnoticed because Eugene McCarthy's surprisingly strong second-place finish was being treated as the most important upset in New Hampshire primary history.

Nixon got everything he wanted in New Hampshire. Ordinarily, he would have felt angry and bitter toward the media for ignoring his huge victory, the dramatic comeback of the two-time loser. But the New Nixon understood that the civil war within the Democratic Party and the collapse of the once invulnerable incumbent president, Lyndon Johnson, was very, very good news for Richard Nixon.

FIFTEEN

"ABIGAIL SAID NO"

I t was 2:00 a.m. on the night the votes were counted in New Hampshire when Bobby Kennedy called Gene McCarthy to congratulate him. It was a brief, awkward call between two men who were never comfortable with each other. The call was made all the more uncomfortable because Bobby was once again thinking about running against Johnson, which now meant running against Johnson and McCarthy.

Lyndon Johnson's reaction to McCarthy's "win" in New Hampshire was numb shock. Over the next few days of reviewing the extent of the damage in New Hampshire, Johnson's team could see clearly what it was all about: the administration's failure in Vietnam. That meant LBJ's campaign strategy was going to be as complicated as his war strategy. He couldn't just swing to the left on the war, because

half the votes the Johnson campaign was counting on in New Hampshire abandoned him because
they believed the president was not being aggressive
enough in Vietnam. That was an obvious opening
for Nixon. Johnson now knew he had to worry about
McCarthy hitting him from the left on the war while
Nixon hit him from the right. And Johnson always
felt that he could never stop worrying about Bobby.
LBJ saw the New Hampshire result primarily as an
opportunity for Bobby.

Bobby Kennedy never publicly announced that
he'd decided not to run for president, but he did
make sure Gene McCarthy and Lyndon Johnson
knew he wasn't running. Four days before the New
Hampshire primary Ted Sorensen went to the White
House and reassured Johnson that Bobby had no
plans to challenge him in the primaries. LBJ was
not convinced. Nothing could persuade him to stop
worrying about Bobby.

In the beginning of 1968, Kennedy had still not
taken a clear position on Vietnam. In January, when
he gave a speech at Brooklyn College, one of the first
things he saw was a student's sign saying "Bobby
Kennedy: Hawk, Dove, or Chicken?"

It sounded to Bobby just like a crack Gene McCarthy might make. It was the image of Bobby that was
forming among many McCarthy supporters. The
idealistic youth movement that Bobby had spent
the years since 1964 cultivating was taunting him

now, heckling him. In their view, it was politically and morally impossible to have one foot in the peace movement. Bobby should have both feet in and those feet should have run against LBJ. Anything less was cowardice and political calculation. A **Newsweek** article referred to Bobby's "artful dodging," and wondered if he could measure up to the standards of his brother Jack's book **Profiles in Courage**.

Even though Bobby concluded the meetings at his home by deciding not to run, and breaking Al Lowenstein's heart in the process, Bobby never stopped thinking about running. The people closest to Bobby knew this. Jack Newfield wrote a piece in the **Village Voice** suggesting that if Bobby didn't run, he would lose his soul and become a robot. Ethel Kennedy cut the piece out of the paper and started showing it around. Bobby had no doubt about how his wife felt about it. In January, Ethel helped her kids hang a "Run, Bobby, Run" banner outside their bedroom window. Also in January, Bobby received on the same day one letter from Ted Sorensen, warning him that if he ran against Johnson his career would be over, and another letter from Arthur Schlesinger, warning him that if he failed to run against Johnson his career would be over.

Bobby went public with his decision not to run two weeks before the New Hampshire primary. He told the press, "I have told friends and supporters that I would not oppose Lyndon Johnson under any foreseeable circumstances." Everyone in politics hears the word **foreseeable** as wiggle room. Johnson, McCarthy, and Nixon certainly did. Al Lowenstein showed up right away in Bobby's office and said, "I'm an unforeseen circumstance!" Lowenstein was deeply disappointed with the Peter the Hermit stumbling of the McCarthy campaign, which had not yet caught fire in New Hampshire. Bobby crushed Lowenstein's dream again. He wasn't going to run.

"Do you understand?" he asked Lowenstein, as if he needed Lowenstein's forgiveness. Lowenstein said he did and left the office fighting back tears.

Adam Walinsky, one of the truest RFK believers on the Senate staff, told Bobby he quit. Walinsky wanted to dump Johnson. That now meant working outside RFK's organization.

Even as his political team was defecting to McCarthy, Bobby kept an experienced eye on the primary situation. Joe Dolan, one of his fervent antiwar staffers, analyzed every poll. It looked to Dolan as if Bobby polled well enough in California to possibly beat Johnson there. In Wisconsin, the next state to vote after New Hampshire, LBJ looked strong. Johnson was polling at 80 percent to McCarthy's 13 percent. The polls were telling Dolan that Gene McCarthy was just a protest candidate who had no real chance of gaining the nomination, and that is what Dolan told Bobby. But then came the Tet Offensive, and in February, LBJ's approval ratings started tumbling.

Suddenly the polls suggested that Bobby might have made the wrong decision. He might have blown it.

On February 8, Bobby gave a major speech in Chicago attacking Johnson's policy in Vietnam. Adam Walinsky returned to the Kennedy camp, with excitement, to write it. But it still wasn't an antiwar speech. Bobby didn't call for U.S. withdrawal. He just presented the hard facts of the war: "Half a million American soldiers, with 700,000 Vietnamese allies . . . with total command of the air, total command of the sea, backed by huge resources and the most modern weapons, are unable to secure even a single city from the attacks of an enemy whose total strength is about 250,000."

Bobby and his staff were hearing increasingly positive reports of how the McCarthy campaign was gaining ground in New Hampshire. Unimaginable things were happening up there. Thanks to Tet, and to a groundswell of sudden, uncharacteristic energy in his campaign, Gene McCarthy was actually looking surprisingly strong in the primary. There was even a chance, RFK's New Hampshire people said, that McCarthy might get 30 percent of the vote. Bobby might be losing his best chance at the presidency.

With sudden urgency, Bobby sent Dolan and another staffer to California to sign up delegates for the state's primary. Five days before the New Hampshire primary, Kennedy rose in the Senate and rejected escalation in Vietnam, which he'd once supported, as a totally failed policy. He went further this time. He compared Johnson's justifications for continued fighting to Nazi Germany's justifications for taking Poland. He took a page straight from the Eugene McCarthy playbook, invoking—for the Senate this time, not just for the kids—national moral and ethical responsibility. Indeed he went further than McCarthy's classical liberalism. Bobby expressed sympathy for what the most radical youth, fans of wars of national liberation, liked to call "the peace-loving people of North Vietnam."

"Are we," Kennedy asked the Senate, "like the God of the Old Testament that we can decide in Washington, D.C., what cities, what towns, what hamlets in Vietnam are going to be destroyed?" After the speech he flew to join Dolan for the delegate hunt in California. Four days before the New Hampshire primary, Bobby called Teddy Kennedy from California with news he wanted Teddy to tell McCarthy. Bobby had changed his mind. He would probably run in the Wisconsin primary after all, and he wanted McCarthy to know.

Teddy Kennedy was still against an RFK run, but he wanted to be helpful to his brother so he didn't do what Bobby told him to do. Teddy thought he had a better idea. He worried that tipping McCarthy off might give the McCarthy people ammunition against Bobby in the final days of the New Hampshire campaign. So Teddy Kennedy ignored Bobby's instructions. He didn't get in touch with McCarthy. Bobby, arriving back in Washington from California only a day before the primary, learned that McCarthy hadn't been warned and asked Richard Goodwin, who had become a McCarthy adviser, to do the nasty job of informing McCarthy that Bobby was thinking about running.

The request made Goodwin nervous. The McCarthy people already thought he was really a Bobby supporter, possibly a traitor to McCarthy and a spy for RFK. Mentioning Kennedy would draw only caustic sarcasm from McCarthy at best and dark suspicions of Goodwin at worst. The day before the New Hampshire vote, Goodwin did reluctantly give McCarthy the news. McCarthy sent a message straight back to Bobby. It was classic Gene—the same message he had given Mary McGrory for Bobby back before McCarthy himself had announced. "Tell him to support me," McCarthy told Goodwin. "I only want one term as president. After that, he can take it over." A meeting between McCarthy and Kennedy was set for the day after the New Hampshire primary in Teddy Kennedy's Senate office.

On the evening of March 12, New Hampshire primary day, Robert Kennedy spoke at a United Jewish Appeal dinner in New York. After the speech, he went to the "21" Club with supporters to await primary results. It was there that he got the news from

New Hampshire. Bobby was ready for McCarthy to
do better than expected, but no one had predicted
anything over 40 percent. McCarthy's vote was stunning, the delegate count even more so. RFK and his
supporters at "21" faced a new set of problems. Right
away they saw that McCarthy's victory was too great.
Kennedy's people had hoped McCarthy would show
that Johnson was vulnerable, but that it would take
a stronger candidate than McCarthy to dump Johnson. Now it looked like McCarthy might be able to
do it himself.

As they thought aloud about it at the table, it
seemed that if Bobby came in now, the "ruthless"
and "cowardly" labels would start to fly. RFK might
look to the public the way he looked to McCarthy:
a cold, calculating opportunist. Now fear of dividing the party meant fear of dividing it three ways:
into Johnson, McCarthy, and Kennedy factions. But
the RFK team believed that McCarthy couldn't win
the nomination or the election. But Bobby could.
George Romney was already out. With Richard
Nixon running unopposed in New Hampshire, he
was the likely GOP nominee, and Kennedy's team
knew how to beat Nixon. At that table at "21" and in
Bobby's mind, the pros and cons battled it out.

After midnight, Bobby went to his New York apart-
ment, called New Hampshire, and spoke to an elated
Richard Goodwin, flushed with McCarthy's victory.
"You never should have trusted the traditional poli-

ticians," Goodwin told Bobby. When Bobby called McCarthy at 2:00 a.m. to offer congratulations, both men knew their real conversation was already scheduled for the next day in Teddy Kennedy's office—a conversation neither one of them was looking forward to. Each was hoping the other would step aside and allow a one-on-one campaign against Johnson for the nomination.

Gene McCarthy seemed positively euphoric speaking to reporters in New Hampshire the next morning. He said, "I think I can get the nomination. I'm ahead now. We'll be able to finance our Wisconsin campaign after what happened." He added, "We'll be able to pay our hotel bills." During the flight to Washington, McCarthy walked the aisle, gabbing happily with reporters. He drank a morning martini.

Earlier that morning Bobby Kennedy flew from New York to Washington and found reporters at the D.C. airport waiting for him. They wanted his response to the amazing McCarthy "win" in New Hampshire. Under the pressure of their questioning, he felt he had to begin to turn over his cards. "I am actively assessing the possibility," Bobby said, "of whether I will run against President Johnson."

The remark blindsided Bobby's perpetually confused and divided advisers. He gave those reporters more forthright information than he had given his team at "21" the night before. By the time he arrived at the Senate office building twenty minutes later, reporters were standing several rows deep in the hall outside his office. Inside, all the phones were ringing. Telegrams were pouring in, seventy-five per hour.

Bobby quickly called a few advisers to give them a heads-up about his off-the-cuff remark. He announced a team meeting for 4:00 p.m. that afternoon, at his brother-in-law Stephen Smith's office back in New York.

McCarthy's plane, meanwhile, landed in Washington, and Jerry Eller, his Senate staff leader, boarded as fast as he could, waving a roll of carbon copies from a news feed. He had Bobby's quote about reassessing his options.

When McCarthy got off the plane and faced the waiting reporters, they noticed a difference. "The happy man was put away somewhere now," wrote a **Minneapolis Tribune** reporter covering the campaign. McCarthy looked grim. The reporters at the airport were vastly outnumbered by the young McCarthy supporters there to welcome their conquering hero. They drowned out questions about Kennedy by simply chanting "McCarthy!" The press conference ended quickly.

As McCarthy rode from the airport to the Senate office building for the Teddy-brokered meeting with Bobby, he knew what the Kennedys wanted. They would congratulate him on his big win in New Hampshire. They would discuss the road ahead to the nomination, making the case that Bobby had a better chance against Johnson and a better chance against Nixon in the fall. They would say this wasn't about ego or ambition, this was about ending the war, running the strongest possible campaign to dump Johnson and end the war. This would be hard to take from someone McCarthy believed was nothing but ego and ambition. Maybe Bobby would offer the vice presidency if the conversation got that far. If there were no history of bitterness between them, if Bobby and Gene were each other's best friend in the Senate, this would still be a difficult conversation. One presidential candidate asking another to step aside happens only after the candidate being asked has just lost a primary. It had never happened to a candidate after he won one. Gene McCarthy knew he was going to be asked to do something that no other "winner" of the New Hampshire primary had ever been asked to do—a request only the Kennedys would make.

The always gregarious Teddy welcomed McCarthy into his office with a big smile and a congratulatory pat on the back. Bobby again congratulated Gene on New Hampshire. He then told Gene what he was sure Gene already knew—that Bobby had just told reporters he was thinking about running. Gene immediately told Bobby he had no intention of getting out. Bobby and Teddy knew Gene well enough to understand that the conversation was essentially over, that Gene didn't want to hear any offer or request from the Kennedys. Gene repeated his delusional-sounding offer of serving a single term and then handing off the presidency to Bobby. Bobby responded only by saying he hoped they would find ways to work together.

That night Blair Clark showed up at the McCarthys' house straight from New Hampshire, a suitcase in each hand. In their front hall, he declared his commitment to Gene and Abigail, no matter what Bobby did now. "We mustn't give up," Clark said. "You can beat him, because he just doesn't have what it takes. He showed that when he wouldn't come in in the first place." Abigail was deeply impressed by Clark's commitment because Clark was a Kennedy family friend.

The next morning, McCarthy cracked to a **Newsweek** reporter, "That Bobby: he's something, isn't he?" Immediately after his meeting with McCarthy, Bobby flew back to New York with Ethel for a team meeting late that afternoon. Teddy arrived ahead of Bobby and wearily listed all of the options being considered by his still indecisive brother.

Ted Sorensen said Bobby must stay neutral in the McCarthy-Johnson battle. Pierre Salinger chimed in to say that neutrality might look as opportunistic as anything else. Schlesinger proposed that Bobby should run in some primaries and support McCarthy in others. There was no consensus in the Kennedy camp.

They watched the CBS evening news to see an interview Bobby had given to the CBS news anchor Walter Cronkite earlier that day in Teddy's office before the McCarthy meeting. In the interview, Bobby heaped praise on the student activists who had pushed McCarthy over the top in New Hampshire. Bobby promised Cronkite he wouldn't make any decision before talking with McCarthy, and then Bobby seemed to all but announce his candidacy.

"What the hell's the point of holding this meeting?" Teddy boomed at the end of the interview. "He's made all the decisions already, and we're learning about it on television!" With the cost of a losing primary campaign in mind, Teddy said, "Bobby's therapy is going to cost the family four million dollars."

When Bobby and Ethel arrived, the meeting turned into a jolly Bobby-and-Ethel cocktail-and-dinner party with a strange feeling of a possible campaign kickoff. To Schlesinger, Bobby looked distracted, uncertain. To the journalist and Kennedy friend Jules Witcover, Bobby seemed relieved, relaxed, confident.

Bobby pulled Teddy and a small group into a room to talk strategy. Bobby told Schlesinger that he would announce a decision within thirty-six hours. Bobby knew he needed every one of those hours before he could make an announcement. He had a plan.

The next morning Bobby and Sorensen flew separately to Washington. They each went straight to the

Pentagon. Together they sat down for a secret meeting with Clark Clifford, the new secretary of defense, who replaced Robert McNamara after LBJ came to believe McNamara was verging on collapse, possibly even suicide. In Clifford's huge office overlooking the Potomac, Sorensen and RFK put forth the names of men they believed should serve on the Vietnam commission that would make recommendations to the president on the war. LBJ seemed interested in that idea—or feigned interest—when Sorensen had suggested it to him. LBJ did the same when Chicago mayor Richard Daley suggested something similar. Daley was now worried that the war was dividing the party. Clifford viewed the list as overpopulated by doves—it included RFK himself—but Bobby and Sorensen insisted that the list contained mostly moderates. Then Bobby floated the deal without actually saying it was a deal: if a credible process emerged from this commission, leading to the end of American involvement in Vietnam, Bobby told Clifford he would support Johnson's nomination, keep the party together, and do everything he could to help Johnson defeat Nixon in November. Otherwise, Bobby told Clifford, he was going to run against Johnson.

Bobby didn't want an impartial commission, he wanted to stack the deck—that's all Johnson could hear when Clifford brought the offer back to him. Johnson, Clifford, and Abe Fortas, LBJ's friend and now a Supreme Court justice, discussed Bobby's proposal and arrived at a flat-out no. After rejecting everything about RFK's offer, the president had his press secretary leak to **Time, Newsweek,** and CBS what LBJ saw as Bobby's weaselly effort at blackmail.

That afternoon, still waiting for Johnson's response, Sorensen and Bobby lunched with George McGovern and three other antiwar lawmakers. They all urged Bobby not to enter the race right now, to instead support McCarthy in the short term. They believed room for common cause with McCarthy might emerge later, but knowing McCarthy as they did, they were certain that if Bobby came in now, McCarthy would never collaborate. Anti-RFK messages from McCarthy supporters were piling up in Bobby's office. Walinsky went through all the telegrams and pulled out only those that were favorable to show to Bobby.

At 5:00 p.m., Clark Clifford called Kennedy's office. Sorensen took the call. Bobby listened in on an extension while Clifford told Sorensen that President Johnson had rejected the offer wholesale.

After all these months, Ted Sorensen knew he'd finally lost the fight. There would be no change in Johnson's Vietnam policy. So Bobby would insist on running. The next day, Friday, March 15, an unhappy Sorensen found himself drafting Bobby's announcement statement.

A press conference was scheduled for Saturday at 10:00 a.m. The Saturday announcement was tactical: Bobby's announcement would make all the Sunday papers and TV news shows. There would be no going back.

At about the same time Friday morning that Sorensen was working on Bobby's announcement, Richard Goodwin and Blair Clark were meeting at McCarthy campaign headquarters in Washington. Both men had once hoped for an RFK run. Now, after all this time, word was out that Bobby would announce the next day. Goodwin and Clark feared that a fight between McCarthy and Kennedy would benefit LBJ and extend the war in Vietnam. With McCarthy on a flight to Wisconsin, the next primary state, Goodwin and Clark called Teddy Kennedy. They had a proposition. Would Teddy join them on a flight to Green Bay to talk to McCarthy before Bobby's Saturday press conference?

Bobby headed to the airport to take the shuttle flight to New York. Frank Mankiewicz accompanied Bobby to the airport. Bobby told Mankiewicz to stay in Washington. "You'd better get the caucus room for tomorrow," he said. That was the room where Jack Kennedy announced his own presidential candidacy eight years earlier.

Bobby boarded the plane with Jack Newfield and **Washington Star** reporter Haynes Johnson. Bobby floated for the two reporters his defense against the inevitable charge of ruthless backstabbing. "Not to run," Bobby told them, "to pretend to be for McCar-

thy, while trying to screw him behind his back—
that's what would really be ruthless. Making speeches
for him, while I'm secretly trying to get delegates for
myself, that's ruthless." Bobby acknowledged Teddy's opposing view of running. "I know my brother
thinks I'm a little nutty for doing this," Bobby went
on, "but we all have to march to the beat of our own
drummer. . . . What has McCarthy ever done for the
ghettos or the poor?"

In New York, they went to a friend's apartment and
Bobby started making calls to supporters and staffers. He called his California operatives working on
the delegate count there. He called many longtime
supporters who needed to know that the race was on,
including Pierre Salinger, Arthur Schlesinger, and
Bill vanden Heuvel. Bobby planned to fly back to
Washington for a gathering of the whole team that
night at Hickory Hill. The gathering would include
one mystery guest. Bobby called the prime mover
behind McCarthy's success and invited him to the
Hickory Hill meeting. His attendance would have
to be secret. "You can keep me off your calendar,"
Bobby told Al Lowenstein.

As the RFK team was gathering at Hickory Hill
that evening, a chartered plane was leaving Washington, heading for Wisconsin. Blair Clark had called
McCarthy directly to say he was bringing Teddy
Kennedy for a meeting that night. McCarthy said
nothing. The private plane carried Teddy Kennedy;

Clark; Goodwin; Curtis Gans; Sam Brown, the national youth coordinator; and Jessica Tuchman. Twenty-one and only five months out of Radcliffe, Tuchman was Gene's assistant campaign manager. As they flew, they came to a rough potential understanding.

To avoid warfare between the antiwar candidates, the plan, as Goodwin, Clark, and Ted Kennedy worked it up, was this: Bobby and McCarthy would divide up the primaries. Each would run unopposed in a designated set of races, with the other supporting him, until California. Then, on June 4, they would square off in California and let the winner of that primary take that big pot of delegates.

Teddy Kennedy had not cleared this deal with Bobby, so he couldn't actually commit Bobby to it. Still, he agreed to kick it around with McCarthy. Kennedy thought the two anti-Johnson insurgents might sign a pledge of reconciliation. Teddy had drawn up a draft document to show McCarthy.

The plane landed in Green Bay late Friday night. McCarthy was staying at the Northland Hotel. It was important to hide this meeting from the press, so Teddy Kennedy and McCarthy's people headed for the Holiday Inn. From there they began trying to make covert contact with McCarthy.

Back at Hickory Hill late that same night, the RFK team was meeting again, and things weren't going smoothly. As was so often the case at Bobby and Ethel's, this all-important meeting had coincided with a long-planned Kennedy-style dinner for Washington society and various luminaries: the mountaineer Jim Whittaker, the filmmaker George Stevens Jr., and the humor columnist Art Buchwald. Bobby and his political team had to hobnob and make merry before getting down to business. Amid the chatter and carousing, some of the Kennedy kids played with two big dogs while Jefferson Airplane blasted from the living-room stereo.

It wasn't until 11:00 p.m. that Bobby finally got upstairs into a room with the team. With the piano playing downstairs and the guests loudly singing, they discussed their challenges. Mayor Richard Daley had confirmed his continued support for LBJ. In the crucial battleground states of Pennsylvania and Ohio, party chairmen had publicly stated that at the convention Johnson would get all of their states' delegates. Big unions were sticking with Johnson, and so, of course, was John Bailey, the Democratic Party chairman. So the establishment was going to stand by the president.

The antiestablishment forces had their candidate already: Eugene McCarthy. The first antiwar senator, Wayne Morse, now a hero to the peace movement, refused to endorse Bobby. John Kenneth Galbraith, having failed to get Bobby to run, had thrown his support to McCarthy and wouldn't go back to Kennedy now. McCarthy's legions of antiwar student supporters were sounding angry at the possibility of Bobby trying to steal Gene's thunder.

The RFK political team's arguments grew loud and tense. Adam Walinsky and Jeff Greenfield, always true believers, talked tough about Bobby's taking on McCarthy in all primaries. Senior team members Sorensen and Schlesinger thought a McCarthy-Kennedy battle would bruise both candidates and only help Johnson. Al Lowenstein, hoping McCarthy would never learn of his presence here tonight, urged cooperation between the two camps. They all knew that Bobby had given Teddy Kennedy the go-ahead to travel to Green Bay with McCarthy's people and see McCarthy personally.

They all hoped that maybe something could still be worked out. As their arguments dragged on at Hickory Hill, RFK's team hoped for some good news from Teddy Kennedy in Wisconsin.

ABIGAIL McCARTHY felt at home at the Northland Hotel in Green Bay. In their early years in politics, she had campaigned for Gene in small towns throughout Minnesota, and she'd stayed in ghostly old hotels just like this, once grand, now midcentury modernized with faux Danish lamps and wall-to-wall carpeting.

The candidate's suite at the Northland had a living room and a bedroom. The head of the Wisconsin chapter of Women for McCarthy had supplied instant coffee, antique china cups, and fresh daffodils, just on the verge of blooming on that Friday, March 15.

Abigail had been campaigning hard all over the state with her daughter Mary. Mary had arrived in Wisconsin outraged at the news of RFK's "reassessing" comment. When Abigail and Mary got back to the hotel that night, they heard that Walter Cronkite had reported on CBS that Robert Kennedy would announce his candidacy the next morning. They knew that Cronkite was friendly with Bobby and must be right. They did not know that a year earlier Cronkite had personally urged Bobby to run. Walter Cronkite was a true believer, too.

Abigail had been watching Bobby's recent moves further away from LBJ's war policy and toward Gene's. Nothing she was hearing now surprised her. When Gene and Jerry Eller returned from campaigning they joined Abigail and Mary in the suite. They had a room-service dinner. Gene seemed exhausted. After dinner, he headed straight for the bedroom to get some sleep. Mary then left and went to her room. Suddenly Mary rushed back into the suite's living room and said Teddy Kennedy was on his way to Green Bay to see Gene. "They're all coming from Washington in a chartered campaign plane!" Mary said.

"All?" said Abigail.

"Yes, all: Blair Clark, Dick Goodwin, Curt Gans, Jessica Tuchman."

Abigail was stunned. Gene hadn't said anything about this. His top people were coming—and bringing Teddy Kennedy with them. Had they all switched to Bobby? Already?

Jerry Eller was disgusted. Senate staffers never trust campaign types. Now Eller, Gene's Senate loyalist, was convinced they were all traitors. Eller never had any confidence in Goodwin, had always thought he was a Bobby man biding his time. Eller had heard rumors from reporters that Goodwin had spent much of the previous day coming and going at Hickory Hill. Clark, too, had always been tight with the Kennedys, and Gans, like Lowenstein, had only come to McCarthy when Bobby had refused to run. Abigail remembered Goodwin telling Gene, "I'm with you all the way." She remembered Clark reassuring Gene, in the McCarthys' front hall, that Bobby wouldn't have the courage to run. Now they were coming with Teddy Kennedy to force a coup.

But Abigail had a plan. She told Mary and Gene's Senate secretary, Susan Perry, to present themselves as the senator's staff on the road. She set Jerry Eller as lookout. He soon got word that the Washington group had checked into the Holiday Inn. Eller sent word to the Holiday Inn that Gene could be found at the Northland. Soon the youngsters Gans, Tuchman, and Brown arrived, ahead of the rest of the Washington group. They went straight up to Mary's room.

Abigail went to see them there. She found Gans reminding Mary that it was really the peace movement that mattered most of all, not the candidate. Abigail directly confronted young Sam Brown: Was he with Bobby now? Brown could only say that he didn't know.

After leaving Mary's room, Abigail found the **Newsweek** reporter Dick Stout trying to listen through the wall in the empty adjoining room. She shooed him out. It was time for Abigail to awaken Gene.

IT WAS WELL AFTER midnight back at Hickory Hill, and the team was still fighting over the announcement speech for the next morning. At one point, Kennedy asked Lowenstein, "Should I put into my statement that I told Gene I was going to run before New Hampshire?"

"Yes, great!" Lowenstein said. "That will save you from looking like a vulture and an opportunist."

There were three separate drafts—Sorensen's, Walinsky's, and Schlesinger's—each making totally different points. Sorensen's minimized differences with Johnson. Walinsky and Greenfield hated that version. Walinsky's draft was all about ending the war. Schlesinger's tried for a tone of cooperation with the McCarthy campaign. All drafts had to get integrated into something cogent by 10:00 a.m., but the arguments were growing harsher. Integration of viewpoints was elusive. Chaos was looming. Bobby read aloud a sentence from Sorensen's draft and said, "Ted, that doesn't make any sense. But then, this whole thing doesn't make much sense either." When Bobby deputized Schlesinger to take everything they had and reconcile all drafts, Walinsky groaned aloud.

BLAIR CLARK AND DICK GOODWIN arrived at Green Bay's Northland Hotel, still in advance of Teddy Kennedy, greeted only by Abigail and Mary. Gene was nowhere to be seen. Clark was upset. "What's all this, Abigail," he said. "I thought this was all arranged."

He had reason to be upset. He had spoken to McCarthy, but Gene had said nothing about it to Abigail. When Abigail had awakened Gene and told him who she thought was coming to see him, he said that he had decided he didn't want to meet with Teddy Kennedy. Then Gene went back to sleep.

"I don't know," Abigail told Clark. "What **is** it about?"

Goodwin took over, more calmly than Clark. He and Abigail began discussing the idea of making a deal with Bobby, and Abigail began to wonder whether making some sort of deal might be the wiser course.

Left to right: Attorney General Robert F. Kennedy, Senator Edward M. Kennedy, and President John F. Kennedy at the White House, August 28, 1963

Left to right: Muriel Humphrey, vice presidential nominee Hubert H. Humphrey, President Lyndon B. Johnson, and Lady Bird Johnson campaigning in 1964

Michigan governor George Romney campaigning with his wife, Lenore, January 1968

Roger Ailes working for the Nixon campaign, 1968

Senator Eugene McCarthy at the Wayfarer Inn the night
he "won" the 1968 New Hampshire primary

President Lyndon B. Johnson working on the speech in which
he announced he would not run for reelection

Memphis sanitation workers trying to avoid the rain, 1968

Dr. Martin Luther King Jr. delivering his last sermon, April 3, 1968

In Indianapolis, Bobby Kennedy announces, "Martin Luther King
was shot and was killed tonight in Memphis, Tennessee."

Gene McCarthy with eighteen thousand supporters at the Veterans Memorial
Coliseum in Madison, Wisconsin, where he began by reciting
Walt Whitman's "I Hear America Singing"

Los Angeles Rams defensive end Deacon Jones holding Bobby Kennedy in a crowd in Oakland in the final days of the California primary campaign

Bobby Kennedy's California victory speech: *(left to right)* Dolores Huerta, Ethel Kennedy *(partial)*, Bobby Kennedy, Roosevelt Grier *(partial)*

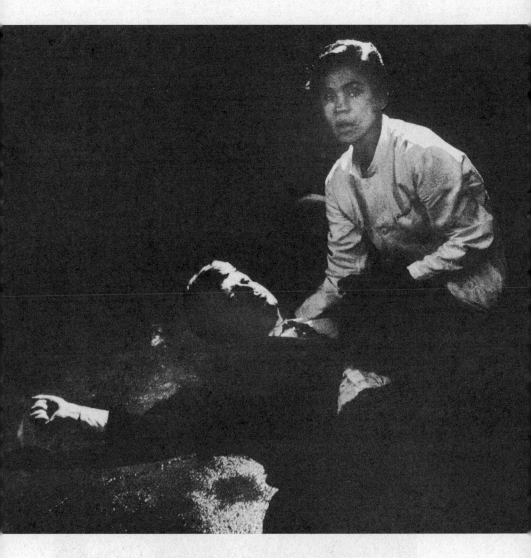

Juan Romero with Bobby Kennedy immediately after he was shot

Allard Lowenstein speaking to the New York State Democratic
Committee about the selection of convention delegates, July 2, 1968

President Johnson meeting with South Vietnam president
Nguyen Van Thieu in Hawaii, July 19, 1968

Richard Nixon makes his first public appearance in Miami Beach arriving at his hotel for the 1968 Republican Convention

NBC News correspondent John Chancellor interviewing California governor Ronald Reagan on the convention floor

Left to right: William F. Buckley Jr. versus Gore Vidal on the ABC News election coverage

Chicago police pushing protesters into police vans in front of the Hilton Hotel

Senator Abraham Ribicoff speaking at the Democratic Convention with Mayor Richard Daley (under Illinois sign) shouting, "You Jew son of a bitch!"

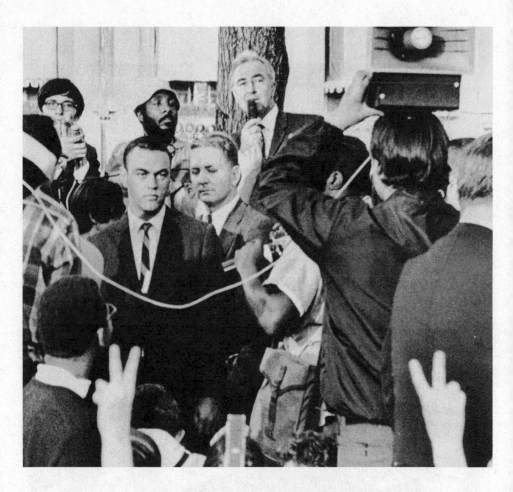

Gene McCarthy speaking to convention protesters in Chicago's Grant Park
with Dick Gregory to his right and Secret Service agents in front of him

Richard Nixon with the New York Republican liberals *(left to right)* Governor Nelson Rockefeller, Mayor John Lindsay, and Senator Jacob Javits, September 11, 1968

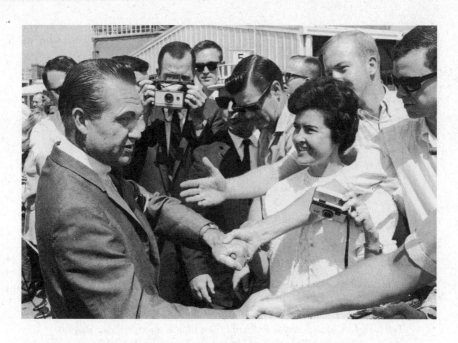

George Wallace campaigning in Lexington, Kentucky, September 15, 1968

Richard Nixon in Philadelphia, September 20, 1968

Left to right: Chicago mayor Richard Daley, Illinois governor Sam Shapiro, Vice President Hubert Humphrey, November 1, 1968

But then Clark lost it. Abigail felt Clark couldn't bear dealing with women, underlings. "Either you wake up Gene or I will," Clark said. He headed for the bedroom. So Abigail never heard the full terms of the deal.

Teddy Kennedy sneaked through the hotel's rear door and went upstairs in the freight elevator at 2:00 a.m. By the time Teddy arrived in the living room of the suite, Gene was awake and dressed. Mary had stopped Clark from storming the bedroom. She had gone instead and somehow persuaded her father to get up and meet with Teddy.

Teddy seemed to Abigail remarkably full of good cheer and energy given the excruciatingly long day he'd had. Teddy sat on a couch with a briefcase laid across his thighs as if in anticipation of handing over some paperwork. Gene sat in an armchair beside Mary and Abigail. The three McCarthys faced Teddy with Goodwin and Clark looking on to referee as needed.

Teddy Kennedy said he came because Bobby wanted McCarthy to know what a fine job he had done so far in campaigning. Then he began to open the briefcase on his lap. With only a small hand gesture, McCarthy stopped him. Having stopped Kennedy from opening the mysterious briefcase—what was in it? Abigail would always wonder—McCarthy spoke with characteristic calmness. He told Kennedy that he appreciated his making the trip. He pointed out that news of Bobby's announcement the next morning had been covered by Cronkite on TV.

Teddy Kennedy said Bobby was interested in helping Gene in Wisconsin anyway.

"From all the indications we have, we're doing very well in Wisconsin," McCarthy said. "We need no help." He wouldn't step out of future primaries unless the people of those states asked him to. But McCarthy did have a suggestion for collaboration. The best way to beat Johnson would be to make an antiwar run in all primaries. There were some primaries McCarthy had not entered. Bobby might want to run in West Virginia and Louisiana, and maybe Florida, where, McCarthy believed, a challenge to Johnson could be highly effective. That was the kind of collaboration he envisioned. McCarthy said beating Johnson had always been his only goal.

Goodwin and Clark were trying to come into the conversation now, but for Teddy Kennedy this meeting was over. He didn't respond to McCarthy's suggestion about the three unentered primaries. Soon all they were discussing was how to get Teddy out without press involvement.

Teddy felt as soon as he entered the suite that Abigail was really running this meeting and that she was opposed to any deal. The whole scene felt hopeless to him from the start, sitting across from the three McCarthys. He believed Gene had let him fly there

for nothing. Jerry Eller came in to say that reporters and photographers were mobbing the hallway
now, cameras trained on the suite's door. They knew
Teddy was in there.

So Abigail escorted Kennedy out in front of the
press like a Washington hostess after a dinner party.
Reporters heard them chat about civil rights while
Goodwin and Eller and others tried to clear their
path. To the reporters' barrage of questions, Teddy
Kennedy only said, as he walked through the crowd,
"It's too late to talk, we just had a pleasant visit. . . .
We all need to get a few hours' sleep. . . ."

The three McCarthys were alone again.

"That's the way they are," Gene said. There was
real bitterness in his tone. "When it comes down to
it, they never offer anything real." But he never gave
Teddy the chance to make an offer.

At Hickory Hill, Arthur Schlesinger was sleeping
in an empty kid's bedroom. The younger men on
the team had finally gone home, but the old-guard
Camelot men had curled up in various corners of the
house. Schlesinger was still working on the speech.
Sorensen had got to it, putting back in some touches
that the absent Walinsky and Greenfield had cut.

At 6:00 a.m., Schlesinger found himself awakened
by a hoarse whisper. "Ted. Ted." It was an exhausted
Teddy Kennedy, fresh off the plane and searching for
Ted Sorensen.

"Very unsatisfactory," Teddy reported in a whisper to Schlesinger about McCarthy. "I think his wife was against it."

Teddy next awakened Bill vanden Heuvel. "Abigail said no," Teddy told him.

By 7:00 a.m., Bobby was wandering around aimlessly in his pajamas. The announcement was only three hours away. Sorensen had taken over reconciling the drafts in light of Teddy's report of no cooperation from McCarthy. Someone asked where Bobby was. "Upstairs," said Sorensen, "looking for someone who agrees with him."

Teddy threw up his hands. It was incredible, the whole thing, just crazy. Maybe they could still talk Bobby out of it. Maybe have him declare for McCarthy, then pick up McCarthy's delegates later.

Bobby overheard that last part. He came through the French doors into the breakfast room and told them not to talk about it anymore. "I'm going ahead," Bobby told them. He left to get dressed.

Teddy took over. "He has to be at his best at this goddamned press conference. We can't talk about it anymore," he said. And that was it.

A barber came in to cut Bobby's hair. "Cut it as close as you can," Teddy ordered him. "Don't pay attention to anything he says. Cut off as much as you can."

The day was warm and cloudy, and the Senate Caucus Room was packed with supporters, photographers, and reporters. Ethel led nine of the ten Kennedy kids to seats in the front row. Members of the old guard, such as Schlesinger, were standing in the crowd, as were members of the new guard, such as Walinsky.

At 10:00 a.m., Bobby came to the microphone accompanied by Frank Mankiewicz. Jack Newfield was nearby.

Robert F. Kennedy, lacking any campaign staff, national organization, committed delegates, or promised support, announced his intention to challenge Lyndon Johnson in some of the primaries. Bobby denied running against anyone personally. There was, he implied, no vendetta with Johnson. He praised McCarthy's success in glowing terms. That was Schlesinger's draft. Bobby also talked about Watts and Mississippi, Vietnam, the anger and outrage of young people.

He concluded his speech on a note of JFK-era triumphalism. It was a Ted Sorensen line that sounded to Walinsky and Greenfield like the imperialism they were fighting. "At stake," Bobby said, "is our right to the moral leadership of this planet."

As the press conference began, a reporter said, "There has been speculation that this is opportunism on your part—" and his question was deliberately drowned in a roar of supporters' cheers. This was to be a celebratory occasion, not an interrogation.

The second Kennedy presidential campaign was launched. A few days later, Jackie Kennedy took Arthur Schlesinger aside at a dinner party in New York. "Do you know what I think will happen to Bobby?" she asked. Schlesinger waited for her to answer her own question.

"The same thing that happened to Jack," she said.

SIXTEEN

THE POOR PEOPLE'S CAMPAIGN

Parallel with the presidential campaign, Martin Luther King Jr. was running a national campaign for economic justice called the Poor People's Campaign. In 1967, when Bobby and Gene McCarthy were thinking about running for president, Dr. King was planning it in earnest. After riots in Newark and Detroit in the summer of 1967, Dr. King cowrote a report aimed at redirecting the rage of rioters into organized nonviolent protest. The report's premise was that "to dislocate the functioning of a city without destroying it can be more effective than a riot because it can be longer-lasting, costly to society but not wantonly destructive." The finish line for Dr. King's campaign was the same as the presidential campaign's—Washington, D.C. That was the city he planned to disrupt.

Dr. King was the most famous, most revered civil

rights leader in the world. He was **Time** magazine's Man of the Year in 1963 at age thirty-four. The next year he won the Nobel Peace Prize and helped push the Civil Rights Act through Congress—a bill that would not have even been written had not Dr. King led a ten-year national crusade for civil rights that included protests and civil disobedience, for which he was arrested twenty-nine times. The next year he pushed the president and Congress to enact the Voting Rights Act. And then many in Washington believed their work with Martin Luther King was done. But justice was always Dr. King's goal, and justice is a never-ending quest.

The Poor People's Campaign was broader than anything Dr. King had done before. In the beginning of 1968, he and his staff were organizing poor people across America—black, white, Latino, Native American—for a massive march to Washington in the spring that would then become a peaceful occupation of the city to demand congressional action. Organized labor supported Dr. King's Economic Bill of Rights, which included "a meaningful job at a living wage" and "a secure and adequate income." AFL-CIO president George Meany would not endorse the campaign if it included an antiwar position.

On the day Bobby Kennedy announced his presidential campaign, Dr. King spoke to the California Democratic Council at the Disneyland Hotel in Anaheim. He made his strongest antiwar statement yet, directly confronting LBJ: The war "has made the Great Society a myth," King said, "and replaced it with a troubled and confused society. . . . How can the administration, with quivering anger, denounce the violence of ghetto Negroes when it has given an example of violence in Asia that shocks the world? . . . I have been working too long against segregation in public accommodations to end up segregating my moral concerns." Back in November, Dr. King had told McCarthy he had to remain publicly neutral in the Democratic primary race because he needed to preserve access to the president.

Now, just days after the McCarthy "win" in New Hampshire, Dr. King seemed to all but endorse the antiwar candidate. The California Democrats loved it.

Dr. King had remained silent on the war in Vietnam longer than he wanted to. Young African American radicals like Stokely Carmichael and H. Rap Brown despised the war as a racist, imperialist adventure of a corrupt and militaristic state. They condemned Dr. King's refusal to speak out. When, at his own Ebenezer Baptist Church, on an April Sunday in 1967, Dr. King preached in opposition to the war, Stokely Carmichael was sitting in the front row to lend his support.

Dr. King hoped the Poor People's Campaign could also get Stokely Carmichael's support. He hoped to bring his economic justice movement together with the more radical demands of young Black Power leaders. The Poor People's Campaign would prove that nonviolent confrontation still offered the only effective way to achieve real, sweeping social change.

"Very frankly," Dr. King told reporters, "this is a search for an alternative to riots."

If the nation didn't respond to the presence of poor people occupying Washington, King predicted, "as we labor there two or three months, however long it takes, God only knows what we will face in terms of chaos." Influenced in part by the teachings of Malcolm X, who was assassinated in 1965, many young black activists found Dr. King's insistence on nonviolence to be old-fashioned. "In order for nonviolence to work," Stokely Carmichael said in 1967, "your opponent must have a conscience. The United States has none." H. Rap Brown said, "If America don't come around, we're gonna have to burn it down." Dr. King well understood the movement's potential for devolving into chaotic violence.

The day after Dr. King's speech to the California Democrats, he took a call from his old friend the Reverend James Lawson. He was calling from Memphis and he needed his friend Martin's help. With few others did King share such a longstanding commitment to the principle of nonviolent resistance. On the phone in a Los Angeles hotel room, Dr. King listened as Lawson described the situation in Memphis, where there was a major strike that had

dragged on for a month. It was sparked by two gro-
tesque deaths. The city's lowest-level sanitation workers were those who carried the trash from homes to
sanitation trucks. They were miserably paid "at will"
workers, lacking any protections or pensions or even
uniforms. And not surprisingly for a segregated city
like Memphis, these lowest-paid, worst-treated workers were black.

Work rules prohibited them even from getting out
of the rain, except by sitting inside the scoop in the
backs of their trucks, which turned out to be a tragedy waiting to happen.

On February 1, 1968, Robert Walker and Echol
Cole, sheltering from a pounding storm, were merci-
lessly dragged by a neglected, malfunctioning truck
compressor into the innards of the truck itself, with
the garbage. The driver desperately tried to make the
compressor stop. He couldn't. Robert Walker and
Echol Cole were swallowed, crushed, and broken
up amid the filthy refuse they had thrown into that
truck.

The horror and degradation was unbearable for
the victims' coworkers. They walked off the job, and
demanded the right to join a union. Their slogan
seemed to resonate for black and poor Americans everywhere: "I am a man."

On the phone, Lawson told Dr. King that the
strike had become deadlocked and had reached a
very dangerous point. The mayor was refusing to

negotiate. The mayor brought in white strikebreakers to pick up the mountains of trash. The strikebreakers were protected by armed police patrols. The Memphis press was harshly condemning the striking workers. Police were beginning to club marching strikers. Within the protest itself, young Memphis Black Power advocates—they called themselves "the Invaders"—were threatening to respond to white oppression with outright violence. The city might soon see the kind of rioting that had torn apart so many other cities. Memphis needed Martin Luther King Jr.

Dr. King immediately saw that the movement against racial inequality was being combined with a new labor movement in the Memphis strike. The striking workers were protesting racial oppression and they were protesting the class oppression of the poorest of the poor. That was the focus Dr. King wanted for his Poor People's Campaign. And he always believed he had to find ways to counter talk of violent protest in these situations. Dr. King feared if the protest in Memphis turned violent, it would be a setback for everything he was trying to accomplish.

Some of Dr. King's staff thought Memphis was a sideshow. They wanted him to stay focused on building the Poor People's Campaign. For years Dr. King had been living his life out of a suitcase with peripatetic, exhausting cross-country jet travel from one protest to another, from one important speech to another. He would make a speech in one city, preach a sermon the next day in another city, stop for a night at home in Atlanta, and take off for another city the next day. His aides called it Martin's "war on sleep." His staff was always more willing to decline the next invitation than he was. It was hard for Dr. King to say no when he knew he was the most credible voice in the country for nonviolent protest. It was hard to say no when he knew he was in the best position to hold the movement together. It was hard to say no when Memphis needed him. And it was impossible to say no when he needed Memphis to show what the Poor People's Campaign was all about. Over his staff's objections, Martin Luther King Jr. decided to fly from Los Angeles to Memphis the next day.

GEORGE WALLACE'S PRESIDENTIAL CAM-PAIGN might have seemed like the dying resistance to Dr. King's already successful civil rights movement. It might have seemed like an extended temper tantrum after Nick Katzenbach rolled over him in the doorway of the University of Alabama with the Kennedy brothers monitoring Governor Wallace's futile gesture from Washington. Though the 1968 Wallace for president campaign was a grudge match from the past, it was also about a present that had not yet publicly revealed itself: hardcore racism in the North and de facto segregation in the North. And it was about the future.

When Tom Turnipseed watched Donald Trump campaign for president in 2016, he knew where he had seen that style before: when he was managing George Wallace's 1968 campaign for president. He said they both used "the politics of fear." After the Wallace campaign, Turnipseed went through a bigger change of heart than most Southern white men his age. He eventually became a civil rights lawyer and fought the Ku Klux Klan. He described Wallace's and Trump's "politics of fear" this way: "You know, it's like you gotta be afraid. You know, the black folks are taking over. And, you know, Trump, the Mexicans are coming. The Chinese are going to get you. And, you know, fear is a motivator in many many incidents—in politics number one and many other ways. And so they are a lot alike in that. You had to play on fear, you know, fear of this group or that group. They are going to get you and so forth. You know, motivate people to vote." Judy Turnipseed, Tom's wife, also worked on the Wallace campaign. When she watched Trump, she saw Wallace. She said, "I think that both of them appeal to the same type of person, to the poor, working class people who really want to make America great again, or in their opinion great again, and their fear of government, fear of people who are not like themselves. And so they are alike that way. They appeal to the same kind of people. I think their style is a lot alike too. They draw a big crowd and get them all excited.

They do not talk much about substance, but more about what the problems are, what they should fear, not so much about what to do about it."

"Niggers hate whites and whites hate niggers," George Wallace once explained to a reporter. "Everybody knows that deep down." And he meant everybody. That is why he believed he could find support for an Alabama segregationist presidential campaign in 1968 years after racial segregation became illegal. Wallace knew that segregation was still real even though it was technically illegal. Wallace knew that Northern landlords like the Trumps in New York City were discriminating against black tenants. He knew that public school systems like Boston's were effectively segregated because of the historically segregated neighborhoods of those cities. He knew that there were white people all over the country who thought about race the way he did: "whites hate niggers." And so a month before the New Hampshire primary, George Corley Wallace announced his candidacy for president of the United States. He was running as an independent. He wouldn't have to fight for a nomination. He was in this all the way. In a close election, the Wallace vote could determine the outcome.

George Wallace left the Democratic Party, but in his view the party had left him. The Democratic Party didn't have a problem with him in 1963 when he was sworn in as governor of Alabama and said in his speech that day, "Segregation now, segregation tomorrow, segregation forever!" Five months later, when Nick Katzenbach backed up by U.S. marshals and the National Guard confronted the governor at the doorway of the University of Alabama, George Wallace must have realized his days in the Democratic Party—the Kennedy party—were numbered.

By the time Wallace made an exploratory trip to New Hampshire in the spring of 1967 with an independent candidacy on his mind, he had substituted the phrase "states' rights" for the word **segregation**. Everyone understood they meant the same thing. Wallace's twin-engine plane came to a stop on a cold, rainy April evening on the landing strip of the small Concord, New Hampshire, airport. As Wallace got out of the plane, he was met by a small group of supporters. They cheered and snapped flashbulbs and waved tiny flags. The flag these New Englanders were waving was the flag of the Confederate States of America.

No New Hampshire officials showed up to welcome Wallace. He stood under an umbrella held by a staffer and spoke briefly to reporters. Ordinary working people, he told the press, were about to run over the politicians. Then he jumped into a limousine.

The next afternoon Wallace held a rally in Concord at the state capitol in front of a statue of New Hampshire's most famous son, Daniel Webster, the congressman, senator, and secretary of state, who did everything he possibly could to hold the union together before the Civil War. Wallace's thick Alabama accent left some words incomprehensible to New Hampshire ears, but there was never any doubt about what George Wallace meant, what was in his heart. His tone ranged from anger to amused anger. His constantly waving and pointing finger was always angry, too, punctuating every sentence. His message to New Hampshire was "If one of these two national parties don't wake up and get straight I can promise that you and me, we gonna stir something up all over this country!" Every Confederate flag-waver cheering on Wallace that day knew what that meant. George Wallace would be coming back to New Hampshire as a candidate in 1968.

Wallace aimed his presidential campaign at the voters he called "the working people," "the common folks," "the people," and sometimes just "the folks." He never got into complex domestic or foreign policy issues. He stuck with feelings instead of facts. There was "too much dignity in government now," Wallace told a reporter. "What we need is some meanness."

Wallace had been rehearsing his 1968 campaign talking points in Alabama for years. It was judges who were ruining America, he told the folks. There would soon be a new civil war, he predicted, literal warfare: rightists versus leftists, whites versus blacks, ordinary people versus bureaucrats, and it was just about to boil over. "Hell," he said, "all we'd have to do right now is march on the federal courthouse there in Montgomery, take over the post office, lock up a few of those judges, and by sunset there'd be a revolution from one corner of this nation to the other." Wallace wasn't talking about right-wing conservatism; he was talking about revolution.

Wallace began his political life as a Southern New Dealer, more than happy in those days to let his state "wallow in the trough" of Washington funding. He still supported Medicare and Social Security but opposed the people who created those popular programs. He was anti-Washington, anti-politicians, anti–the system.

Wallace did not begin his career as a vicious public racist. In his first campaign for governor in 1958, he made speeches condemning the Ku Klux Klan's violence against black citizens. His Democratic opponent in the primary ran with the Klan's support. After losing the primary election, Wallace vowed that "no son of a bitch will ever outnigger me again."

In 1962, Wallace won the Democratic primary for governor. In those days, Republican opposition was nonexistent in Alabama, so Wallace won in November with 96 percent of the vote. He took his oath of office standing on a gold star marking the spot where Jefferson Davis took the oath as president of the Confederacy. Governor Wallace invoked the language of the Civil War in his war to preserve segregation.

In the Wallace war, there were two enemies: civil rights leaders, especially the most visible, Martin Luther King Jr., whose organization was registering black voters throughout the South, and the federal government, which for Wallace and his supporters meant the president and attorney general named Kennedy. According to Wallace there was a straight-up conspiracy at work in Washington against the South and its traditional values and institutions. In his first year as governor, Wallace barked, "The President wants us to surrender this state to Martin Luther King and his group of pro-communists who have instituted these demonstrations." Wallace always blended anticommunist rhetoric with anti–civil rights rhetoric, usually in the same sentence. He wanted to make communism and civil rights synonymous. When people heard politicians talking about civil rights, Wallace wanted them to think "communist."

Governor Wallace entered the Democratic presidential primaries in 1964 on the strength of Southern opposition to LBJ's civil rights bill. He did surprisingly well in Wisconsin, Indiana, and Maryland. Wallace's speeches in the 1964 campaign drew protests from civil rights activists and liberal college students. That was exactly what he wanted. In Cincinnati in '64, Wallace shouted to his crowd about the protesters outside. "When you and I start marching and demonstrating and carrying signs," he told his folks, "we will close every highway in the country!" He called the protesters "little pinkos." Nearly a thousand of Wallace's folks ran for the exit to attack the protesters.

That reaction surprised even Wallace. Since that day in Cincinnati, Wallace masterfully toyed with the anger of his audiences. He drove them to fits of outrage, always trying to bring them to the brink of violence before holding them back. He made sure there was more than enough tension at his events that it always felt like anything might happen at any moment. And that always made news.

Wallace's strategy for a third-party run in 1968 was not to win the presidency. Running as an independent would eliminate party competition and keep public attention on Wallace all the way to November, allowing him to criticize policies of both major parties at will. The dream was to get his name on the ballot in as many states as possible—a huge task, with more than four hundred thousand signatures needed in Ohio alone—and then win enough votes in November to prevent an electoral college victory, throwing the election into the House of Representatives. That would make George Wallace the ultimate national power broker. He would extract big policy concessions on race in exchange for conceding the office. Even if Wallace couldn't win a single state, he expected to pull enough votes away from LBJ and the Republicans that one or both of them would have to lean his way on the issues.

Like Gene McCarthy's supporters, Wallace's support could skew young and attract volunteers with little campaign experience. In Nevada, a twenty-six-year-old man from Reno became the campaign's vice chairman. Some campaign operatives were Klansmen. A sixty-four-year-old real estate agent in Washington state who volunteered for Wallace said without embarrassment, "I am a racist. I don't even believe in Irish marrying Germans."

The complex national effort to get Wallace on the ballot achieved startling success. The Wallace phenomenon began to look like a groundswell of rage. When Wallace made a semiformal announcement of his candidacy on **Meet the Press** in April 1967, denying any racism and condemning big government, the response was overwhelming—letters, checks, and cash poured in from around the country. People in every state volunteered to help get him on ballots. He began getting more TV invitations than he could accept. A woman living in a working-class suburb of San Francisco, long concerned about law and order, communism, welfare, and hippies, told a reporter she had written to Wallace and told him, "This is the time and you are the man to lead us."

When he stood in front of Daniel Webster's statue that day in Concord, Wallace was riding the wave of support his **Meet the Press** comments had provoked. That evening he went on to Dartmouth College, Daniel Webster's alma mater. Wallace had spoken there before in 1964 when he'd campaigned on an outspokenly racist platform. In that first appearance at Dartmouth, he drew boos of outrage for describing Southern blacks as "easygoing, basically happy, unambitious, incapable of much learning." He also heard some applause that night. Dartmouth has always been the most politically conservative Ivy League school, perhaps the only one where Wallace could have gotten any applause. This time at Dartmouth, Wallace's racial rhetoric was coded in the language of "law and order," but the image he wanted to convey was still clear: he was the leader of the war between the races, the war between the elites and the workers, the war between government and the folks.

Inside the Dartmouth auditorium there was a steady roar. Outside, students ran toward the sound. A crowd gathered under the windows and on the steps. It was standing room only inside and the noise never ceased, a howl of urgent emotion. There was outrage and there was approval. It was a new kind of crowd intensity, not heard before in American politics. Amid pandemonium, Wallace was pacing the stage, spitting into his handkerchief before responding to student questions shouted from index cards by one embattled student. Every time Wallace spoke, the roar intensified. Jabbing the air with his finger, Wallace called anyone who expressed support for the Vietcong a traitor.

Suddenly a long-haired young professor was leading a group of students down the center aisle to charge the stage. Shoved back by campus security, the teacher yelled up at Wallace, "Get out of here! Get out of here!" as students yelled and cheered and booed.

When it was over, Wallace sat calmly in the back of his car as his driver began pulling away and students overran the vehicle. They banged on the hood, kicked the fenders. A police officer got knocked down in the crowd. A student jumped up with the officer's hat and waved it around. Wallace's car moved slowly through the crowd.

Wallace was used to this by now. The law-and-order candidate was causing near riots everywhere he went. His Dartmouth speech would get a lot of news coverage, and the folks Wallace was championing would see him once again fearlessly bringing it to the communists, the black people, the antiwar protesters, and the Ivy League elites. As his car pulled away leaving chaos in its wake, Wallace knew he'd had a good day in New Hampshire.

SEVENTEEN

"SOMETHING BAD IS GOING TO COME OF THIS"

Bitterness engulfed Richard Nixon as he sat staring at the TV in a hotel in Portland, Oregon, on the morning of Saturday, March 16, as Robert Kennedy announced his candidacy in the packed Senate Caucus Room. With Nixon were John Ehrlichman and other aides. When the Kennedy press conference was over, they turned off the TV and Nixon just sat there.

He kept staring at the empty screen. The rested, relaxed, upbeat Nixon of the day before was gone. Nixon had spent every day since the JFK assassination in 1963 pulling every puppet string, pushing every lever, manipulating every Republican presidential contender so that the 1968 presidential race would be a contest between Lyndon Johnson and

Richard Nixon. It was Johnson he positioned himself against. It was Johnson he baited. It was Johnson he was supposed to be running against in the general election. Not a Kennedy. Not again.

Gene McCarthy's surprising insurgency didn't worry Nixon. He thought a protest candidate hurling himself against LBJ's war policy would only weaken Johnson for the general election. Now Nixon worried that Bobby could actually beat Johnson. Nixon had not spent years developing a strategy to beat Bobby. He didn't have one.

Nixon was sure Bobby would not just run against Johnson for the nomination; he would run against Nixon at the same time. Nixon expected Bobby to use him to win the nomination by essentially saying the best way to beat Nixon is with a Kennedy. Nixon believed Bobby would exaggerate how big his brother's victory over Nixon was, and, of course, ignore Nixon's graciousness in not demanding a recount in Illinois or Texas. Even when Bobby wasn't attacking Nixon, there was no better reminder of the Old Nixon, the loser, than a Kennedy in the race. Bobby would try to make Nixon look like a paranoid old dinosaur from the 1950s.

Nixon finally broke his grim silence with Ehrlichman and the aides standing around the TV. "We've seen some terrible forces unleashed," he told his people. "Something bad is going to come of this."

Wallace was the only candidate in the race who

was glad to see Bobby jump in. Wallace thought Bobby could beat LBJ for the nomination and that this would open up more possibilities for Wallace's third-party run. Southern Democrats would never vote for a Kennedy again, and they wouldn't want to vote for a Republican unless they had to. Wallace believed he could sweep the South in a three-way race with Bobby and Nixon. Reagan was the only Republican who worried Wallace. If Johnson and Reagan were the nominees, that would leave little room for Wallace even in the South. But Wallace thought that if he got to run against Bobby the liberal and Nixon the establishment Republican, then all he would have to do is pick off a few states in addition to the South, and he could actually win. Wallace never dreamed the day would come that he was rooting for Bobby Kennedy, but he now was.

George Wallace was not the only one who saw an opening with Bobby now officially in the race. Nelson Rockefeller, the perennial on-again, off-again candidate, was sure Republicans would now worry about losing to another Kennedy. Rockefeller had always been hoping for a draft-Rockefeller movement. He had given Romney public and practical backstage support, but in January, when a reporter asked Rocky off the record about Romney's tendency toward impulsiveness, Rockefeller had said, "You'd better ask a psychiatrist."

Rockefeller's chief adviser was George Hinman,

who now found himself trying like hell to control his boss's excitement about getting into the race. Hinman thought Rockefeller had a good chance of exerting a major influence over the platform and the convention, but only if he stayed out of the race. Hinman figured the odds of a draft were twenty to one. But Rockefeller couldn't stop looking at polls.

A Rockefeller presidential candidacy was going to have, as always, a lot of obstacles. Rocky was a New Deal liberal taking big government to extremes that the party's burgeoning right wing was rejecting. He was a clear hawk on the Vietnam War, when opposing LBJ or Bobby would require highly focused and shifting criticisms of current war policy while offering what would sound like a new plan for peace.

And, of course, there was always the Mrs. Rockefeller problem. Happy had two children with Rockefeller now but still suffered public criticism for giving up custody of her children from her previous marriage. She knew that she had been a liability to Rocky in 1964 and was now very reluctant to campaign.

Rockefeller started excitedly looking at the race immediately after Gene McCarthy's March 12 "win" in New Hampshire. He immediately dispatched Republican campaign consultant John Deardourff to Oregon, which was only ten days away from finalizing the names on the state's presidential primary ballots. Deardourff met with state party leaders to assess Rocky's chances there. Hinman told Rockefeller that if he announced so quickly it would look as if he had not been sincere in supporting Romney. On Friday morning, March 15, the day before Bobby announced, Deardourff arrived back in New York on an overnight flight and went straight to the governor's office, where he found Hinman.

"We can win," said Deardourff.

"You really think that?" said Hinman.

Deardourff reported that everyone important in Oregon Republican political organizations said they would support Rockefeller. Hinman called Rockefeller, and Rockefeller called a meeting at his apartment at 812 Fifth Avenue for the next day.

As Bobby Kennedy stood in the Senate Caucus Room the next morning, Rockefeller's team was preparing a draft statement for Rockefeller's run in Oregon. As they watched Bobby's announcement, they felt a sudden urgency for a Rockefeller campaign, as did liberal Republicans throughout the country.

The next day, a Sunday, St. Patrick's Day, Deardourff shepherded a delegation of Oregonian supporters he had just flown to New York into Rockefeller's palatial apartment. The only home that could say "winner" to them louder than Rocky's was the White House. With the Oregon filing deadline only five days away from locking in the names on the state's primary ballot, the Oregonians outlined the road to a Rockefeller victory in their state. Two statements were drafted.

One version announced a run. The other announced that Rocky had no higher ambition than being governor of New York.

As the Rockefeller team continued to debate their options, they looked down on Fifth Avenue from the apartment windows and saw none other than New York's Senator Robert Kennedy grabbing hand after hand on the St. Patrick's Day parade route. As Rocky watched Bobby already campaigning, he seemed to finally make up his mind. Rocky grabbed the version of the statement announcing he would run and started working on it.

The next day, Monday, March 18, Rocky went to Washington for meeting after meeting with GOP members of Congress to gauge their support. It looked good. That night, he hosted a dinner at a mansion he owned on Foxhall Road in Virginia, not far from Bobby Kennedy's Hickory Hill home. By evening's end, everyone at the dinner was sure that Nelson Rockefeller was running for president.

The next day's **New York Times** made it virtually official. The paper reported that "Governor Rockefeller will announce Thursday afternoon that he is a candidate for the Republican nomination for President and that he will enter the Oregon Republican primary on May 28." It was the traditional heads-up leak that governors and senators usually give their state's biggest newspaper before announcing a presidential campaign. Finally, Rocky was using the

314 PLAYING WITH FIRE

conventional playbook for launching a serious presidential campaign.

With each passing day since Bobby's announcement more political columnists were opining that Rockefeller would be a stronger candidate than Nixon against Bobby Kennedy in the general election. Rockefeller scheduled a press conference for Thursday, March 21, at 2:00 p.m. in the New York Hilton ballroom.

Right on time, Rocky entered the packed room and pushed his way through the cheering throng. Reaching the microphones, he signaled the crowd for quiet. The liberal Republicans in the room, along with those watching on TV around the country, finally had their candidate, their salvation from Tricky Dick.

"I have decided," Rockefeller told them, "to reiterate unequivocally that I am not a candidate campaigning directly or indirectly for the presidency of the United States."

Rockefeller had not told most of his top supporters about his shocking last-minute decision. They were stunned. And hurt. Some felt deceived. Some were bitter. That bitterness would come back to haunt Rocky.

To Richard Nixon, however, the explanation for Rockefeller's reversal was simple enough. "He has the same figures as we have for Oregon," Dick explained to Bill Safire. In February, the Oregon prediction had been Nixon 35 percent, Rocky 35 percent, Reagan 8 percent. Now it was Nixon 47 percent, Rocky 26 percent, Reagan 3 percent.

"It's all over for him," Nixon said. "The only one who can stop us is Reagan."

No one other than Nixon seemed to be taking Ronald Reagan seriously as a contender for the Republican presidential nomination. Reagan was only in his first term as governor, his only elective office other than president of the Screen Actors Guild. He wasn't being taken seriously even as a governor yet. The constant jokes about the actor-turned-politician all shared the premise that Reagan was just an actor whom Republicans had cast to play a governor. The idea of Ronald Reagan having executive command of anything struck most politicians and voters outside of California as surreal. Reagan was the Donald Trump of the 1960s—his connection to voters and political skills were always underestimated before he made a serious run for the White House. Reagan and Trump were underestimated for the same reason: they were both TV stars trying to be taken seriously as national politicians.

California was more accepting of actor politicians than the rest of the country. Helen Gahagan Douglas was an actress before being elected to Congress from a Los Angeles district. George Murphy, like Reagan a former president of the Screen Actors Guild, ran for Senate as a Republican in 1964 and won. To the rest of the country that seemed like something that could happen only in California.

But even in show business—especially in show business—eyes rolled at the thought of a Reagan presidential run. Inside show business, actors are the least respected people in the industry. People in show business generally accept the cliché of actors as self-absorbed know-nothings even more than people outside the industry do. The only respect actors do get in the business is based almost entirely on the importance and seriousness of their roles. If Hollywood had to imagine an actor running for president in real life, it would have to be someone like Gregory Peck or Henry Fonda, someone whom Hollywood would cast as president. Ronnie Reagan was an undistinguished movie actor with credits like **Bedtime for Bonzo**, in which his costar was a chimpanzee. He never had the talent or the gravitas to play a president, not in a serious movie.

Richard Nixon never underestimated the opposition. He had been underestimated, and he knew how much that had helped him. It allowed him to surprise his opponents with things they never saw coming. He saw Reagan as a threat he hoped to manage. When Bobby Kennedy entered the race, Nixon watched the Reagan threat even more closely. He knew some Republicans would want to fight glamour with glamour. That would mean Ronnie versus Bobby in the general election.

Ronald Reagan began his political life as a Democrat. The first vote he ever cast for a Republican was
for Eisenhower in 1952, and like a lot of other Eisenhower Democrats he had mixed feelings about jumping the party ship. He had become deeply concerned
about communism at home and abroad, and as the
head of the Screen Actors Guild he had been helping
the FBI purge suspected communists in Hollywood.
That kind of anticommunist hysteria was bipartisan
then. Reagan's biggest hesitation in voting for Eisenhower in '52 was his choice of running mate.

An errand boy—that's what Reagan thought of
Nixon then. Dishonest, an opportunist, a phony fa-
çade with nothing behind it. Reagan had strongly
supported Helen Gahagan Douglas for Senate in
1950 and knew just how low Nixon could punch.
So Reagan voted for Ike in 1952 and prayed that Ike
would stay healthy. Having Richard Nixon as president, Reagan wrote a friend, would be as bad as having "Uncle Joe" Stalin.

Reagan's transformation from Eisenhower Democrat to right-wing Republican began when he became
the spokesman for the General Electric Company.
General Electric hired Reagan to play a role much
more involved than that of a mere spokesman in
advertising. The company was already a corporate
behemoth delivering energy and technology on a
massive scale to municipalities and the defense industry and dominating electric lighting for both private

and public spaces, as well as the burgeoning market for electrical appliances—electric servants, GE's advertising called them. GE was leading the evolution from the age of the icebox to the age of the refrigerator. GE was going to make America the first country to stop washing clothes by hand and hanging them out to dry on clotheslines and start washing and drying clothes in machines. At home! Soon machines would be washing dishes, and Texas summers would be bearable thanks to a machine stuck in a window blowing cool air into the room. GE needed a friendly face to guide America through all these innovations so that they would be watching a GE television while drinking an ice-cold Coke from a GE refrigerator as their clothes were being washed and dried by GE machines. Ronald Reagan's job at GE was to guide America to a better life.

GE had already begun not merely sponsoring but actually overseeing production of a weekly radio show called **General Electric Theater** with advertising built into the content. Each week it presented a different stand-alone story, starring well-known actors, with introductions, segues, and breaks read by a host promoting GE products. The show often adapted well-known, accessible works of literature, hastily converted to radio drama. Scripted conversations followed the stories. The host and one of the stars would share their amazement at how convenient life had become thanks to affordable electrical appliances.

Following one radio episode the actor William Holden informed the host, Ken Carpenter, "I want you to know, Ken, that in our family, General Electric appliances rate pretty high. We wouldn't be without them." Then Ken Carpenter promoted Holden's latest film, **Stalag 17**.

For the big move to TV, GE took that approach a step further. Reagan's style as presenter was fresher and more natural than the booming style of the invisible radio announcers of the 1940s. On **General Electric Theater**, he spoke in normal tones that made it feel like he meant what he said. Reagan would appear at the beginning of the show, partway through, and at the end. Reagan's presence was the only constant. The show itself was still an anthology, with episodes often written to showcase rugged American individualism and what would later be called family values. Top Hollywood stars knew and liked Reagan and were easy to get. James Dean, Natalie Wood, and Eddie Albert sometimes performed live. Production soon moved from New York to California, and **General Electric Theater** aired on CBS on Sunday nights following the immensely popular **Ed Sullivan Show**. Ratings were high.

At age forty-five, Ronald Reagan had gone from fading movie actor to big star in the new medium. He wasn't up on a big screen in a dark theater, he was right there in people's living rooms more often than their neighbors. America was getting to know Ronald Reagan in a relaxed, intimate way, not in the way they got to know politicians, by listening to boring monotone speeches and reading newspapers. With only three networks to choose from, each week more viewers saw Ronald Reagan on TV in their homes than ever saw him in one of his movies.

If GE's use of Reagan had stopped there, his political career might never have happened. But GE's Reagan strategy quickly became more comprehensive. The presenter was to serve not only as the TV face of GE but also as the embodiment of a new approach to corporate communication.

Lemuel Ricketts Boulware was Reagan's boss at GE. Lem Boulware made all the decisions about how to deploy Ronald Reagan. He had been given a mandate in 1947, following a difficult strike, to do whatever he believed necessary to prevent more strikes without giving the workers too much in negotiations. In the 1950s, Boulware developed an overall plan for accomplishing that goal.

When Reagan wasn't on TV, Lem Boulware kept sending him on the road—the railroad, because Reagan feared flying. Reagan began crisscrossing the country to visit GE plants. Since he was the host of a TV show, a Reagan visit to a GE plant generated excitement. The workers and managers were all fans of **General Electric Theater**. Headlines in plant newspapers and the town's newspapers announced Reagan's imminent appearance. He would arrive to much fanfare, tour the plant, chat with workers and managers in tightly scheduled sessions, smile and shake hands and tell tales of old Hollywood. All of that was reported in company organs, building anticipation for future visits elsewhere. Reagan was the star, of course, and a corporate representative, but also, like the workers, he was a GE employee. Just as he did on the show, in person Ronnie was able to project regular-guy ordinariness and showbiz star power all at once.

At each plant, Reagan gave a prepared talk for a large group. At first the talks only covered GE's paternalistic relationship with its employees, but soon they developed a bigger picture. The overarching message was to cast liberal, federal social policy friendly to organized labor as the enemy of American business and American freedom. The details were folksy and accessible. Some people, Reagan joked, "can't see a fat man standing beside a thin one without automatically concluding the fat man got that way by taking advantage of the thin one." The climaxes were soaring: Americans were at a crossroad and could only go "up to man's age-old dream, the ultimate in individual freedom consistent with law and order or down to the ant heap of totalitarianism." Soon Reagan combined plant visits with presentations at local Rotary clubs and other organizations delivering the same message. He found his voice as a conservative. The speeches GE wrote for him became his belief system. There was a timbre and a rhythm to Reagan's speech voice that made him instantly recognizable and easy to follow. It was a blend of dadlike authority, laying down the law, and delighted, gosh-and-golly Americana. He could swing from his furrowed-brow sternness over the dangers of what he had begun to call collectivism, to a big, open cowboy smile as free as all outdoors. He smiled not only with his mouth but also with his eyes, the brows sweeping upward. He warned of dangers to liberty while extolling the beauty of freedom. And despite what the underestimators said, Reagan could think on his feet.

Reagan was carefully driving home the message that collective bargaining and government regulation hampered not only the company's business profits but also the workers' liberty. Lem Boulware believed that in any labor-contract negotiation, the company should listen sincerely to labor's desires and concerns and then make a bottom-line offer with no fallback position: take it or leave it. If the company took enough care to keep employee satisfaction high—with pay, of course, but with other things, too—and worked hard enough to align the workers' allegiance to the company's goals, then the workers would naturally want to collaborate with a system that had their best interests at heart. The unions wouldn't be busted. They'd be marginalized.

Enemies of this approach, in Boulware's view, included prolabor legislation, mandatory union membership, worker solidarity, high corporate tax rates, and a general suspicion of corporations. GE workers had to be taught to view such efforts as disrupting the balance that made for a healthy company on which the workers' future depended. Boulware commanded a vast budget for doing things that the GE consumer never saw. GE published four major periodicals for its workers, employing writers, editors, and designers. The company ran classes and created curricula on free-market economics and decentralized management systems. GE educated thirty-two thousand employees at a headquarters in Ossining, New York. Classes were offered at every GE plant on company time. After work, employees were encouraged to join weekly book clubs, open to spouses as well. The books were free and they covered free-market thinking, philosophies of liberty, the dangers of communism, the benefits of decentralized management, and other subjects dear to Lem Boulware's heart. Discussions led by employee-relations managers allowed Boulware to get a sense of issues of concern to both workers and managers.

At a hectic travel pace, Reagan brought Boulware's management, political, and economic philosophy to thousands of GE people, even as he was bringing GE branding to millions every week on TV. Ronald Reagan became what a later era would call an integrated brand voice.

Like many a new religious convert, Reagan showed intense zealousness for conservatism. He was a quick study. Train travel gave him time to read. He was trying to memorize everything he read: newsletters, management charts, books by free-market economists of the Austrian school like F. A. Hayek and Ludwig von Mises. In midlife he was reborn not only into a new kind of job that Boulware and he were inventing together—business theater, it would later be called by marketeers—but also as a thinker and leader. Reagan projected what he took in. There was a kind of method acting involved. Reagan was not faking it; he was feeling it and the feeling showed. If this was acting, it was acting in real life with America as the set and the American people as the supporting cast.

In 1958, Lem Boulware took Reagan away from plant visits and sent him almost exclusively on what Reagan called the mashed-potato circuit. He did dinner speeches for business groups and political clubs around the country. Boulware believed that the time to move the electorate came between, not during, presidential campaigns. **General Electric Theater** was at the top of the ratings and Reagan was one of the most recognized men in the country. While Reagan spoke in banquet halls, Boulware traveled the country talking to elites. He helped fund William F. Buckley's conservative start-up magazine, **National Review**. Reagan began writing his own speeches about the national debt, socialized medicine, federal programs, and especially the "confiscatory taxation" that paid for it all.

In 1962, Reagan began citing the Tennessee Valley Authority as a prime example of government spending run amok. And that was a big problem for GE. The TVA was a classic New Deal program of the FDR era. Its dams had prevented floods, provided hydroelectric power, and enhanced economic development in the rural Tennessee River Valley. Reagan told audiences that annual interest on the TVA debt added up to five times as much as the annual flood damage it had sought to correct.

At the time GE was bidding on $50 million of TVA business. GE considered firing Reagan but instead told him to take the TVA references out of his speeches, which he did.

Attorney General Robert Kennedy took an interest in a waiver that the Screen Actors Guild issued in 1952 under Reagan's leadership. The waiver exclusively permitted one agency, MCA, to engage in unlimited film production, contrary to SAG bylaws; Reagan had also negotiated a deal giving away actors' residual rights in films made before 1960, and again MCA benefited, having bought Paramount's film library. Did Reagan violate labor laws and betray his union's interest in making sweetheart deals with MCA? The attorney general might not have been so interested in that question if Reagan hadn't been attacking his brother. At a speech in Pasadena Reagan accused JFK and Arthur Schlesinger, by name, of bringing collectivist statism to America and cringing before the Kremlin. Reagan was subpoenaed to testify before a grand jury on potential conflicts of interest when running SAG. Reagan testified under oath that he simply could not recall the details of the events in 1952.

GE got increasingly worried about where Reagan's rhetoric was taking him. Controversy is not good for the face of a company. So GE fired Reagan. **General Electric Theater** folded up. Reagan soon found himself flailing. He tried to get back into movie acting. He published a memoir. He finally registered as a Republican—despite the intensity of the conversion, he'd never bothered to switch parties—and campaigned for a right-winger running for reelection to Congress. For a year he had a job introducing **Death Valley Days**, a western-themed anthology TV series sponsored by 20 Mule Team Borax. Reagan also acted in twenty-one of the **Death Valley** episodes. In 1962, he endorsed Richard Nixon, the man Reagan used to despise, for governor of California.

In 1964, Reagan campaigned for Barry Goldwater and he campaigned hard. He didn't play the chess game Nixon did with the Goldwater campaign— one step forward, two steps back, simply to maintain the appearance of campaigning for Goldwater while keeping enough distance to avoid the stain of defeat. For right-wing conservatives, Reagan's fierce commitment to the Goldwater campaign followed by his election to governor two years later made Ronald Reagan the only and obvious choice for president in 1968.

In the closing weeks of the Goldwater campaign, Reagan was asked to do a stump speech for Goldwater on TV for national broadcast. Reagan asked for a large studio audience so he could feel the crowd's reaction to his speech. He wanted to be able to see people's eyes, not just a camera lens. In that speech, called "A Time for Choosing," televised as paid Goldwater advertising, Reagan said everything he'd been saying for years. For the 1964 election he cast the choice as occurring in a moment of extreme crisis. This was the stern, even grim, Reagan. He barely smiled. It wasn't a time for charm, it was a time for choosing.

"No nation in history," Reagan told his audience in a studio and viewers from coast to coast, had ever "survived a tax burden amounting to a third of is national income. . . . You and I are told we must choose between a left or right, but I suggest there is no such thing as a left or right. There is only an up or down. Up to man's age-old dream—the maximum of individual freedom consistent with order—or down to the ant heap of totalitarianism."

The phrase "consistent with order" was the first draft of what was to become "law and order" in 1968.

Republicans knew what "order" meant—no more riots, no more demonstrations and protests, the stuff that "permissive" liberal Democrats like Bobby Kennedy tolerated and sometimes even supported, the stuff that was tearing the country apart in the eyes of conservatives. For them, order had completely broken down, and it had to be restored with no compromise. Ronald Reagan looked like the man for that job.

"A Time for Choosing" became known among Reagan's supporters simply as "the speech." During "the speech" Reagan held a big piece of the national mood in his hands. "The speech" raised an astonishing $8 million for Goldwater.

Ronald Reagan won the governorship by beating the man who beat Richard Nixon for the governorship. Therefore, Reagan was a stronger candidate than Nixon. That's what Reagan people were telling themselves and anyone else who would listen in 1968. But Reagan had served only one year as governor by then and no one thought that was enough governing experience to be president. Reagan knew he had to counter that, so he became an earnest student of government. At a governors' conference, Reagan asked simple questions about taxation that tried Nelson Rockefeller's patience. "Oh, Christ, Ronnie!" blurted Rockefeller. Whenever Governor Reagan was in New York, he always met with the master of big-state governing, Governor Rockefeller. Reagan learned to bring pragmatism to governing. Despite his antigovernment rhetoric, he signed into law the biggest budget in history along with the biggest-ever tax increases to pay for it.

Unlike Nixon, there was no ambiguity in Reagan's positions. Tricky Dick was always leaving himself escape routes from his policy positions. Reagan wholeheartedly embraced the blend of spiritual and economic revivalism preached by those favoring free markets, white communities' right to exclude black people, and militant aggression against the Soviet Union and global communism, including in Vietnam. This meant doing battle with the enemy within, American liberalism. The right-wingers wanted to put an end to all big-government, civil rights liberalism within the Republican Party. As Barry Goldwater proved in 1964, it was easy to make their positions sound angry, harsh, and old-fashioned. Only Ronald Reagan could make right-wing Republicanism sound good-natured and friendly.

Reagan was always resolute, reassuring, smooth. He spent years as the face of GE perfecting the sound of the reliable neighbor who's just here to help. He gave his words a warm, almost romantic, almost religious, and always American glow.

The Reagan glow seemed to come naturally. He was, all Republicans agreed, a great communicator. Never close to being the best actor in Hollywood, Ronald Reagan was the best actor in politics.

EIGHTEEN

"STAND UP AND BE COUNTED"

Bobby Kennedy's campaign announcement angered Gene McCarthy, worried Richard Nixon, excited Nelson Rockefeller and Ronald Reagan, and haunted Lyndon Johnson.

On the day Bobby announced, the president's planned big speech on Vietnam was still making the rounds of the executive department for review and suggestions. The Tet Offensive made the Vietnam speech both necessary and impossible. Johnson couldn't say anything in the speech about Tet other than claiming victory, which the public did not believe. He couldn't say anything about seeking peace without sounding like Tet was forcing him to retreat or he was bending to the antiwar candidate who just "beat" him in New Hampshire. And now Bobby.

Every policy speech is a political speech. LBJ's Vietnam speech had to describe a war policy everyone except the Peace Now crowd could support and thereby cut off lines of attack against Johnson by the presidential candidates. LBJ knew there was no one in the Defense Department or State Department or the White House who was going to find the words to cut off Bobby Kennedy's line of attack on Lyndon Johnson's war. LBJ knew Bobby was in a unique position to make him the sole owner of the war. Bobby was the only candidate who was there at the creation inside the Kennedy administration. Only Bobby could take JFK's fingerprints off Vietnam and say President Kennedy never intended to escalate U.S. assistance to all-out war. LBJ knew that no speechwriter could take that knockout punch away from Bobby.

He had secretly been writing resignation letters since 1948. It was Lady Bird who always made sure those letters remained secret. Perhaps those letters were just his way of getting his wife to sympathize with him. He always seemed to feel sorry for himself before anyone else did. LBJ didn't mention a resignation letter when Bobby announced. He didn't show his staff any fear of Bobby the way Nixon did when he sat there in that hotel room staring silently at the TV screen. The Bobby announcement seemed to energize Johnson. Maybe it was adrenaline. Maybe hatred. Maybe both.

The day after Bobby's announcement, the president had to give a speech to the National Farmers Union in Minneapolis. Johnson knew everyone would be studying his words and tone for the effect of the McCarthy "win" and the Kennedy announcement. LBJ had nothing new to say about Vietnam, so he kept it simple and talked more about his Great Society proposals. There was no doubt for anyone in that room that Lyndon Johnson was all in. He banged both fists on the lectern and boomed, "Make no mistake about it, I don't want a man in here to go back thinking otherwise: we are going to win!" He ordered the farmers to "stand up and be counted!"

The Vietnam speech, scheduled now for the end of March but not yet announced, was becoming more belligerent. The worked-over draft now insisted there would be no bombing halt without reciprocal concessions from North Vietnam, and that 50,000 more reserves would be called up. But Johnson was still looking for a new approach, and when Secretary of State Dean Rusk suggested reducing the rate of bombing North Vietnam during the rainy season, Johnson seized on the idea as an incentive for getting the North to the negotiating table.

LBJ convened Dean Rusk; Clark Clifford; Dean Acheson; Walt Rostow; Harry McPherson, now LBJ's special counsel; McGeorge Bundy; and others, joined by top military men like retired general Omar Bradley. They all had been strong supporters of the war. Now they were nearly unanimous in advising the president to find a politically acceptable way out of the war. Credible steps toward peace would serve American interests while knocking down the candidacies of Nixon, Kennedy, and McCarthy all at once. Handled properly, Johnson might emerge victorious in Vietnam and in the election. That became the new objective of the Vietnam speech. And so the speech scheduled for the end of March had to be ripped apart and put back together. Fast.

THERE WAS NOTHING JOHNSON could say in his Vietnam speech that would change the plans for massive protests at the Democratic Convention in Chicago. Tom Hayden and David Dellinger were once again working with Abbie Hoffman and Jerry Rubin to merge their forces into one huge constant demonstration covering every aspect of the convention. They were trying to duplicate the success of their March on Washington in October 1967, but amplified across four convention days. The idea was to attract a critical mass not just for protest but for a kind of temporary, alternative, festive, confrontational street society, at odds with the police, the war, politics, capitalism, and Lyndon Johnson.

As the plans for Chicago developed, the seriousness of Hayden and Dellinger's National Mobilization Committee to End the War in Vietnam (MOBE) and the psychedelic kookiness of Hoffman and Rubin's Yippies began coming into conflict. The unity of the strands of the radical New Left about exactly what to do in Chicago was challenged first by the success of Gene McCarthy in New Hampshire and then by Bobby's announcement that he was running. What if LBJ was not the Democrats' nominee in Chicago?

MOBE's vision for the Chicago demonstration came out of a long tradition of careful tactical planning by generations of American radicals. Tom Hayden and his friend Rennie Davis defined themselves as revolutionaries in a fairly familiar way. Beginning by attacking Johnson on Vietnam, they wanted the McCarthy supporters to look beyond the playing-by-the-rules tactic of supporting an antiwar candidate and to imagine new ways of overturning the existing political system.

The MOBE and SDS plan for Chicago was to cause an overt confrontation between what Hayden called "a police state and a people's movement." Rennie Davis predicted that when the world saw tens of thousands of unarmed young protesters held away from the Democratic Party's convention site by tanks, barbed wire, and uniformed troops, America would see that "the Democrats can't hold a convention without calling in the army." But that tactic would only work for McCarthy's supporters who had gotten "clean for Gene" and campaigned for him door-to-door in New Hampshire if LBJ was being nominated. Only then would the McCarthy kids get it—the system was irredeemable. They would stop listening to insider liberals like Al Lowenstein.

MOBE and SDS had lost all hope in electoral politics. "Perhaps a small minority," Tom Hayden said, "by setting ablaze New York and Washington, could damage this country forever in the court of world opinion. Urban guerrillas are the only realistic alternative at this time to electoral politics or mass armed resistance." Hayden called the communist society in North Vietnam more democratic than the United States. He was one of the few Americans who had been to North Vietnam. Hayden made the first of several trips to North Vietnam in 1965. He visited factories and villages. He coauthored a book about that trip titled **The Other Side**. On his second trip to Hanoi in 1967, he secured the release of three American prisoners of war whom Hayden was allowed to pick up in Cambodia and escort home.

That Tom Hayden and Rennie Davis were open to guerrilla violence disturbed Dave Dellinger, the pacifist in MOBE leadership. Dellinger was a radical but also a true believer in principled nonviolence and war resistance. The three MOBE leaders all believed in the same objectives. Their only difference of opinion was on tactics. Picking out the MOBE guys at the large group planning meetings for Chicago was easy. They were the clean-shaven ones. Dellinger looked like a professor and Hayden and Davis looked like perpetual grad students.

The Yippies were easy to spot, too. Abbie Hoffman, thirty-two, and Jerry Rubin, thirty, were explosions of hair, sideburns, beards, dazzling headbands, and kaleidoscopic clothes that seemed randomly selected. Since the March on Washington, they had been amplifying their trademark mix of silly stunts and social confrontation. With leaders like the anarchic comedian and writer Paul Krassner and the postbeat poet and psychedelic garage bandleader Ed Sanders, the Yippie was a New York City phenomenon, matching the Haight-Ashbury peace-love vibe with the snark, profanity, and daring of the East Village. Yippie actions focused on New York landmarks such as the New York Stock Exchange. Abbie and Jerry showed up there one day and dropped one-dollar bills from the gallery to the trading floor. The brokers and traders scrambled to grab up the cash. When the police came to remove the Yippies, the stock-market men started booing the cops. That was Yippie nirvana: absurdist chaos.

Like Hayden and Davis, Hoffman and Rubin saw themselves as guerrillas, but theirs was really guerrilla theater, a revolution of the mind. Their medium was the modern publicity machine. Richard Nixon said, "This campaign is about television." Abbie Hoffman said, "A modern revolutionary group heads for the television station, not the factory." Where members of MOBE were organizing for a showdown with the state by drawing on texts from Karl

Marx to Herbert Marcuse to Frantz Fanon, Abbie and Jerry called ideology a brain disease. The real secret meaning of the term "Yippie," according to Jerry Rubin, was "It's nonsense. Its basic informational statement is a blank piece of paper. . . . Yippie is just an excuse to rebel."

So to Abbie and Jerry, guys like Tom Hayden and Rennie Davis and their sometime mentor Dave Dellinger looked a lot like the same uptight grown-ups the Yippie revolution was dedicated to humiliating. "They all wear suits and ties," Abbie complained of MOBE and SDS. "They sit down and talk rationally."

The Yippies' plan for action in Chicago in August was to think up outrageous public statements, wild gestures, and one-liners, put them on posters, run them off on mimeograph machines in East Village basements, and hand them out at the convention. Their overall plan was reduced to one big poster announcing "Festival of Life: Music. Lights. Free. Theater. Magic. August 25–30, Chicago."

Consistency was for squares, so the Yippies deliberately sent mixed messages. "We will burn Chicago to the ground!" was combined with "We will fuck on the beaches! We demand the Politics of Ecstasy! Acid for all! Abandon the Creeping Meatball! YIPPIE! Chicago, August 25–30."

These communiques actually parodied both the sober rhetoric of the New Left and the idealistic new spiritualism of the counterculture. When the Yippies presented agenda items for Chicago that included a dawn ass-washing ceremony, they didn't crack a smile, but they imagined the youth of America giggling themselves silly over that one. The Yippies announced they would schedule daily meetings in Chicago in which "psychedelic longhaired mutant-jissomed peace leftists will consort with known dope fiends, spilling out onto the sidewalks in pornape disarray each afternoon."

Abbie Hoffman worked up a single 8½-by-11-inch poster that brought Yippie communications to the ultimate. The page crammed together so many brief expressions that it seemed to say it all, while saying nothing. A small representative segment:

— ENERGY—MRS. LEARY'S COW—BLOOM—JIM FOURATT—NO CENSORSHIP—BEAUTY—KISS—NIRVANA—FLASH —SHIRLEY CLARKE—BEADS—BIRDS—GO—BEWARE LOCAL POLICE ARMED AND CONSIDERED DANGEROUS—FOOD—GAMES—DICK GREGORY—HUG—TENTS—LOVE—CARAVAN—WONDERFUL—FUGS—SKYDIVING—BLACKS—FREE CITY . . .

The list went on and on—something for everyone in the target audience. All of it, every word from the

Yippies and MOBE, was aimed at Lyndon Johnson. But what if Johnson wasn't the nominee?

Now a Kennedy would be attending the Democratic National Convention in Chicago. The New Left had cast that convention as a Festival of Death, presided over by chief pig Lyndon Johnson for his ongoing murderous war machine in Vietnam. Bobby Kennedy, running against the war, would cast a new glow of life and hope and youth over politics as usual in Chicago.

Gene McCarthy was one thing. But Bobby was something else. Hayden scorned McCarthy as a weak reformer, a shill for the system, while the Yippies expressed a condescending affection for Gene. Rooting for McCarthy, Abbie Hoffman said, was like rooting for the New York Mets. McCarthy couldn't win, and once he lost, the Clean for Gene kids were sure to go radical: that was the way everyone planning demonstrations at the convention saw it. Then came Bobby.

Even for Tom Hayden the Kennedy mystique still played. Some of it might have been tribal. They were both from Irish American families. When Bobby was scoping out the New Left, they had actually met. That was in February 1967, when Bobby's position on Vietnam was still to support the president. Hayden was working as an organizer in the black community in Newark and had already moved far to the left of his earlier hopes for radical reform. Jack Newfield set up the meeting because Bobby wanted to connect with the brightest people on the radical left. Hayden found himself grudgingly impressed with Bobby's sincerity about the problems of poverty and racism. Hayden had no problem talking about guerrilla tactics against Lyndon Johnson while ignoring Gene McCarthy. But if Bobby won the nomination, Hayden knew he was going to need a plan B for Chicago.

From the Yippie perspective, Bobby was going to ruin their fun. "We expected concentration camps," Jerry Rubin said, "and we got Bobby Kennedy." Abbie Hoffman openly envied Bobby's public style, which he called "participation mystique." Abbie thought Bobby was the only politician who encroached on the Yippies' turf. He said Bobby was a master of "theater in the streets. He played it to the hilt."

And on March 23 and 24, in a suburb outside Chicago, MOBE, the Yippies, various Black Power organizations, and others convened to coordinate their plans for the August convention. The mood was uncomfortable and strained. MOBE tried to hold serious planning sessions, while Abbie and Jerry kept interrupting to propose making the protests' chief goal the elimination of pay toilets. Black militants expressed skepticism that anything about this protest would further any radical cause. They all agreed to reject both McCarthy and Kennedy as real peace candidates. But everyone inside and outside the meeting knew that agreement would be meaningless if McCarthy or Kennedy did win the nomination. Most of the protesters would become supporters of the convention's nominee.

That same week, Jerry Rubin wrote an article in the **Village Voice** hoping to dampen enthusiasm for Bobby. He wrote, "We all live the dream of the celebrity candidate. Yet only massive populist revolution can liberate the imprisoned soul of the people of America. . . . The most aware attitude toward the election is (1) not to vote; (2) to vote for yourself, a national 'Vote for Me' campaign; (3) to vote for a close friend." Jerry Rubin's final line of the piece was a prediction: "Today's shaved nice McCarthy-RFK collegians will be tomorrow's yippies!"

NINETEEN

"IT'S NOT IMPORTANT WHAT HAPPENS TO ME"

Nothing about Bobby's coming into the race could visibly ruffle Gene McCarthy. His pride ran too deep for that. Privately, he was calling Bobby destructive, vindictive, a coward. Millions of McCarthy supporters now felt the same way.

Publicly, McCarthy did get off some insults thinly disguised as jokes. "I got an A in economics," he told reporters, "and Bobby got only a C. . . . He plays touch football, I play football. He plays softball, I play baseball. He skates in Rockefeller Center, I play hockey."

Bobby had barely started campaigning, with virtually no organization, wasn't even on the ballot in the Wisconsin primary, and suddenly all the admiring attention aimed at McCarthy's upset in New Hampshire shifted over to Bobby. On March 24, a Gallup poll had RFK beating Johnson 44 to 41, and Johnson beating McCarthy 59 to 29. Richard Goodwin was secretly planning to leave the McCarthy campaign. He'd always been a Kennedy man, and McCarthy's aloof approach to politics had never sat well with him. And there was the Gallup poll saying Bobby could win and McCarthy couldn't. Goodwin began secretly writing speeches for Kennedy.

Al Lowenstein felt he couldn't in good conscience leave McCarthy now, despite the lack of a real relationship with him. Lowenstein hoped to find ways to merge the two campaigns. He saw himself as forming the key link. The huge problem for Lowenstein was that after struggling for so long to get one Dump Johnson candidate, now there were two and that was only good for Johnson. A split in the antiwar vote in the Democratic primaries would guarantee Johnson the nomination. Lowenstein was sure there would have to be a coalition. Gene and Bobby would simply have to unite against LBJ. The California primary in June would tell that story. The candidate who did best in California would have to take the lead against Johnson, and the loser would have to support him. That was Lowenstein's plan. McCarthy true believers were not ready for Lowenstein's plan and might never be. The people closest to Gene, from Abigail and Mary and many of the kids working closely with them, considered mere tolerance of RFK a form of heresy. Some McCarthy supporters were showing up wherever RFK campaigned just to heckle him.

America had never seen a candidate like Gene McCarthy, a genuine antiwar candidate credibly challenging a war-making president. McCarthy supporters were watching the first brave presidential candidacy they or anyone else had ever seen. It was also the most important presidential candidacy they had ever seen—the only one that was about life and death. Gene was the only one who understood what this election had to be about, and he was the only one brave enough to run himself to make it about the most important thing his supporters cared about: the war. Life and death. His supporters admired him and loved him for that. Getting them to vote for someone else would be as painful as a divorce.

Al Lowenstein began to despair. Instead of forming a key link, he found himself under suspicion from both sides. McCarthy supporters suspected Lowenstein of treason, hypocrisy, sophistry; Kennedy people found him naively loyal to McCarthy in the face of polls showing only Bobby could win. Lowenstein started looking at a suburban New York congressional seat on Long Island to make a run for Congress himself.

SOME OF McCARTHY'S PEOPLE with Kennedy ties were not confused. Blair Clark, despite Kennedy friendships since college, was staying on as McCarthy's campaign manager. Lowenstein's partner Curtis Gans did not share his dual loyalties. Gans was sticking with McCarthy and was running the campaign with Clark. And the battle for Wisconsin was going amazingly well, despite Bobby's announcement.

The Wisconsin primary election was coming on April 2, and Bobby wasn't in it. Despite all the breathless national attention on Bobby's new campaign, the McCarthy campaign was flying high in Wisconsin on the optimism and energy coming out of New Hampshire. The "Clean for Gene" student volunteers were pouring into Wisconsin and going door-to-door. With all the new tension about the Kennedy campaign distracting McCarthy's national campaign office in Washington, Gene, Abigail, and Mary were amazed to see that the local Wisconsin organization ran itself better than the national organization did. There in the heartland, where the McCarthys' Catholic social liberalism had been born, tireless local volunteers carried on a true people's effort, taking the spirit of New Hampshire to the next step.

Establishment Democrats kept trying to write New Hampshire off as a fluke. They still try to do that whenever an insurgent suddenly poses a real challenge to the Democrats' presumed front-runner in presidential primaries. They did that when Barack Obama beat Hillary Clinton in Iowa in 2008. And they did it again when Bernie Sanders beat Hillary Clinton in New Hampshire in 2016. Establishment Democrats are always the last to know when something new and important is happening in their party. One LBJ campaign memo suggested that they hire "one of those electric guitar 'musical' groups" to play at rallies, "some kids with long hair and fancy clothes, giving them a name such as 'The Black Beards' or 'The White Beards.'" When Larry O'Brien went personally to Wisconsin to inspect the Johnson campaign office in Milwaukee, he found it listless, but the most important thing happening in the Johnson campaign was not happening in the primary states. It was happening in the speech-writing shop at the White House.

They were working on the Vietnam speech. It was scheduled to be nationally televised at the end of the month, right before the Wisconsin vote. The speech was intended to bring voters back to LBJ on the eve of the Wisconsin primary.

Gene McCarthy appeared at a rally at the Veterans Memorial Coliseum in Madison, Wisconsin. He had just received the endorsement of Madison's **Capital Times** newspaper. The overflow crowd swelled to eighteen thousand, his biggest ever. His audience was composed not just of antiwar students from the University of Wisconsin at Madison. There were people of all ages—people who appeared to be from all walks of life. The cheering in the auditorium was deafening, but the coliseum grew silent and intimate when the crowd needed to hear their hero's words. The optimism in the air was palpable. In that room it was easy to get the feeling that there were no other candidates in the race. On that stage it seemed like even Gene could forget about Bobby. The McCarthy team at the coliseum had the same feeling they'd had in the closing days of the New Hampshire primary: hope for the redemption of American democracy. At the podium, the poet running for president began by reciting Walt Whitman's "I Hear America Singing":

> Poets to come! Orators, singers, musicians
> to come!
> Not today is to justify me, and answer what I
> am for;
> But you, a new brood, native, athletic,
> continental, greater than before known.
> Arouse! Arouse—for you must justify me—
> you must answer.

Eugene McCarthy was the last American presidential candidate who thought flattering an audience's intelligence was the way to win their hearts and their votes.

Martin Luther King Jr. was also going to have his spirits lifted when he addressed a huge crowd after landing in Memphis on the evening of Monday, March 18. He was met at the plane by his old friend the Reverend James Lawson, accompanied by Jesse Epps, a young union organizer from Mississippi, there in support of organizing the sanitation workers. With Dr. King were Andrew Young, Ralph Abernathy, and others.

The group went straight to Memphis's Masonic Temple. Lawson had promised King that ten thousand people would turn out to hear him that night, but he was wrong. There were more than fifteen thousand. There was nowhere left to stand. The aisles were filled. The building pulsated with energy in anticipation of the arrival of Dr. King.

As Martin's group approached the building, they realized they needed more muscle to get him inside. The overflow crowd outside was as thick as the lucky ones packed inside. So they formed a protective wedge of local preachers and sanitation workers to get Dr. King inside as the hall seemed to be vibrating. At the sight of Dr. King, the place began erupting with an endless, rolling roar that filled the space with deafening approval. Hung from the rafters was a huge banner: "Not by Might, Not by Power, Saith the Lord of Hosts, but by My Spirit."

Moving toward the stage inside the human wedge, Dr. King could see local ministers already gathered up there along with union officials. There were also three garbage cans on the stage, filled with cash donations for the striking workers.

When Dr. King finally turned toward the microphones and faced the crowd, the roar abruptly dropped to a hum. They didn't want to miss a word. They knew they were seeing a man who was already a legend. They knew they were about to hear the most gifted public speaker of his time. They knew they would be telling their children and grandchildren about this speech for the rest of their lives. They knew they were witnessing history. The crowd was beyond anything Dr. King expected. This was the largest indoor gathering in the history of the civil rights movement. This was the Poor People's Campaign.

Dr. King said, "You are demanding that this city will respect the dignity of labor. So often we overlook the worth and significance of those who are not in the professional jobs, in the so-called big jobs, but let me say to you tonight, that whenever you are engaged in work that serves humanity, for the building of humanity, it has dignity and it has worth." He promised to return to Memphis soon to lead a march in support of the strikers.

BOBBY KENNEDY'S ABRUPTLY LAUNCHED campaign was bringing him a rush of attention good and bad that was already overwhelming. It ranged from a thrill among the Kennedy lovers, to outrage for dividing McCarthy's peace movement, to reenergized hatred from permanent Kennedy haters. In the second half of March, Bobby traveled all over the country, and mostly it was like the New York Senate campaign all over again on a far bigger scale. He was mobbed at the airports, on the college campuses, in the shopping centers.

Often young women led the way, screaming, "Bobby! Bobby! Bobby!" Among the rallying crowds, he could see the signs: "Bobby Is Groovy," "Sock It to 'Em, Bobby."

He was heckled and razzed, too, by McCarthy supporters. They had signs of their own: "Gene for Integrity. RFK: Leader of Youth or Rebellious Opportunist?" They yelled, "Where were you in New Hampshire?"

"At least McCarthy was on time!" shouted a student in Oregon.

"Yeah, but I'm worth waiting for," Bobby said, drawing laughter and cheers. He was relaxed. The difficult decision was behind him. Now the campaign team had to make Bobby look unstoppable, the voice of the people. "We're going to do it a new way," Adam Walinsky told reporters. "In the streets."

The young staffers Walinsky and Jeff Greenfield went on the road with Bobby. In many ways, they knew his audience better than Bobby did. The crowds were mostly ecstatic explosions of the New Politics. Bobby's presence invoked Jack Kennedy, but his words did not. The JFK political and governing legacy was Old Politics now. And Bobby admitted it. "The answers of the New Frontier," Bobby told students in Utah, "are not necessarily applicable to the problems of the future." The space race, containment of communism, and covert intervention were replaced by racial justice, economic opportunity, and no more war.

Old Politics still worked for getting delegates. The older generation, the JFK men Schlesinger, Sorensen, Salinger, were working on that. The public, grass-roots, groundswell feeling was meant to show the party establishment that RFK could win the general election. At campaign headquarters, the elders counted and figured and reached out to power brokers in key states.

To go into the convention with a majority, Bobby would need 1,312 delegates. It was hard to see where more than 800 would come from. Richard Daley could deliver the entire Illinois delegation en masse. Despite Daley's Kennedy connections and support for JFK, the mayor was establishment all the way, so he would probably stick with LBJ. Most states didn't have primaries, so getting their delegates was purely an inside game. In thirty-seven states, governors and party officials controlled the delegates and told them how to vote. That's how most of the delegate votes at the convention would be delivered. The governors would be betting on who would win in November. They wanted to place safe bets, so if polls showed LBJ and Bobby both beating Nixon in November, they would stick with LBJ. If they went with Bobby at the convention and LBJ still got the nomination and won the election, they would expect President Johnson to find every way he could to hurt them and their states in federal funding formulas for the next four years. They would always stick with the incumbent president unless he was a sure loser in November. That's what Bobby was hoping to prove with wins in the primaries.

The party chairman, John Bailey, told Bobby directly that the only way he could imagine the party ever giving him the nomination would be if Bobby won an overwhelming Kennedy sweep of the primaries.

Everyone agreed that the most important upcoming primary was California. It was the biggest state having a primary, and its voters resembled the national electorate more than smaller homogenous states like New Hampshire. And California came toward the end of the primary season on June 4, giving California voters a longer look at the candidates. Bobby was already campaigning in California in late March and the Kennedy magic was working.

In Sacramento, Bobby reached for the support of white working-class voters who were increasingly suspicious of liberal Democratic Party politics. In the blazing sun at a shopping center, fifteen thousand people jammed into a space for five thousand. They cheered Bobby's attack on the Vietnam War and mobbed him afterward, grabbing his clothes, ripping off buttons, almost climbing on his car. That evening in San Jose a crowd of seven thousand, almost all Mexican Americans, cheered Bobby so loudly that most of the crowd couldn't hear a word he said. Again he lost his cufflinks as the crowd reached to touch him. His shirttail was pulled out. In wealthy Republican Monterey, the highway to the airport where Bobby's plane was scheduled to land became a parking lot of people wanting to welcome him. Local police had never seen anything like it. At the Greek Theatre in Los Angeles, the huge crowd behaved exactly as they would at a Rolling Stones concert, creating a frenzied uproar that drowned out much of what the candidate had to say on racial justice, poverty, and the war. At all of the big crowd events, the next Kennedy presidency seemed inevitable.

When Bobby jumped into the race, it was already too late for him to compete in Wisconsin. The Wisconsin filing deadline had already passed and the March 28 deadline for getting into the May 7 Indiana primary was fast approaching.

Bobby was closely watching polls in Wisconsin. What he saw made him hopeful for his chances in Indiana. McCarthy was looking very strong against Johnson in Wisconsin. McCarthy could really win this one, actually get more votes than LBJ this time. That would badly wound Johnson's campaign. Still, stealing the nomination from an incumbent president was going to take some kind of miracle. On March 24, the **New York Times** predicted that Johnson would get more than 65 percent of the delegate votes at the convention.

With his national tour proving that he could thrill huge crowds, and with McCarthy poised to possibly beat LBJ in Wisconsin, Bobby saw Indiana as his first, best chance to stake his claim to the nomination. On the evening of March 31, nearly the eve of the Wisconsin primary, Bobby ended his national tour. He boarded a plane for New York, hoping for a big McCarthy win over LBJ in Wisconsin. After McCarthy weakened Johnson, Bobby would be ready to take on both of them in Indiana.

That same evening, President Johnson was finally ready to deliver his Vietnam speech to the nation. It was scheduled for 9:00 p.m. All three networks would interrupt regularly scheduled programming and broadcast the speech live. Most of that day, like all days now, the president could hear protest chants outside the White House. "Hey, hey, LBJ! How many kids did you kill today?"

The speech drafts had undergone so many changes that its early drafters wouldn't recognize it. There would be some surprises tonight for the nation and for the speechwriters.

The LBJ campaign team had been stunned by Wisconsin poll numbers giving McCarthy an outright majority of the vote over Johnson. The Democratic establishment, of course, publicly disagreed with the polls. The Republican establishment in the person of Richard Nixon did, too. Nixon had told reporters that he believed LBJ would win Wisconsin. LBJ found some time in the afternoon before the speech to sit down with his campaign people and review their plans for victory. If Johnson was going to win Wisconsin, tonight's speech on the war was going to have to do it.

The final drafting was done at the cabinet level by Clark Clifford and Dean Rusk. They worked on new drafts until late the night before. It was almost all Vietnam now. Very little had survived on the economy. A reference to the Alamo was cut. At the last minute, Johnson added some words of his own. The cabinet didn't know about them. They were fed into the teleprompter separately. The president had not even made up his mind whether he would say them.

Lady Bird would be standing by, off camera. She and Lyndon had a signal. If the president did decide he would say the additional words, he would forewarn his first lady by lifting his right hand.

At 9:00 p.m. that night, when the president began his address to the nation, Gene McCarthy was making a speech in a Wisconsin auditorium. Bobby Kennedy was in the air headed home to New York. Richard Nixon was especially tense and expectant. He had planned his own Vietnam speech, which he'd postponed. He wanted to hear what Johnson had to say first. Anything sounding like a peace announcement would be a problem for Nixon.

Everyone working on all of the campaigns who wasn't on a stage or a plane watched the LBJ speech on TV or listened on the radio. At McCarthy's Wisconsin campaign headquarters at the Schroeder Hotel in Milwaukee, Richard Goodwin and Blair Clark, along with the journalist Theodore White and several campaign staff, gathered in front of a TV. Throughout the hotel, the "Clean for Gene" kids were putting aside their work to switch on the TV sets. Blair Clark was enraged by Johnson's timing, saying the broadcast was an abuse of presidential power. It was clearly a massive blast of LBJ campaign advertising on the eve of the Wisconsin primary.

The single camera feeding all the networks found the president seated at his desk in the Oval Office. That was the only thing about the speech that wasn't a surprise.

For months, Johnson had looked haggard and ailing. Now he looked fine. His voice was strong and clear. He spoke with calm and confidence. The president announced he would halt the bombing of North Vietnam. He would unilaterally de-escalate American war making in Vietnam. American attacks would cease throughout 90 percent of Vietnam. He would seek a negotiated peace with North Vietnam. New U.S. troops would still go to Southeast Asia, but only in relief and support of troops already there. Johnson defended the commitment to liberty in Southeast Asia. He insisted that this commitment was the only motivation for American involvement there.

Johnson designated the diplomat Averell Harriman to lead a delegation in conducting talks with North Vietnam. Without making specific promises or offering a timetable, Lyndon Johnson predicted the arrival of peace in Southeast Asia.

Clark and Goodwin, watching in Milwaukee, saw this presidential reversal as both a victory for the McCarthy antiwar campaign and a smart campaign move by Lyndon Johnson. LBJ announcing an unprecedented unilateral de-escalation would cut into McCarthy's lead in Wisconsin. This speech might hurt the McCarthy and Kennedy campaigns. This could be the night that Johnson secured the nomination.

Then the president lifted his right hand. The camera was in close-up now, the signal invisible to viewers.

Going off what his staff knew was the script, Johnson began reviewing the privileges and challenges of his career as president. It wasn't clear where he was going. "It is true that a house divided against itself by the spirit of faction, of party, of region, of religion, of race, is a house that cannot stand," the president said. Everyone working on every campaign, including Johnson's, wondered what that could possibly mean. He's not going to compete in any primaries—does he just expect the convention to give him the nomination? That could work for the nomination, but what about November? Does he just expect the voters to give him the election because he is a wartime president who is too busy trying to make peace to campaign? Was this a Rose Garden strategy taken to a wartime extreme?

"With America's sons in the fields far away," he continued, "with America's future under challenge right here at home, with our hopes and the world's hopes for peace in the balance every day, I do not believe that I should devote an hour or a day of my time to any personal partisan causes or to any duties other than the awesome duties of this office—the Presidency of your country."

This was crazy. FDR campaigned for reelection during World War II. The other candidates were going to have to find ways to force LBJ to engage with them.

At the White House, Clark Clifford and Dean Rusk leaned forward, suddenly realizing that they were not the final authors of this speech. "There is division in the American house now. Believing this as I do," LBJ said, "I have concluded that I should not permit the Presidency to become involved in the partisan divisions that are developing in this political year."

Then, with all the sudden shock of a lightning

bolt, it all made sense. "Accordingly," Johnson said calmly, smoothly, eyes level with the camera, "I shall not seek and I will not accept the nomination of my party for another term as your President."

Every TV and radio in America that was turned on had people staring at it in stunned disbelief. Could they possibly have just heard what they just heard?! Drivers pulled to the side of the road to wait for someone on the radio to repeat what they thought the president had just said. Families hugged their draft-age boys. Cheers shook the windows of college dormitories everywhere. Conservatives looked on sadly at another win for the liberals, a softening of American military power.

In Milwaukee, Goodwin leaped to his feet. From other rooms in the hotel, student volunteers were pouring into the hallways, whooping, yelling, dancing, the whole place bursting into an impromptu party of sheer joyous pandemonium.

Fifteen miles away, McCarthy was winding up his speech when someone in the crowd yelled, "He's not running, he's not running!" Reporters mobbed the stage and stopped the speech to get a statement from McCarthy. He compared the collapse of his former friend's presidency to Greek tragedy.

McCarthy rushed from the auditorium to a series of late-night network-affiliate TV studios to give his response to the history-changing decision of the president not to seek reelection. The partying at McCarthy's hotel wasn't going to end anytime soon. The kids had dumped Johnson.

And they forced Johnson into a reversal on Vietnam—a bombing halt and a de-escalation with no preconditions. The impossible quest McCarthy had committed himself to after the Katzenbach hearing the year before had worked. As he made the TV rounds that night, it was occurring to McCarthy that Johnson might actually feel relieved, liberated to have finally put the good of the nation above personal ambition.

When McCarthy finally got back to the hotel, he went to Mary McGrory's room. They celebrated as only McCarthy would—with poetry. They recited some Robert Lowell, then some Yeats. McCarthy began reciting his own poetry. Blair Clark started transcribing McCarthy's poems on McGrory's typewriter as McCarthy spoke and the pandemonium of the kids' celebration filled the halls of the hotel.

Bobby Kennedy's flight home was in the air during LBJ's speech. As soon as the plane landed at LaGuardia, Bobby's staff rushed onto the plane, pushing their way through deplaning passengers to tell him the news. "You're kidding" was all he could manage. The same thing Bobby had said when he was told Gene McCarthy was running for president.

Once at home, Bobby said, as if talking to himself, "I wonder if he would have done this if I hadn't come in." The campaign staff was popping corks and celebrating at his apartment. Bobby saw nothing to celebrate in the collapse of a presidency. He tried to watch the news on TV. He was pensive. Finally, Ethel said, "He didn't deserve to be president anyway."

Only one person at the McCarthy hotel in Milwaukee thought of something else. The first call Lyndon Johnson received after announcing his withdrawal from the campaign came from Abigail McCarthy. She made the call on impulse, intending to ask for Lady Bird. They'd known each other apart from their husbands as members of the Senate Wives Club, which developed much closer bonds than the gender-neutral remnant of it that exists today. Abigail wanted to say something positive about Lyndon. Abigail was startled when the president came on the line before handing the phone to the first lady. Abigail told him how much she admired his sacrifice.

"Honey," Lyndon Johnson said, "I'm just one little person. It's not important what happens to me."

TWENTY

"I'VE SEEN THE PROMISED LAND"

Twelve hours before the Lyndon Johnson speech that rocked the world, on Sunday morning, March 31, the vice president was packing for a trip to Mexico City to sign a nuclear non-proliferation treaty. The president and first lady dropped by. Leaving the wives in the living room, LBJ and his aide Jim Jones took Hubert Humphrey into the study and had him close the door. Johnson gave Humphrey a copy of the speech he would deliver to the nation that night. Humphrey started reading. The cessation of bombing and a call for peace talks gave him hope. Then Johnson handed him the secret alternate ending, announcing his withdrawal from the race. The aide Jim Jones saw tears in Humphrey's eyes. "If you're going to run," Johnson told Humphrey, "you'd better get ready damn quick."

In the days right after his announcement of withdrawal from the campaign, the president seemed a changed man: relaxed, satisfied, relieved. Finally, some good will flowed his way. Senator Fulbright, Johnson's great antagonist on Vietnam, praised the president as a great patriot. Bobby Kennedy called his worst enemy's decision not to run "truly magnanimous." Mary McGrory, one of LBJ's biggest critics in the press, called him a statesman. The president giving up another term was received by the public better than his landslide victory in 1964, which was never really his. It was always viewed as a sympathy vote for the assassinated president. Suddenly, 57 percent of the country approved of President Johnson's job performance. To his friends, LBJ seemed twenty years younger. He cracked jokes again. "It's easier to satisfy Ho Chi Minh than Bill Fulbright," he said.

Gene McCarthy and his team spent the day after Johnson's announcement—April Fools' Day— campaigning in Wisconsin against no one. The next day he won the Wisconsin primary, as many predicted he would even before LBJ dropped out. But the vote totals were confusing. McCarthy won 56 percent of the vote to LBJ's 35 percent with a 6 percent write-in vote for Bobby. With LBJ dropping out, why didn't McCarthy win by even more? Why did 35 percent cast their votes for a candidate who wasn't running? Was that the size of the prowar vote or the moderate vote in the Democratic Party that neither McCarthy nor Kennedy could win? Would those hard-core Johnson voters move to the other winner of the Wisconsin primary if McCarthy or Kennedy won the nomination? Richard Nixon won 79 percent of the Republican vote in Wisconsin. Ten percent wrote in votes for Ronald Reagan and 1.6 percent wrote in Nelson Rockefeller's name. No one was quite sure what to make of the Wisconsin vote, so it was mostly ignored. Everyone was waiting for the next real primaries—the ones with Bobby on the ballot.

The day after the Wisconsin primary, Bobby requested a meeting with the president. Bobby and Ted Sorensen waited in the Cabinet Room. LBJ entered with his national security adviser, Walt Rostow. Both LBJ and RFK made gestures toward a truce. Bobby said, "Your speech was magnificent." He said a lot of their feud was his fault. Johnson said the press always exaggerated it. Bobby asked, "Can I ask about the political situation? Where do I stand in the campaign?" He meant, was LBJ planning to work against him? Johnson professed neutrality for now but said he expected Humphrey to run and he would probably support his vice president. Bobby and Sorensen raised the question of allowing cabinet members to take sides in the primaries. Johnson launched into a reminiscence about his own loyalty to JFK. As president, he never fired a Kennedy appointee. He said no one appreciated that he carried on JFK's policies on civil rights and poverty and had been repaid only with dissatisfaction from black people and protests from students.

Very softly, Bobby said, "You are a brave and dedicated man." Bobby cleared his throat and said it again, more audibly.

With Johnson out of the race, the question of who Martin Luther King Jr. might endorse became only a bit less complicated. Now he didn't have to worry about offending an incumbent president he would need to work with for the rest of the year. Now he just had to worry about offending McCarthy or Kennedy. Dr. King had a better history and relationship with McCarthy. Their wives were friends. Dr. King had strong reason to believe that as attorney general, Kennedy personally authorized the initial FBI wiretaps and surveillance of him. Bobby personally told Dr. King that he had nothing to do with the wiretaps. McCarthy was a bit better than Kennedy on Dr. King's issues, but Bobby was vastly more popular among black voters. McCarthy remained very weak with black voters.

After speaking to that massive crowd on his first night in Memphis, Dr. King flew back and forth to Memphis for the next two weeks, squeezing in speeches and sermons in Harlem and Washington and even managing to sleep at home in Atlanta three nights. He returned to Memphis the day after the Wisconsin primary and spoke again that night at the Masonic Temple.

Every Martin Luther King Jr. speech had political context and most had the emotion and rhythm and religious context of a sermon. Tonight's speech was classic Dr. King: more than forty minutes long, no notes, political argument and strategy, prayers and predictions. Dr. King addressed the injunction obtained by the mayor preventing a scheduled protest march in Memphis. He said the injunction was something he would expect from the totalitarian governments in China and Russia and promised to fight the injunction in court. He very explicitly called for nonviolence above all else in Memphis. He outlined some of the elements of economic justice that he planned to focus on in the Poor People's Campaign. He suggested that boycotts of some local banks and big companies like Coca-Cola might be necessary to get mayors to pay attention to them.

He told the story of how he almost died years earlier when he was stabbed at a book signing in New York City. He revealed that the airline pilot on the flight from Atlanta that morning told him that the plane had been thoroughly searched for bombs, and because they knew he was reserved on the flight, the plane was guarded all night. Then King said, "Like anybody, I would like to live a long life. Longevity has its place. But I'm not concerned about that now. I just want to do God's will. And He's allowed me to go up to the mountain. And I've looked over. And I've seen the Promised Land. I may not get there with you. But I want you to know tonight, that we, as a people, will get to the promised land! And so I'm happy, tonight."

These were the last words publicly spoken by Martin Luther King Jr. At 6:01 p.m. the next afternoon, as he stood on the balcony of his room at the Lorraine Motel, he was hit in the neck by one bullet from an assassin's rifle and was pronounced dead at St. Joseph's Hospital at 7:05 p.m.

Black leaders all over the country urged calm and nonviolence as the news of Dr. King's assassination spread. Mayors of major cities and their police chiefs braced for riots.

When Dr. King was shot, Bobby Kennedy was campaigning in Indiana. He had just given a speech at Ball State University and was on his way to the airport in Muncie for a quick flight to Indianapolis. A kid at the Muncie airport asked Bobby if he had heard about Martin Luther King. Immediately, Bobby asked, "Was he shot?"

When Bobby's plane landed in Indianapolis, he was still in his seat when he got the news that Dr. King had been pronounced dead. His head jerked backward, then he covered his face with his hands.

Bobby was scheduled to speak at a campaign rally in the heart of the city's black neighborhood at Seventeenth and Broadway. Republican mayor Richard Lugar said he could not guarantee Senator Kennedy's safety that night. The safe choice for Bobby was to cancel the event. With assassination in the air, everyone would understand. That was the politically safe choice, too. If rioting broke out at or near the Kennedy campaign event, would Bobby be accused of inciting the crowd? Bobby decided to go straight to Seventeenth and Broadway without any police protection. The Indianapolis police chief advised Bobby to cancel the rally for his own safety. Bobby told the chief, "I could take my wife and family and we could sleep on the middle of the street at Seventeenth and Broadway and there would be no problem." Impoverished black urban America was not where Bobby feared a bullet. There was no place he felt safer.

When the crowd saw Bobby step up on the rally stage, the back of a flatbed truck, most of them cheered and hoisted Kennedy campaign signs. News spread more slowly in those days when no one had phones in their pockets. Most of the people there did not yet know what had happened in Memphis. Bobby would have to tell them. "Give a very short speech," said Frank Mankiewicz. He handed Bobby his speech notes. Lost in thought, Bobby put them in his pocket. A light mist was falling. The spot where Bobby was going to speak on the back of the truck was lit by two bright white floodlights mounted on poles. Most of the crowd was left in the dark.

Bobby was the only presidential candidate who had to deliver the awful news publicly and he had to do it with the people whom it was going to hurt the most. Adam Walinsky had just arrived from the airport, having landed on a separate flight. He handed Bobby some hastily written speech notes. Bobby waved them away. Just before he stepped toward the microphone, he asked, "Do they know about Martin Luther King?" hoping he would not have to personally break the news. All the heads around him shook the silent answer no. He nodded and took the microphone.

"Ladies and gentlemen," Bobby began as cheers grew louder and signs waved higher. "I'm only going to talk to you for a minute or so this evening because I have some very sad news for all of you. Could you lower those signs please?" The crowd grew quiet. "I have some very sad news for all of you and I think sad news for all of our fellow citizens and people who love peace all over the world. And that is that Martin Luther King was shot and was killed tonight in Memphis, Tennessee." Screams of pain, howls of rage came out of the crowd in the darkness. "No!" was the only clear word.

Everyone wanted to hear Bobby's soft-spoken words, so those who could control their moans of agony quieted enough to hear Bobby continue: "Martin Luther King dedicated his life to love and to justice between human beings, and he died in the cause of that effort."

Bobby paused to try to contain his emotion and there was a moment of pure silence. Bobby's eyes were wet. He had never made a public comment about what had happened in Dallas on November 22, 1963, never a word about how he felt that day, not a direct word about his brother being shot in the head and killed. Until now.

"For those of you who are black and are tempted to be filled with hatred and distrust at the injustice of such an act, against all white people, I would only say that I feel in my own heart the same kind of feeling. I had a member of my family killed, but he was killed by a white man. But we have to make an effort in the United States, we have to make an effort to understand, to go beyond these rather difficult times. My favorite poet was Aeschylus. He once wrote: 'Even in our sleep, pain which cannot forget falls drop by drop upon the heart until, in our own despair, against our will, comes wisdom through the awful grace of God.' What we need in the United States is not division; what we need in the United States is not hatred; what we need in the United States is not violence and lawlessness; but love and wisdom, and compassion toward one another, and a feeling of justice toward those who still suffer within our country, whether they be white or they be black. So I shall ask you tonight to return home, to say a prayer for the family of Martin Luther King, that's true, but more importantly to say a prayer for our own country, which all of us love—a prayer for understanding and that compassion of which I spoke.

"The vast majority of white people and the vast majority of black people in this country want to live together, want to improve the quality of our life, and want justice for all human beings who abide in our land. Let us dedicate ourselves to what the Greeks wrote so many years ago: to tame the savageness of man and make gentle the life of this world. Let us dedicate ourselves to that."

There were some cheers at the end of Bobby's speech. Only a few people in the crowd reached out to him. They didn't want to just touch him the way the frantic crowds always did. They wanted to hold his hand the way you hold hands at a funeral, at a grave site. Most people just stood—some silent, some crying. They didn't move.

Rioting broke out that night in cities all over America. Indianapolis was not one of them.

The rioting lasted a week. Tens of thousands of people were arrested. Thousands were injured. Dozens were killed. America has never seen anything like that scale of nationwide rioting before or since.

The day after the King assassination, Washington was a war zone. Smoke from burning buildings hid the dome of the U.S. Capitol. Vehicles packed with soldiers and marines patrolled debris-strewn streets. Row after row of stores were looted and burned. Broken glass was everywhere.

Stokely Carmichael said, "White America made her biggest mistake when she killed Dr. King last night. . . . She killed the one man of our race in this country . . . who the militants and the revolutionaries and the masses of black people would still listen to." Thirty cities were burning.

More than six thousand people were arrested in Washington in the days following King's murder, ten killed. A convoy of military trucks crossing into the district on the Memorial Bridge the second night had to fight an opposing tide of tens of thousands of people—in cars and buses and on foot—fleeing the devastation. Then came the 3rd Infantry. The 6th Armored Cavalry Regiment. The 91st Engineering Battalion. The 82nd Airborne. These and other units converged on the capital. Some rode straight up Pennsylvania Avenue to seal the White House gates, bivouac in defensive posture on the lawn, and pile up sandbags in the spooky glow of klieg lights. Others bounced their jeeps all the way up the Capitol steps and settled there, establishing radio communications, turning machine guns toward the Lincoln Memorial to command the Mall, taking over nearby offices to gain fields of fire from the high roofs nearby. Only a week after withdrawing from the campaign and announcing a military de-escalation in Vietnam, President Johnson was commander in chief of a massive military operation to seize back control of Washington, D.C.

So began the militarization of American police forces. The Army Operations Center (AOC) in the

Pentagon had originally been established to handle any and all domestic military operations, such as counterattacking a Soviet invasion. In July 1967, when the Michigan National Guard found itself overwhelmed by the rioting in Detroit, President Johnson had deployed the 82nd Airborne from AOC to restore domestic order. He then appointed former deputy secretary of defense Cyrus Vance to manage the use of the military in domestic disturbances. Cyrus Vance created a guidebook on using the U.S. Army in coordination with local and state police. The "Vance Book" was distributed widely to law-enforcement personnel all over the country. Eighteen army brigades were dedicated to handling civil control exclusively. Units were preassigned to specific cities. Commanding officers at all levels coordinated with local police, getting tours to determine the lay of the land where riots might occur and acquiring intelligence on local militants and other leaders. They drew up detailed operational plans for deploying in each city.

At the U.S. Army Military Police School in Fort Gordon, Georgia, the army established the Senior Officers Civil Disturbance Orientation Course (SEADOC). They brought together teams of law enforcement from the FBI, National Guard, and local police. They built a practice area that looked like a ghetto. They named it Riotsville. In war games, army MPs played the role of rioters.

A special intelligence branch known as the U.S. Army Intelligence Command (USAINTC), operating out of Fort Holabird, Maryland, fanned a thousand agents throughout the country, in cooperation with the National Security Agency, to infiltrate, spy on, and report back on activities of organizations deemed dissident and militant. Many of the organizations targeted were African American groups and included, obviously, nonrevolutionary groups like the NAACP. MOBE and other known planners of the 1967 March on Washington were infiltrated by army intelligence.

The president was in the Oval Office planning a trip to Hawaii as a halfway meeting location for his military commanders flying in from Vietnam when he got the news that Martin Luther King Jr. had been killed. He canceled the Hawaii trip. Almost immediately, the president's top staff, with Cyrus Vance at the helm, shuttled from the White House command to the District Building, where both the city's police and the military commanders coordinated operations. The Department of Justice was another command center. City police precincts were transformed into urban fortresses. Military units hunkered down in Washington's lobbies and laundromats and auditoriums.

Four thousand National Guardsmen enforced a curfew in Memphis. Newark had nearly two hundred fires. Detroit, Baltimore, Pittsburgh, and Kansas

City burned. More than a hundred American cities saw some burning, looting, and destruction. More than 50,000 troops were deployed against American citizens, with twenty thousand arrests nationally and thirty-nine deaths.

When Coretta Scott King accompanied her husband's body home to Atlanta from Memphis, Abigail McCarthy was at the Atlanta airport to meet her friend. Bobby Kennedy had very publicly provided a chartered plane for Mrs. King's flight. Gene and Abigail McCarthy did not want to compete politically with Kennedy over Dr. King's death. Abigail was invited to join Atlanta's mayor at the foot of the ramp where the coffin would be lowered, which meant she would be among the first to greet the widow, but Abigail politely declined. This was personal. She was not seeking attention. She respectfully hung back. When Mrs. King approached Abigail, they embraced without speaking. To avoid publicity, Abigail declined Mrs. King's invitation to the funeral home. Instead, Abigail went to the King home and amid the bustle of funeral preparations, Abigail rolled up her sleeves and helped prepare food for hundreds of people who would be visiting. When Mrs. King arrived home, she was shaking. She went straight to bed.

Later, Abigail joined Mrs. King in the bedroom. The singer and activist Harry Belafonte also went into the room. Abigail McCarthy sat by the bedside, holding the widow's hand. None of this McCarthy-

King family connection was made known to the public.

In the aftermath of the riots, Richard Nixon leaned much more strongly on law-and-order rhetoric. George Wallace's poll numbers went up. Even Bobby Kennedy, campaigning in conservative Indiana, started working law-and-order notes into his speeches and reminding voters of his own experience at the top of American law enforcement as attorney general. Only Gene McCarthy resisted joining the competition for demonstrating toughness on law and order. As he watched the riots on TV, McCarthy said, "If I were a Negro, I don't know what I'd do."

Two funeral services were held in Atlanta for Martin Luther King Jr.—the first for the King family and friends was at Ebenezer Baptist Church, where Dr. King and his father had served as pastor. A second service for the public was held three miles away at Dr. King's alma mater, Morehouse College. The church was packed with 1,300 people, including foreign dignitaries, movie stars, sports heroes, the first black Supreme Court justice, Thurgood Marshall, and most of the presidential candidates. Richard Nixon, Nelson Rockefeller, and George Romney were there along with Gene and Abigail McCarthy. Jackie Kennedy accompanied Bobby Kennedy. Hubert Humphrey attended in his own right and in his official capacity for the president. George Wallace was not invited, and Ronald Reagan apparently made no effort to be invited. Two hundred thousand people marched behind the casket from the church to the college. There was some singing and there were some long painful silences. Once again in the 1960s, the country was transfixed watching the funeral of another assassinated leader.

There was something disturbingly regular about this now in America. Assassination was not wildly outside of our expectations. Martin Luther King Jr. anticipated it publicly and privately, including in his last speech. Bobby Kennedy anticipated it, too. On the night Dr. King was killed, Bobby told an aide, "That could have been me."

TWENTY-ONE

THE HAPPY WARRIOR

O n the day of Martin Luther King Jr.'s funeral, eight hundred miles north at Columbia University in New York City, a memorial service for Dr. King was under way in St. Paul's Chapel when the leader of the university's SDS chapter, Mark Rudd, rushed the altar, grabbed the microphone, and started shouting. Mark Rudd had been planning a step-by-step action against the university, beginning with protest, leading to harassing Reserve Officers' Training Corps instructors. SDS wanted to heighten tensions between radicals and jocks, climaxing in a general student walkout that would shut down the school. Throughout March, Mark Rudd had been bringing a radical student strike closer to some kind of major action. At the King memorial, he saw his chance. "If we really want to honor this man's memory, then we ought to stand together against this racist gym!" Rudd yelled about Columbia's plans to displace some of its poor Harlem neighbors for the construction of a new athletic building. Rudd led a small group of students in a walkout from the memorial. Most stayed in their seats.

On April 22, Rudd published an open letter to the Columbia administration. In it, he flatly rejected university president Grayson Kirk's call for obedience. Taking a page from the pants-down Yippie approach to revolution, he got threatening while trying to be comedic.

"We will destroy at times," Rudd said, "even violently, in order to end your power and your system." And Rudd ended his letter to "Uncle Grayson" with this: "Up against the wall, motherfucker, this is a stickup."

Everything that happened at Columbia was under the glare of the New York news media. The news spread fast. Suddenly Tom Hayden was in the thick of it and the university was calling him an "outside agitator" on their campus. This made Bobby Kennedy more nervous about the New Left. He had thought Hayden was someone he could talk to because he had talked to him. But now any association with Hayden would make Bobby look like a supporter of chaos to moderate voters.

Hayden was sleeping on the floor of Mathematics Hall, which the outside groups had stormed and occupied. In Hamilton Hall, radical students had burst through a barrier set up by students who dissented from the rebellion. The radicals took over Hamilton and made a hostage of one of the deans.

There were only about eighty black students attending Columbia. They, along with Black Panthers from the neighborhood, demanded that the white students evacuate Hamilton and hand it over to them, which the white kids did. The black students and the Harlem Black Panthers took over Hamilton while other students took over Low Library. Students broke into President Grayson Kirk's office. They hung posters of Che Guevara and Chairman Mao. They declared Columbia a revolutionary zone.

When the university finally brought in the police on April 30, Rudd, Hayden, and the other leaders got what they wanted. New York City police were caught on camera beating the students with clubs as they arrested them. As more vans full of club-wielding cops arrived, the students screamed, "Motherfuckers!" The New York news media produced all the images Mark Rudd was hoping would show a police-state crackdown on the white middle-class kids of Columbia University.

To Bobby Kennedy, expressing any sympathy for any adventure anything like the Columbia uprising did not look like a good path to the Democratic nomination. He was campaigning in Indiana, where he wanted to establish credibility with Midwestern moderate Democrats who were worried and frightened by all the rioting they saw on TV. His speeches played down the leftist antiwar lines. "We can do better in Vietnam" became the slogan. He began connecting his efforts to end poverty with a concomitant effort to end "lawlessness and violence."

He meant ordinary crime, of course. Its national rise was one of the outrages that middle-of-the-road voters were most concerned about. But he also meant rioting and rebellion and politically inspired disorder of all kinds. Amid the growing chaos after the King assassination and the Columbia uprising, Robert Kennedy repeatedly reminded his Indiana audiences that he'd once been the nation's chief law-enforcement officer.

The student riot at Columbia gave Old Nixon an opportunity to set some of the New Nixon's tone. Nixon said the student revolt at Columbia was part of a plot to "seize the universities of this country and transform them into sanctuaries for radicals." He also accused Johnson's attorney general, Ramsey Clark, of denying the national rise in crime. If things continued at the present rate, Nixon predicted, rape, robbery, assault, and theft would double in four years. "The city jungle will cease to be a metaphor," he said. "It will become a barbaric reality." Poverty may have "played a role" in rising crime, Nixon said, but liberalism "grossly exaggerated" that role. He announced that as president, he would cut the crime rate by doubling the conviction rate—impossible because federal prosecutions were a small percentage of the country's criminal cases, most of which were prosecuted by the states.

Ronald Reagan reshot the end of his film biography to add some up-to-date law-and-order material after the King assassination, which Reagan said was a "great tragedy that began when we began compromising with law and order and people started choosing which laws they'd break."

George Wallace had always been law and order and nothing but law and order. He needed no changes in his rhetoric. After the King assassination and the riots, Wallace's poll numbers just kept rising.

Hubert Humphrey had to wait a decent interval after Martin Luther King Jr.'s funeral to announce that he would run in Johnson's place for president. The riots extended that decent interval. Humphrey lost valuable weeks waiting for the right moment. Every lost day mattered to a candidate getting in the race so late. He was going to need every possible minute to remind voters who Hubert Horatio Humphrey really was.

Starting with the first vice president, John Adams, occupants of the office a heartbeat away from the presidency have been marginalized, humiliated, made invisible. That's what happened to Hubert Humphrey. That's what happened to Lyndon Johnson during the Kennedy administration. During the Eisenhower administration, that's what had happened to Richard Nixon. Most vice presidents suffered that fate until

1993, during the Clinton administration, when Al Gore became the first vice president to be an active participant in government. Every vice president since then has been a strong partner of the president's. Gore was followed by Richard Cheney, Joseph Biden, and Mike Pence. All of these strong vice presidents had much more experience in Washington and in governing than the presidents they served. They all maintained high public profiles. Humphrey would not recognize the Obama-Biden working and personal relationship. That's what Humphrey craved—a respectful, working friendship, with Humphrey always getting in the last word of advice with the president. But in the 1960s, the vice presidency was still the place politicians were sent to be forgotten. With a larger-than-life president, two Kennedys in the Senate (one running for president), McCarthy's exciting insurgent campaign for president, colorful governors like Rockefeller and Reagan, and flamethrowers like George Wallace, Hubert Humphrey was the forgotten man of American politics in 1968.

"Whatever became of Hubert?" sang the satirist Tom Lehrer:

Once a fiery liberal spirit,
Ah, but now when he speaks he must clear
    it. . . .
Did Lyndon, recalling when he was VP,
Say "I'll do unto you like they did unto me"?

The "Happy Warrior" of Midwestern liberalism, the brave man who challenged the Democratic Party in 1948 to alter its shameful legacy on race, had now spent four years doing what the public perceived as nothing. Johnson deployed Humphrey as chief defender of the Vietnam War. Vice President Humphrey addressed leaders of the Americans for Democratic Action, the liberal group he had once dominated, and was criticized by former allies like John Kenneth Galbraith. When Gene McCarthy openly broke with the incumbent president and party leader over the war, the break was really with Humphrey-style liberalism, the old liberalism of the cold warrior. When Bobby Kennedy broke with Johnson over the war, it remained Humphrey's job—pretty much his only job—to travel the country defending Johnson's Vietnam policy.

Humphrey felt trapped. He had come to see the war as a political loser for Johnson and for himself. In 1965, when the president was becoming committed to escalation, Humphrey had tried to get him to cut his losses in Vietnam. He had sent Johnson a long memo cautioning the president about his prowar advisers. "Many key advisors in the Government," Humphrey wrote, "are advocating a policy markedly similar to the Republican policy as defined by Goldwater." He noted that a large-scale land war would tend to shift the administration's emphasis from its Great Society–oriented programs to further military outlays and "damage the image of the President of the United States—and that of the United States itself." The president not only ignored his vice president's advice but angrily consigned Humphrey to what the vice president thought of as Johnson's doghouse. Humphrey was never asked to serve as one of the president's advisers on Vietnam, only as spokesman for the failing policy. When Johnson finally did listen to reason, and began to seek de-escalation in Vietnam, Humphrey was the last person who could expect to get any credit.

Humphrey had nevertheless given the president unshakable loyalty. He could see his political future only in terms of his role as vice president. His only hope was to see LBJ reelected for another four years. Then, as the incumbent vice president, Humphrey would be the front-runner for the presidential nomination. Suddenly, the time to succeed Johnson was now—1968—four years sooner than Humphrey was preparing for.

A vice president running for president enjoys incumbency, but Humphrey's 1968 incumbency differed from Nixon's in 1960. The president wasn't concluding a successful eight years and handing his successor his blessing, a record to run on. In Humphrey's case, the president was quitting and handing his successor a mess. Humphrey was not even sure he would have Johnson's support. With Johnson out, Humphrey could not be sure he would be the default choice of the Democratic Party establishment. Some of the old party bosses didn't know what to do, and Kennedys always looked like winners. The Democratic Party establishment remembered JFK easily beating Humphrey in the 1960 nomination race. It was already too late for Humphrey to be competitive in the primaries. Too many filing deadlines had passed. The only way left for him to win the nomination was the inside game. He had to go after all those delegates who showed up in Chicago free to vote for whomever they wanted. He was going to need Johnson's help with them. And so twenty-seven days after the president withdrew from the race, the vice president announced he was running for president to a hall filled with Humphrey supporters at the National Press Club, two blocks from the White House.

One of the Humphrey supporters at the Press Club was Walter Mondale, the man who was appointed by the governor of Minnesota to replace Humphrey in the Senate when Humphrey became vice president. Senator Mondale had a problem no other senator had to deal with—two Democratic presidential candidates from his state, one his senior senator, the other his vice president and political patron. Gene McCarthy never expected his junior partner in the Senate to endorse him. Mondale was still a strong supporter of LBJ's war policy, and Mondale was a Humphrey man all the way. Mondale entered Minnesota politics at age twenty, working on Humphrey's first Senate campaign in 1948. There was never a doubt that Mondale would stick with the Johnson-Humphrey ticket in 1968. When Johnson dropped out, Senator Mondale, like so many who were clinging to the wreckage of the Democratic establishment that spring, simply waited for Hubert Humphrey to take Lyndon Johnson's place in the campaign.

There was nothing surprising about Senator Walter Mondale, a future vice president and future Democratic nominee for president, being there the day the Democratic establishment candidate launched his campaign. And it wasn't surprising that Humphrey thanked Mondale at the beginning of his speech. What he said about Mondale **was** surprising. Humphrey looked at the junior senator from Minnesota and said into the microphone, "Thank you, Senator Mondale, thank you, my champion." It didn't make any sense. Walter Mondale wasn't anyone's hero. He was seventeen years younger than Humphrey. His two years in the army during the Korean War were spent safely inside the United States. Mondale had never done anything politically brave. Humphrey had got it backward. If there was a political hero in the room, it was Humphrey—the Hubert Humphrey of 1948, who bravely took on his party on civil rights. But by 1968, no one seemed to remember that Humphrey, not even Hubert himself.

Calling Walter Mondale a hero was not in Hum-

phrey's written speech text. It was improvised. It was
what came to him when he said thank you to Mondale, which was in his prepared text. He seemed to
blurt out "my champion" to show some enthusiasm
about something or someone at the beginning of a
speech that had no enthusiasm. And there was a nervous desperation about "my champion." It sounded
as if Humphrey were surprised that any senator, even
one who owed his career to him, would be willing to
publicly support him.

What followed was a very long speech using the
old rules of Washington speech writing that made
Americans hate political speeches. It was so careful
that the speech left hundreds of boring words between what seemed to be references to the campaign.
When Humphrey said, "The time has come to put
aside selfish ambition," it sounded like he was referring to Bobby. Or did he mean McCarthy? Or both?
The audience watching on TV had plenty of time
to think about it because it was several minutes before he said anything as interesting. The speech, of
course, used the word **patriotism** but not the word
Vietnam. The committee writing Hubert Humphrey's first campaign speech clearly feared Vietnam
to the point where the speech did not mention Vietnam in a campaign that was about Vietnam, about
life and death.

The speechwriters gave Humphrey nine sentences
in a row that began with the phrase "I believe." But

they said nothing. Democratic primary voters in 1968 wanted to hear the candidate say "I believe we can win in Vietnam" or "I believe we should withdraw from Vietnam," and then they would vote accordingly. The primary voters were not responding to Humphrey lines like "I believe that this strong, rich and idealistic nation of ours can help to create a broader world society in which human values will one day rule supreme."

Humphrey did not specifically say that he would not compete in the primaries, but he offered this explanation for voters in primary states who weren't going to get to shake his hand: "The people who voted for me for Vice President have every right to expect a full four-year service in that office. Thus in the weeks ahead I want you to know that I shall place high priority upon that call to service and I shall continue to fulfill, to the best of my abilities, the duties of my office and the responsibilities that have been placed upon me." The country was reasonably sure that LBJ, like all presidents they had watched before him, placed no responsibilities upon his vice president. This was not McCarthy-like respect for the intelligence of the audience.

Humphrey never mentioned the existence of other presidential candidates, Democrat or Republican. But in one line, it was very clear he was talking about the most successful Democratic candidate so far in the primary season, Gene McCarthy: "The man who wins the nomination must be able, first, to unite his party. The man who unites his party must be able above all to unite and govern his nation. . . . I do not, and will not, divide either my party or my country." There was more than a whiff of bitterness in that, as if it were a personal offense to Humphrey that the man he helped launch in Minnesota politics dared to challenge the reelection of the Johnson-Humphrey ticket.

By the end of Humphrey's speech it was clear that the Democrats now had an Old Politics candidate to run against two New Politics candidates, but nothing else was clear. You didn't know whether Humphrey wanted to raise or lower taxes. You didn't know what his foreign policy would be in relation to the Soviet Union or China or Israel or even France, because not a single foreign country was mentioned—surely a by-product of the fear of mentioning Vietnam. And you didn't know whether your sixteen-year-old son or boyfriend would grow up to be an eighteen-year-old who got drafted, sent to Vietnam, and killed in the second or third year of a Humphrey presidency. You didn't have a reason to vote for Hubert Humphrey.

There must have been enough good politician left in Humphrey for him to recognize how empty his speech was. He definitely knew how unwelcome he was going to be in a campaign with a majority of Democrats already supporting McCarthy or Kennedy. The speech lacked confidence, so much so that when he said, "I shall seek the nomination of the Democratic Party," he paused for applause. Then as chants of "We want Humphrey!" broke out, Humphrey, in a burst of nervous self-awareness, leaned into the microphone as if speaking directly to the TV audience, and after the last "We want Humphrey" chant, he said, "Like it or not, you have him."

TWENTY-TWO

DON'T LOSE

With Hubert Humphrey sitting out the primaries, the public stage of the Democratic presidential campaign was simply Gene McCarthy versus Bobby Kennedy, while Humphrey played the inside game where most of the delegates could be won. With thirty-seven states not conducting primaries, McCarthy and Kennedy had reason to worry that Humphrey could be locking in more delegates on the phone from the White House than they could win by nonstop flying around the country giving speeches to primary voters.

Humphrey could not afford to ignore the primaries entirely. If Bobby won huge victories, they would be highly publicized expressions of what the voters wanted. Grabbing the nomination away the old-fashioned way from a proven vote getter would feel like an antidemocratic process that overruled Democratic primary voters. If the combined vote total of McCarthy and Kennedy was big enough, it would appear that Democratic Party voters were insisting on an antiwar candidate. Watching Humphrey emerge as the nominee after an overwhelming combined antiwar primary vote for McCarthy and Kennedy would have a Soviet feel to it. So Humphrey did run in the primaries, but he did it under various aliases through the favorite-son method. Florida's Democratic senator George Smathers was on the Florida primary ballot as a favorite son. Voters dissatisfied with McCarthy and Kennedy could vote for Senator Smathers, thereby delivering delegates to their senator, who would then decide how those delegates voted at the convention.

George Smathers had been one of Jack Kennedy's best friends in the Senate. He was an usher at Jack's wedding, the only one not related to Jack or Jackie. In 1967, it was leaked that JFK had been considering dumping Johnson as his reelection running mate in favor of another Southern Democrat—George Smathers. He was elected to the House of Representatives the same year Jack Kennedy and Richard Nixon were. He moved up to the Senate with them and befriended both. Senator Smathers was a segregationist in the 1950s. He said the U.S. Supreme Court's historic ruling against segregation, **Brown v. Board of Education**, was a "clear abuse of judicial power." He voted against the Civil Rights Act of

1964. He voted against LBJ's nomination of Thurgood Marshall as the first African American Supreme Court justice. Marshall was the lead lawyer on the winning side of **Brown v. Board of Education**. Then, in 1965, Smathers was one of only four Southern Democratic senators who voted for LBJ's Voting Rights Act. He might have known then that he was not going to run for a fourth term in 1968. George Smathers was not a Kennedy man like Sorensen, Schlesinger, or Galbraith, whose loyalties extended to all of the Kennedy brothers. Smathers was only a Jack Kennedy man. The delegates he won in the 1968 Florida presidential primary were all going to be ordered to vote for Hubert Humphrey at the convention. With George Smathers on the ballot, the Kennedy campaign decided not to compete in Florida. The Florida primary would be McCarthy versus Smathers (Humphrey).

Bobby had to stay out of the Florida primary because Bobby's primary strategy was very simple: don't lose. Bobby had to emerge from the primary season and head for the Chicago convention looking like a winner. To do that, he chose to compete only in states where he would win. It was a simple-sounding strategy that was not easy to execute.

Bobby entered the race too late to get on the ballot in Pennsylvania and Massachusetts, the next two primaries after Wisconsin. McCarthy won both of those states, but with Kennedy and Humphrey not competing, McCarthy supporters celebrated the wins with a muted news media reaction as it waited for the first McCarthy-versus-Kennedy contest in Indiana on May 7.

Indiana's governor Roger Branigin was on the ballot as a favorite son, so the worst-case scenario in Indiana was to come in third. McCarthy was popular on college campuses, but only Bobby was popular on the campuses and in the ghettos and with the white working class. Bobby told each of those groups what they wanted to hear. The students heard about stopping the war in Vietnam. African Americans heard about Bobby's hopes for their future. White rural audiences heard about "jobs not welfare" and, of course, "law and order."

The Kennedys launched the Indiana campaign on the fly and ran it at full throttle for four weeks. The state had never seen anything like it—a modern major-league presidential campaign devoted entirely to Indiana voters, complete with chartered planes, motorcades, TV ads, paid telephone canvasses, huge crowds, and Kennedys. Kennedys everywhere.

The Kennedys were sensitive about two things in Indiana: their money and their religion. Indiana had a significant bloc of anti-Catholic sentiment. Bobby knew ignoring it would be a mistake, so he tried to demystify and humanize Catholicism with a joke. He repeatedly told his crowds that he had just met a nun who wished him luck. "She said she had been praying to St. Jude for me," he said. "I thanked her, then asked somebody who St. Jude was. And then I learned he is the patron saint of lost causes." And the Catholic politician from Boston by way of Washington and New York got a big laugh about Catholicism from a non-Catholic Indiana crowd.

Bobby and Teddy were sensitive about how much money the family was spending in Indiana. Teddy ducked the question when he was on the campaign trail in Indiana. His mother did not. When seventy-eight-year-old Rose Kennedy campaigned in Indiana for Bobby and was asked about the cost of the campaign, she said, "It's part of this campaign business. If you have money, you spend it to win. And the more you can afford, the more you'll spend. The Rockefellers are like us—we both have lots of money to spend on our campaigns." Rose Kennedy's campaign handlers were horrified at the elitist sound of that, but everyone in Indiana already knew the Kennedys were rich, and for many voters Bobby's mother might have sounded refreshingly honest. In the next century, Donald Trump would fly into Indiana in his private plane, brag about how rich he was, and win the state in the primary and general election.

Gene McCarthy felt the pressure of the Kennedy campaign. It was like nothing he had competed against before. Taking down Johnson in New Hampshire was an extraordinary achievement, but it didn't feel so difficult in those last two weeks in

New Hampshire. He had the state to himself. It was
McCarthy against a mirage. Johnson wasn't campaigning in the New Hampshire primary and wasn't
even on the ballot. McCarthy also had Wisconsin to
himself. By the last day of campaigning in Wisconsin, Johnson had officially dropped out of the race.
Now Bobby was campaigning everywhere in Indiana. And if Bobby wasn't there, Teddy was. Or Rose
Kennedy. Or Ethel Kennedy. McCarthy was discov-
ering the hard way that everything he had ever heard
about campaigning against the Kennedy machine
was true. In what sounded like an attempt to trans-
plant the urgency of McCarthy's New Hampshire
campaign into Indiana and his Indiana supporters,
he said, "As Indiana goes, I think that's the way the
Democratic Party will go in Chicago."

On election day, sound trucks rolled through the
black wards in Indianapolis and other cities with the
last words of the campaign coming through a loud-
speaker in a familiar voice: "Go to the polls as early
as possible. Indiana can choose the next President
of the United States. I ask your help. This is Robert
Kennedy." One of the governor's men covering the
black wards passed along the bad news: "Everything
that moves is voting."

On election night, Governor Branigin was refreshingly honest. "I got whipped," he said. "I got taken
to the woodshed." Bobby Kennedy took him there.
Bobby won 42 percent of the vote. Governor Brani-

gin won 31 percent. And Gene McCarthy came in third with 27 percent.

Gene McCarthy was far too smart and self-aware to be good at denying the obvious—something candidates sometimes have to do. Finishing third behind the second-place candidate who said, "I got whipped," McCarthy tried to say the exact opposite. He said the Indiana vote was his "most significant achievement" because he did better than he expected. Everyone knew that coming in third in Indiana was not McCarthy's "most significant achievement," but admitting an outright loss to Bobby just wasn't in him and he had to say something. The McCarthy team tried to spin the hypothetical that McCarthy would have beaten Kennedy one-on-one. But a **Newsweek** primary-eve poll showed that "Kennedy would have trounced McCarthy 61 to 39 percent in a two-way race." **Newsweek** said the Indiana results were ambiguous enough "to keep McCarthy alive to fight another day." When he began his concession speech in a ballroom at the Claypool Hotel in Indianapolis, McCarthy said, "I didn't come here to dismiss the troops." His crowd cheered as if he had just announced victory.

Bobby's supporters saw an exhausted candidate deliver a victory speech that was more modest than victorious. He didn't want to offend McCarthy or Humphrey. He knew he was going to need support from both of them in the general election. Later that night, Bobby commented on the McCarthy campaign spin that Gene had done better than expected in Indiana. "Well," said Bobby, "I don't know whether people think it's so good to be second or third. That's not the way I was brought up. I was always taught that it was much better to win. I learned that when I was about two."

Three days after Humphrey entered the race, the Republican field also added a candidate. Nelson Rockefeller stepped up to a microphone at the capitol in Albany and this time he announced what everyone had expected him to announce six weeks earlier at the Hilton in Manhattan: "Today I announce my active candidacy for the nomination by the Republican Party for Presidency of the United States." He got a big burst of applause, leaned over to kiss Happy, then delivered his prepared remarks. Rockefeller said he was getting in the race because he believed the party wanted to have "a choice of candidates and programs" and because he was "deeply disturbed" by "the course of events, the growing unrest and anxiety at home, and the signs of disintegration abroad." The next day's **New York Times** referred to unsourced "private conversations" in which Rockefeller said LBJ's decision to drop out, Bobby Kennedy's decision to jump in, Martin Luther King Jr.'s assassination, and "subsequent racial disorders" all helped change his mind about running.

One of Rockefeller's staff told the **Times** that "the

campaign boiled down to two things: the polls and the Republican Governors." Like Humphrey, Rocky knew it was too late to compete in the primaries. He was going to play the inside game with the twenty-six Republican governors who controlled enough delegates to deliver the nomination. His argument to them was going to be electability. Rockefeller was their best bet in the general election. No one wanted to watch Nixon lose to another Kennedy. Rockefeller was betting that polls would show him stronger than Nixon by the time Republicans gathered for their convention in Miami. At the press conference immediately following his announcement, Rockefeller was asked if he would accept Governor Ronald Reagan as a running mate—the dream ticket for some Republicans. Rocky said that would "be a matter of later decision." Anything was possible. Rocky said he spoke to Reagan by phone before the announcement. He laughed as he told reporters that Reagan wished him the best of luck. Rocky said he had not called Nixon before the announcement.

Happy Rockefeller played the dutiful role of the smiling wife throughout her husband's announcement and all the reporters' questions except one. Her smile disappeared when a reporter asked if the governor was concerned about his family being subjected to the "indignities" of a presidential campaign. Rockefeller said that when you are in public life, you are "in a sense public property."

Rockefeller didn't mention the most surprising adviser who helped talk him into running. It happened at the White House. The president invited Nelson and Happy Rockefeller to a secret meeting. Johnson told Rockefeller that he wouldn't be able to sleep at night if Richard Nixon became president. And Johnson wasn't all that high on Humphrey. Johnson wanted someone who would hang tough, both on continuing urban renewal and on avoiding defeat in Vietnam, and Johnson saw Rocky as more that man than either of the parties' front-runners.

Rockefeller told Johnson that it would be Happy who made the ultimate decision.

"Let me talk to Happy," Johnson said.

Coming in so late, Rocky needed a strategy that didn't depend on strength in primaries. To get delegates to bolt from Nixon to him, he would have to demonstrate his appeal not only to liberal Republicans but also to Democrats and independents. Rockefeller needed greater electability than Nixon against Humphrey in November. The only way to prove to delegates and party bosses that Rocky was electable would be by citing not primary numbers but polls. Pushing poll numbers up called for a modern, sophisticated advertising campaign.

Rocky had the money for that. Nixon had said his campaign would be waged on television, but it was Rocky who now put that idea most flamboyantly to the test. The advertising agency McCann-Erickson, owned by the massive holding company Interpublic, supported Rocky. One of McCann's subsidiaries, Jack Tinker & Partners, seemed just the team to give the Rockefeller campaign staff a jolt. Suddenly fifty people at Tinker were assigned to the Rockefeller campaign: creatives, media buyers, sociologists, researchers, strategists, budget people.

The Tinker team pitched Rocky a simple concept: leadership. The current national crisis, in this narrative, represented a failure of taking wise yet bold action, and liberalism now equaled leadership. So Rocky shouldn't run away from his own liberalism, the Tinker men argued, but embrace it as the hallmark of leadership.

It wasn't hard to get client buy-in for that concept. The more important thing Tinker had to offer was expertise in targeted ad campaigning. In '68, the audience was gathered in one place. With TV, 90 percent could be reached at once. Based on Gallup and Harris polls, the agency knew just where to reach the people who would respond favorably to sixty-second TV spots in thirty key markets. They would add three minutes per week of national TV advertising. Poll numbers would go shooting up and Rocky would have his electability argument for the delegates and bosses. Total media price tag for this effort: $4.5 million, the most expensive effort to affect the polls ever undertaken. Rocky could afford it.

The other tactic, of course, was approaching delegates the old-fashioned way. It was in that process that Rocky's hard-nosed old pros beating the bushes for delegates around the country in May and June began colliding with the Tinker admen.

The old pros' job was to bring Rocky out to meet with the groups of delegates. Rocky's job was to tell them that he had not really tried to undermine Nixon in '60, and that while he didn't support Goldwater in '64, at least he didn't work against him. Rocky was a party man was his message. If the delegates couldn't pledge themselves to him now, then Rockefeller hoped that they would keep an open mind and see how things shaped up in the polls and at the convention. But the Tinker ads were not about Rocky the party man. They were not just unabashedly liberal but also intense, attention-getting ads from a modern ad agency. One ad showed an African American Vietnam veteran walking a dark, rainy, garbage-littered street. People didn't know how to take that. Rocky's delegate hunters didn't know how to explain that.

On the campaign trail there was no doubt about Rocky's charisma. His biggest problem was that there was just no way to pull big press attention from the all-consuming McCarthy-Kennedy battle in the West Coast Democratic primaries. So Rocky's campaign began slowly and bumpily. May was a tough month. Emmett Hughes, a hard-drinking journalist and long-time political adviser to the Rockefeller family, served at times as head of media, at other times as campaign manager. There was no clear hierarchy. The whole Rockefeller effort on the ground felt simultaneously chaotic and slow.

A week before he announced his candidacy, 18 percent of Pennsylvania voters wrote in Nelson Rockefeller's name on their Republican presidential primary ballots. Richard Nixon won 60 percent and Ronald Reagan got 3 percent of the vote. On the day he announced, across the border in Massachusetts, Rockefeller actually won the primary as a write-in candidate with 30 percent of the vote to Nixon's 26 and favorite-son governor John Volpe's 29 percent. Reagan took 2 percent of the vote. No one considered Massachusetts a real test of a Republican candidacy. A week later, Richard Nixon got 100 percent of the vote in Indiana, and the Republican world seemed to be back to normal.

A week after the Indiana primary came the Nebraska primary, where Bobby Kennedy won by a bigger margin this time: 53 percent to Gene McCarthy's 31 percent. Hubert Humphrey got 9 percent as a write-in candidate. On the Republican side, Richard Nixon won 70 percent of the vote, Ronald Reagan won 22 percent as the write-in candidate, and only 5 percent wrote in Nelson Rockefeller's name. Rocky was obviously in trouble in the more conservative states.

The Kennedy victory was so big in Nebraska that even Gene McCarthy was forced to admit that Bobby had won "a significant victory." Bobby was elated and tried to find the diplomatic words to suggest that McCarthy no longer had a path to the nomination. In trying to put it in a way that wouldn't deeply offend McCarthy, Bobby said there might be a way to "go in together." Bobby offered no specifics. Did he mean a Kennedy-McCarthy ticket? Or did he simply mean cooperation on dividing up the rest of the primaries so that only one of them would make a serious run in each remaining state? McCarthy offered no opening that night. He said, "We did just about what I estimated, about thirty percent. Now we'll go on to Oregon and California."

Oregon was the state Bobby was hoping to avoid. He worried that Oregon was the state that could ruin his "don't lose" strategy. Oregon looked good for McCarthy and all uphill for Kennedy. That's why Bobby was hoping they could have an open agreement about which states they would compete in, which would lead in the end to their combining their forces to block Humphrey's nomination. That way, if Bobby was publicly not competing in Oregon and came in second, it wouldn't count as a loss. If it did, it would be the first time a Kennedy had lost an election. But McCarthy wouldn't consider such an agreement. That left Bobby with no choice: he had to compete in Oregon. As soon as you announced a presidential candidacy, Oregon automatically put your name on its ballot. You didn't have to get thousands of signatures to get your name on it. You didn't have to file anything. Oregon automatically put your name on the ballot, and you couldn't get it off unless you withdrew your candidacy nationally. You could not just withdraw only from the Oregon primary.

Oregon was one of the strongest antiwar states in the country. Oregon's Wayne Morse was the first United States senator to oppose the Vietnam War and was one of only two senators who had voted against the Gulf of Tonkin Resolution. Gene McCarthy was the Wayne Morse of presidential candidates. After losing two in a row to Kennedy, McCarthy went on the attack in Oregon. He reminded voters of Kennedy's longstanding support for the war. He mentioned Attorney General Kennedy's approval of the FBI's wiretapping of Martin Luther King Jr.—long rumored but yet to be proved. McCarthy's condescending humor went public. He said Bobby threatened "to hold his breath unless the people of Oregon voted for him." At the Portland Zoo, both candidates appeared coincidentally at the same time. When Bobby realized it, he had his driver hit the gas to get out of there fast. McCarthy's supporters yelled after him: "Chicken! Coward!"

Flying into Coos Bay, Oregon, an exhausted McCarthy mentioned vaguely to **New York Times** reporter Ned Kenworthy that if Humphrey changed his Vietnam policy, McCarthy could endorse him. The **Times** reported the story, and Gerry Hill, Al

Lowenstein's California partner, now cochairman of McCarthy's California campaign, was furious. Supporters were calling McCarthy headquarters outraged at the idea that, as Hill put it, "Gene was playing footsie with Hubert." Secretly, the McCarthy campaign, having been contacted by Humphrey's people in April, had accepted money from the Humphrey campaign in an effort to stop Bobby in California. Now the whole West Coast McCarthy operation was in an uproar over McCarthy's suggestion in the **Times** that he might step aside for Humphrey.

The next night, with California and Oregon voters in mind, McCarthy spoke to seven thousand excited but unsettled supporters at the Cow Palace in San Francisco. California's primary would be a week after Oregon's. In New Hampshire, McCarthy entered the halls where he spoke as inconspicuously as possible. He entered the Cow Palace by walking down a center aisle in the huge audience. His student admirers reached to touch him. He joked with them as he moved through the crowd. This had the feel of a Kennedy event. Until he spoke.

McCarthy got personal. He directly attacked Kennedy and Humphrey. It was his most serious speech of the campaign and, for antiwar voters, it was his best. McCarthy did something no major politician had done since November 22, 1963: he attacked JFK. He didn't attack him directly. Instead, he reminded his audience that Robert Kennedy played "a prominent role" in developing Kennedy administration policies, "which resulted in disastrous adventures." McCarthy said those policy failures "found in the past three years a new champion in Vice President Humphrey."

McCarthy, in effect, dared Bobby to directly attack his brother's policies when he said he was not convinced that Bobby had "entirely renounced" his support for the war because Bobby never criticized Dean Rusk and Robert McNamara, both JFK cabinet members. The press concentrated on how harshly McCarthy went after Kennedy and Humphrey, but the speech's analysis was, decades later, going to become the generally accepted history of the Vietnam War: "At the very time when American policy grew most disastrous, Vice President Hubert Humphrey became its most ardent apologist. Not merely did he defend the war, he defended every assumption which produced the war—America's moral mission in the world, the great threat from China, the theory of monolithic conspiracy, the susceptibility of political problems to military solutions and the duty to impose American idealism upon foreign cultures." He said this was "a direct result of America's conception of itself as the world's judge and the world's policeman." McCarthy said that "the American people," by which he meant voters, "will fix responsibility [for the war] charitably but firmly, not to be vindictive but rather to assure themselves that errors will not be repeated." By now there was no one left in the Cow

Palace still thinking Gene McCarthy could ever endorse Humphrey or Kennedy. To remove all doubt for McCarthy supporters everywhere, he said he "will not offer any deals or accept any deals but will carry my fight to the finish." He closed with "I will prove to the world that the politics of courage, commitment and reason can be the politics of success."

With Bobby winning his first two primaries in a row with an increasing victory margin, McCarthy started getting questions about being a spoiler who could only help Humphrey by splitting the antiwar vote. McCarthy said, "You can say that Bobby spoiled it for me by coming in." As Bobby rose in the polls in Oregon, he said, "If I get beaten in any primary, I am not a viable candidate." McCarthy reminded reporters, "Bobby was for Lyndon Johnson until a few days after New Hampshire."

The last NBC poll in Oregon showed Bobby with a slight lead within the margin of error at 34 percent. McCarthy was at 32 percent, and Humphrey was polling at 10 percent with Lyndon Johnson still at 9 percent. In the last contested Democratic presidential primary in Oregon, Jack Kennedy decisively beat favorite son Wayne Morse by 51 percent to 32 percent. Maybe Oregon was Kennedy Country.

When the votes were counted in Oregon, history was made once again in the 1968 Democratic presidential primary campaign: Bobby became the first Kennedy in history to lose an election. The family had celebrated victories twenty-seven election nights in a row—primaries and generals. Then came Oregon, where Gene McCarthy won what the press called "a stunning upset victory." Bobby sounded stunned. He said, "I congratulate Senator McCarthy for what appears to be a significant victory." When he was asked what the loss meant to his campaign, the best he could come up with was "I would say it is not helpful." He couldn't find a way that night to reverse what he'd said in a CBS television interview earlier that day when he was feeling more confident: "I can't afford to lose if I'm going to remain a very active and viable candidate."

Gene McCarthy told his joyous election-night crowd in Portland, "I think we've demonstrated who had the real staying power, the real strength, the real commitment." The California primary, with its huge prize of 174 delegates, was a week away. California would decide the winner of the primary campaign. And now Gene McCarthy had the momentum.

TWENTY-THREE

"EVERYTHING'S GOING TO BE OKAY"

California was the primary that most resembled the general election. First, it is huge. The candidates could easily drive from one end of New Hampshire to the other in a day with campaign stops along the way. Every other state they campaigned in had only one big city, one leading newspaper, and one television and radio market. California had three major media markets, each selling very expensive TV advertising slots, in San Francisco, Los Angeles, and San Diego. Second, California's population was as diverse as the country's. The white homogenous population of New Hampshire could all be approached the same way. But the voter appeal that worked in the black neighborhoods of Los Angeles would not work in Beverly Hills, or in conservative Orange County, or with Central Valley farmers or dock workers or Latino grape pickers or surfers. To run statewide in California meant you had to know something about every racial and ethnic group in the great melting pot of American culture. Minnesota was a good training ground for New Hampshire, Wisconsin, and Oregon. But California was something else, and Gene McCarthy was going to have to learn how to deal with that overnight.

McCarthy found himself forced to focus on issues other than the war. He moved to Bobby's left on domestic issues. Where RFK proposed rebuilding the crumbling neighborhoods where many African Americans lived, McCarthy began calling for bolder steps toward real integration. McCarthy wanted to help people move out of ghettos. That sounded threatening to white voters who feared black people moving into their neighborhoods and their suburbs. Bobby was not willing to go that far. He didn't think he could afford to lose any more of the white Kennedy voters of 1960 who didn't like how far the Democrats had moved on civil rights in the last eight years.

By the time the campaign reached California, even Democratic Party bosses were shaken and confused. The Democratic establishment was supposed to be managing the easy reelection of an incumbent president who won four years ago in a landslide. Now they were spending every day trying to do something they had never considered before: contain chaos and see their way through it to a win in November. Parties were invented to eliminate chaos. America's two major parties had long ago extinguished chaos and replaced it with predictability. It doesn't take long for predictability to be boring. **Boring** was the first word most Americans would probably associate with politics. Until 1968.

When looked at as a business, a political party craves predictability as much as General Motors does—no surprises on the assembly line. In the twentieth century, no party suffered worse surprises than the Democrats did in the 1960s. They lost two incumbent presidents—one to assassination, the other to a strangely intractable war and an insurgent challenge within the party. Watching Gene McCarthy go to New Hampshire to campaign for the nomination against the incumbent president of his own party was disorienting enough for the establishment. No one had ever seen that. The establishment explained it to themselves mostly in personal terms—McCarthy is a bored crank with nothing better to do in the Senate; McCarthy craves attention; McCarthy is still angry that LBJ didn't choose him for VP; McCarthy can't get along with anyone. The party bosses were confident in their analysis of why McCarthy was in New Hampshire because decades of predictability breeds confidence. Everything is predictable because we have everything under control. That confidence means the establishment is always the last to know that it has lost control of a process that it created, like nominating a presidential candidate. And so the political establishment is always inclined to believe, with confidence, that nothing is ever happening that it does not understand. They believed that Gene McCarthy launched a presidential campaign because he was a jerk, not really one of them, and that LBJ would crush him and leave McCarthy's political career buried in a snowbank in New Hampshire.

The establishment is always the last to know it is wrong. When McCarthy "won" in New Hampshire, the Democratic establishment did not say or think they were wrong. Thus, they explained away New Hampshire: LBJ wasn't even on the ballot; McCarthy could flood a small state with volunteers, but that wouldn't work anywhere else. They were sure LBJ would come back and crush McCarthy in Wisconsin. There was nothing Gene McCarthy could do to wake the party establishment from their dream that everything was under control. It was Johnson who woke them up when he dropped out of the race. Since then, each day brought a new worry for the party bosses.

They were shaken by Bobby's jumping into the race right after New Hampshire, but they still expected to go all the way with LBJ. Bobby was a real challenger in the establishment's view. Unlike McCarthy,

Bobby could probably win a general election. But even if Bobby polled better against Nixon than LBJ, you don't abandon an incumbent president, because you just don't. They expected to crush Bobby, too. They expected Bobby to get out as soon as the going got tough. They knew Bobby had a family winning streak to preserve and, unlike McCarthy, a political future. Most of them expected to be working for Bobby as their presidential nominee in 1972.

Johnson dropping out exploded everything the party establishment thought they knew about nominating a presidential candidate. They did not know what to do. Humphrey passed the word immediately that he would run, and so they waited for Humphrey. There was nothing in Humphrey's announcement speech for anyone to get excited about. Every Humphrey supporter watching knew instantly that their candidate was the most boring man in the race, including Nixon. The speech foreshadowed everything he would do on the primary campaign trail when he insulted voters' intelligence by pretending he wasn't campaigning, just touring the country in his official role as vice president, making speeches. He smiled too much. It was a nervous forced smile that made a stiff politician seem all the more fake. He seemed to think he had to constantly look happy to live up to his old and largely forgotten unfortunate political nickname, the "Happy Warrior." It was the wrong nickname and the wrong image for the defender of a war policy that was ripping the fabric of American society. What did he have to be so happy about? Did he not attend the White House meetings that day about the war? Did he miss that day's body count? The antiwar candidates smiled a lot, but that was in response to the enthusiasm of their huge emotional crowds. McCarthy and Kennedy did not say they were running on "the policies of happiness," as Humphrey had done just weeks after the assassination of Martin Luther King Jr. Humphrey actually said in the middle of the year that had already endured the King assassination, nationwide riots, and thousands of Americans killed in action in Vietnam, with millions of young men fearing they would be the next sent to die there, that "it should be a time of great confidence and, above all my friends, a time for public happiness in this nation." As much as they wanted to, it was impossible for the Democratic establishment to feel confident or happy about their new candidate Hubert Humphrey.

And so they turned to Bobby. They didn't defect; they just watched. They watched Humphrey try to force happiness on a troubled country and they watched Bobby beat Gene McCarthy in Indiana and Nebraska. If Bobby kept this up, redefining the establishment choice as the man who used to be a leader of the party establishment until he challenged the president just a few months ago was not going to be too difficult. They had all supported a Kennedy presidential campaign before. The establishment's switch from Johnson to Humphrey was never a comfortable one. How could it be? They'd never had to switch before. But now that they were forced to switch, switching the next time to a candidate who was on a winning streak—a candidate they knew and respected—should be a bit easier. Then came Oregon.

Losing Oregon held off any establishment defections to Bobby. They would only have to wait a week to see whether there was an alternative to Humphrey. California voters would decide that.

The day after the first Kennedy loss in history, when Bobby's motorcade drove through downtown Los Angeles, thousands of people lined the streets. Confetti showered down on him as he waved from the backseat of a convertible. People rushed to the slow-moving car to touch him. Later he said, "After last night in Oregon I'm going to call Los Angeles Resurrection City."

The California Kennedy campaign was what the Democrats were hoping their presidential campaign would look like—exciting, fun, glamorous, serious, and important all at the same time. Bobby was in the backseat of top-down convertibles waving to crowds on the sidewalk as if he already were president. Sometimes it was a family affair with Ethel and the kids and their dog Freckles. Sometimes Freckles sat beside Bobby on the plane or in a motorcade. If Freckles wasn't beside him, then a movie star might be—Sidney Poitier, Lauren Bacall, Warren Beatty, or countless others. When he was in the barrios—jacket off, tie loosened, sleeves rolled up—Bobby listened intently. When he walked the streets of Watts on the last day before the California vote, Bobby didn't look like other politicians who dropped into a black neighborhood for a photo op. He looked welcome. The crowds that turned out for him in Watts were enormous and awestruck. They seemed to feel connected to this man whose brother's picture was in so many of their homes beside a picture of Martin Luther King Jr.

McCarthy had his own troupe of stars—Paul Newman, Dustin Hoffman, Paul Simon, and Art Garfunkel—but McCarthy knew he couldn't compete with a Kennedy show. He concentrated on the college and university campuses, where he was always given a hero's welcome.

Bobby avoided direct mention of McCarthy, but he kept reminding California that he was also running against the candidate who wasn't there: "If the Vice President is nominated to oppose Richard Nixon, there will be no candidate who has opposed the course of escalation of the war in Vietnam. There will be no candidate committed to the kinds of programs which can remedy the conditions which are transforming our cities into armed camps. There will be no candidate committed to return government to the people, or returning to the economic policies which gave us rising prosperity without destructive inflation."

On the final weekend before the California primary, McCarthy and Kennedy appeared together in a nationally televised debate. Kennedy had been refusing to debate McCarthy—the standard choice of a front-runner in the polls. When he arrived in Los Angeles the day after the Oregon primary, Bobby immediately agreed to a debate. He explained to the press his sudden eagerness to debate: "I'm not the same candidate I was before Oregon."

ABC's Frank Reynolds sat at the center of a table with McCarthy to his right and Kennedy to his left. Reynolds asked questions and the candidates avoided direct comment to each other. The press was disappointed to report that there were no fireworks. **New York Times** columnist Jack Gould wrote that it was "an electronic tennis game, in which Senators Robert F. Kennedy and Eugene J. McCarthy played on the same side of the net." Neither side claimed victory in the debate.

Bobby knew the California primary could be his last election night of the year. On his first day of campaigning in California after Oregon, he made coast-to-coast front-page headlines by promising to drop out of the race if he didn't win California. He also said that "under no circumstances" would he accept a vice presidential nomination. Even if Bobby won California, if the establishment all stuck with Humphrey, Bobby would not be the nominee. And so he ran in California as if it were his last race—all out all the way through that last day in Watts.

The last polls before the California primary showed the race too close to call. The cooler heads in each campaign knew that only one antiwar candidate would be viable tomorrow. Bobby was the only one to publicly admit that by vowing to drop out if he didn't win California. But then what? Would he endorse McCarthy? Could he endorse Humphrey? Would he stay neutral? Bobby had already promised to endorse the Democratic nominee, but the party wouldn't have a nominee for almost three months. It looked like McCarthy would have very little chance of winning the nomination even if he won California. Endorsing McCarthy would be personally difficult for Bobby after all of McCarthy's insulting jokes about him. But if Bobby didn't endorse him, it would look as if he were not really committed to the cause of peace. But if Humphrey was going to be the nominee, Bobby could exact concessions on the war before endorsing him. That would get America closer to peace than endorsing a losing peace candidate would. Such were the difficult questions swirling around the Kennedy campaign on election day.

If McCarthy lost, he would face the decision to drop out and endorse. Dropping out of the race that he'd started in favor of the candidate who took advantage of the opening against LBJ that McCarthy created would be excruciating for McCarthy. It would feel as if he were surrendering to that Kennedy sense of entitlement that he abhorred. But if McCarthy stayed in the race, he really would be nothing but a spoiler for Bobby. He would be preventing the leading antiwar candidate from going all the way. Then McCarthy would look as if he were committed only to his campaign, not to peace. If he dropped out and didn't endorse Bobby, then how could he claim to be committed to peace? Endorsing Humphrey was clearly out of the question for McCarthy. An option some discussed on election day was McCarthy technically staying in the race but not seriously competing. That way he could avoid the pain of endorsing Bobby. No one wanted to bring up these questions to the candidates, but they wanted to be ready to help their man face these questions tomorrow if he had to. The dreamers in both campaigns, such as Al Lowenstein, continued to dream of some kind of unification of the two campaigns tomorrow, but no one was sure how to describe that or exactly what their demands would be to agree to a unification. Everyone knew that tomorrow was going to be a completely different campaign from what it was today. And no one knew what to do about that when the polls closed in California at 8:00 p.m.

Juan Romero was a seventeen-year-old high school student working as a busboy at the Ambassador Hotel in Los Angeles on election night. He was ten years old when he moved to California from Mexico in 1961. Juan Romero delivered a room service dinner to room 514. It was dinner for four: Bobby and Ethel Kennedy and the singer Andy Williams and his wife. It was Juan Romero's first time in Senator Kennedy's room. "He made me feel like a regular citizen," Romero said decades later. "He made me feel like a human being. He didn't look at my color, he didn't look at my position." What impressed Romero the most was the handshake: "He shook my hand. I didn't ask him."

At 9:00 p.m., the early returns left the election too close to call. At 10:00 p.m., it could still go either way. Then Bobby took a small lead. By 11:00 p.m., Bobby's lead was holding, and soon it was clear that in the precincts that had not yet been counted there would not be enough McCarthy votes for him to catch up. Bobby Kennedy was a winner again.

Roosevelt "Rosey" Grier, the former New York Giants and Los Angeles Rams defensive tackle, was one of the celebrities with Bobby on election night, as he was every day and night of the California campaign.

Rosey Grier had been a Kennedy family friend for years, and he'd appointed himself Bobby's bodyguard for the campaign. Grier instantly became the most famous bodyguard in the world because he was the only famous person to take on a task like that. Grier presented a challenge to campaign photographers because Bobby frequently disappeared behind Grier's six-foot-five-inch frame, but at least the photographers got shots of a hugely popular NFL star. Sometimes Bobby asked Grier to speak at rallies, but he preferred to stay at Bobby's side, ready to protect him from anything.

Roosevelt Grier was a rich former NFL star turned Hollywood actor and entertainer, one of the first to follow that path. He wasn't being paid to be a bodyguard. He was doing it for a friend. Whenever you saw Grier using his body to provide a safe space for Bobby in a crowd, you knew he was doing it for love. He wasn't going to let us lose this man. We had lost too many in the 1960s to assassins' bullets—Jack Kennedy, Medgar Evers, Malcolm X, Martin Luther King Jr. With the country still reeling from the loss of Dr. King, Grier wasn't going to let that happen to his country again. He wasn't going to let that happen to Bobby. There was no doubt that Rosey Grier would take a bullet for Bobby.

When Bobby stepped up to the microphone at the Embassy Room in the Ambassador Hotel on the night of the most important win of his life, Rosey

Grier stepped back to protect Ethel, who was then three months pregnant with her eleventh child.

Across town at the Beverly Hilton Hotel, Gene McCarthy was to hear that Bobby was beginning his victory speech without following the tradition of waiting for the loser to give the concession speech first. It was 3:00 a.m. on the east coast, and Bobby had to rush it to have any chance of having his victory photos on the front pages of the late editions of tomorrow's papers. As Bobby spoke, McCarthy started typing the speech he would never give.

Juan Romero was off duty when Bobby began his speech at two minutes to midnight, but like many of the off-duty hotel workers, he stayed to hear Bobby speak. It was a short speech. Almost twelve minutes. Nothing written. Nothing prepared. He thanked Cesar Chavez and Dolores Huerta, the founders of the United Farm Workers, who were standing beside him on the podium. He thanked Olympic decathlon champion Rafer Johnson and Rosey Grier. There was cheering after every sentence. He thanked the campaign staff and the volunteers. He thanked black voters for delivering his 46 to 42 percent victory, which could have gone the other way without them. Then he said: "What I think is—what I think is quite clear is that we can work together in the last analysis and that what has been going on in the United States over the period of the last three years, the division, the violence, the disenchantment with our society, the division whether it's between black and white, between the poor and the more affluent or between age groups over the war in Vietnam, that we can start to work together. We are a great country."

The final words Bobby Kennedy spoke publicly were: "So, uh, thanks to all of you and on to Chicago, and let's win there!"

The applause and "We want Bobby" chants didn't last long. Gunfire turned the applause to screams. Eight shots that sounded like firecrackers. Bobby had moved quickly off the podium and was going to pass through the kitchen on the way to another room where he would face reporters in a press conference. He was shaking hands with waiters and cooks when he was shot. "I saw Kennedy lurch against the ice machine, and then sag, and then fall forward slowly," wrote Pete Hamill in his eyewitness account in the **Village Voice**.

Rosey Grier was guarding Ethel on the opposite side of the podium from where Bobby exited. When Grier caught up to where the shots were fired, he saw men struggling with the shooter, who still had the gun in his hand. Grier reached for the gun. He said, "I put my hand under the trigger housing and I pulled back the hammer so it couldn't strike." He wrenched the gun away. "Now I have the gun in my hand, so I shove it in my pocket." Then the crowd went after the shooter. Grier said, "They were going to tear him to pieces. I fought them off." The last person Rosey Grier protected that night was the man who'd shot Bobby Kennedy.

When the crowd was rushing away from the sound of the gun, Juan Romero rushed toward it. He saw Bobby lying on the floor. He knelt down beside him and lifted Bobby's head off the floor and held him. The picture of Juan Romero holding Bobby Kennedy was on the front pages of newspapers around the world the next day. Romero never spoke to a reporter until four years later, when he said he felt something warm like water flowing in his hands. "I wasn't sure what it was, if it was the emotion I felt touching him or something, I wasn't sure of myself so I moved my hand to look at it and there was blood on it."

"Is everybody okay?" Bobby asked.

"Yes, everybody's okay," said Romero.

"Everything's going to be okay," said Bobby.

His eyes were still open when Ethel Kennedy knelt beside him and whispered, "I'm with you, my baby."

It took twenty-two minutes for the ambulance to arrive. "Don't lift me" was the last thing anyone heard Bobby say as he was moved onto a stretcher. Then he lost consciousness.

At the hospital, a doctor passed a stethoscope to Ethel so she could hear Bobby's heartbeat. Bobby clung to life all the next day as the country absorbed the agony of another shooting. There was very little shock this time. Not after Jack Kennedy. Not after Martin Luther King Jr. just two months earlier. In the place once occupied by shock was the sickening feeling that this is what America had become— assassination was now a routine of American life, assassination was, as Pete Hamill put it, in "the secret filthy heart of America."

Twenty-four hours after he was shot, Bobby Kennedy was still clinging to life as America went to sleep worried about what tomorrow's news would bring. The next day, Frank Mankiewicz had to make the most painful announcement any campaign press secretary has ever had to deliver: "I have a short announcement to read which I will read [pause] at this time. Senator Robert Francis Kennedy died at 1:44 a.m. today, June 6th, 1968. With Senator Kennedy at the time of his death were his wife, Ethel, his sisters Ms. Stephen Smith, Ms. Patricia Lawford, his brother-in-law Mr. Stephen Smith, his sister-in-law Mrs. John F. Kennedy. He was 42 years old. Thank you."

On the evening news that night, NBC's Chet Huntley said this: "Senator Kennedy's body was taken to Los Angeles International Airport in a cortege of relatives and close associates. At 1:28 p.m. a White House airplane took off bearing the body and the Kennedy party. Even as the great jet wheeled out over the Pacific to make its turn and head out toward New York, the final votes were coming in from remote precincts of the state, swelling the count which the senator had established in the state only two days ago. He won the election, tasted briefly the satisfying fruit of achievement and then lost his life."

TWENTY-FOUR

STOP NIXON

The funeral was at St. Patrick's Cathedral in midtown Manhattan. President Johnson was there. Hubert Humphrey and Gene McCarthy were there. Richard Nixon and Nelson Rockefeller were there. Teddy Kennedy delivered the eulogy: "My brother need not be idealized, or enlarged in death beyond what he was in life; to be remembered simply as a good and decent man, who saw wrong and tried to right it, saw suffering and tried to heal it, saw war and tried to stop it. . . . As he said many times, in many parts of this nation, to those he touched and who sought to touch him: Some men see things as they are and say why. I dream things that never were and say why not."

The casket was moved from the cathedral to a special funeral train filled with Kennedy family and friends headed to Washington for a burial at Arlington National Cemetery near JFK's grave. Two million people lined the tracks as the train headed south through New Jersey, Delaware, and Maryland.

All the presidential candidates suspended their campaigns. The president ordered Secret Service protection for all of them. Gene McCarthy had the most trouble adjusting to the loss of his opponent. For the others, the adjustment was just a matter of finding the proper timing for returning to the campaign trail. But McCarthy was at home in Washington with Secret Service agents suddenly occupying his basement while he lay awake at night in bed staring at the ceiling, regretting so many things he had said about Bobby. Of course, with Gene McCarthy, even his regrets were complex. While he regretted having left those attacks against Bobby in the record of the campaign, he also regretted that he would never be able to prove they were true. There would be no room for McCarthy's accusations in what he was sure would become the quick and lasting mythologizing of Bobby Kennedy.

Three days after the assassination, McCarthy met with Humphrey. The meeting was inconclusive and proved nothing other than how disoriented McCarthy was. He seemed physically and emotionally exhausted. Humphrey listened as McCarthy rambled. It sounded as if he were almost apologizing for taking his campaign as far as he had. He said something about feeling overburdened by Abigail's commitment to the campaign and the "Clean for Gene" kids' enthusiasm. He did offer Humphrey a word of advice: don't take Ted Kennedy as a running mate. That sounded like McCarthy was giving up, but it was too late for that. Two weeks later, the McCarthy campaign picked up sixty-two New York delegates, leaving Humphrey only twelve.

The only candidate who found a new energy after the assassination was the other New Yorker, Nelson Rockefeller. In the weeks after the assassination, voters started to notice there was another liberal New Yorker running for president, a fighter for civil rights, a son of an American dynasty. Rockefeller seemed to be reaching a quickly regrouping coalition of liberal Republicans, Democrats, and independents.

Now there had to be two Nelson Rockefellers. Talking to party delegations, Rocky used his indoor voice. Ever the master of budget and policy, he could summon flurries of numbers with total recall. To soothe those Republicans growing suspicious of big government, Rocky could make all problems seem solvable with nothing more than good bookkeeping.

But outdoors, it was a different story. Young people, working people, and black people began flocking to Rocky's rallies. They carried signs like the ones seen in Bobby's crowds: "Rock Rock Rock with Rocky" and "Go Go Go with Rocky." A real visionary image was growing around Rockefeller. The excitement was authentic.

Rocky had always loved the backslapping, the joshing, the back-and-forth with a crowd. He had the policies and the record that made sense on the street. Instead of lecturing urban crowds about law and order, he talked about jobs, schools, equality. Black audiences would yell "That's right!" and he'd say it back, "That's right!"—sometimes even taking on an urban dialect of his own. "Thass right, man, thass right!" Rocky would yell, and instead of turning away from such weird appropriations, they made Rocky, for this crowd in this moment, almost a Kennedy.

On Saturday, August 3, stepping off the ramp of his plane at the Coast Guard's Opa Locka Airport near Miami, with Happy by his side, Nelson Rockefeller was met by an excited crowd that included many transplanted New Yorkers. Many at this rally weren't Republicans. This was the cross-party coalition that could demonstrate Rocky's likely success in the general election. The candidate addressed the crowd, and he did not back off his liberalism.

"The Republican Party," Nelson told the cheering throng, "must become once again a national party, the voice of the poor and the oppressed."

That was the Rockefeller Republican Party. He was in Miami Beach to save it. His campaign was against Old Nixon conservatism, and against New Nixon vagueness. Rocky was there to rescue the party from its right wing. The crowd loved him.

By 1968, two and a half million visitors were

flocking every year to Miami Beach, joining eighty-five thousand permanent residents, with a median age nearing sixty. Miami Beach had no factories, no railroads, no airport. Miami Beach had no cemetery. What it did have was more than 2,500 apartment buildings and more than 350 hotels, crammed into seven square miles of turgid humidity and scorching sun, where Americans happily paid to frolic. They came to flop in the pools, retreat to the chill of air-conditioning, and for the daring, attend nude reviews supposed to rival those of Paris.

Off the island of Miami Beach, across the bay in the real big city of Miami and beyond, the heightening national divisions and violent shocks, called out by daily headlines, along with the mundane realities of daily life itself, seemed a universe away. Insulated by water, Miami Beach made a natural American mecca for business presentations and conventions of all kinds.

On Monday, August 4, 1968, in Miami Beach, the Republican National Convention started the business of nominating its presidential candidate in what party officials hoped would seem a confident display of unity. The public action was in the Miami Beach Convention Center, with executive and administrative operations ensconced at the Fontainebleau Hotel, and GOP delegations from every state filling suite after suite in hotels up and down the beach and along Collins Avenue. It was the first national nominating convention ever held in Miami Beach. The hall had been expanded the year before specifically to accommodate the Republicans. This paradise of the American imagination ideally suited the Republican Party's developing vision of itself: vanguard of a conservatism as ordinary as dirt and yet aspiring to glitter. In Miami Beach, there was nothing all that wrong with America that couldn't be fixed with a little law and order out there in the cities, and a little indulgence in the leisure and entertainment that are the just rewards of honest effort.

The Chamber of Commerce had been working hard to burnish the local image in advance of the GOP arrival. The chamber warned the hotel business to refrain from upcharging this influx of state delegations. That would spread a bad reputation throughout the whole country. The state of Florida brought in almost fifty alcohol-control agents. They were there to monitor and control the price gouging and drink watering they expected to go on. In Miami Beach the GOP had found a patch of hyper-Americana well protected from all of the upheavals of past months. As seen on TV, here was a place to forget all your troubles.

The police department intended to keep it that way. The police chief deployed what he called "maximum security with minimum visibility." Amplifying the city's two-hundred-man police force were Florida Highway Patrol officers, the FBI, the U.S. Army, the

Bureau of Narcotics, and the IRS. Security personnel in Miami Beach outnumbered convention delegates. The convention hall was defended by a six-foot
chain-link fence, guarded by police. A compound
nearby was designated as a holding pen for any protesters. In a departure from freewheeling conventions of years past, new systems of tickets, passes,
badges, and hand stamping controlled all movement
around the convention floor. The Northeastern press
was duly disgusted, both by the garishness of Miami
Beach and by the control exercised over the press
within the hall. Convention security had never been
so tight and intrusive.

This was the summer of 1968—the summer of
riots and assassinations. The city of Miami Beach
and the Republican Party could not afford to take
any chances with control of the convention.

The story that the Republican Party had to tell the
public, in four days of droning speeches and maniacal
cheering and sign pumping, all covered on network
television in prime time, was of an amazing comeback from the worst electoral disaster of the twentieth century, after Barry Goldwater, only four years
earlier. Ideological passion was muted. What Nixon
had become adept at presenting as a pragmatic, conservative centrism was the message of the day.

Barry Goldwater was in Miami Beach with the mission of bringing his fervent right-wing base into the
Nixon mainstream. Goldwater's payback for Nixon's

support four years ago was to calm the excitable, aiding the feeling of unity around Nixon. All of the convention's public display, including the manufactured eruptions of cheering and demonstrations of joy, amped by ringers hired to cheerlead, was meant to be soothing. Even boring. Boring would do the job, too. In 1968, boring would be just fine for a change.

Out of view of TV cameras, Republican Party unity was a total illusion, and as he planned for arrival in Miami Beach, Richard Nixon knew it. After all he'd done to frame himself for the press, the party, and the public as the only viable candidate, Dick knew he would once again have to grunt and sweat his way to the nomination. He would have to make promises. He would have to blend the Old and New Nixons. While his team went about shoring up the delegate count, Nixon himself carefully calibrated his appeal, tailoring it to each group and each person he spoke to. No one knew better, as he liked to say, how the game is played. He was ready.

The political dance that Dick and his people now had to perform reflected the peculiar point that national party conventions had come to in 1968. They were on TV, of course, but within recent memory they had not been. In those pre-TV days, sweaty delegates—overwhelmingly men, overwhelmingly white—sat around in shirtsleeves, ties askew, hats lost, eating peanuts out of paper sacks and throwing cigar butts on the floor while making deals. From the high galleries, an audience booed and drank and cheered and threw stuff down in response to speeches. In 1952, CBS and NBC began providing the public with gavel-to-gavel coverage. By '68, the parties were trying to make their conventions predictable multi-day TV commercials for the party. The deal making had to go on but instead of taking place in public with nobody watching, now it had to take place in back rooms while everyone was watching the show on the convention stage.

While the GOP wanted to give the public a carefully orchestrated display of party unity, for the nominees and bosses and delegates, the whole trick, and really the whole point of having a convention at all, still came down to wrestling delegates to the ground, tying them up with commitments, protecting them from being stolen by other candidates' teams, and stealing delegates that the other candidates' teams were trying to protect. That's what a convention was. That's how conventions had always been. The New Politics was soon going to end all that by awarding enough delegates during an expanded primary season to lock in the nomination months before the convention. In 1968, there was still room for drama at a convention.

The state chairmen and delegates now flooding Miami Beach were considering how the winds were blowing, how much the winds had changed since New Hampshire, even since California. Reasons could arise for switching candidates.

The GOP nominee would need 667 delegate votes. If Nixon could line up at least that many delegates, he would go "over the top," as the saying went, and win the nomination on the first ballot. A second ballot would then be only a formal ritual of party unity with the other candidates happily releasing their delegates so the second ballot would become a near-unanimous vote. But if Nixon fell short of 667 on the first ballot, more rounds of balloting would become necessary, and the drama would go public. A slight shortfall could be pretty harmless to the front-runner. There were a number of state favorite-son candidates to be placed in nomination on the first ballot, as a sign of party and state regard, but if the front-runner fell short, any favorite son loyal to him would release delegates and endorse him. The front-runner would go over the top easily on the second ballot. If things were looking really rough for the front-runner, tractable favorite sons might be pleaded with or ordered by bosses to hand over their delegates even before the first ballot. If a first-ballot shortfall was deep, his support might erode quickly as the delegates regrouped to cast the second ballot. Favorite sons, seeing power shifting, might agree to endorse the runner-up, or even a third-place candidate. Delegates supposedly pledged to the front-runner might see an insurgency in the making and abandon the front-runner in panic at being left out of whatever might be brewing. Between the balloting rounds, aggressive floor operators would be courting delegates, and the front-runner would have to start offering policy concessions, at the very least.

If Republicans didn't have a winner on the first ballot, anything could happen, as it did in 1860 when Republicans nominated Abraham Lincoln, the president they've always been most proud of. New York's Senator William Seward arrived at the convention in Chicago with the most delegates, thanks to New York being the largest delegation. Thirteen names were put in nomination. On the first ballot, Senator Seward was way out in front with 173 votes to Lincoln's second-place finish at 102. By the third ballot, it was a landslide for Abraham Lincoln.

Ronald Reagan arrived in Miami Beach having refused, again and again, to compete in the primaries. But he had been campaigning in other ways all along. The Goldwater crowd began the year pressuring Reagan to at least hint publicly that he might be serious about challenging Nixon, to keep right-wing hope alive.

Reagan kept making right-wing speeches while waiting and watching. If this was going to be his year, Reagan figured, any maneuvering would have to remain secret. After the Goldwater disaster of 1964, party unity was all most Republicans cared about.

Reagan couldn't openly go against Nixon and divide the party.

It wasn't only Western and Californian Republicans who saw Reagan as their last, best hope. Paying Reagan important attention now was a new group, Southern Democrats turned Republican. Representing the only bloc of states Goldwater had won in '64, Southern Republican delegations had new power in the party, and as they convened in Miami Beach, they were driven by one thing: opposition to civil rights. They wanted to obstruct and even one day roll back federal civil rights laws and restore the old ways of Southern life and politics. Their new code language for all of this was "freedom of choice" and "states' rights." A liberal integrationist like Rockefeller was naturally out of the question for them. To the GOP South, blocking Rocky was an unambiguously clear goal.

The Nixon question was more complicated. Sold to Southern delegations as the one man who could actually win in November, Nixon did have strong conservative credentials. Still, the South and the far right were spoiled. In Goldwater they'd had a candidate they knew was one of their own in his heart and soul, a true believer. Nixon had been around too long, an establishment politician, with multiple political personalities and a flexible ideology. In the name of party unity Southern delegations were being dragged grudgingly toward victory over the integrationist Democrats through Nixon. But the New Nixon had not won their hearts. Ronald Reagan did.

Segregationist Southerners saw in Reagan one of their own, too, and they loved him for it. Though supposedly not campaigning, Reagan had been traveling widely. It was in the white South that the California governor met with a level of excitement that almost matched Bobby Kennedy's appeal in black neighborhoods and barrios. Going into Miami Beach, some Southern Republicans' strategy was actually more complicated and devious than Reagan himself could have realized, as tricky as anything Nixon could have come up with.

Spearheaded by a loose affiliation known, because it had first met in Greenville, Mississippi, as the Greenville Group, the sharpest Southern Republicans knew that an enthusiastic Goldwater-style campaign could only lose the GOP another election. If that happened, a civil-rights-supporting Democrat would be president for the next four years and the cement of civil rights law would harden. Those Southern Republicans were just as committed as the rest of the party bosses to a boring, apparently unified, convention.

But they also wanted the GOP nominee in their debt and subject to their demands. They wanted "states' rights." To get that, they would have to withhold certainty from the front-runner. They had to keep Nixon from believing he had Southern delegations locked up. The leaders of the Greenville Group had told Nixon that he had their support, but they still wanted him nervous enough to have to listen to them on civil rights. That's why they kept urging Reagan to announce. They wanted Nixon running scared of Reagan—running in their direction. They were taking a big risk. Southern delegates were already swooning over Reagan, but Reagan seemed to have no chance of winning in November. They didn't really want to nominate Reagan, just use him to control Nixon.

In the spring, Nixon had played straight into the Southerners' hands. Nixon had been getting worried about George Wallace, and at the end of May he met with the GOP's Southern state chairmen in Atlanta. The Southerners, irritated that the Republican National Committee had been turning deaf ears to their own concerns about Wallace's allure, were impressed. Nixon actually listened. The GOP was bleeding support in the South, they told Nixon. Voters were going over to Wallace.

"What can I do?" Nixon asked.

They told Nixon he had to talk to Strom Thurmond. "Well, where is he?" Nixon asked.

The next day, the South Carolina Democrat-turned-Republican senator was sitting in the back of a limo coming in from the Atlanta airport deep in discussion with Richard Nixon. It was Strom Thurmond who had led the "Dixiecrat" walkout at the Democratic convention twenty years earlier, when the young firebrand Hubert Humphrey led the fight for a civil rights plank. In 1948, Thurmond had run, as Wallace was running now, a third-party segregationist campaign. After that, many of the Southern Democrats went back to the Democrats, but Strom Thurmond didn't. Having filibustered the 1957 civil rights bill in the Senate for a record-setting twenty-four-plus hours, reading recipes and anything else to keep his mouth moving, he finally switched parties to endorse Goldwater in 1964. Now the great segregationist was the leader not only of his South Carolina GOP delegation but of most Southern Republicans. Senator Thurmond's main issue was obstructing civil rights enforcement in the South. "All the laws of Washington and all the bayonets of the Army," Thurmond said in 1948, "cannot force the Negro into our homes, into our schools, our churches and our places of recreation and amusement."

In the limo beside Thurmond on the way to meet the GOP governors, Nixon was nervous. He couldn't tell Thurmond that as president he would publicly support "states' rights" regarding federal integration laws. Nixon couldn't publicly promise that outright and win the election.

Thurmond told Nixon there was one thing he wanted. Tense, Nixon waited to hear what it was.

Thurmond leaned in. He said, "Never let up on the Communists."

That was easy. Nixon wholeheartedly agreed.

Thurmond made Nixon also agree that at the convention he would meet with every Southern delegation—every Southern delegate, if necessary!—and answer any question they might see fit to ask. Nixon played, in turn, to Thurmond's vanity. Nixon didn't just ask for support—he told Thurmond that he was the one man who could save the Republican Party from George Wallace.

Flattered, and eager to dictate Southern terms to Nixon, Thurmond took the stop-Wallace mission to heart. Throughout the summer Thurmond worked one idea again and again into the heads of the Southern Republican delegations: Nixon's the one. Thurmond had to stop not only Southern impulses to support George Wallace but also the swooning of many Southern delegates over Ronald Reagan.

"I love Reagan," Thurmond would say. It was true. He wouldn't deny it. Ronnie was the party's future. But to vote for Reagan this year, Thurmond constantly repeated, would be the kiss of death. Either Rockefeller would be the next president, or Humphrey would. Reagan was the long game for Thurmond. In 1968, for Strom Thurmond, for the South, Nixon must be the one.

Thurmond was succeeding in holding Southern

support for Nixon. Then, just before the convention, Reagan began making moves that excited the Southern delegations and made them harder to control.

Reagan had kept saying he wasn't running. Sometimes he said it with an offhand, gee-shucks attitude that made you think he was open to suggestions. Other times, seemingly stricken with fear of how he would look if he seemed to be running, he protested his lack of interest with an intensity that turned off his fans. When the head of Texans for Reagan, the enthusiastic J. R. "Butch" Butler, flew to Massachusetts and startled Governor John Volpe by offering him the vice presidential spot on Reagan's ticket— a ticket that didn't exist—it wasn't only Volpe who was surprised, Reagan was, too. Volpe expressed cautious interest; he said he "reserved his position." The Reaganites like Butch Butler kept hustling about to promote a Reagan candidacy.

What these Reaganites were hoping for in Miami Beach was a Nixon-Rockefeller tie on the first ballot. That would give Reagan the chance to come forward as the unifier, the breaker of the deadlock. But Rocky had started too late to get enough delegates to pull it off. So if Nixon was really to be denied an over-the-top win on the first ballot, Reagan would just have to start grabbing delegates on his own.

Flying quickly about the country, Reagan dropped in on eight state delegations just to have a chat. Most were in the South. And on July 31, well before either Rockefeller or Nixon, he arrived in Miami Beach. He checked into the Deauville Hotel, went to the Fontainebleau to address the Platform Committee, flew away to drop in on more delegations just preparing to head for the convention, flew back to Miami, and prepared to make his powerful presence felt in meetings with all the state delegations arriving in Miami Beach. He still hadn't declared his candidacy, but a lot of Southerners now believed Ronnie was running.

To the Greeneville Group's dismay, some of those delegates were talking "Ronnie or bust." The group's strategy for using Reagan to pressure Nixon on civil rights might be spinning out of control.

When Nelson Rockefeller checked into the Americana Hotel in Miami Beach after his airport speech, he had to face some bad news. A Gallup headline told the story: NIXON OVERTAKES HUMPHREY AND MCCARTHY; ROCKY RUNS EVEN AGAINST BOTH DEMO-CRATS. The multimillion-dollar Tinker advertising campaign had not done the trick. After an initial bump for Rocky in the polls, on the eve of the convention, a Gallup poll now showed that Nixon had the edge against both possible Democratic nominees. But Rocky had his own poll. It showed him ahead of Nixon in the nine key industrial states where the November election would really be decided. Nixon had a big lead in delegates now, too. Rocky did not have enough active delegate support to stop Nixon on the first ballot. Still, this was Nelson Rockefeller, and he had hope. That hope was Ronald Reagan.

Just as the Reagan people were hoping for a Rocky-Nixon first-ballot deadlock, so Rocky now hoped for Reagan to put together enough delegates that, when combined with Rocky's, would hold Nixon not just below the winning 667 but below 600 on the first ballot. If that happened, the game would instantly change. The best projections Rocky's people could come up with showed Rocky taking the lead on a third ballot with 481 delegates to Nixon's 387 and Reagan's 336. If that happened, a long night would follow, and in the end, one man and one ideology would triumph. The nominee would be either Ronald Reagan, backed by the South and the right wing, or Nelson Rockefeller, backed by the North and a revived Republican liberalism.

This alliance of Rockefeller, out to save the party for liberalism, and Reagan, the hope of the New Right, wasn't as impossible as it might sound today. The idea of balancing the ticket with left and right had been floated many times. Rocky thought Ronnie had a good chance of putting together a strong challenge to Nixon; meanwhile, Rocky's team would work on "erosion," grabbing as many of Nixon's delegates as possible, one at a time and in small groups, and bringing them into either the Reagan or the Rockefeller camp, it didn't matter. The whole game was to stop a Nixon win on the first ballot. The very meaning and purpose of the Republican Party was at stake. And yet the TV networks previewing their gavel-to-gavel coverage were telling the public that this would be the least ideological convention in American history.

TWENTY-FIVE

"GREAT TELEVISION"

The front-runner arrived in Miami Beach on Monday, the day before the convention would officially open. About six hundred people gathered to greet Richard Nixon outside the Hilton, where his headquarters was set up. As the candidate arrived, two bands played the campaign song "Nixon's the One," while the Nixonettes, chirpy high school and college cheerleader types, wearing straw boaters, and with "Nixon" banners over their miniskirts, bopped along. Two thousand balloons were released and ascended to the heavens.

Nixon was not just tanned but slightly sunburned. While Reagan and Rocky had been dashing from hotel to hotel working delegates in closed rooms, Nixon had been working on his acceptance speech in Montauk on Long Island. He smiled and shook hands and then disappeared into the hotel. No speech, no press conference. He was saving it.

Above the fray. That was the strategy. That's what the TV news cameras showed at the hotel—Nixon was so confident he didn't have to say a word. He knew he was facing a Rocky-Reagan challenge to deny him a first ballot victory, but the New Nixon was not going to be seen nervously speechifying for delegates in the Hilton driveway. Invincible and inevitable was the image of the day for Nixon. He had a huge lead in delegates won in the primaries. He had the support of state party leaders all over the country. He had private assurances from the Southern bosses. He had Oregon senator Mark Hatfield persuading the liberals while Barry Goldwater calmed the right wing and Strom Thurmond buttonholed the Southern Reagan fans. But by the summer of 1968, there was no such thing as inevitable in America, and Nixon knew it.

Nixon had a nation in crisis and a law-and-order platform to deal with it. He had Johnson's failure to end the war in Vietnam. He had been the vice president in what most Republicans thought of as a better time. And in a party desperate for success through unity, he had the party chairman and he had Congressman Gerald Ford, minority leader of the House, the chair of the convention.

Nixon headquarters at the Hilton reflected the savvy, calm, data-driven, businesslike mood that John Mitchell had imposed on the campaign. While

Rocky's headquarters at the Americana was all creative chaos, and Reagan's at the Deauville was simply a tortuous, slow-drip delegate-counting machine, Nixon's hummed with steady, confident activity.

Everyone wore a lapel badge. The badges revealed the wearer's level of access to floors of the hotel. Few could enter the penthouse where the Nixon family was staying. Also in that penthouse was a big, emptied solarium that provided space for the campaign's command post. Outside that room was a seventy-two-line switchboard. Inside were overlapping, wired communication networks integrating individuals on the floor of the hall and a command trailer outside.

A gigantic blackboard took up a whole solarium wall: there, every state's delegate totals would be entered, state by state, on each day of the convention. Fifty chairs arranged in front of the blackboard gave each state captain a reserved seat. State captains would report twice a day on totals for their state. In the center was a seat for Richard Kleindienst, Nixon's commander for convention operations.

There was reason to be cheerful, and in their pragmatic, corporate, well-groomed way, that's what Nixon's men and Nixon himself were being. They had their worries. They might well fail to go over the top on the first ballot. Their key to success, however, was copied from the modern corporate strategy of always appearing certain of success. Controlling both fear and enthusiasm was job one.

On Sunday, before Nixon had even arrived, John Mitchell had a visit at the Hilton with a group of Southern delegations concerned about Nixon's commitment to pushing back public school and other forms of federally enforced racial integration. These Southerners had heard something horrifying, they told Mitchell. Nixon's press man Herb Klein had told reporters that Nixon was looking at Mark Hatfield, the liberal senator from Oregon, as a running mate. It wasn't true, Mitchell knew. Klein had only been trying to keep Nixon's liberal delegates from bolting for Rocky. But if the Southerners continued to believe the Hatfield story, they would bolt for Reagan.

Mitchell, surrounded by Southerners jealously protecting their rising party status and plans for enforcing states' rights against racial integration, chewed on his pipe and played it cool while offering vague reassurance. While he couldn't give guarantees about specific running mates, Nixon would not, Mitchell promised the delegates, "split the ticket." He wouldn't mitigate his own Western conservatism by choosing a running mate with Northern liberal credentials. The delegates left only partially mollified.

All day Monday, with the festivities and procedures beginning, Southern suspicion of Nixon stayed alive. The delegations were on the convention floor, the speeches were droning from the podium, the numbers men were moving around, notepads in hand, walkie-talkies at the ready, and Reagan was busy exploiting the Southerners' worries.

Reagan was making the rounds of the delegations in their hotel suites. His delegate counters were privately optimistic. Publicly, they made a show of the difficulty involved in building delegate-by-delegate support. That would allow them to spin any minor success as a burst forward. Now things were looking up. Reagan gave a TV interview aimed at Southern delegates. "It's very difficult to disagree with most of the things that Mr. Wallace is saying," said Reagan. At lunch on Monday in his suite at the Deauville, Reagan met with the Greenville Group. Still hoping to use him to pressure Nixon and still worried about losing control of Reagan fever, the Greenville Group once again encouraged Reagan to announce his active candidacy. This time he told them he would.

Reagan had been sensing restlessness in his own California delegation. Some of those delegates were Nixon people, and Reagan needed to keep the delegation with him. If the California delegation started splintering, Reagan would have nothing. Reagan had always hoped to announce as late as possible. This might be it. At 4:00 p.m. Monday, one of Reagan's men came out of a California delegation meeting at the Deauville and spoke to the press. The breaking news: California had just declared that Ronald Reagan was now an active candidate for the presidency. Then, Reagan himself popped up and tried to give his best performance. "Gosh, I was surprised!" he said. "It all came out of the clear blue sky."

Only two days before nominating and balloting were scheduled to begin, Ronald Reagan started openly campaigning. If even one state switched from Nixon to Reagan, Nixon might be stopped on the first ballot.

Monday evening, Reagan started moving from delegation to delegation. He kept things loose. The enthusiasm for him was nearly religious. He didn't have to amp it up. In keeping with the unity theme, Reagan grinned and furrowed his brow and looked like a cowboy in a business suit with no personal ambition, just ambitions for the country. He made no demands, asked for no hard commitments. Taking a page from Rocky's book, Reagan said only that he thought it would be more productive to have an open convention instead of a coronation. Holding off nominating anyone on the first ballot would give every voice a chance to be heard. That was the best way to unify the party for November. It went over well. It was in small groups, one of the delegates said, that Reagan was always truly irresistible.

Nixon's people knew what was going on. They had the situation on the floor closely covered. In keeping with the Nixon campaign's modern approach, John Mitchell's team was always a step ahead. There were three hundred Nixon staffers—Reagan only had eighty—with enough manpower on the floor to keep the delegations hemmed in at each end of the rows of seats. If you even got up to go to the men's room, a Nixon man would be on you like glue, giving you all the reasons it would be bad for you to switch, pitching unity, offering favors, and, if it came to it, making threats. Mitchell had at least one man inside each delegation sending intelligence to the command trailer outside. They even had a fleet of houseboats docked nearby, "Nixon's Navy." Delegates were invited to relax there, take the edge off.

As Reagan's moves heated up the convention, the show viewers were watching at home had none of that excitement. The hall they were watching couldn't have been more bland. Gavel-to-gavel coverage meant presenting each long speech and each orchestrated reaction. TV viewers were missing huddled pockets of Southern delegates in sudden, heated discussion around the floor. Nixon walkie-talkies crackling. Reagan peeling off Southern delegates. Maybe a lot of them. What the TV coverage did offer was hour-by-hour delegate polling. CBS News had the best. Soon the network put up numbers showing Nixon at 626, Rockefeller at 243, Reagan at only 192. Nixon was still way ahead but not at the winning 667, and Reagan's was the only total that was steadily rising. And there still were two days until balloting began. That wasn't good for Nixon, or for displaying party unity. The South might be starting a big defection. Somehow, Nixon had to push Reagan back.

By 10:00 p.m. Monday night, Strom Thurmond was with Nixon and Mitchell in Nixon's penthouse. On TV, Barry Goldwater was at the podium making a bland appeal for unity. In the Nixon penthouse, the tone was muted panic. Maybe the campaign had been too businesslike, too dispassionate. Nixon had spoken only with Southern party bosses, not with delegates themselves, who found it so easy to get caught up in the glow of Reagan's promises. Thurmond insisted that Nixon now live up to his promise and speak to all Southern delegations. And Thurmond needed to be able to tell the Southerners something new.

Thurmond walked Nixon quickly through the next steps. First, Nixon must sign on to what the South called guidelines, leaving it to local communities to decide for themselves how to enforce federally mandated school integration. Second, Nixon must not take a running mate who was unacceptable to the South.

As coached and prodded by Thurmond, Nixon the above-it-all front-runner now got down into the fight for the nomination. On Tuesday, Nixon met with the Southerners. Instead of Nixon's making the rounds of the delegations, as Rockefeller and Reagan did, Nixon had the delegations come to him, the way they would come to an incumbent president.

The Southern delegations came in two sittings. In both, Nixon did everything he could to give them what they needed. This pair of meetings represented a high point in everything Nixon had been working for since 1962. Just that morning, the New Nixon had given a press conference, hitting all the New Nixon themes: with stability restored by his presidency, with peace and honor in Vietnam, he could see a time coming when the United States might use its global power not for war but for newly productive, democracy-enhancing relationships with the Soviet Union, maybe even with China. The moderate Manhattan conservative, sharing a big foreign policy vision, was now, in his suite with the South, letting the Old Nixon do the talking. On school busing—the court-ordered method of integrating schools—he was against it. Sending children from one side of a city to another just to satisfy some civil rights lawyers wasn't the kind of thing Nixon would support as president. On the federal courts—which had mandated those processes—they were supposed to be interpreting the law, not making it. That got applause. This was pure pandering by Nixon, who knew there was nothing the president could do to change the outcomes of civil rights litigation other than the long game of appointing federal judges who might make more conservative rulings.

Nixon told the Southerners that the problem of race relations wasn't Southern only, it was national. The Southern delegates left feeling they had a strong candidate. The next day and night, Strom Thurmond followed up, going to the delegates' suites and around the convention floor exaggerating the power he had personally been given over the choice of running mate. Strom sort of suggested that Nixon had given him outright veto power. That little lie helped a lot. Six years after his humiliation in the California governor's race, Richard Nixon was nearing the mountaintop.

On Tuesday afternoon, Nelson Rockefeller began publicly denying hard facts. He told CBS TV that his own polls showed Nixon couldn't get over 550 on the first ballot.

"What about the second, Governor?"

"An erosion of fifty votes in his strength."

"And the third?"

"The dam will break!" said Rocky.

No one but Rocky had those numbers, and on Tuesday night, with Strom Thurmond bustling from delegation to delegation in company with Nixon's floor manager, the Maryland congressman Rogers Morton, both Rocky's and Reagan's delegate counts began to stall. Nixon's assurances to the South on civil rights and school busing seemed to be working.

One fact that Rocky had to face was especially painful. He could have had much of the Maryland delegation, maybe even the whole thing. That would have made a big difference. It might have stopped Nixon. But Rocky didn't have Maryland and could never get it—not on a third ballot, not on a tenth ballot, not ever—because of a simple but important phone call that Rockefeller should have made four months earlier.

Spiro Agnew, the governor of Maryland, was once Rocky's most enthusiastic supporter. Known as Ted, he was one of the few GOP politicians with any recent immigrant heritage. Agnew's father was born Anagnostopoulos in Greece, and Ted grew up in Baltimore in an era of anti-Greek prejudice. His mother was a Virginia Protestant. Ted declined to join the Greek Orthodox Church.

Agnew studied at Johns Hopkins and was drafted in both World War II and the Korean War. After having begun as a registered Democrat, he switched to the Republican Party in the late 1950s, serving in elective offices in Baltimore. In those offices, he always seemed modest to a fault. Spiro Agnew appeared to be one of the few American politicians with an accurate sense of his own limitations and little ambition to rise.

But as the GOP gubernatorial candidate in 1966, Agnew came out swinging surprisingly hard. On the advice of his ad agency, Agnew attacked his Democratic opponent's anti-integration platform as racist.

Agnew hit a nerve. Suddenly Spiro Agnew seemed, to Maryland civil rights liberals, a voice of reason. Democrats crossed party lines to vote for him. Questioned on whether his victory had any national significance, he said, "I have difficulty imagining myself as a national leader, and sometimes I have difficulty imagining myself a state leader." At a celebratory lunch, an old friend ribbed him by saying he would one day be introduced as the president of the United States. Everybody, including Ted Agnew, laughed.

By the time he began connecting with Nelson Rockefeller, at the GOP governors' conference in 1967, Governor Agnew was already disappointing the civil rights advocates who had voted for him. He had succumbed to a dull centrism, at odds with the sunny liberalism of a Rockefeller. With the threat of urban rioting, Agnew was an early adopter of law-and-order rhetoric.

Despite their political differences, Ted Agnew adored Rocky. Charisma, wealth, energy, dynastic lineage, ambition—Rocky had everything Agnew admired. And Rocky had something Agnew had tried to grab and failed to hold: the loyal support of both blue-collar urban white voters and African Americans. As leader of the Republican governors—in that unofficial sense Agnew's boss—Rockefeller enjoyed immense national power that impressed Agnew to no end. Nelson Rockefeller, Agnew came to believe at the end of 1967, was the only Republican who could win the presidential nomination decisively and then beat Lyndon Johnson in November 1968. Agnew wanted more than anything to be part of that.

Agnew's certainty became unshakable, nearly a mania. As early as the spring of '67, Agnew announced that he wanted Rocky to commit to running and that he'd assigned himself the job of persuading the forever vacillating candidate. If the GOP governors formed a united front, as Agnew urged them to do, they would control the nomination for their leader, Nelson Rockefeller. In the early weeks of the 1968 primary season, when no one could tell if Rocky was supporting George Romney only as a stalking horse for an eventual Rockefeller campaign, Ted Agnew was sure that, in the end, Romney would be out and Rocky would be in. Throughout all those weeks and months of vacillation, when Rocky was denying any intention of running—"I am not a candidate," he told Agnew personally, "and under no circumstances will I be"—Agnew refused to give up. With no ambition to become king himself, he hoped to be kingmaker.

The other governors saw their junior Maryland colleague as a dreamer of a Rockefeller Camelot. Governor Jim Rhodes of Ohio was a Rocky supporter, but he barely gave Agnew the time of day. Governor Rhodes wasn't about to get involved in anything organized by Spiro Agnew.

Rockefeller found Agnew's insistent, unrelenting enthusiasm for him weird and disconcerting. Ted must be smoking opium, Rocky told the press. Agnew responded by proposing a Rocky-Reagan ticket. Reagan wasn't buying that. Reagan kept saying that he had no interest in the vice presidency.

On the same nine-day governors' cruise where

George Romney and Nelson Rockefeller spent so much time discussing Romney's primary campaign, Rocky met with the press on the sun deck and responded to their questions about Agnew's insistence. "I don't want to be president," Rocky said. This time there was open irritation in his tone.

"That's pretty definite," Agnew generously conceded, when asked about it, on that same cruise. "But I still say . . ." And then he was off, yet again pitching the idea of a convention draft. There was nothing Rocky could say that would deter Agnew's optimism.

Then it happened. As George Romney's campaign began to fall apart, and Rocky began admitting to the possibility of a draft, Spiro Agnew suddenly started looking prescient. Governor Jim Rhodes, once so chilly, linked arms with Agnew at a Palm Beach governors' conference and talked about a stop-Nixon, draft-Rockefeller movement. At the end of February, when Romney dropped out of the race, Agnew's excitement really took off.

He met with Rocky. By then, Rockefeller had reached the point of being willing to discuss the nomination, and this time, Agnew came away feeling better. Agnew was not invited to Rockefeller's Fifth Avenue apartment on St. Patrick's Day, when the inner circle debated the question of running. Agnew wasn't in Rocky's inner circle. He could only try to pick up gossip from Maryland about Oregonians suddenly arriving in New York to explain the outlook for their primary to Rocky. Agnew did get invited to the Rockefeller dinner the next night in Washington at the Foxhall Road house, where with all the other guests he got the unshakable impression that Rockefeller would soon announce. When the **New York Times** ran the story saying that Rockefeller would announce his campaign the next day at a press conference, Agnew scheduled his own press conference for the same day.

On March 21, the governor's staff at the Maryland State House prepared to celebrate, upon Rocky's announcing his candidacy, the revelation that their boss was one of the savviest and most prophetic political minds in the Republican Party. Agnew invited the Maryland press into his office to watch Rocky's announcement together. Agnew's staff turned on the TV. Agnew sat in a chair in front of the TV and members of the press stood in an arc around him. Everyone awaited the triumph of Agnew. Instead Rockefeller delivered utter humiliation for Governor Agnew, who watched in horror as Rocky said, "I reiterate unequivocally that I am not a candidate campaigning directly or indirectly for the presidency of the United States."

It was an oversight. Al Abrahams was the head of the Maryland office of the Rockefeller exploratory team, working in partnership with Agnew. Abrahams had gotten a call from Rocky's man George Hinman at 11:30 a.m., hours before Rocky's scheduled announcement.

"Close down," Hinman said.

"Has anybody told Agnew?" Abrahams asked.

"The governor talked to him this morning," Hinman said.

Abrahams didn't know that Hinman was wrong. Nor did Abrahams know that Agnew had set up a TV in his office, and invited the press to watch the announcement on TV with him. Rocky did call Ted that afternoon, full of apologies. Six weeks later, when Rockefeller finally entered the race, many former supporters went back to him. Spiro Agnew did not.

As the spring went on, Agnew endorsed no one. He held his delegation back, putting himself forward as a favorite-son candidate. Rockefeller actually went to Maryland and tried to get Agnew and the delegation back, but Richard Nixon had already started calling Agnew periodically. Nixon flattered him by asking his advice on this or that matter. Agnew liked that. During Rockefeller's Maryland trip, Agnew snubbed him.

Agnew praised Nixon while retaining his own favorite-son position. In early May, a Maryland reporter asked Agnew, "Are you available for a draft for second place?" meaning as Nixon's running mate.

"Very seriously," Agnew said, "no."

It was Wednesday in Miami Beach, the nominating process would begin in a few hours, and when Nixon's people looked at the numbers, they felt only okay, not great. All legitimate delegate counts showed

Nixon at or near the magic number 667 on the first ballot. "At or near" was by no means good enough.

Just as Strom Thurmond had been helping Nixon against Reagan, Spiro Agnew had been making every effort to help Nixon against Rockefeller. Nixon made Agnew feel that he was deep inside the inner circle. Nixon's people had asked Agnew as early as July to take the role of placing Nixon's name in nomination at the convention. Everyone regarded that assignment as an honor. Within his own delegation, Agnew held eighteen Nixon votes. On Monday, he stopped his favorite-son campaign and released them, but he couldn't stop eight of them from going over to Rocky. Agnew was now "vigorously" endorsing Nixon, in the interest of their "deep ideological bonds," he told the press.

Still, the Nixon team needed more votes. They were worried by the unruliness of the South. For all of Strom Thurmond's efforts, the Florida delegation had remained especially volatile and Reagan-happy. The Florida delegation had been staying not in Miami Beach but at the Doral Country Club on the mainland, harder to get at. Its power brokers were divided three ways: for Nixon, Reagan, and weakly for Rockefeller. Nixon's people thought that the seventeen Florida delegates who were women all had big crushes on Reagan.

Bad news from the Florida delegation had come earlier in the day directly from their boss, the Nixon man Bill Murfin. He reported by phone to Strom Thurmond's associate Harry Dent that two of the most zealous California Reaganites were coming over to the Doral to pitch Reagan to the Floridians. Some of the women were sure to be swayed.

"If you want to stop this thing falling apart," Murfin told Dent, "you'd better get Strom's ass over here before they turn up."

Strom Thurmond headed for the mainland, barely beating Reagan's men to the Doral. "I have a veto over his vice-presidential choice," Thurmond falsely assured the Floridians. But even that wasn't enough to swing the whole delegation, so at noon Nixon himself was sitting with sixteen of the Florida Reaganites in his suite offering them the same reassurances he had given the rest of the Southern delegations the day before.

In the afternoon, with the nominating process set to begin in a few hours, the Florida delegates met again at the Doral, and Murfin, the Nixon man, invoked a "unit rule," requiring the minority to back the majority so that the entire delegation voted as a unit for one candidate. Some of the Reagan women were crying. Murfin threatened to resign as GOP state chairman if they rebelled.

It was time to go to the convention hall. With four members abstaining, the Florida delegation agreed, under protest, to commit as a unit to Nixon.

Even after they arrived at the convention hall emotionally spent and took their seats, their psychodrama didn't end. Reagan sat in his command trailer just outside still trying to work the Florida delegation. The Nixon team saw what was happening, and Florida delegates leaving Reagan's trailer got pounced on by Nixonites. The Floridians were reaching an emotional breaking point.

Alabama, supposedly solid for Nixon, began acting up at the eleventh hour. The Nixon plan had been to pressure Alabama—alphabetically first—to yield to South Carolina, where Strom Thurmond was a favorite son. South Carolina would then nominate Thurmond, inspiring a long celebration that would kick off the nominating process by giving the entire segregationist South its big moment.

A Nixon man within the Alabama delegation, Jim Martin, sensed that the Alabamans would resent the suggestion that they yield to South Carolina for the benefit of Nixon. That kind of highhandedness might send Alabama running straight to Reagan, Martin warned Nixon's team. Southern Reaganites would go for Nixon in the end, he believed, but only if they felt their deep emotional connection to the California right-winger had been fully heard and honored.

So the only viable Nixon strategy now, Martin argued, was to make a demonstration to the whole GOP South that deep down inside, everybody here loved Ronald Reagan just as much as the South did.

Don't ask Alabama to yield to South Carolina, Martin counseled the Nixonites. Alabama should instead yield to California, with the exact words "out of respect for that great conservative Ronald Reagan." The ensuing celebration would feel as if the whole convention were bowing down before Ronnie. The GOP would be saying we love you, but this is not your year. Getting segregationists to hold firm for Nixon, as Martin saw it, meant bowing down not to Strom Thurmond but to Ronald Reagan.

Even as the Nixon team's wrestling of the South into submission went on, and as the minutes ticked down toward entering names in nomination, Nixon people on the floor remained keenly aware that to go over 667 on the first ballot, they couldn't focus on the South alone. Nixon needed to nail down a bundle of delegates from the industrial North, too.

With time running out, where could they hunt? New York was solid for its governor, Rockefeller. It was time to look at Northern favorite-son candidates. Some of them might, in order to keep Nixon on the safe side, release delegates before the first ballot. Maybe their delegates could also be peeled off in batches even without being officially released. Looking northward, what favorite-son delegation could the Nixon guys raid?

How about George Romney's? Unlike other favorite sons, Romney had been a real candidate, for a time the media's favorite. Though he withdrew before the New Hampshire primary, he had been stung by Rocky's treatment of his campaign and had not endorsed anyone yet. The Michigan delegation was expected to vote unanimously for Romney, a kind of consolation prize for their local hero. So might George Romney, John Mitchell's people now wondered, be begged or pressured to release his delegates to Nixon now, before the first ballot, in the name of party unity? Under time pressure, they figured it was worth a shot.

No! George Romney made that loud and clear. He had already been urged by Agnew to release his delegates to Nixon, but Romney wasn't about to release them to anyone. Romney was playing his last hand. Nixon's people started trying to pick off individual Michigan delegates, but it was just too much to ask. Only four of forty-eight Michigan delegates—rightwingers from Grosse Point—jumped over to Nixon.

What about Ohio? Governor Rhodes was its favorite son, and he was holding his entire delegation with an iron fist for Rockefeller. Rhodes, too, had resisted Agnew's efforts to pull much of Ohio toward Nixon.

That left New Jersey. The alphabet played a role here: New Jersey would vote about halfway through the roll call. If that state went for Nixon, later delegations, sensing a possible landslide, might feel they had to jump on it. So in the final hours before nominating began, the Nixon people went after New Jersey.

New Jersey's favorite son was Clifford Case, a liberal senator lacking a governor's power to advance and ruin careers, thus weak in holding his delegates together. He supported Rockefeller and planned to use his favorite-son votes to stop Nixon. Upon arrival at the convention, only two of forty in Case's delegation were for Nixon. One of those was Frank Farley, the political boss of Atlantic City, who knew how to work delegates. During the convention, the delegation split, leaving twenty-four for Case, eleven for Nixon, five undecided.

At the New Jersey delegation's hotel suite, the Nixonites made their pitch. If New Jersey voted for Nixon tonight, the state would become the convention powerhouse, the delegation that pushed the winner over the top on the first ballot. For many delegates, that was a strong draw.

Senator Case pulled the other way, but Farley and Nixon's people had a stick to go with the carrot. With the South now holding strong, they argued that New Jersey risked being left out of a big Nixon win if it went for Case in hopes of going to Rocky on a second ballot that was never going to happen.

By the time the New Jersey delegation arrived at the hall, it had been ripped apart. New Jersey held twenty votes for Nixon now. The Nixon team was making similar last-ditch efforts with other delegations.

At 5:30 p.m., all the delegations were gathering on the floor for the nominating session. At the podium high above, Gerald Ford called the convention to order. The nominations began.

The nominating process wouldn't end for almost eight hours. Beyond the three major candidates, there were eight favorite sons to place in nomination, plus Harold Stassen, who ran pointlessly every four years. After each long and windy nomination speech, everything had to stop for up to half an hour of intense jumping up and down by the supporters of each man who was nominated. Bands played, balloons descended, noisemakers honked. And then another speech and then more dancing and singing and clapping.

As the process began, Alabama did yield to California, and Reagan was indeed placed in nomination first, to the delight of the whole South, just as planned. During Reagan's celebration—some called it the most intense of the night—the band played "Dixie."

Then, given the need for similarly preplanned displays of ecstasy for favorite sons from Alaska, Arkansas, Hawaii, Kansas, and Michigan—and with delegations nominating out of order by yielding to others—it took more than two and a half hours just to get from Reagan's nomination to that of the next major candidate, Nelson Rockefeller.

Finally the front-runner, Nixon, was placed in nomination by Spiro Agnew, with merciful brevity, and Nixon's celebration erupted. But it was already late and the other favorite-son nominations were still to come.

ABC, UNABLE TO AFFORD full coverage, was running only a ninety-minute wrap-up that included a convention coverage novelty that pulled in surprisingly large audiences—intense ten-minute nightly debates between William F. Buckley Jr., the leading intellectual conservative, and the liberal author and essayist Gore Vidal.

William Buckley was already well known from his sophisticated discussion-debate show on public television called **Firing Line**. He would invite liberals, friends of his like John Kenneth Galbraith, for polite, thoughtful discussions. Buckley never worried whether some of the exchanges went over the head of the viewer. If the audience couldn't keep up with the intellectuals, too bad. Buckley's show had no imitators because the size of its audience never suggested that imitation would be profitable.

Gore Vidal was known to the late-night audience who could stay awake for Johnny Carson's **Tonight Show**. Quick-witted intellectual authors of popular novels such as Gore Vidal and Truman Capote were a favorite guest category for Johnny Carson. They were his intellectual nourishment among the usual parade of movie stars, singers, dancers, and comedians. While Buckley sounded strictly aristocratic, Vidal sounded like the naughty boy in an aristocratic family—more playful, warmer, and far more willing to talk about sex. Gore Vidal's latest novel, **Myra Breckinridge**, published in February 1968, was about a transsexual, a word most Americans did not yet know. Some called it pornographic. It quickly became a worldwide best seller, much to William Buckley's horror.

When ABC signed Buckley for the convention debate segments, they asked for names of liberals he would prefer to debate. Gore Vidal was one of the people Buckley did not want to debate, which was all the ABC executives needed to hear. They were hoping for fireworks to pull viewers away from the boring convention proceedings on CBS and NBC. It worked.

ABC viewers who knew Buckley's debate style were shocked the most. This was not the genial, respectful conservative-versus-liberal chat they had watched with Buckley and Galbraith. In exchanges moderated by ABC's venerable anchorman Howard K. Smith, Buckley seemed at times genuinely angry, but it was hard to be sure because he kept forcing a smile whenever he could. Buckley didn't have the same control he had on his own show. On **Firing Line**, when Buckley interrupted, the guests politely endured it. Not Gore Vidal. He interrupted right back and never stopped smiling, as if the whole thing were fun, even though he was the only one who seemed to be enjoying it. This looked like hard work for Buckley. He was straining. His Yale-honed debate skills were not working. He was frustrated. No one had ever seen William F. Buckley Jr. frustrated. And anyone who did couldn't stop watching. ABC had a hit on its hands. A hit that changed television history. Every angry political argument you've seen on television since then, every conservative trying to shout over every liberal and vice versa, owes its origin to the simple budgetary fact that ABC couldn't afford major-league convention coverage.

Gore Vidal: Tonight the key question for every patriot is can an aging Hollywood juvenile actor with a right-wing script defeat Richard Nixon, a professional politician, who currently represents no discernible interest except his own.

William Buckley: Mr. Gore Vidal, the playwright, saying that after all Ronald Reagan was nothing more than a quote "aging Hollywood juvenile actor." Now, to begin with, everybody is aging . . .

Gore Vidal: Even you are, Bill. Perceptibly, before our eyes.

William Buckley: Therefore, that adjective didn't contribute anything extraordinary to the human understanding. Then he said, "Hollywood." Now one either acted in Hollywood during the time Mr. Reagan acted or one didn't act at all.

Mr. Vidal sends all of his books to Hollywood, many of which are rejected, but some of which are ground out and put on.

Gore Vidal: Now Bill, I don't send any there.

William Buckley: He called him a juvenile actor, which is presumably to be distinguished from an adult actor. My point is . . .

Gore Vidal: Yes, get to it.

William Buckley: If you play this sort of a game you can say, "Look, I don't think it's right to present Mr. Gore Vidal as a political commentator of any consequence since he is nothing more than a literary producer of perverted Hollywood-minded prose."

Gore Vidal: Now, now Bill. Careful now.

William Buckley: I'm almost through.

Gore Vidal: In every sense.

Howard K. Smith: Let Mr. Buckley finish this sentence then, Mr. Vidal, I assure you time to refute.

William Buckley: [If] ABC has the authority to invite the author of **Myra Breckinridge** to comment on Republican politics, I think that the people of California have the right when they speak overwhelmingly to project somebody into national politics, even if he did commit the sin of having acted in movies that were not written by Mr. Vidal.

"Great television." That's what ABC executives called Buckley versus Vidal. It was "great" because it was edgy and unpredictable and, of course, because people watched it and kept coming back for more. It was good television because Buckley and Vidal were well-informed smart people discussing the issues of the day from opposing political positions. It was "great television" because they genuinely hated each other. The audience wouldn't fully catch on to how much they despised each other until Buckley exploded at the Democratic convention, an explosion Buckley regretted for the rest of his life.

And so in 1968, a new kind of television talk was born—premeditated confrontation, bought and paid for by the networks. Thirty years later, Roger Ailes's contribution to the genre was to hire conservative Republican anchormen at Fox News who could easily shout louder than their occasional liberal guests. In 2016, when Donald Trump's campaign manager was fired and then hired by CNN the same week to argue with and interrupt Democrats already on the CNN payroll, he had William Buckley and Gore Vidal to thank for his new paycheck.

DELEGATE HUNTERS FOR REAGAN, Rockefeller, and Nixon were sweeping the floor, making and fending off attacks on delegates. Reagan was in his trailer, grandly receiving a steady flow of waverers.

At around 8:00 p.m., the Reagan people found new hope. Amid all the noise and ballyhooing on the floor, Reaganites could be seen moving through the Southern delegations. They were handing out the late edition of the **Miami Herald**, which had a shocking story: Nixon would choose the liberal Mark Hatfield as his running mate after all.

Alabama and Mississippi objected the loudest. Their delegations' leaders, Nixon men, rushed to Thurmond. They had to shout to be heard above the relentless noise. They told Thurmond that their delegates were rethinking their commitments. When the time came to vote, the Alabama and Mississippi delegates wanted to pass in order to see how the other states voted before they committed.

Thurmond knew that this would collapse everything he had been working for. He yelled back over the noise that the Hatfield story was false and demanded they get their delegations under control right away. Thurmond grabbed a megaphone so that everyone around him could hear him say he would never let the South be fooled in such a way. To a passing TV crew, Thurmond said, "The South loves Reagan, but it won't break!"

The head of the Mississippi delegation went back to his troops and offered to bet any delegate $100 that Hatfield wouldn't be Nixon's running mate. No takers? Okay: $200. No? $500, then. The delegates' silence made his point, and the Alabama leader borrowed the tactic but started the betting at $1,000. Delegates began getting back in line.

Strom Thurmond's friend Harry Dent found Don Oberdorfer, the reporter who had written the **Herald** story. Dent grabbed Oberdorfer and pulled him over to the Georgia and Louisiana delegations. He offered to bet the reporter $300 that his story was wrong. Oberdorfer couldn't even hear Dent. He laughed and walked away. Word spread that the reporter refused to bet on the truth of his own story.

It wasn't until 1:19 a.m. that the roll-call vote began. The convention secretary began the process by saying "Alabama?"

Happy and Nelson Rockefeller were in their hotel suite with the core team watching the TV coverage. When the roll call reached the emotionally battered Florida delegation, the totals told the story, and Rocky knew it. Florida abandoned the beloved Reagan. The Florida delegation went thirty-two for Nixon, only one for Rocky, and amazingly, only one for Reagan. If Reagan could pull only one vote out of Florida, nothing could stop Nixon now.

Rockefeller watched as Spiro Agnew's Maryland delegation delivered seventeen votes for Nixon. He watched as George Romney held all but four Michigan votes. Rockefeller knew that if he had treated those two men with the respect he now realized they deserved, their delegations might have been his. That might have made the difference in stopping Nixon.

Then came New Jersey. Favorite son Clifford Case, angry about losing control of his delegation, demanded a poll: each New Jersey delegate had to stand up and announce his or her own vote. Case was hoping that the embarrassment of being seen as a defector would bring back some of his delegates. Senator Case was able to hold twenty-two of his New Jersey delegates but lost eighteen to Nixon.

It was all over. Nixon played the game perfectly, Rockefeller thought. Nixon got Thurmond to hold the South and all hopes for a Reagan insurgency had been defeated. And Nixon crushed Rockefeller liberalism at the same time.

Rocky joined Happy on the sofa and put his arm around her. It was a bad night for Republican liberals. No one knew then that it was their last night. The Republican Party turned away from its liberals in Miami Beach in 1968 and never looked back.

TWENTY-SIX

THE LAST LIBERAL STANDING

Richard Nixon was in his penthouse at the Hilton watching TV. The room was quiet. He sat calmly in a chair, steadily noting the growing delegate tally on a yellow legal pad. Pat Nixon sat on the other side of the room.

Nixon had not yet hit the magic number of 667. Then Wisconsin cast all 30 of its votes for Nixon, and he went over the top on the first ballot. The final score: 692 for Nixon, 277 for Rockefeller, 182 for Reagan. Nixon was the one, but not by a landslide. In the end, only 26 votes stood between Nixon and first-ballot failure. In 1964, Barry Goldwater had gone over the top with 203 more votes than that. It was an unusually close first ballot win for a front-runner opposed by only two candidates who joined the race late and very late.

But looked at from the starting point of the day

after the 1962 California election when Nixon sounded like he was quitting politics, Nixon and his team pulled off a stunning political feat. Leonard Garment, John Mitchell, Pat Buchanan, John Ehrlichman, Bob Haldeman, Maurice Stans, Richard Kleindienst, Roger Ailes, and all the rest, with Nixon teaching most of them every step of the way, had brought a two-time loser, a political punch line, to the pinnacle of his party once again.

The phone rang. It was Rocky, congratulating Nixon and complimenting his prowess.

"Ronnie didn't do as well as I thought," Rocky told Nixon. "I was counting on him for a little more muscle."

These two knew the game. They loved it. They both knew Rocky made unforced errors and that Nixon's campaign was, to their eyes, a thing of beauty.

Ronald Reagan left his trailer and was striding toward the stage. His smile was lighting up the convention hall. At the podium, Gerald Ford was trying to insist on following parliamentary procedures, but Reagan had the star power. He wanted to be the first to call for unity and a unanimous vote on the second ballot. As Reagan took the microphone, the crowd went wild for him one more time. He asked for unity in the party and called for a new ballot.

George Romney did, at last, release his delegates. Only a few holdouts remained, so sickened by the thought of Richard M. Nixon as their party's nominee that they couldn't get on the unanimity bandwagon. On the second ballot Rockefeller got ninety-three votes. Reagan got two.

"I won the nomination," Nixon was already telling the TV reporters, "without having to pay any price, making any deal with any candidate or any individuals representing a candidate." He was free, he told them, to choose his running mate. The big night wasn't over yet.

John Lindsay had come to this convention with mixed feelings. The mayor of New York City, Lindsay was a poster-ready icon of the Eastern liberal wing of the Republican establishment. A lean six feet four with blue-green eyes, he was the Republican with the most Kennedy style. Mayor Lindsay walked the streets of New York's ghettos during the "long, hot summer" of 1967, suit coat slung over his shoulder, sleeves rolled up, talking to people. The suburban right wing saw Lindsay as a bleeding-heart liberal for the welfare-dependent poor, a spendthrift in a decaying city, and soft on crime. Liberals around the country saw him as the Republican face of the New Politics. Many liberals saw John Lindsay as presidential material. Nixon called John Lindsay, like Ronald Reagan, a glamour boy.

This emerging national Lindsay phenomenon mingled image with reality. Before seeking office, he'd been a partner of Webster, Sheffield, Fleischman, Hitchcock & Chrystie, a law firm founded in the

1930s. John Lindsay could make anyone he happened to be speaking with, at any given moment, feel like the only person in the room. That talent made his rise in politics swift. In the early 1950s, Lindsay was president of the New York Young Republican Club. After serving in the Justice Department, at the age of twenty-seven, he won the congressional seat for New York's Silk Stocking District, the liberal Republican enclave of Manhattan's Upper East Side. John Lindsay had become the Northeast liberal Republican par excellence. But as mayor, he was often at bitter odds with the better-known New York liberal Republican Nelson Rockefeller. John Lindsay had begun his political career under Rocky's sponsorship, and at the 1968 convention he naturally supported his governor's nomination, but there wasn't room enough for both of them in the rapidly shrinking space of Republican liberalism.

John Lindsay's mission in Miami Beach in '68 was building delegate relationships for a run in 1972 or 1976 and making himself visibly available as this year's running mate, while, of course, shying away from any reporters' questions about the VP nomination. That modest effort required seven Lindsay hotel rooms at the Americana, nine walkie-talkies, and even a far-fetched projection of Lindsay's capturing the presidential nomination on the sixth ballot.

The hopes of many convention liberals for maintaining liberal strength in a party about to nominate

Richard Nixon had settled on making John Lindsay Nixon's running mate. Herbert Brownell, Eisenhower's attorney general, was one of Lindsay's mentors. Brownell was in Miami Beach and was pushing Nixon hard on Lindsay for VP. So was Governor Jim Rhodes of Ohio. Lindsay himself had made it clear to Nixon that while he'd naturally been publicly supporting his own governor, he might be available as the liberal balance for Nixon's ticket.

Lindsay's feelings were mixed. His liberal instincts feared any association with Nixon. On Wednesday morning, Lindsay sent Nixon a note via the ever-present power-broker journalist Theodore White. The note said that Lindsay would accept the second spot on the ticket only if acceptance was presented to him as a party duty. Lindsay would then reserve the right, when vice president, to make his opinions on policy known even when they differed from Nixon's. A note like that to Nixon should have resolved the question of John Lindsay's vice presidential candidacy for good. Still, something was brewing.

At 2:10 a.m., Richard Nixon officially received the nomination of his party for the presidency. His floor men had been circulating a note from Nixon to certain GOP dignitaries, inviting them up to his penthouse to discuss the vice presidential nomination. Privately, Nixon had arrived at a plan. No one else knew about it. Success would require slow playing of his hand.

He met with his team—Mitchell, Haldeman, Ehrlichman, Kleindienst, Garment, Klein, Stans, and
Buchanan—to narrow the running-mate list. Then
the delegation leaders and other party players began
arriving at the suite. It was around 3:00 a.m. They
poured bourbon and scotch and lit cigars. These
bosses were exultant but tired. It had been a long
season. Nixon began the meeting by stating, "I have
brought no names to Miami." Everyone knew that
wasn't true, but they didn't know what he was thinking. Nixon did say he wanted someone with urban
credibility, maybe an "ethnic" background. Jim
Rhodes and Herb Brownell were the only important liberals present. They proposed John Lindsay as
a running mate. Strom Thurmond rejected Lindsay
out of hand and Barry Goldwater agreed with him.
Thurmond and Goldwater, in turn, proposed Ronald Reagan. The Northerners said that the industrial
states would never accept Reagan. And Reagan had
already said publicly that he wouldn't consider the
second spot on the ticket. Nixon said he was against
choosing a glamour boy. That meant Lindsay and
Reagan were out.

So the group sat, stumped, amid the cigar smoke.
It was time to look at lower-profile candidates. Gov-
ernor John Volpe of Massachusetts, Senator Howard
Baker of Tennessee, and Governor Spiro Agnew of
Maryland were three names that had survived only
because nobody took any of them seriously. And

Agnew was only on the list, some staffers thought, because in the earlier meeting, Nixon had said, "How about Agnew? That was a hell of a nominating speech he gave." It wasn't, but no one argued.

The North leaned toward Massachusetts governor John Volpe, the South toward Tennessee senator Howard Baker. Strom Thurmond called all three acceptable to the South. So around 6:00 a.m., on Thursday, these GOP leaders headed for bed, thinking it was over. John Volpe seemed to have the lead, given his greater experience. They were in for a surprise.

Nixon went to bed at 6:30 a.m., got up at 8:30 a.m., and went downstairs to a meeting with Gerald Ford, Illinois senator Everett Dirksen, Texas senator John Tower, and other power brokers. Nixon reviewed the outcome of his earlier meetings. The idea now was simply to determine which running mate might win Nixon more votes.

Some of these men were ready and willing to ignore Strom Thurmond and the South because George Wallace might peel away so many votes that Nixon might fail in the South. Strom Thurmond might not even be able to get reelected in South Carolina.

Gerald Ford pushed Mayor Lindsay again. John Tower thought Nixon could beat Wallace in the South with Reagan as his running mate. Once again, Nixon said he wasn't comfortable with glamour boys.

So this second group also had to start thinking

about compromise candidates. They came up with three people who were sitting in the room: Senator Tower; Robert Finch, who had managed the 1960 Nixon campaign and was now Ronald Reagan's lieutenant governor; and Nixon's convention floor manager, Maryland congressman Rogers Morton. Now Nixon had a totally different batch of names than those from the first meeting, and not one of these new names seemed viable, even to the prospects themselves.

Only Nixon knew what was really going on. All of these meetings were smoke screens. Nixon understood something the party bosses didn't. They wanted to "strengthen the ticket," as they put it, but there was no way to do that. This ticket couldn't be strengthened. Nixon had taken private polls. They showed that with literally any running mate, his numbers went down. The New Nixon had made himself so opaque, so vague, that the clarifying presence of anyone else on the ticket could only turn off some segment of the electorate.

He'd do better alone. The optimal running mate: nobody.

Nixon already knew who that nobody would have to be. Still, he kept this show going. When it was all over, Nixon could say meetings had occurred, everyone's voice had been heard, and the party had unified around a consensus choice.

The three new compromise candidates—Tower,

Finch, and Morton—were called upstairs to the penthouse. Nixon sat them down with Mitchell, Haldeman, and Ehrlichman. None of these three supposed choices thought for a minute that Nixon would pick them. The staffers, too, didn't get what Nixon was up to. It was approaching midday. The nomination of the VP was hours away.

"We seem to have come down to you three," Dick told the compromise men. "Or Ted Agnew."

So it was Agnew. Now they all got it.

Still Nixon sat there, going over each man's qualifications and weaknesses, at times taking each one into another room for private consultations. Finally, about noon, Nixon ended the show.

"Rogers," he said to Congressman Morton, a Marylander, "would you put in a call to Ted Agnew?"

Even Strom Thurmond got played. On the way upstairs, Nixon had asked John Tower to call Thurmond and ask him which one he would prefer if it came down to John Volpe or Spiro Agnew.

It might have seemed a weird question. By now, Volpe wasn't even under close discussion, and Agnew had barely come up. Both were on Thurmond's "acceptable" list, and Nixon knew which way he would jump. Maryland was a Southern state compared to Massachusetts. And Agnew had been sounding more Southern as he stressed law and order after the riots. Without hesitation, Strom Thurmond chose Spiro Agnew.

So Nixon got Strom Thurmond to believe that Thurmond's lie had come true—that Thurmond really was picking Nixon's running mate. Acting as his own strategist, Nixon had outmaneuvered the entire party establishment and ended up with a running mate no one wanted . . . except Nixon.

Pedestrians were asked hours later by TV interviewers if they could identify the meaning of "Spiro Agnew." "It's some kind of disease," said one.

"It's some kind of egg," suggested another.

That gave the media and the Democrats plenty to chuckle about, but, as usual, Nixon knew something they didn't. Agnew might not win Nixon any votes, but he wouldn't lose votes the way Rockefeller or Reagan would. Having lost a presidential race by less than two-tenths of 1 percent, Nixon wasn't willing to allow his running mate to lose him a single vote.

Governor Agnew had been relaxing with his wife, Judy, in his suite at the Eden Roc, planning a quick flight to Grand Bahama for early the next morning. A little after noon, the phone rang.

"Are you sitting down?" Congressman Morton asked Agnew. Then he put Nixon on the line.

Soon Nixon was giving a press conference to announce his decision to the nation. Agnew watched on TV, still overwhelmed. Nixon drew out the announcement, torturing his old enemies in the press by withholding the running mate's name, rambling on about the importance of the office of the vice president. When at last Nixon let the bomb drop, there was an audible gasp in the room. Many on Nixon's staff, standing at the back, were shocked, too.

"Spiro who?" would soon become a well-worn joke. At that first moment, it was a perfectly sincere question.

The right wing got in line quickly. Ronald Reagan called Agnew "a darn good man." Strom Thurmond said Agnew stood for law and order. But some of the liberals started rebelling. And they saw a chance to fight back.

A vice presidential candidate had to be nominated, too, just like a presidential candidate. The process was usually only a formality. By 1968, a nominee's choice of running mate had been sacrosanct for generations. Delegates were expected to give that choice a unanimous vote. The running mate would deliver an acceptance speech, then the presidential nominee would bring the convention to its climax with his acceptance speech. But it always remained technically possible to have a floor fight over a vice presidential nomination. A cadre of GOP liberals, on Thursday night in Miami Beach, decided this was finally the time to start one.

This wasn't just about Spiro Agnew. This was about the future of the party, specifically the future of liberalism within the party. The liberals knew what was happening. The South now felt itself in control of both nominees on the Republican ticket. "This is wonderful!" said a boss of the Louisiana delegation. "It shows the South did have veto power!" The liberals thought Agnew looked like the seal on a deal to relax civil rights enforcement. Some liberals decided that the Agnew nomination would not stand.

This last-ditch rebellion against Richard Nixon was started by Congressman Charles Goodell from upstate New York. Congressman Goodell had been bucking the overall trend of his party by becoming ever more liberal, especially on Vietnam. Charles Goodell began a series of quick discussions all over the convention floor. None of this was seen on the TV coverage. A coalition was quickly forming, and not only of liberals. Goodell found allies against Agnew among conservatives from Iowa and Pennsylvania. Some of Rockefeller's men were interested, along with Jim Rhodes of Ohio. Together they could control a lot of delegate votes.

Goodell came up with a plan. During the nominating session, the Nevada and Rhode Island delegations would nominate John Lindsay. That would force a vote—a real vote, not ceremonial. Enough delegates might line up for Lindsay, in protest of Nixon's choice, to deny Agnew a first ballot win. That would force Nixon to reconsider and ultimately withdraw the Agnew nomination. The liberals would at least put the right wing and the South back in their places. American liberalism might yet survive in two parties.

Congressman Rogers Morton was scheduled to nominate Agnew. The Nevada and Rhode Island delegations notified the chair that they, too, wanted to nominate a vice presidential candidate.

That tipped off Nixon's people that something was up. Quickly they considered their parliamentary options to block the move. The head of the Nevada delegation, George Abbott, warned Charles Goodell that he really couldn't get out on a limb by nominating John Lindsay unless he was sure Lindsay would accept the nomination. Abbott wasn't willing to stand there looking like a fool with no committed candidate. They had to get Lindsay on board. The insurgents sent Congressman Charles "Mac" Mathias—a liberal, Agnew-hating Maryland congressman—to find Lindsay.

Lindsay was in the makeup trailer. The Nixon team had reached him first. Nixon asked Lindsay to second Spiro Agnew's nomination. Lindsay was getting ready, with mixed feelings, to do just that. In exchange for seconding Agnew, Nixon had offered Lindsay something he had been wanting for years: permission for New York City to buy the Brooklyn Navy Yard for a very low price. Spiro Agnew had also called Lindsay to personally request that the mayor second his nomination. Agnew understood the power of the personal call, the show of respect.

Mac Mathias, along with Governor John Chafee of

Rhode Island and Senator Edward Brooke of Massachusetts, the only African American in the Senate, arrived at the makeup trailer. Lindsay's younger staff were vigorously protesting Lindsay's agreement to second Agnew's nomination. When Mathias, Chafee, and Brooke blurted out Goodell's hastily conceived plan, Lindsay listened carefully.

"How many votes do you have?" Lindsay asked Mathias. He wasn't going to mount an insurgency without strong support.

Mathias wasn't yet sure how many. Maybe 450—a serious showing.

Lindsay wavered. The party was going conservative. Rockefeller wasn't able to save it. Right now, in fact, out on the floor, Rocky was having none of this stop-Agnew uprising—perhaps out of personal jealousy of Lindsay becoming the surprise star of the convention. As Lindsay's visitors saw it, John Lindsay was the last liberal standing who could save the Republican Party.

The trailer door opened.

In came Herbert Brownell.

Everybody out! That was Brownell's order. Everybody, he said, and that included Mathias, Chafee, and Brooke. The room emptied. Brownell put the situation to Lindsay clearly.

This scheme for a running-mate floor fight was political suicide. The liberals would never get the votes to win, and if they did somehow manage to force Agnew off the ticket, the South would flee, splitting the party and causing a loss in November.

Brownell had just been with Nixon himself. Nixon wasn't going to take this. Nixon told Mitchell, "If the sore losers get away with something like this now, they'll do the same damn thing during my presidency."

Brownell warned Lindsay that after all that had been done to bring the party back from the Goldwater near extinction, if things shattered now in a floor fight over a vice presidential nomination, only one person would get the blame. Not Charles Goodell. Not Mac Mathias. Not John Chafee. Not Ed Brooke. John Lindsay would get all the blame. It would all be on him.

When Brownell and Lindsay came out of the trailer, Mathias, Chafee, and Brooke were waiting hopefully. Saying nothing, Lindsay walked away with Brownell.

Lindsay went to the podium, and to the shock and dismay of liberals not only in the convention hall but all over the country, John Lindsay played out the theme of GOP unity. He seconded the vice presidential nomination of Spiro Agnew.

John Lindsay was the last liberal standing at the Republican convention of 1968. He was literally the last liberal to stand at a Republican convention podium. When John Lindsay finished speaking that night, liberalism in the Republican Party died.

One of the most remarkable effects of the Agnew nomination is that it produced something of an agreement between William Buckley and Gore Vidal.

> **William Buckley:** The choice of Mr. Agnew is in my judgment a sophisticated choice. It seeks to do two things simultaneously. One, to nominate somebody whose position on civil rights is impossible to challenge. He was enthusiastically endorsed by the **Washington Post** and the **Baltimore Sun**. Two, somebody who since his election has insisted that civil rights is not a mandate for civil disorder.
>
> **Gore Vidal:** I think, of the lot, Agnew was probably the least disturbing compromise.

Richard Nixon and Spiro Agnew accepted their nominations to thunderous acclamation—Nixon was escorted to the podium by Strom Thurmond—and as the New Nixon gave his acceptance speech, riots broke out across the bay in the Miami neighborhood of Liberty City. Liberty City is a black neighborhood six miles from the convention hall, but it might as well have been a thousand miles away. No one in the hall knew there was rioting nearby during Nixon's speech.

Trouble had started in Liberty City earlier in the week. There were reports of a white man driving through Liberty City with a George Wallace bumper sticker on his car. He fled from his car and it was burned. Police used tear gas to disperse crowds on Wednesday. Thursday night, the situation got completely out of control with looting and gunfights with police in which three black men were killed. As Nixon was speaking in Miami Beach, America was coming apart again just a few minutes away in Liberty City.

The next day's **New York Times** reported, "The rioting was the first major racial trouble in the history of Miami."

It would not be the last.

TWENTY-SEVEN

THE PEACE PLANK

The Stevens was the biggest hotel in the world when it opened in 1927. It occupied an entire city block on Michigan Avenue across from Grant Park, which was known as Chicago's front lawn. The hotel had three thousand guest rooms and what it called a City Within a City: a bowling alley, movie theater, a miniature golf course on the roof. The first registered guest was Charles Dawes, the vice president of the United States. By the time Vice President Humphrey checked in for his week at the Democratic convention in 1968, the Stevens was a Hilton, and Grant Park was the planned location for the biggest protests in the history of American political conventions. Since Vice President Dawes spent that first night in the Stevens, most vice presidents had stayed at the hotel. Hubert Humphrey would be the first to smell tear gas in his suite.

When Eugene McCarthy arrived in Chicago on Sunday, August 25, he checked into the Hilton, too. It was more than big enough for both of them. McCarthy and Humphrey were in separate wings with separate elevator banks. McCarthy did not arrive in Chicago with the customary political entourage. He flew on a chartered plane from Washington with the poet Robert Lowell, the novelist William Styron, and four journalists. No political types allowed. When someone on the plane asked if he thought he could still win the presidency, McCarthy wearily replied, "Who would want the job?"

The phrase "midlife crisis" was not yet in wide circulation in 1968, but Gene McCarthy had all the symptoms: indecisiveness, confusion about life goals, mood swings, and a strained marriage. That can happen to fifty-two-year-old men in any occupation. If it can happen to men who are surrounded by stability, what happens to men who are surrounded by crisis? For Gene McCarthy, 1968 began with shock followed by crisis followed by more shock and more crisis. Through it all, there was the applause, the adoration—an intoxicant that has left no man unchanged.

McCarthy's year began with him far off into the unknown challenging the incumbent president of his own party for the nomination. Then came the surprise of the kids getting "clean for Gene" and pouring into New Hampshire, followed by the shock of "winning" New Hampshire, followed immediately by the crisis of Bobby and Teddy Kennedy trying to get McCarthy to step aside, then Bobby announcing his challenge to McCarthy and Johnson. Then three days after McCarthy's fifty-second birthday came the shock of LBJ dropping out and the strategic crisis of how to run against Bobby. Four days after that, Martin Luther King Jr. was assassinated and the entire country was in crisis. Two months after that, Bobby was assassinated and Secret Service agents were suddenly protecting McCarthy. By the summer, McCarthy had lost two Democratic opponents in shocking ways, which threw his campaign into crisis. Then he picked up one new opponent, who was his first important friend in Minnesota politics. And every day, the body count in the war McCarthy was trying to stop was going up. Every day, young men who hoped Gene McCarthy could save them were being drafted and shipped out to Vietnam. Every day, McCarthy felt the weight of expectation from those kids, from the country, from his daughter, from his wife. He felt the enormous weight of his supporters' fervent hopes that he often doubted he could fulfill—hope that he would win the presidency, hope that he would end the war, hope that he would bring peace to the world.

Millions of voters of all ages very seriously believed there would be no more war after Vietnam. America would never be this stupid again, they thought. All they had to do was elect Gene McCarthy, so the

United States could get out of Vietnam and never again think it could militarily control countries that didn't threaten it. When the "Clean for Gene" kids looked at McCarthy as a superman, he sometimes felt like a charlatan. If any man ever earned a midlife crisis, it was Gene McCarthy.

By the time he arrived in Chicago, this man who was supposed to be fighting for the presidency was asking who would want the job. Only a candidate much less sensitive, introspective, and philosophical than Gene McCarthy could run for president and never have doubts about the goal along the way. Even Jesus of Nazareth in the Garden of Gethsemane had his doubts.

The candidate wasn't the only one in the McCarthy campaign who was emotionally frazzled by the end of the primary season in June. They had all gone through the same shock and crisis cycle of the campaign. They all grieved for Martin Luther King Jr. and for Bobby Kennedy. After every shock, after every crisis, they all knew what to do—get back to work on the next primary. But after Bobby was killed, there was no work to get back to for most McCarthy people. The primaries were over. There were no more get-out-the-vote phone banks to staff. Most of the volunteers drifted away as the campaign turned to the inside game of chasing delegates. Very few of the senior campaign staff who were left had any experience with the inside game, and they were all still dealing with their own grief as well as their candidate's dark moods and erratic behavior.

Everyone who has worked at the highest levels of highly pressurized campaigns knows that the candidate needs room to deal with pressure. The candidate will get angry under pressure and make mistakes. The staff hopes that all of those mistakes are made behind closed doors, where they can be muffled by the staff and, when possible, fixed. One of the common mistakes that candidates under pressure make is to say impulsive things like "You're fired" to the wrong person. The senior staff's job is to sort out the candidate's good impulses from the bad and to understand exactly which angry exclamations the candidate means and which should be ignored. The best staff know they need to give the candidate room to feel things and say things that they should ignore. Blair Clark, who didn't need the job of McCarthy campaign manager and whose loyalty was tested and proved when Bobby entered the race, was fired four times. Curtis Gans was fired five times. They never missed a day of work and those incidents never became public.

The Humphrey campaign had the better inside game because they had the best inside players and their candidate loved it. As with so many politicians, Humphrey's onstage awkwardness disappeared in private. He enjoyed the backslapping. He was clear about what he wanted and how you could help him and, most important, how grateful he was for your help. What the McCarthy campaign lacked in experience of the inside game it tried to make up for with ingenuity. The weakest link in the McCarthy campaign's inside game was the candidate. Decades later, McCarthy said that after Bobby's assassination, he felt like he was "just going through the motions." But there were some very simple motions that he overlooked. When Senator George McGovern called to offer his endorsement, McCarthy never called him back. McCarthy canceled three scheduled meetings with Mayor Richard Daley, who'd delivered the presidency to JFK in 1960. He ignored calls from John Kenneth Galbraith. Worst of all, Gene and Abigail were barely speaking.

Abigail was the one person who could get the candidate to do things he didn't want to do. Now she was increasingly frozen out. Inside the campaign, there were rumors of the candidate having an affair or affairs. Many presidential campaigns had such rumors, but in those days, the unwritten rule of the news media was that those stories were off-limits. Reporters allowed politicians to have private lives. Abigail's absence from the campaign was covered by health problems. She was ailing with gallstones. Abigail felt that she was losing Gene and that Gene was losing his way.

The city of Chicago had been gearing up for the Democratic convention all year. By the middle

of summer—after the assassinations and riots—
Chicago was bracing for the convention the way
small Caribbean islands brace for the worst hurri-
canes. The convention no longer seemed like a prize
for the city. The other cities that had hoped to host
the 1968 Democratic convention now considered
themselves lucky that it wasn't headed their way.

A broad countercultural New Left, having already made its protest mark in Washington and at
Columbia, announced its plan to bring hundreds
of thousands of protesters into the city, disrupt the
convention, and turn Chicago into a mixture of war
protest and love-in. Nothing like that had ever happened before, and coming out of the shocks of the
McCarthy insurgency, the Wallace campaign (which
was now polling at 15 percent), the president's withdrawal, the King and Kennedy assassinations, and
the burning cities, the American public was steeling
itself for one more unprecedented event in Chicago.
The news media busily searched for synonyms for
unprecedented all year. As Chicago approached, the
only thing they were sure of was the new unpredict-
ability of American politics and American life. The
columnist Theodore White said, "What was different was the entire nature of American life."

The convention was held at the International Amphitheatre, a 1930s sports-and-concert arena near
the city's famous stockyards. That was a good location from the city's point of view. The hall was a few

miles from Grant Park, where the protesters would gather. The protesters could easily be stopped from marching on the convention.

Al Lowenstein, working outside the McCarthy campaign, had founded a new ad hoc organization, the Coalition for an Open Convention (COC), dedicated to stopping the nomination of Humphrey. Dump Johnson had become "Dump the Hump." COC wanted to bring what Lowenstein hoped would be a hundred thousand "Clean for Gene" kids to Chicago to protest the undemocratic process that had awarded Humphrey delegates in defiance of the primary voters. McCarthy vetoed Lowenstein's idea. McCarthy saw violence and chaos on the horizon. He didn't want his young supporters on the front lines. As the McCarthy kids still working for the campaign began setting up shop at the Hilton, McCarthy told Lowenstein he did not want to see thousands more pouring into the street.

Too late. They were already on their way. McCarthy assigned his youth coordinator, Sam Brown, to a storefront office on Wabash Avenue. Brown was to coordinate the McCarthy kids' activities, keep them focused on productive projects, protect them from recruitment by Yippies and radicals, warn them against violence.

Mayor Richard Daley thought he had everything he needed to control the protesters and prevent violence. The one thing that Yippie Abbie Hoffman,

Black Panther chairman Bobby Seale, MOBE's Tom Hayden and Rennie Davis, and the McCarthy college students could agree on was that Daley epitomized the heavy-handed, brutal authoritarianism they were trying to overthrow. Mayor Daley was a central-casting idea of the big-city political boss. He was sixty-six years old, in his thirteenth year as mayor, and on his way to eight more years in city hall before dying in office in 1976 at age seventy-four. He got his first taste of politics as a protester in the streets of Chicago marching as a boy at his mother's side demanding women be given the right to vote. His mother didn't live to see how her son treated protesters on those same streets in 1968.

Richard Daley went to work at the Union Stock Yards, whose horrible working conditions were exposed by Upton Sinclair. Daley's mother wanted more for her only child than fulfilling an Irish American occupational cliché. She once said, "I didn't raise my son to be a policeman." After eleven years of night classes, Richard Daley earned a law degree. He was elected mayor in 1955 with 708,222 votes. For the rest of his life, the license plate on his car was 708 222.

Richard Daley grew up in an Irish American political machine whose motto was "Vote early and often." Authorship of that motto is hard to pinpoint, as it spread among big-city Irish political machines in the early twentieth century. In Boston, it was put to song with a rhyme for the legendary mayor James Michael Curley—"Vote early and often for Curley." It was really an alternative phrasing for "The ends justify the means." If a little chicanery had to be tolerated to give the (Irish) workingman a better chance, then so be it. The big-city Irish mayors were expected to take care of their friends—their close friends as well as everyone who voted for them. The number on Daley's license plate wasn't a boast; it was a promise never to forget who'd sent him to city hall.

The Daley-style Irish mayors delivered the jobs to build the country's biggest public school systems, the most complex mass transit systems, and state-of-the-art public hospitals, and the lives of everyone in those cities were improved a little or a lot. The mayors packed the police and fire departments with their voters. For all that, they were usually rewarded with reelection and the constant whiff of scandal. Mayor Daley was never indicted, but he knew a lot of people who were. Daley's clean criminal record did not prove beyond a reasonable doubt that he was never corrupt, but it was an indicator that he wasn't nearly as criminally inclined as all the Illinois politicians who went to prison before, during, and after the Daley era.

Richard Daley never polished his speaking style as he moved from the stockyards to city hall. There was a rough sound to everything he said, even when he didn't intend it. Often words didn't come out quite the way he wanted them to: "They have vilified me, they have crucified me, yes, they have even criticized me." He delivered so many malapropisms that his press secretary told reporters, "Write what he means, not what he says." There was no doubt about what he meant after Martin Luther King Jr. was assassinated and rioting swept through American cities. He met with the police superintendent at city hall. Then the mayor announced to the press: "I said to him very emphatically and very definitely that an order be issued by him immediately to shoot to kill any arsonist or anyone with a Molotov cocktail in his hand, because they're potential murderers, and to shoot to maim or cripple anyone looting." The Reverend Jesse Jackson said that that was "a fascist's response."

"Shoot to kill" made Daley a hero to many law-and-order voters. They didn't know that most bullets fired by police miss their target completely and that the precision of shooting "to maim or cripple" a moving person is impossible. "Shoot to kill" horrified liberal Democrats who planned to attend the convention. Some Democratic Party operatives pushed for moving the convention to Miami Beach. LBJ would not consider moving the convention. Crossing Richard Daley was unthinkable for establishment Democrats. If Illinois were a safe Democratic state, Daley's power might have remained local. But Illinois was a swing state with 27 electoral votes. The votes Daley's machine delivered in Chicago often decided the outcome in Illinois. Taking the convention away from Daley could mean taking the election away from the Democrats.

When the demonstrators began seeking permits for a week of protests in Chicago, they found themselves up against Fort Daley. Rennie Davis and Tom Hayden of MOBE began reaching out in June to Mayor Daley's office to get permits. Rennie Davis, already on the ground in Chicago, called the mayor's office every day and left messages that weren't returned. In early July, Davis assigned an assistant to call constantly until he got someone on the phone. The assistant kept calling steadily for two weeks. He never got through. Tom Hayden started talking publicly about a revolutionary takeover of the city of Chicago while he was in Paris serving as a self-appointed liaison between antiwar America and the North Vietnamese government. Davis gave an interview to CBS calling for the Chicago Police Department to be investigated before the convention began. Around the country, organizers from the Yippies to Dave Dellinger were attacking LBJ's peace talks, the Democratic Party, and the Chicago Police Department and ending their interviews and speeches by dropping the phrase "See you in Chicago."

"Nobody is going to take over this city," said Mayor Daley. By August 1, having failed to make contact with the mayor or any key officials, Rennie Davis met with liberal go-betweens who told him in no uncertain terms that Mayor Daley was not interested in issuing permits. So as the convention neared, the motley revolutionary coalition and the Chicago mayor's office and police department were all preparing for confrontation.

Everywhere Hubert Humphrey went that summer he heard the chants: "We want Gene!" and "Dump the Hump!" His rallies became volume contests between the cheers and the boos. Humphrey's crowds were sparse at best, hostile at worst. On campuses, the students yelled insults. In Watts, young black activists chased him out of a hall chanting, "Honky, go home!" Humphrey's old-fashioned campaign enthusiasm reeked of phoniness and/or obliviousness.

To the McCarthy team, it felt like Humphrey had an unfair advantage in the delegate hunt, but to Humphrey his position seemed painfully and unfairly precarious. All of Humphrey's delegates would have to hold firm, and in 1968 nothing ever seemed to hold firm. The party was splitting over race, with some Southerners fleeing to George Wallace, and over Vietnam, with McCarthy and the New Left allying.

Humphrey believed he would not win the nomination without the president's support. Johnson's tone was not reassuring. He deliberately tried to keep Humphrey in suspense. After Bobby Kennedy's assassination, Johnson felt no need to soften war policy to help Humphrey with the antiwar crowd, even though Humphrey was trying to pick up Kennedy delegates. LBJ wanted his VP to sell the Johnson war policy.

Even while telling the press he had no involvement, LBJ was micromanaging the convention preparations. The convention was scheduled to coincide with Johnson's sixtieth birthday, and he planned a big birthday celebration at the convention whether he attended or not. Johnson vetoed all of Humphrey's proposals for convention officers and put in his own people. Johnson controlled the day-to-day program, making sure, among other things, that a film memorializing Bobby Kennedy was scheduled for after the nominations so that it would not fuel any sudden notions of drafting Teddy Kennedy, who, at age thirty-six, was only in his second year of constitutional eligibility for the presidency.

Johnson slighted Humphrey in subtle ways with reporters, which always kept Humphrey off balance. Privately, Johnson told friends that Humphrey was too old-fashioned for 1968. Humphrey never knew from one day to the next what Johnson was really thinking. He was never sure if he could even count on a clear endorsement from the president. Mayor Daley was no more excited about Humphrey than LBJ was. Daley hated the McCarthy insurgency, but Bobby had been a possibility for Daley in a choice between Humphrey and Kennedy. Humphrey was always the most publicly enthusiastic candidate, but he always had the least enthusiastic supporters.

Humphrey campaigned that summer as if he were a suspect in a crime and everything he said could and would be used against him. He barely commented on the urban riots or the RFK assassination or Vietnam. The McCarthy campaign saw Humphrey as the tool of a rigged system that could hand him the nomination without his running in a single primary. Humphrey felt like the prisoner of that system, a system controlled, like everything else in his life, by Lyndon Johnson. By the time Humphrey arrived in Chicago, Johnson had not endorsed him.

Each party always has preconvention meetings that are usually ignorable. The Rules Committee decides the rules of the convention, which are mostly or entirely duplicates of their convention's rules of four years earlier. The Credentials Committee rubber-stamps the credentials of all the state delegations. The Platform Committee produces a policy document that no one reads and the presidential nominee is not bound by. Nothing to see here. Nothing to fight about. But in 1968, all of these committees found themselves battling for the soul of the Democratic Party. The outcome changed the party and the nominating process for every Democratic candidate for president since then.

The Rules Committee was the scene of the seemingly calmest fight. The Rules Committee governs how delegations and individual delegates may vote at the convention. The debate in the Rules Committee presaged the more openly explosive conflicts that were about to roil the other committees and then blow up during the convention.

The objective of McCarthy's people on the Rules Committee was to expose to the press and the country how undemocratic and machine-driven the nominating process was. McCarthy won primaries. Humphrey didn't even run in the primaries. Humphrey's apparent delegate lead was the work of party officials unaccountable in any democratic way to the electorate. That is exactly what the rules allowed, and that's why the McCarthy people said the rules had to be changed. Were the Democrats the party of the people or the party of the bosses?

On Thursday, August 22, the McCarthyites on the Rules Committee challenged the "unit rule." Manifestly undemocratic, this was more of a trick than a rule. It was popular in the smaller states, especially in the South. It allowed the leaders of the state delegations to force their delegates to vote as a bloc for the candidate who had the most votes in the delegation. The purpose of the rule was to strengthen a state's impact on the nomination. McCarthy's people demanded the unit rule be abolished.

As an old-line Northern liberal, Hubert Humphrey had a clear position on the unit rule. He opposed it.

But in the weeks leading up to this Rules Committee meeting, Humphrey began waffling on it. Humphrey's problem was Texas governor John Connally. Humphrey needed Governor Connally's Texas delegation and Connally needed the unit rule.

Some of Humphrey's people had given Connally the strong impression that Humphrey would take Connally's position on the unit rule: keep the rule this year, possibly abolish it for 1972. But the day before the Rules Committee was to meet, the Humphrey campaign issued a statement calling for immediate abolition of the unit rule. Humphrey's reversal of position infuriated Connally and the Southerners. Humphrey's people told Connally that the campaign statement was a mistake, just organizational ineptitude. Connally didn't believe it and began threatening Humphrey with losing the Texas delegation.

Richard Goodwin saw an opening. Goodwin had returned to the McCarthy campaign after Bobby Kennedy was killed. He was working at McCarthy headquarters in Chicago when the Humphrey campaign publicly opposed the unit rule.

What if, Goodwin wondered, Gene McCarthy offered John Connally the vice presidency? With the Texas delegation, McCarthy could deny Humphrey a first ballot nomination at least. Connally could attract enough establishment support on a second or third ballot to win the nomination. In the general election, the Democrats would have a ticket balanced with North and South, liberal and moderate, antiwar and pro-LBJ peace negotiations. Goodwin met with Connally. The governor discussed the idea for two hours. Any shrewd politician would be fascinated by the idea. This wasn't how idealists ran campaigns, but it was how realists won campaigns. Goodwin's problem in closing the deal was not Connally, it was McCarthy.

McCarthy refused even to consider running with John Connally. Humphrey's people kept begging Connally's forgiveness. Humphrey promised Connally that he would retreat on the unit rule and that he would continue to support LBJ on the war. The Rules Committee decided to avoid a showdown and leave it to the convention to decide on the unit rule. All the delegates could vote on it. The Humphrey campaign's confusion about the unit rule did not look good to party professionals on the Rules Committee. Was Humphrey for it or against it? Humphrey's campaign seemed chaotic when he was supposed to be selling the party on his stability.

The Credentials Committee had to decide who gets to serve as delegates and why. There was nothing controversial about the delegates in most of the state delegations headed for Chicago. Most delegates were chosen for their faithful service to the party and were very good at following orders. Those delegates liked the system the way it was. Most of them saw the McCarthy campaign as a threat. Many Democratic

Party regulars could accept a Nixon win in November more easily than a McCarthy nomination in August. Nominating McCarthy would hand over control of the party to the McCarthyites. Party regulars could lose status at the local level. Incumbents everywhere would surely face primary challenges modeled after the successful McCarthy insurgency. Power would shift to a younger generation. For many delegates, that could make 1968 their last convention. For his part, McCarthy did nothing to make those delegates feel more comfortable.

McCarthy seemed to be going out of his way to offer the party regulars nothing. His people didn't seem to care about party unity. Some of them seemed to scorn the party. In a preconvention meeting in New York about choosing delegates, Al Lowenstein said to party loyalists, "I implore you not to be so stupid." McCarthy did not even pledge to support the eventual nominee, something Bobby Kennedy had no problem doing.

Many of the McCarthy people, new to politics, had been outraged to discover the inside workings of party operations, especially the selection of delegates. Only about a third of the delegates were selected based on the outcome of the primaries. In three states, a single man was empowered to fill nearly an entire delegation. "You mean this is how the system works?" said one Missouri McCarthy delegate after a committee meeting. The writer and cartoonist Jules Feiffer, a

McCarthy delegate in the New York delegation, remarked, "I said all along the system doesn't work. So I got in the system. And now I know I was right."

The McCarthy strategy in the Credentials Committee was, as Jerry Eller put it, "Achieve panic. Then win." The McCarthy campaign wanted to challenge the legitimacy of as many of the state delegations as possible, then force the committee to replace them with McCarthy people. They would at once expose the illegitimacy of the system and establish a new system.

To win the nomination, McCarthy had a choice of long shots: attack the system or work within the system. Democratic strategist Tom Finney was trying to persuade uncommitted delegates to come over to McCarthy. That would be impossible if those delegates' credentials were being challenged by McCarthy people. "You've got to stop those kids," Finney told Tom Mechling, the campaign's top delegate hunter. "They're tearing this party up by the grass roots."

Sam Brown and Curtis Gans led the McCarthy forces in the Credentials Committee hearings. They were joined by twenty-six-year-old Dave Mixner, who studied the rules and had an easier time mastering them than he expected. "A kid out of kindergarten could do it," he said. Another twenty-six-year-old at Yale Law School, Geoffrey Cowan, quickly wrote a handbook on credentials for the McCarthy team.

The most experienced strategist on the team was thirty years older than the rules whiz kids.

Joseph Rauh was a fifty-seven-year-old labor and civil rights lawyer who was also a founder of Americans for Democratic Action. As the Credentials Committee hearings began, Joseph Rauh served as the McCarthy point man in presenting challenges to the committee. Rauh expected to have open conflicts with the committee chairman, Governor Richard Hughes of New Jersey, a tough party-establishment man, but he also found himself in conflict with some of the young McCarthy supporters who looked skeptically at Rauh's plan for victory with credentials challenges.

Rauh's strategy was not to mount a frontal assault on the whole system of delegate selection, as many McCarthy people wanted. Rauh believed this would make McCarthy supporters temporarily feel good as they headed for certain defeat in the Credentials Committee. Rauh wanted to mount a narrowly focused attack that no one would realize had the power to bring the whole system crashing down if successful. If anyone could pull this off, it was Joseph Rauh.

The son of German immigrants, Joseph Rauh had been the center on Harvard's basketball team. In 1932, he went straight from Harvard College to Harvard Law School, where he finished first in his class. He went to the U.S. Supreme Court as a clerk, then decided to specialize in civil rights law. He wrote the civil rights plank that Hubert Humphrey fought for in the 1948 convention. He walked with Martin Luther King Jr. in the March on Washington in 1963.

At the 1964 Democratic convention, Rauh challenged the credentials of the segregated Mississippi delegation. He was the lawyer for the Mississippi Freedom Democratic Party, which sent its black delegates by Greyhound bus to the Democratic convention in Atlantic City to challenge the all-white Mississippi delegation. Martin Luther King Jr. testified to the Credentials Committee in support of the Mississippi Freedom Democratic Party, but he was not the star of the hearings. Fannie Lou Hamer, who once said, "I'm sick and tired of being sick and tired," captured the country's attention with her testimony of being fired after she tried to register to vote. The huge hearing room fell into stunned silence listening to her account of being arrested and beaten in her jail cell. Her testimony was broadcast live on network television. President Johnson was watching in the White House and immediately rushed to the press briefing room to hold an impromptu press conference just to seize the network coverage from Fannie Lou Hamer. Later, all the networks showed her testimony in its entirety. She was near tears at the end of her statement and most people watching were, too, when she said, "All of this on account we want to register to become first class citizens, and if the Freedom Democratic Party is not seated now, I question

America. Is this America, the land of the free and the home of the brave?"

LBJ knew that after Fannie Lou Hamer's testimony, a majority of the convention's delegates would vote to unseat the Mississippi delegation. Johnson wasn't going to let them have that chance. He asked Humphrey to negotiate with the Mississippi Freedom Democratic Party. Humphrey was then in the thick of his competition with Gene McCarthy to be chosen as LBJ's running mate. LBJ feared that if the Mississippi delegation was not seated, then all the Southern delegations would walk out with Mississippi. Johnson wasn't going to let Barry Goldwater win the South so easily.

Hubert Humphrey was no match for Fannie Lou Hamer, who was the vice chair of the Mississippi Freedom Democrats. She and the rest of the negotiators refused Humphrey's offer of two nonvoting seats in the Mississippi delegation. When Humphrey pleaded with them, saying that his position on the ticket with LBJ was at stake, Fannie Lou Hamer said, "Do you mean to tell me that your position is more important than four hundred thousand black people's lives? Senator Humphrey, I know lots of people in Mississippi who have lost their jobs trying to register to vote. I had to leave the plantation where I worked in Sunflower County, Mississippi. Now if you lose this job of Vice-President because you do what is right, because you help the MFDP, everything will be all right. God will take care of you. But if you take it this way, why, you will never be able to do any good for civil rights, for poor people, for peace, or any of those things you talk about. Senator Humphrey, I'm going to pray to Jesus for you."

Humphrey got no deal. The Mississippi delegation did not lose their credentials. The South did not walk out of the 1964 convention. And as Fannie Lou Hamer predicted, the South voted for Goldwater in November. One of Humphrey's promises to Fannie Lou Hamer and the Mississippi Freedom Democrats was that segregated delegations would not be seated at the next convention in 1968. Joseph Rauh was there in '64 when Humphrey made that promise.

Rauh wanted to challenge the 1968 Mississippi, Georgia, and Alabama delegations for flagrant violation of the party's new position on fair racial representation. Rauh was the perfect lawyer to remind the Credentials Committee of the promise of four years ago. He hoped to unseat those delegations and replace them with McCarthy people. Rauh believed the fight over the Southern delegations could shatter the Humphrey coalition, and then anything could happen.

"When Strom Thurmond escorted Richard Nixon to the podium," Humphrey said in a speech on August 9, "you saw the birth of a new political party: the Nixiecrats." If Humphrey's people on the Credentials Committee fought to keep segregationist delegations, Humphrey would be trying to keep the Strom Thurmond types in his own party. There were 212 black delegates coming to this convention. They could split from Humphrey and take some Northern liberals with them. And if Humphrey chose not to fight to keep those black Southern delegates out, the South would run from him, all the way out of the party to George Wallace. Rauh's strategy had the potential to put Humphrey in an impossible bind.

But the younger staff favored a broader assault on the party. They wanted to use the Credentials Committee to challenge the whole system.

Northern delegations were run by racist bosses, too. Rauh countered that the Northern delegations "aren't worth the gunpowder that's needed to blow them up." Rauh thought going after Northern delegations would unify the North and South in fighting all the challenges.

McCarthy insurgencies in every state had the right to bring challenges to the Credentials Committee, and they didn't need Rauh's or anyone else's permission to do that. There was no top-down discipline from McCarthy. On August 19, at the Credentials Committee's first meeting, the committee faced an unheard-of number of challenges. A total of fifteen state delegations came under direct attack by the McCarthy insurgents, including Northern delegations such as Connecticut, Pennsylvania, Indiana, Michigan, and Minnesota.

The Humphrey people joined the McCarthy team in challenging the white Mississippi delegation's credentials. Humphrey knew the Mississippi challenge would be successful this time, so the Humphrey campaign wanted to save its strength to fight off other challenges.

Georgia's governor, Lester Maddox, stacked his delegation with segregationists. Governor Maddox captured national attention in 1968 for refusing to fly the flag at half-staff at the capitol in Atlanta while Martin Luther King Jr.'s funeral was taking place across town. Julian Bond was a twenty-eight-year-old member of the Georgia House of Representatives, its first African American member since Reconstruction. Representative Bond was planning to challenge the Maddox delegation. In July, Curtis Gans, Sam Brown, and Dave Mixner went to Atlanta to coordinate the Georgia challenge with Julian Bond. The Mississippi Freedom Democrats' example of four years earlier was Julian Bond's model. He put together a challenge slate of delegates with twenty-one white and twenty black people with strong McCarthy commitments.

At the Credentials Committee hearing in Chicago, Bond calmly urged that his delegation be seated instead of Governor Maddox's. Governor Maddox was interrogated sharply by the African American California legislator Willie Brown. The committee chairman saw that something was going to have to be done about Georgia. Humphrey and everyone else knew Lester Maddox was going to support George Wallace in November. Humphrey didn't have anything to lose with Maddox. Chairman Hughes insisted on a compromise. He split the Georgia delegation into half Bond's people, half Maddox's. Neither side was satisfied.

On August 20, the Credentials Committee voted 84 to 10 to deny credentials to the Mississippi delegation and replace it with a new Mississippi delegation divided between Humphrey and McCarthy delegates. The strong vote against Mississippi combined with the compromise on Georgia gave Chairman Hughes the coalition he needed on the committee to stop rocking the boat. Governor Hughes shut down all the challenges to Northern state delegations, just as Joseph Rauh expected.

The Credentials Committee did recommend to the national committee that it review all delegate selection procedures and make new recommendations for 1972. Those recommendations would change the nominating process so that a candidate like Hubert Humphrey could never have a chance at the nomination without running in the primaries. The year 1968 would be the last time the primaries would be less important than the inside game.

All Joseph Rauh could do after the Credentials Committee was wait a week until the convention opened. He planned to leave the Northern delegations alone and bring stronger Southern challenges to a vote on the floor. It was a long-shot strategy for instant reforming of the party at the convention, but Rauh would try.

The Credentials Committee battles were minor compared to what happened in the Platform Committee. The platform is supposed to be a written outline of the party's positions on the issues and its promises of what the party's candidates hope to achieve in office. Platforms tend to be bland and vague so that candidates from Maine to Hawaii can run at varying distances from the platform without having to directly contradict it. The night Gene McCarthy "won" New Hampshire, every professional Democrat knew the party was headed for a historic battle over what the platform would say about the Vietnam War. A week before the convention, the Platform Committee saw what McCarthy had seen a year earlier: the 1968 campaign was about war and peace, life and death.

McCarthy wanted a "peace plank" in the platform, and Humphrey wanted whatever LBJ would allow him to have.

The antiwar movement saw little progress in President Johnson's pursuit of peace talks with North Vietnam, which he had announced the night he dropped out of the race. He made his big speech. He stepped aside as a candidate. But he still seemed to be hoping for some kind of military victory.

Preliminary talks between the United States and North Vietnam began on May 10 in Paris. Johnson had ordered a temporary halt in the bombing of North Vietnam. Hanoi's position was that the bombing must end permanently before North Vietnam would talk at all. Johnson had three conditions for ending the bombing. He kept the conditions secret, so that if North Vietnam accepted them, they could claim there were no preconditions to a bombing halt. LBJ's conditions were de-escalation of Northern attacks on South Vietnam, a demilitarized zone (DMZ) between North and South, and acceptance of South Vietnam as a party to any talks. Accepting South Vietnam into the talks was impossible for the North and the Vietcong. South Vietnam also refused to join talks that included the Vietcong. The United States and North Vietnam were the only parties at the table in the beginning of the summer, and they publicly spent their time arguing about the shape, literally, of the conference table. North Vietnam wanted a big circular table with all parties seated equally with no one at the head of the table. South Vietnam wanted a rectangular table with the North and South across from each other and no Vietcong. The Vietcong did not want South Vietnam at the table. At this pace, there would be no progress before the election. If the peace talks showed more progress, the Platform Committee might have comfortably produced a vague plank saying the party fully supports the peace process under way in Paris. No progress in Paris put all the more pressure on the Democrats in Chicago.

John Gilligan thought a peace plank would help Humphrey. Gilligan was an Ohio congressman who was campaigning to move up to the Senate that year. Gilligan wanted the platform to move to the left of LBJ's position on the war—a move that would be difficult for Humphrey to make on his own as a member of the Johnson administration. Gilligan saw this as the only route to party unity, the only way to get McCarthy kids to vote for Humphrey in November.

Gilligan and other antiwar regulars lined up a high-profile coalition in favor of the peace plank. In early August, before the Platform Committee meetings began, a lunch at the Carroll Arms Hotel in Washington brought together McCarthy staff and former Kennedy staff—Blair Clark, Joseph Rauh, Frank Mankiewicz, Ted Sorensen—along with a group of Fulbright's antiwar senators. John Gilligan presented the peace-plank strategy to push Humphrey away from LBJ. The key, everybody at this lunch agreed, would be to maintain unity within the peace-plank group itself. To get adopted, this plank would have to feel more establishment than insurgent. Any direct criticism of President Johnson would force Humphrey into a defensive position, and he would reject the peace plank.

Such an agreement for unity was tough on McCarthy's people. McCarthy's entire campaign had been run against LBJ on the war. Blair Clark said he would make the pitch to McCarthy.

In the tense weeks that followed, the peace-plank coalition tried to whip up support. Back in Ohio, Gilligan promised his union supporters that the peace plank wasn't an anti-Humphrey effort. He faced strong opposition. Most union bosses saw any effort for a negotiated peace as appeasing the communists. Others in the peace-plank group reached out to Humphrey's staff. Ted Sorensen got so close to David Ginsburg, a Washington lawyer charged with drafting Humphrey's Vietnam position, that McCarthy people in the peace group began to think Sorensen was serving as a secret agent for Humphrey.

Despite some mutual suspicion, peace-plank unity generally held. The coalition members began to believe they might be able to force a peace plank on Humphrey. John Gilligan put it this way: "It would be like throwing a child into a swimming pool. He'd swim."

Hubert Humphrey knew his future depended on coming up with something on the war that distinguished him from Johnson. To convince delegates and the American people that he was, as he kept claiming, "his own man," Humphrey would have to arrive at an original plan for peace. It never occurred to him to actually be his own man and not get LBJ's approval for whatever he said about the war.

Humphrey's position paper titled "Vietnam: Toward a Political Settlement and Peace in Southeast Asia" had been through five drafts by late July. The paper was vague. It called for "de-Americanizing" the war. It referred to some recent lulls in the fighting as possibly meeting the conditions under which LBJ had hinted he would make the bombing halt permanent. The latest draft had Humphrey saying that if such trends continued, he would, as president, carry out a permanent bombing halt.

On July 25, his staff read him that draft. He liked it. Then he added, "I'll have to show it to the President."

Johnson didn't just tell Humphrey that the position paper was no good. He told Humphrey that if he made this commitment to a bombing halt, Humphrey would be placing in danger the lives of Johnson's own sons-in-law serving in Vietnam. Their blood would be on Humphrey's hands. Humphrey knew that Johnson used his sons-in-law in private when he was most emphatically trying to crush any hint of dissent on Vietnam. Johnson said the position paper would destroy Humphrey's chances of becoming president. Humphrey came away so humiliated by the president's comments that at first he didn't tell anyone. He simply handed the Vietnam paper over to David Ginsburg to fix.

The day after Johnson's meeting with Humphrey, the president met with Richard Nixon. It was treated as a normal briefing for the presumptive Republican nominee on the Vietnam War and the status of the peace talks in Paris. Nixon had publicly needled Johnson on the war from every direction, but Johnson thought his legacy in Southeast Asia might be safer with Nixon as president. He couldn't imagine Nixon cutting and running out of Vietnam. He thought Nixon was much tougher than Humphrey. Johnson worried that if the Democratic or Republican candidate called for an unconditional bombing halt, it would kill any progress toward a negotiated peace. If the North Vietnamese believed the next president would stop the bombing, then why negotiate with LBJ? Johnson had Humphrey locked up tight. Now he needed to lock up Nixon, too.

They met in the Cabinet Room on Friday, July 26. Secretary of State Dean Rusk was there along with National Security Adviser Walt Rostow. Johnson knew that to convince Nixon this was a real meeting, not just a courtesy, he would have to tell Nixon something he couldn't read in the newspaper. Johnson told Nixon about his secret conditions for negotiating peace, something Johnson had not told Humphrey. Hoping he had won Nixon's confidence, Johnson told him he was hoping Nixon would agree not to call for a bombing halt or anything that would suggest to North Vietnam that they would get a better deal if Nixon were president. Here was the Democratic president asking the Republican candidate for president to limit his choices of possible campaign tactics on the most important issue in the campaign. As wily as Johnson was, he didn't understand how easy it was for Nixon to agree to this request. Nixon had no intention of calling for a bombing halt. He never proposed anything that specific on Vietnam. He just promised to do a better job on Vietnam than LBJ. For that to continue to work, Nixon needed a quagmire.

Nixon did express concern that Humphrey, pressured by the McCarthyites, might call for a bombing halt, or even withdrawal, and get a boost in the polls from that. Johnson reassured Nixon that he had Humphrey under control. That information alone was worth the visit to the White House for Nixon. He didn't have to worry about Humphrey's moving left on Vietnam.

Johnson and Nixon had a deal. Nixon said he would not advocate a bombing halt, and that he would refrain from criticizing Johnson directly, as long as Johnson stayed firm on Vietnam and didn't make any moves toward arriving at peace without informing Nixon. Johnson agreed. And they agreed to stay in touch.

Johnson kept the most important recent development about Vietnam to himself when he met with Humphrey and Nixon. Johnson believed he was on the verge of a breakthrough after receiving a secret message from Soviet premier Alexei Kosygin.

The Russian leader told Johnson that if the United States stopped the bombing, the Soviets would get North Vietnam to agree to Johnson's three conditions. Johnson could go ahead and announce an end to the bombing and still get what he wanted from the North.

The Soviet Union supplied North Vietnam with 80 percent of its war supplies. Johnson believed the Soviets had the leverage it would take to get the North to accept Johnson's conditions. As Johnson slowly and carefully explored the possibility of a secret deal with the Soviets on Vietnam, he felt himself edging toward the kind of breakthrough that could deliver what he called peace with honor.

Richard Nixon was keeping his own secret about Vietnam. It was not a possible path to peace. It was the darkest secret of Nixon's life, a life filled with dark secrets. It was a secret that would not be fully revealed until long after Nixon's death. When Lyndon Johnson eventually found out about it, the president was shocked. It was much worse than the worst Johnson could have imagined about Nixon.

While Johnson was hoping for a breakthrough for peace in Vietnam, Nixon was trying to prevent one. Two weeks before Nixon's meeting with the president, he had a secret meeting with South Vietnam's ambassador to the United States, Bui Diem. The ambassador flew from Washington to New York with Washington hostess Anna Chennault.

Anna Chennault was born in China in 1925. She was the daughter of a Chinese diplomat. Her name at birth was Chen Xiangmei. She was a nineteen-year-old reporter when she met and interviewed an American air force general in China in 1944. Three years later, after the general's divorce, they were married. She took his last name and became Anna Chennault. Her husband was thirty-two years older. They had two daughters. The marriage lasted ten years, until her husband's death in 1958. Anna Chennault lived the rest of her life as a very wealthy widow, thanks to her husband's postmilitary business success. In Washington during the 1960s, with the United States completely cut off from China, no one had better contacts in the region than Anna Chennault. Her first involvement in a presidential campaign was when she campaigned for Nixon in Chinese American communities in 1960.

The entrance of Anna Chennault in the 1968 presidential campaign now seems like the work of a Hollywood screenwriter cutting to the entrance of the beautiful, mysterious Asian woman to thicken the plot.

The Nixon campaign asked Anna Chennault for help in establishing direct, secret communication with the government of South Vietnam, so she introduced Nixon to the South Vietnamese ambassador. A presidential candidate meeting with a foreign ambassador was not in itself strange. The candidate might want to listen to the ambassador's view of trade relations with that country. That is the most innocent version of such a meeting, as is the ritual of presidential candidates routinely visiting Israel and publicly meeting with Israeli government officials. In 1968, no foreign government had a greater interest in the American presidential election than South Vietnam. Their future as a government depended on it.

Nixon used the secret meeting with Ambassador Diem to establish points of contact. Nixon made it clear to the ambassador that he had known Anna Chennault for years and trusted her. She was to be considered the sole contact between the Nixon campaign and the government of South Vietnam. On the Nixon side, John Mitchell was to be Chennault's contact.

Nixon wanted South Vietnam to keep him informed of any secret developments in the peace talks. Nixon and the South Vietnamese government feared the same thing: withdrawal of U.S. troops. The South Vietnamese feared invasion from the North without U.S. troops to protect them. Nixon feared that any significant steps toward peace would be good for the Democrats in November and bad for him. South Vietnamese president Nguyen Van Thieu already believed a President Nixon would be tougher on North Vietnam than a President Humphrey, who would be beholden to the growing antiwar wing of his party.

While the Democrats were trying to write a peace plank, Nixon's message to South Vietnam was: Hold on, don't agree to anything in Paris, you'll get a better deal with me. That message had to be kept secret because it was a crime. Since 1799, the Logan Act has prohibited private citizens from negotiating with a foreign country on behalf of the United States. As Richard Nixon saw it in the summer of 1968, for him to win the presidency more American soldiers were going to have to die.

After Nixon was nominated in Miami Beach, Johnson called him with congratulations. Johnson invited the new nominee, along with his running mate, to his Texas ranch for another presidential briefing. Nixon and Agnew arrived on August 7. Secretary Rusk, CIA director Richard Helms, and Paris peace negotiator Cyrus Vance were there. Nixon had publicly been saying what Johnson wanted to hear, including that it would be wrong to say anything that might affect the Paris peace process. Nixon was now using the Paris talks to maintain his always vague position on the war. At the ranch, Johnson had some new information for Nixon and Agnew: President Thieu was proposing a face-saving way of allowing the Vietcong to join the negotiations. Thieu suggested that the parties simply refer to "our side" and "your side" without specifically mentioning who was included on each side. Before agreeing to accept South Vietnam as a guest of "your side," the North was demanding that the Vietcong have its own seat at the table independent of "our side." Johnson said he would not allow a separate seat for the Vietcong.

Nixon told Johnson that he remained concerned that Humphrey, under increasing pressure from McCarthy as the convention approached, might call for a unilateral bombing halt or even unilateral withdrawal. Johnson was concerned about that, too. He knew the Platform Committee was going to have to deal with a peace plank. Johnson and Nixon congratulated each other on their mutual devotion to the national interest over and above petty, partisan electoral politics.

On August 8, the day after his meeting with Nixon and Agnew, Johnson summoned Humphrey to the ranch. Humphrey brought the latest draft of his Vietnam position paper. At lunch, Humphrey praised Johnson's record so fawningly and fulsomely that his young aide Bill Connell grew embarrassed and Johnson's young aide Doris Kearns felt "saddened." When the president did finally look over Humphrey's latest draft on Vietnam, he said it was all right. Then LBJ threw up a new roadblock. He said there were things in the works that might lead to peace in Vietnam in the next few weeks. Johnson said there was a real breakthrough in Paris that he couldn't reveal to Humphrey. It was the kind of insult Johnson knew Humphrey would accept—there was something so important happening that the president couldn't tell the vice president, never mind the dozen or more administration officials from Paris to Washington who had to already know in order for the information to reach the president. LBJ asked Humphrey not to release his Vietnam policy paper now because it could jeopardize the president's secret, which could be a huge lift to Humphrey's candidacy when LBJ was ready to make the secret Paris developments public. Humphrey left the LBJ ranch that day feeling much better. He told his people that he had regained good communication with the president.

Senator George McGovern was one of many antiwar Democrats who were troubled by Gene McCarthy's erratic behavior after the primaries. On August 10, Senator McGovern announced his candidacy for the Democratic nomination for president. Two months after Bobby Kennedy's assassination, McGovern said his campaign was about "the goals for which Robert Kennedy gave his life." Senator McGovern made his campaign announcement in the same Senate Caucus Room in exactly the same spot where Senator Kennedy had announced five months earlier. McGovern said "that war must be ended now," to the applause of many former Kennedy supporters in the room. McGovern specifically said he was not trying to claim "the Kennedy mantle," but that's exactly the way it looked to the news media and most of the country, especially when three important Kennedy men immediately endorsed McGovern—Frank

Mankiewicz, Arthur Schlesinger, and Pierre Salinger. With only two weeks left before the convention, the McGovern campaign had to be entirely an inside game of chasing delegates.

McCarthy and his supporters once again felt betrayed by another peace candidate trying to steal the movement McCarthy created. Ted Kennedy taking his brother's place in the campaign would have been understandable, but George McGovern? Everyone outside of South Dakota said, "George who?" McCarthy people saw McGovern as a shill for Humphrey. Splitting the antiwar delegates at the convention could only help Humphrey. But McCarthy supporters outside of campaign headquarters did not know how much McCarthy was ignoring the inside game of running for president that summer. If McCarthy had returned McGovern's call, if McCarthy had kept his antiwar Senate allies close to him, this probably would not have happened. But there was also the problem of the many Kennedy supporters who became political orphans after the assassination. They couldn't bring themselves to support McCarthy after his public insults to Bobby during the campaign. Some Kennedy supporters went to McCarthy, some to Humphrey, and McGovern was offering the rest of them a political home. McGovern gave the least believable campaign announcement performance of the year when he delivered the standard line "I'm in it to win." The **New York Times** reported a more credible objective for Senator McGovern: "He indicated that he would be satisfied if his candidacy led only to a stronger antiwar plank in the Democratic platform."

The chairman of the Platform Committee was Congressman Hale Boggs of Louisiana, the House majority whip. Hale Boggs was an experienced congressional vote counter and an LBJ loyalist ready to shut down the peace plank. The platform hearings convened on Monday, August 19, not in Chicago but at the Statler Hilton Hotel in Washington. Two days earlier, Humphrey went off script during a speech in New York City. Amid the usual mix of cheers and boos, Humphrey protested that he had "remarkably similar views on Vietnam" as Bobby Kennedy.

Kennedy men reacted with outrage. Walinsky, Mankiewicz, Schlesinger, and Goodwin together published a **New York Times** op-ed calling Humphrey's statements "false and misleading." They quoted RFK on the necessity of Vietcong participation in any peace talks. They quoted Humphrey calling RFK's proposal "rewarding murderers and assassins." But some members of the peace-plank coalition were hopeful that Humphrey might really be trying to move in Bobby's direction on Vietnam.

Hale Boggs told Humphrey's man David Ginsburg that he wanted the Vietnam plank to be whatever Humphrey wanted it to be. Humphrey had asked Senator Edmund Muskie of Maine to present the Humphrey position at the Platform Committee hearings. The peace-plank coalition enlisted Senator Fulbright and Senator McGovern to testify along with John Kenneth Galbraith. They wanted a strong show of establishment support for the peace plank. About forty of the one hundred committee members were ready to support the peace plank. That would entitle them to at least bring a minority report to the convention floor and get a vote from the entire convention on a peace plank. If they could pull Humphrey their way, the peace plank would be the majority position.

The day the peace-plank debate began, Johnson called Nixon. The president offered Nixon some talking points for criticizing the peace plank.

"You can take this down if you want to," Johnson said, "I think it's a good phrase."

"I'll jot it down," said Nixon.

Johnson said peace-plank advocates should be challenged to rephrase their position: "Why don't they say, 'You should stop bombing men and arms moving southward across the DMZ to kill U.S. and allied forces. . . .' Now, that's what it means, Dick."

"That's the crux of the matter," Nixon agreed.

The next day, August 20, 1968, Soviet tanks rolled into Czechoslovakia.

Lyndon Johnson was stunned. Defense Secretary Clifford was not. Clark Clifford believed the president had been too slow in accepting the Soviets' offer to help with the Vietnam talks. In Clifford's view, Johnson had blown it, but he didn't tell the president that. Johnson called Nixon that night to give him a heads-up about the Soviet invasion. Nixon pointed out that now they had an even stronger hand to play against the peace plank. Then Johnson called Humphrey in and harangued him until after 3:00 a.m. on standing firm on Vietnam.

Naked Soviet aggression hit the peace-plank group hard. Gene McCarthy called the Soviet invasion "not a major crisis." To most voters, that made the peace movement look tuned-out and unserious. When Galbraith called McCarthy to urge him to make a stronger statement on the invasion, McCarthy said, "Ken, I expected all the other fools to call me, but I never thought you would." Soon McCarthy did, as they say in the Senate, revise and extend his remarks but not enough to erase his first comment. McCarthy's reaction to the Soviet invasion did not help hold the peace-plank coalition together.

The Platform Committee moved to Chicago on Thursday, August 22, four days before the convention was to begin. Chairman Boggs denied spots on the platform-drafting committee to two of three leaders proposed by the peace group. With its members' confidence eroding, unity in the peace group itself also began to shred, and in the final peace-plank drafting session on Friday, the group turned on itself. They refought the battles Bobby Kennedy's team used to have. Ted Sorensen pushed for a mild draft that wouldn't scare Humphrey. Richard Goodwin wanted a strong statement for peace based on a draft McCarthy had written. Humphrey's people weighed in with their concerns. John Gilligan, the Ohio congressman who had started the whole thing, was trying to referee. The plank that emerged from the peace coalition's final session, as presented to the whole committee late Friday night, was a mixture of compromises.

It called for an unconditional bombing halt and, implicitly, a government in South Vietnam that would recognize and possibly include the Vietcong. Now they had to see whether Hubert Humphrey could live with it.

Hale Boggs was flying back to Washington as the peace group was coming up with its draft. Boggs brought along two other key convention officers, Carl Albert of Oklahoma, the convention chair, and Senator Jennings Randolph of West Virginia, an influential member of the Platform Committee. They were on their way to see the president.

Boggs asked Johnson what effect a bombing halt in Vietnam would have on the war. Johnson read Boggs and the others a classified telegram from the new U.S. commander in Vietnam, General Creighton Abrams, saying a bombing halt would increase the enemy's capability by 500 percent. The president warned them that the Vietcong might already be

gearing up for another offensive. That was all Hale
Boggs, Carl Albert, and Randolph Jennings needed
to hear. They had their message for the Platform
Committee: the peace plank would cost American
lives.

John Gilligan took the peace-plank draft to Humphrey's headquarters at the Hilton. He had a positive meeting with Humphrey's aide David Ginsburg.
They went over the plank point by point and found
themselves surprisingly close. Ginsburg told Gilligan
that he believed he could get Humphrey on board.
Thinking they might be on the verge of saving their
party and showing their country the way out of Vietnam, Gilligan and Ginsburg left their meeting feeling very optimistic.

Boggs arrived back in Chicago on Saturday and
officially gave the Platform Committee a warning,
based on classified intelligence received directly
from the president: any halt in the bombing would
only empower the enemy and kill U.S. troops, and a
new enemy offensive might be in the works. An LBJ
staffer named Charles Murphy appeared at David
Ginsburg's hotel room. Murphy asked for a copy of
the peace plank that Ginsburg was asking Humphrey
to agree to. The next day Murphy brought Ginsburg
to a meeting with Boggs. The peace plank was unacceptable to the president, Murphy told Ginsburg.
Humphrey couldn't support it. Murphy handed a
revision to Ginsburg. Johnson himself had rewrit-

ten the section on stopping the bombing to make its timing contingent on not endangering any men in the field. That was obviously Johnson's way of saying never stop the bombing. Ginsburg had nothing to say. He realized his mistake was thinking that Humphrey did have something to say. LBJ was obviously in complete control.

On Sunday afternoon, Boggs resumed committee hearings and offered the LBJ plank on Vietnam. Boggs then ended debate. The Platform Committee voted 35 for the peace plank and 65 for the Johnson plank. That was enough to bring both planks to the convention floor for a vote. Peace still had a chance in the Democratic Party.

When Gene McCarthy arrived at Chicago's Midway Airport that afternoon, he told his welcoming supporters, "We're not asking for too much, just a modest use of intelligence."

TWENTY-EIGHT

"THE WHOLE WORLD'S WATCHING"

On the eve of the Democratic convention, President Johnson wasn't just keeping control of the Platform Committee, bullying his vice president, and having secret phone calls with the Republican nominee, he was reconsidering his decision not to run.

Johnson was watching his chosen successor, Hubert Humphrey, run behind Gene McCarthy in the polls. Humphrey was also running behind Nixon. Johnson kept telling people that other influential politicians wanted him to change his mind and run, as if he were trying to create a rumor mill that could produce a draft-Johnson groundswell at the convention. "Nixon can be beaten," Johnson said. "He'll do something wrong in the end."

Richard Daley was all for drafting Johnson. "I'm for a draft," Daley told White House aide Jake Jacobsen, "and I'll start it." Governor John Connally was also in favor of drafting Johnson because Humphrey seemed like such a weak candidate. During the week leading up to the convention's opening, the president secretly made tentative plans to travel to Chicago.

That same week, the situation on Chicago's streets began to change. The protest groups made it clear that they would proceed without permits. The Chicago Police Department was preparing for twelve-hour shifts. At precinct roll calls, police officers were issued gas masks. More than 7,000 U.S. Army troops at Fort Hood were training for riot control. The mayor, the governor, and the Pentagon had also decided to call out the National Guard from nearby Fort Riley. A total force of about 40,000 armed men in Chicago and in the surrounding area was poised to contain and control the protesters.

The protesters kept raising the rhetorical stakes. They informed Daley's office that three hundred thousand protesters would arrive in Chicago even though they expected less than a hundred thousand. Rumors flew of plans to put LSD in the Chicago water supply, attack the convention hall, and trash high-priced stores in the Loop. "The North Vietnamese are shedding blood," Tom Hayden said. "We must be prepared to shed blood." MOBE assigned a raft of protest marshals to teach protesters not only how to resist passively but also how to fight back if necessary, and how to break through police lines.

By midweek before the convention, the Yippies were headquartered in Lincoln Park on the shore of Lake Michigan, four miles north of the candidates' headquarters at the Hilton and eight miles north of the Amphitheatre, where the convention was to be held. "Headquartered" meant the Yippies had two folding tables set up near the street. A local theater company had given them mimeograph access, and on the tables were stacks of maps of Chicago, a program of planned events, lists of hotels where the convention delegates would be staying, and a notice that the Yippies were looking for "chicks who can type" and "cats who have wheels." Yippies also had access to the office of the biweekly newspaper **Chicago Seed**, where Abbie Hoffman and Jerry Rubin held court and gave interviews.

The SDS set up in Lincoln Park. Many SDS members had become more militant and were practicing oppositional maneuvers. The MOBE marshals came to Lincoln Park to teach confrontational tactics and self-defense.

The police put up signs announcing that the park would be officially closed after 11:00 p.m. No sleeping overnight would be allowed in Lincoln Park. Patrolling to enforce that curfew, in the early hours of Thursday, August 22, four days before the convention, officers stopped two long-haired kids near the park. One of the kids, seventeen-year-old Dean Johnson, a member of a South Dakota Sioux tribe, pulled a pistol, according to police. The officers shot him three times and killed him. The reaction among the Lincoln Park radical leadership was immediate. The first Chicago convention protest was actually a memorial in the park for Dean Johnson.

The Yippies planned to hold their own convention on Sunday, the day before the Democratic convention. They were going to nominate a pig as their candidate for president. At 10:00 on Friday morning, the 145-pound animal rolled into town with Jerry Rubin, who named it Pigasus. First stop was a public courtyard downtown where the Yippies had the press gathered for photos of the pig. Police grabbed Jerry Rubin almost as soon as he began speaking. They were surprised to discover that Rubin did not have any drugs with him because minutes earlier an undercover officer had handed a girl a bag and told her to give it to Jerry. She opened the bag, saw that it contained hashish, and dropped it.

The police charged Rubin and six others with disturbing the peace and hauled them off to jail. Police took the pig to the Humane Society, and Abbie Hoffman assembled the press to announce that if he couldn't get Pigasus freed, he would nominate a lion. The pig story was covered in newspapers and on TV news throughout the country. The police released Jerry Rubin and the others on a $25 bond.

MOBE, in keeping with the old-school sobriety so annoying to Hoffman and Rubin, occupied an office downtown, where Tom Hayden, Rennie Davis, and Dave Dellinger were trying to figure out how to organize the protests. Hayden, Davis, and Dellinger could already tell turnout wasn't going to be anywhere near the few hundred thousand they'd predicted. There was only one permit for a demonstration on the third day of the convention, Wednesday, August 28. Peace organizations such as Women for Peace and the American Friends Service Committee weren't getting much sign-up for buses to bring their nonviolent protesters to Chicago.

On Saturday morning, while Hale Boggs was telling the Platform Committee that a bombing halt in Vietnam would cost American soldiers' lives, more than 5,000 National Guardsmen assembled at armories around Chicago armed with M-1 rifles, carbines, shotguns, and tear gas. A few hundred FBI agents moved into Chicago. The Army Security Agency (ASA) had undercover agents in African American neighborhoods, the parks, and downtown. They planted listening devices in offices that the activists were using. All information the army intelligence agents gathered went straight to the Pentagon.

The Chicago police established a command post in a building close to Yippie headquarters in Lincoln Park. Intelligence photographers snapped pictures of protest leaders. By Saturday morning, Lincoln Park was under twenty-four-hour surveillance. By noon, there were more police in the park than protesters.

On Saturday afternoon, MOBE arrived in Lincoln Park for their regular training sessions for protesters. Press photographers couldn't get enough of these training sessions. Local people out for a nice Saturday afternoon were also converging on the park, playing guitars, picnicking, watching MOBE's tactical training. The strategic question of the day for the protest groups was what to do when the 11:00 p.m. curfew came and they were ordered to vacate the park.

As evening fell on the park, the poet Allen Ginsberg arrived. At forty-one, he was a mature counterculture star. With his big dark beard and wild, balding dark hair, he personified the nonviolent wisdom and sensitivity of the peace movement. Ginsberg sat at the Yippies' folding tables and listened to the strategy discussion with his friend, poet Ed Sanders. Abbie Hoffman and Jerry Rubin argued for staying in the park after the curfew. Ed Sanders accused them of telling people to get killed for nothing. Ginsberg said, "The park isn't worth dying for."

The Yippies, SDS, and MOBE arrived at a joint statement urging everyone to vacate the park when ordered by the police. Hoffman and Rubin also urged them to "do what is necessary—make them pay for kicking us out of the park."

When darkness fell at around 9:00 p.m., fewer than a thousand people were still in the park. Hoping to calm the crowd, Ginsberg and Sanders sat on the ground and began chanting the mantra "Om."

About a hundred people joined in the chant. Police began moving into position to enforce the curfew. Some of the protesters started bonfires. Small groups of police rushed into the park, extinguished the fires, and withdrew. Ginsberg and Sanders kept chanting. At exactly 11:00 p.m., as the police announced through bullhorns that the park was closed, Ginsberg rose and led the crowd out of the park.

The police moved in. They pushed out a few protesters who had stayed behind. Seventy-five officers were stationed to guard the park. MOBE and SDS led a few hundred people into the streets, briefly stopping traffic and chanting before disappearing into the usual Saturday-night crowd.

On Sunday morning, MOBE began its first official demonstration. Tom Hayden's tactic was to march on the delegates and disrupt their meetings and partying. The MOBE-led march combined forces with the Yippies and SDS. With no permit for a march, the protesters walked on sidewalks as they approached the Hilton. The police let them keep moving. Downtown streets were filled with chants: "Hey, hey, LBJ, how many kids did you kill today?" MOBE organizer Lee Weiner established a protest location on Michigan Avenue across the street from the Hilton at the edge of Grant Park, with the apparent acquiescence of the police. As Hayden and Davis and the chanting marchers began arriving to join his picket line, Weiner could see police arriving en masse in buses. Weiner quickly moved the picketers away from Michigan Avenue into Grant Park.

Rennie Davis addressed the crowd assembled in Grant Park and declared victory. Tom Hayden told the crowd that the police had no choice but to let them march. "We had the power," said Hayden. Then it was time to hustle back up to Lincoln Park for the Yippies' music festival.

The music festival was a disappointment. Only one band showed up— MC5, from Detroit. The police wouldn't allow a flatbed truck to enter Lincoln Park to be used as a stage. Then the sound system failed. When Abbie Hoffman announced to the crowd of about five thousand that the police had shut down the concert, the crowd reacted with angry boos. Yippie organizers started arguing with the police about getting the sound back on. Once again, Allen Ginsberg sat down, assumed the lotus position and started chanting "Om." Night fell as Ginsberg chanted.

Across the twelve hundred acres of Lincoln Park, groups of various sizes formed in the darkness. Some lit bonfires. Police came in, stamped on the fires, and retreated. New fires were set. Marijuana was passed around. Drumming on overturned garbage cans became the soundtrack of the night. SDS advised people to obey the curfew and leave the park at 11:00 p.m. Abbie Hoffman agreed. Hayden and Davis thought it might be a good tactical test to stay put, see what the police would do, and only then leave the park.

At 9:00 p.m., two hours before the curfew, the police formed a line around the park's bathrooms. Protesters approached them to see what the police were doing. As word spread that something was happening, more protesters approached. Soon there were hundreds of people moving near the police in the dark. Some started throwing rocks. It was impossible to see exactly where the rocks came from.

The police began removing their nameplates. More rocks flew. The police pulled down their face shields. More rocks. The police charged the crowd. For the next few hours, the Chicago police rained down violence on protesters beginning in the darkness of Lincoln Park and continuing into the surrounding streets. Reporters also fell victim to the Chicago Police Department's first effort at convention crowd control. "Get the bastard with the camera," said one officer as they went after a news photographer. Police used tear gas when the crowd moved into the streets. Protesters chanted, "The streets belong to the people!" Protesters overturned garbage cans, blocked intersections, jumped on cars stopped in traffic, then retreated into Lincoln Park before rushing back out for more of the same. Around 2:00 a.m., order was finally restored. Seven hours after he'd started, at 4:00 a.m., Allen Ginsberg stopped chanting.

When the convention opened at the Amphitheatre on Monday night, U.S. Army troops from Fort Hood were taking up positions. Mayor Daley was determined to keep control both outside and inside the convention hall. President Johnson and Mayor Daley devised a seating chart that relegated to the outer reaches of the floor the New York, Wisconsin, California, and other delegations where antiwar and anti-Johnson sentiment dominated. Down front near the podium, Mayor Daley would have the best seat in the house, allowing him eye contact with convention chairman Carl Albert. Daley could control proceedings with a glance or a gesture, signaling Albert when to cut off debate. The microphones for Illinois and Texas were set at full volume. The microphones for the antiwar delegations were muted.

The Massachusetts delegation arrived in Chicago without the state's Democratic senator. Ted Kennedy had publicly announced he would not attend the convention. That was no surprise. It was too soon after his brother's death. He was still in mourning. He was making very few public appearances. But he did give a speech at Holy Cross College in Massachusetts less than a week before the convention that got the Democratic Party's attention. He called for a unilateral bombing halt in Vietnam and a peace process for U.S. withdrawal. He said, "Like my three brothers before me, I pick up a fallen standard. Sustained by their memory of our priceless years together I shall try to carry forward that special commitment to justice, to excellence, to courage that distinguished their lives." That was enough to spark open talk of drafting Ted Kennedy for the vice presidency or even the top spot on the ticket.

Two days after Teddy Kennedy's speech, his brother-in-law Stephen Smith went to Chicago and met with Mayor Daley, hoping to gauge Daley's enthusiasm for another Kennedy candidacy. Smith decided to wait for Daley to bring it up. Smith went directly from Chicago to the Kennedy summer home on Cape Cod and told Teddy that the mayor didn't bring up the nomination. Then the phone rang. It was Mayor Daley calling. He told Teddy that Humphrey was in trouble and that Teddy should enter the race. Teddy told Daley he would not run. Daley asked for some assurance that he would accept a draft. Teddy said he wouldn't accept a draft. But he added that Stephen Smith was coming back to Chicago as a New York delegate and Daley could communicate with Teddy through Smith.

On Sunday morning, with the convention only a day away, Daley met with Stephen Smith again. Daley told Smith the Illinois delegation would hold off for forty-eight hours from formally expressing a nominee preference. That would give Kennedy time to agree to a draft. Smith consulted with Kennedy and came back to Daley. Any Kennedy draft would have to be real. That was the word from Teddy. Smith could not play any role in getting it started.

Smith then spent the rest of the day and night phoning members of every delegation where Kennedy might find supporters. By midday on Monday, hours before the first session was set to open, dozens of excited delegates were coming into a draft-Kennedy office, set up overnight in the Sherman House Hotel. Fully one third of the Pennsylvania delegation, supposedly so strong for Humphrey, came by the office. Even the South was expressing guarded interest in a Kennedy candidacy. When Lyndon Johnson got wind of the Kennedy draft, he made sure that security officials refused to let draft-Kennedy people circulate their petitions or place flyers on delegates' seats. There was a real groundswell.

On Monday afternoon, Stephen Smith's delegate hunting showed that if Ted Kennedy's name were placed in nomination, Hubert Humphrey would fail to go over the top on the first ballot. They could dump Humphrey. They could stop Johnson. They could adopt the peace plank. They could save the party and, after Kennedy beat Nixon in November, they could stop the war. Hope surged.

Smith's phone was ringing. Kennedy was calling. Smith didn't take the call. He didn't want to hear no.

Then came a telegram from Kennedy insisting that his own people must not place his name in nomination.

But what if Richard Daley did the nominating?
Or Gene McCarthy?

On Monday afternoon, as the draft-Kennedy movement was hitting its stride, Gene McCarthy asked Richard Goodwin about it. Goodwin told him he thought Teddy wouldn't go up against him.

"Well," McCarthy said, "we might do it together.

"After all," he mused, "experience isn't really important in a president. Of course he's young, but those fellows were young—Jefferson and Hamilton."

Goodwin didn't know what to make of this. McCarthy had told Humphrey two months ago not to make Teddy Kennedy his running mate. McCarthy's mood had become so cloudy and passive that he was harder to read than usual. Was he offering to endorse Teddy right now and get out of the way? Was he offering to switch positions and become Teddy's running mate?

Goodwin talked to Stephen Smith. Smith wanted to know whether McCarthy would accept an offer to be Kennedy's running mate. Goodwin did not want to deliver another Kennedy message to McCarthy. Goodwin was always suspect in the McCarthy campaign. He'd left Bobby to join McCarthy when Bobby refused to run. Then he'd left McCarthy when Bobby did run. Then after Bobby's assassination, Goodwin returned to McCarthy. Goodwin told Stephen Smith that he couldn't ask McCarthy about running as Teddy's VP. Smith would have to do it himself. Goodwin suggested that Smith come over to McCarthy's suite. Smith said he would think about it.

Shortly after Aretha Franklin sang "The "Star-Spangled Banner" to open the Monday evening convention session, a furious floor fight erupted over the unit rule. Southern delegations were shouting "sell-out" at the Humphrey people because Humphrey had promised no change in the unit rule that year. Then, when it was put to a vote of the entire convention, the unit rule was abolished.

The hall's air-conditioning had stopped working, and now it was the Credentials Committee's turn to turn up the heat. The majority report of the committee recommended seating half of Julian Bond's Georgia delegation and half of Governor Maddox's delegation. Southerners reacted with howls. Then there was a move to seat only Julian Bond's delegation followed by a demand to seat only Lester Maddox's delegation. Liberals booed Maddox. Joseph Rauh challenged three more Southern delegations, including John Connally's Texas delegation. Some McCarthy delegates shouted that all of Humphrey's delegates should be unseated, which infuriated party regulars, both North and South. Sweaty delegates tried to grab microphones from one another, then found they couldn't be heard or Chairman Albert was refusing to recognize them.

No one had ever seen anything like this before on

TV. Then the TV coverage cut to much worse brutality outside the hall. When the 11:00 p.m. Lincoln
Park curfew was enforced, the scene was a rerun of
the night before, only worse. The TV cameras were
ready this time to cover it all—rocks shattering police
car windows, protesters choking on tear gas, police
with no nameplates or badges clubbing everyone they
could reach. For Daley's police force, it looked as if
there were no such thing as an innocent bystander.

At close to 3:00 a.m., Carl Albert finally gaveled
the first session to a close. There had been no resolution on the credentials fight.

News of the rioting outside the hall slowly made
it into the hall. Delegates following the news on
portable radios passed the word. Democrats were
beginning to realize that Richard Daley's strong-
arm tactics were making their national convention
a war zone.

To the draft-Teddy movement, there was only one
answer to the horrors that were now publicly defin-
ing the party's convention: a peace plank and a party
reunified under a Kennedy. On Tuesday morning,
Gene McCarthy asked Dick Goodwin yet again
what they should do about Teddy. Goodwin suggested McCarthy should meet with Stephen Smith,
ostensibly to talk about the peace plank, which was
going to be the big issue in that night's convention
session. Goodwin set up the meeting. Later that afternoon, McCarthy staff in Goodwin's room were

surprised to see the Kennedy man Stephen Smith arrive and go off to huddle with McCarthy.

Goodwin, Smith, and McCarthy were the only people in the room. McCarthy began by saying that he didn't think he could win the nomination.

"I can't make it," McCarthy admitted.

That was the moment when Gene McCarthy officially gave up. It was an emotional moment for McCarthy and Goodwin and even Smith. McCarthy offered to step aside and urge his delegates to support Teddy. McCarthy knew that the Kennedy people who still opposed him would never change their minds, but he believed a lot of his people would go for Teddy. That should add up to enough votes to stop Humphrey from going over the top on the first ballot. McCarthy thought the antiwar coalition could only prevail with Ted Kennedy.

To keep faith with his own supporters and to let them down gently, McCarthy did want his name placed in nomination. He said he would then withdraw before the first ballot. He asked for nothing in return. He never brought up the running-mate slot.

Dick Goodwin walked out of that room with Stephen Smith, deeply moved by McCarthy's sacrifice. He was awed by McCarthy's giving it all up so that Ted Kennedy could achieve what McCarthy had first set out to do—stop the war.

"While I'm doing this for Teddy," McCarthy told Smith, "I never could have done it for Bobby."

No one in the Kennedy camp trusted Gene McCarthy. Now they had to trust him with Ted Kennedy's political career. In order for the McCarthy endorsement plan to work, the draft-Teddy movement would have to go public without Ted Kennedy's shooting it down. All Kennedy would have to do is say nothing when asked for comment on the draft. That would give enough life to a Kennedy candidacy so that McCarthy would have something real enough to endorse. The convention's anticipation of a Kennedy candidacy would grow every minute that Ted Kennedy stayed silent on a draft. If Gene McCarthy and his campaign remained silent in the face of the threat of a new McCarthy opponent, that would double the anticipation. Then when McCarthy's name was placed in nomination and he took the stage, McCarthy endorsing Kennedy would be the stunning climax of all that anticipation. Then and only then, with McCarthy himself drafting Kennedy, could Teddy acknowledge the draft movement and, after considering it, fly to Chicago and accept the nomination. All of this was necessary to protect Teddy from appearing to crave the presidency to the point where he would exploit the opening created by his brother's death to seize the Democratic nomination as if it belonged to the Kennedy family. The basic elements of the plan had the advantage of being true: Ted Kennedy did not personally encourage his own draft and Gene McCarthy's endorsement was freely offered by McCarthy himself. The only problem the Kennedy people saw was Gene McCarthy.

If this was going to be the last Kennedy's first step on the presidential campaign stage, everything had to be perfect. Everything.

Teddy's last conversation with McCarthy was that odd night in Wisconsin before Bobby announced. McCarthy's people had given Teddy enough encouragement to fly out to Wisconsin to discuss what Bobby's candidacy could mean for McCarthy. The vice presidency? A deal on which primary states to compete in? Teddy came away with nothing, without even having a real conversation about anything, without even opening his briefcase when he saw McCarthy gesture that he wouldn't look at whatever Teddy wanted to show him. That's who Teddy had to trust now—an erratic, moody man who had become more unpredictable in the months since their last meeting. The last Kennedy was going to have to trust Gene McCarthy with the Kennedy dream.

If the scheme worked, on Thursday night, Edward Moore Kennedy might be on his way to being the next president. If something went wrong, if Gene McCarthy didn't handle his end perfectly, Ted Kennedy could be humiliated as a desperate, last-minute candidate, and the Kennedy dream could die on the convention floor.

The Kennedy camp's worst fear was that once McCarthy's name was placed in nomination, McCarthy might take in the cheering and the love and emotion of his supporters and decide not to release his delegates to Teddy. Tuesday evening, as Stephen Smith and the Kennedy team worked on the plan, a CBS reporter covering the McCarthy campaign reported that Smith had asked for McCarthy's support for Kennedy. Smith lit into Goodwin over the leak that obviously came from the McCarthy campaign.

The CBS report was all Ted Kennedy had to hear. It didn't matter that it wasn't true. Smith and Kennedy knew they would never be able to convince anyone that McCarthy endorsing Teddy was McCarthy's idea. It looked like this wasn't a real draft. It looked like Teddy was trying to push McCarthy aside. Even if McCarthy denied the story about Smith asking him to step aside, no one would believe it. Teddy knew the damage could not be undone. He was out. The draft had to be shut down immediately. The next morning Teddy called Humphrey and promised that he would not be a candidate. It would be twelve more years before Ted Kennedy ran for president.

Tuesday night's TV convention coverage once again delivered chaos into America's homes from inside and outside the hall. It took seven hours for the convention to finally resolve all the credentials fights. John Connally's Texas delegation survived a challenge and was seated with cheers from the South and boos from liberals. The compromise version of the Georgia delegation was seated with half of the del-

egates awarded to Julian Bond and half awarded to
Governor Maddox. The California delegation began
chanting "Julian Bond! Julian Bond! Julian Bond!"
Antiwar delegates all over the hall took up the chant
while Southerners booed them. CBS reporter Dan
Rather tried to interview a rowdy Georgia delegate
being removed by security guards and was shoved to
the floor as astonished TV viewers watched. Rather
kept talking into his microphone to the studio anchorman Walter Cronkite, who was visibly shocked
at what he was watching. Everyone covering the convention, including Cronkite, knew that Mayor Daley
was in charge of security inside the convention and
out. When Dan Rather got back on his feet, Walter Cronkite told the country, "I think we've got a
bunch of thugs here, if I may be permitted to say so."
Lester Maddox had already left town. All the other
challenges were defeated. George McGovern spoke
in favor of every challenge. McGovern and the challengers didn't know it that night, but they were only
one convention away from changing the Democratic
Party forever. The nominating process would never
look like this again.

Everyone expected the Vietnam platform debate
to be the convention's most difficult fight. The credentials fight took so long that it wasn't until 12:35
a.m. that Chairman Albert turned to the Platform
Committee's report. When Hale Boggs started reading the Platform Committee's majority plank on

Vietnam aloud, Wisconsin delegates stuck way in the back of the hall started making noise to drown him out. Other peace-plank delegates gathered around Wisconsin clapping and shouting. The noise forced Boggs to stop reading. After a long pause in the action filled with booing, jeering, and yelling, Chairman Carl Albert returned to the podium and recognized the Wisconsin delegation leader.

When Wisconsin moved for adjournment until the next afternoon, a roar of approval went up. Antiwar delegates believed the bosses were hoping the lateness of the hour would hide from the viewing public the rawness of the party's division over Vietnam and that peace-plank supporters would surrender to exhaustion. Albert, visibly infuriated by the idea of adjournment, ruled the motion unrecognizable. Booing filled the hall and a chant broke out: "Let's go home! Let's go home! Let's go home!"

Congressman Albert refused to close the session. He recognized Mayor Daley, who shouted into the microphone that the convention was "held for the delegates, not for anyone in the balconies trying to take over this meeting!" He threatened to have people removed, but the demonstration was coming from the floor, not the galleries. The booing and handclapping got louder as the TV cameras zoomed in on the action.

Democratic Party chairman John Bailey realized that the most important thing was to get this angry circus off TV. He signaled to Daley to shut down the convention. Daley signaled to Albert, who recognized Daley, and the mayor moved to postpone debate until tomorrow. Albert gaveled the chaos to a close at 1:15 a.m.

As the delegates headed back to their hotels, many of them came face-to-face with the chaos in the streets. By the second night of the convention, rioting in Lincoln Park had become ritualized. Each night was worse than the night before. At a press conference Tuesday afternoon, Rennie Davis said MOBE had come to Chicago to expose what they saw as the violent coercion of a police state. He believed they had already accomplished that goal. "The whole world's watching," Davis said. That soon became one of the protesters' chants.

Reporters who had been beaten up on Monday night were organizing now, too. All major news organizations sent letters of protest to Mayor Daley's office. Daley responded by telling the press that reporters must obey the instructions of the police. The **Chicago Tribune** defended Daley and said that some of the newsmen looked like hippies and "perhaps they refused to obey police orders to move."

Bobby Seale, the national chairman of the Black Panther Party, arrived in Chicago and headed straight for Lincoln Park, where he was introduced to the crowd on Tuesday afternoon by Jerry Rubin. Some Black Panthers had been in shootouts with police in

California. Seale had not come there to calm things down. He advised protesters to "pick up a crowbar. Pick up a piece. Pick up a gun." He added, "If you shoot well, all I'm gonna do is pat you on the back and say 'Keep shooting.' You dig?"

No matter how bad things got in the streets around Lincoln Park, four miles south in Grant Park, across the street from the Hilton, the situation remained calm. On Tuesday night in Grant Park, there were a few hundred people. They were young McCarthy supporters and older pacifists. For protesters who weren't looking for trouble, Grant Park was the place to be. They gathered in groups, nursed wounds, commiserated, and waited to see what would happen next. The police did not enforce the curfew in Grant Park. It was the specified site for the only city-permitted demonstration scheduled for the next day. As the delegates arrived back at their hotels late on Tuesday night, some of them stopped to listen to the speeches in Grant Park. Tom Hayden announced that the next day the protesters would march without a permit from Grant Park "to the Amphitheatre, by any means necessary."

At 5:45 p.m. on Tuesday, Lyndon Johnson had told reporters that he was undecided about making the trip to the convention. This was news. Johnson had not been expected to attend. The draft-Johnson movement was alive, at least in Johnson's mind. On Tuesday night, the president watched as his future slipped away on TV, as convention coverage once again cut from anger and bitterness in the hall to rioting in the streets around Lincoln Park. LBJ knew the Secret Service couldn't guarantee the president's safety in Chicago now. No draft could be successful without a personal appearance by the candidate. Johnson knew that Carl Albert hadn't had an enemy in the Democratic Party until he stood at the podium in Chicago and started getting shouted down by antiwar delegates. Johnson now knew that Chairman Albert and Mayor Daley could not control the reception the president would get at the podium. LBJ had too many enemies in that hall. LBJ couldn't be the peacemaker at a convention that was being ripped apart by his war. Lyndon Johnson watched TV and finally realized that he couldn't save his party and he couldn't save his presidency. He faced the fact that he was done. His thirty-eight-year career in politics really was finally over.

The only thing left to fight for was his legacy. That meant he was going to have to try to hang on to control of the convention.

TWENTY-NINE

"THE GOVERNMENT OF THE PEOPLE IN EXILE"

People who watched all of the 1968 Democratic National Convention on TV remember only Wednesday night. The unforgettable images inside and outside the hall that night overwhelmed everything else that had happened. People's lives changed on Wednesday night. America's understanding of itself changed on Wednesday night. Hopes changed, none for the better. Richard Daley on the convention floor and William F. Buckley Jr. in a TV studio each had the worst, the ugliest, the most hateful public moment of their lives. All of it was televised. All of it happened in the shocked living rooms of America. Wednesday was the darkest, most dangerous night in the history of American political conventions.

Too much had to get done inside the convention hall on Wednesday. A convention's third day, Wednesday, is always supposed to be for nominating the candidates for president and vice president. The ritual takes time even in an uncontested convention. Each delegation has to have its TV moment announcing its votes. In a contested nomination, there's no telling how long it can take. But Tuesday night's platform business was left undone. So on Wednesday, the delegates had to debate and vote on the platform, then put the candidates' names in nomination and vote on them. And, by Wednesday, everyone knew none of this was going to go smoothly.

Debate on the Vietnam plank of the platform had to begin early. It got started around 1:00 p.m.

The delegates found on their seats a mimeographed list of bullet points in support of the LBJ-approved plank on Vietnam supported by a majority of the Platform Committee. Humphrey's aide David Ginsburg, who tried to get Humphrey to support John Gilligan's peace plank, had to supervise distribution of the LBJ fact sheet as if it were Humphrey's. The sheet condemned the peace plank as a threat to national security. Wisconsin congressman Clement Zablocki, a Humphrey delegate, informed the convention that he was authorized to say that Hubert Humphrey fully supported the majority plank. No one mentioned LBJ's authorship of the plank.

The debate took three hours with powerful speakers alternating pro and con. Pierre Salinger said that if Bobby Kennedy were alive, he would support the peace plank. Once again Bobby got huge cheers and applause at a Democratic convention.

Ohio congressman Wayne Hays linked the pro-testers outside to the peace-plank supporters inside. With Richard Daley clapping hard, Hays suggested that both the protesters and the peace-plank delegates "would substitute beards for brains . . . pot instead of patriotism, sideburns instead of solutions." Platform Committee chairman Hale Boggs ended debate with a reading of the same intelligence report that LBJ had read to Boggs at the White House. Boggs said he had special permission from the president to make this classified information public at the convention. It was the opinion of General Abrams, Boggs told the delegates, that the bombing halt proposed by the peace plank would increase enemy strength by 500 percent.

At 4:30 p.m. on Wednesday, the vote on the two Vietnam planks was taken. It was 1,567 for the Johnson-approved plank and 1,041 for the peace plank.

Lyndon Johnson won. Or so he thought.

The peace-plank vote revealed an extraordinary number of delegates willing to buck the incumbent president and the party establishment to vote for peace. Many of those 1,041 peace-plank delegates were more than disappointed. They were distraught.

Their 1968 political crusade for peace had just crash-landed on the floor of the convention. They were angry and anguished. There were tears. The New York and California delegations at the outer reaches of the hall put on black armbands and covered their badges with crepe. Theodore Bikel, the star of **Fiddler on the Roof** on Broadway, was a New York delegate. The folk singer began leading his delegation in a mournful but powerful "We Shall Overcome." Other delegates joined in the singing. The song swelled as more and more delegates sang through their tears.

Hundreds of posters started popping up around the floor reading "Stop the War!" The rear of the hall started booing the power brokers up front. Chants of "Stop the war!" broke out.

Carl Albert banged his gavel and called for order and got nowhere. New York, California, Wisconsin, Colorado, Oregon, and New Hampshire delegates were standing on chairs as they sang. A Catholic priest in the New York delegation was kneeling on the floor praying.

Chairman Albert put the convention into a temporary recess. The antiwar voices chanted and sang louder. The convention band was ordered to play "We Got a Lot of Livin' to Do," from the Broadway musical **Bye Bye Birdie**. But it didn't work. The antiwar voices were louder than the band.

In the afternoon, while the peace plank was being

debated, the one legal, city-permitted demonstration went on in Grant Park across from the Hilton. MOBE had the permit and organized the event. About fifteen thousand people showed up. An afternoon rally downtown on a weekday attracted a much more diverse crowd than Lincoln Park's Yippie-SDS protests. Men in suits and ties from nearby offices were there along with "Clean for Gene" students and older pacifists, as well as some Yippie and SDS veterans of Lincoln Park. Hayden, Dellinger, and Davis had said they would violate their permit and leave Grant Park to march to the Amphitheatre. The police were ready for that. They surrounded the area and passed out leaflets threatening arrest if the protesters tried to march. Hundreds of National Guard soldiers were ready in a nearby parking lot.

A protester climbed a flagpole and started lowering the American flag. Police pushed through the crowd, pulled the protester down, beat him with clubs, and dragged him away. Protesters started throwing rocks at police. There were more arrests near the flagpole. Rennie Davis moved the trained MOBE marshals to the flagpole area. He tried to position a line of marshals as a buffer between the crowd and the police. Thirty police formed a wedge and flipped down their face shields. Under orders of a sergeant, they charged the line of MOBE marshals in a club-swinging assault.

Rennie Davis was known to the police, a target. He

was telling the crowd to remain calm when five cops singled him out, rushed him from behind, and beat him to the ground with their clubs, opening bloody wounds on his head. Davis passed out. The police kept beating him. When he regained consciousness, Davis was blood-soaked. Protesters took him to a hospital. Police reinforcements came in and a new wedge formed. One officer was heard saying, "Go in, fella, and have some fun."

Mayor Daley's response to two days of reporters documenting excessive use of force by the Chicago police was to increase the force. Protesters saw it as the mirror image of LBJ's Vietnam policy—when met with more resistance than expected, increase the troop strength. This was exactly what Tom Hayden and Rennie Davis were hoping the world would see.

Dave Dellinger, always the pacifist, wanted the violence to stop. He urged Hayden to try to calm the crowd. Hayden did tell them to get out of the park, but as he put it, "Let us make sure that if blood is going to flow, let it flow all over this city." He said, "Don't get trapped in some kind of large, organized march. . . . I'll see you in the streets."

As Hayden spoke to the crowd, the National Guard was moving into the park. Dellinger yelled through a bullhorn, trying to get marchers lined up and urging them to remain nonviolent. The police yelled through bullhorns that this was now an unlawful assembly. The guardsmen flanked the protesters on one side, the police flanked the protesters on the other side, and as the protesters became quickly surrounded by this massive military force, Hayden and others left the park hoping to avoid being penned in and kept off the streets.

Allen Ginsberg now addressed the crowd. Once again, he led a chant of "Om."

The National Guard launched tear-gas canisters, trying to prevent the protesters from leaving Grant Park. Despite every police tactic for containment, the crowd did soon break out at the northern end of the park onto Michigan Avenue with reporters and photographers following them.

At 6:30 p.m., with protesters defiantly filling the streets, suddenly three mule-drawn wagons came down Michigan Avenue toward the convention hall. The wagons were part of a legally permitted march by the Reverend Ralph Abernathy. He was leading Martin Luther King's Poor People's Campaign on a march to the Amphitheatre.

The protesters from Grant Park fell in with Abernathy's march, filling Michigan Avenue. Observers packed the sidewalks, too. For a moment, it seemed the streets did belong to the people. The mood on the street turned positive for the first time. "Join us! Join us! Join us!" chanted the protesters. People on the sidewalk did join them. The demonstration felt huge now, and unstoppable.

Just before the Hilton, police had formed a line obstructing the march. For about half an hour, thousands of marchers stopped and milled about. The lines of police stood calmly. The marchers in front started getting pushed forward to make room for those still marching toward the roadblock. They were pushed right up against the police line.

The crowd started chanting, "Peace! Now! Peace! Now!" and "What's holding us up, let's go, let's go! What's holding us up, let's go, let's go!" and the perennial "Fuck you, LBJ! Fuck you, LBJ!"

The police opened ranks to let the mule wagons through and quickly closed ranks to cut the marchers off from Ralph Abernathy and the Poor People's Campaign.

Gene McCarthy was on the twenty-third floor of the Hilton in his campaign's command suite. He heard the chanting. He went to the window. He had a perfect view of the crowd and the police maneuvers. The police had the crowd surrounded on three sides. McCarthy could also see something in the distance that the protesters couldn't see. More National Guard troops were arriving. The crowd was trapped.

McCarthy watched as lines of twenty and thirty police officers suddenly charged straight into the crowd, mowing people down. The police used tear gas, Mace, and clubs. Police trucks began pulling up. The police threw their beaten victims into the trucks. The trucks sped off to be replaced by new trucks. A group of police reinforcements exploded from their truck yelling, "Kill! Kill! Kill!"

McCarthy was enraged by what he was watching. He didn't know what to do. Should he go down there and try to stop it? Would anyone even hear him down there? He had worried that this would happen to his supporters in Richard Daley's Chicago. Those "Clean for Gene" kids in New Hampshire on election night who'd chanted "Chicago! Chicago!" were down there now. They were risking their lives because of Gene McCarthy.

McCarthy campaign volunteers rushed into the campaign suite and asked McCarthy's permission to create a clinic in the campaign's other offices on the fifteenth floor. McCarthy gave permission. If McCarthy went down to the street, he couldn't possibly accomplish anything. He couldn't be heard or even seen amid the out-of-control violent chaos. He couldn't stop thinking about going down there though. He was heard saying, as much to himself as anyone else, "If I go down I claim them. And they're not mine anymore."

Outside the Hilton, police set up barriers between the street and the sidewalk. Police crashed their own barriers and crushed rows of bystanders up against the plate-glass window of the hotel's restaurant. As the stunned tourists and bystanders were pressed against the glass, the window shattered. Men, women, and children screamed as they fell through the glass into the restaurant. Diners were hit by the shower of glass. Police poured through the shattered window to beat people in the restaurant.

When a white-uniformed doctor with a Red Cross armband ran to help a police victim, two officers tackled the doctor and clubbed him. Police once again attacked the press, breaking cameras and beating reporters.

The vast Hilton lobby was filling with dozens of battered protesters, bystanders, and reporters, all dripping blood and smelling of tear gas. The injured were taken up to McCarthy campaign rooms on the fifteenth floor for first aid. Richard Goodwin was in the lobby. "This is just the beginning," he said. "There'll be four years of this."

Watching from the window of another hotel, Theodore White noted the time, 8:05 p.m., in his reporter's notebook, then wrote, "The Democrats are finished." The chant through the tear gas–filled night became, "The whole world is watching!"

The whole world began to watch at about 9:30 p.m., when the networks had film of rioting ready to show. That's when most delegates in the hall got their first reports of what was happening in the streets.

The convention had begun the nominating process at about 6:00 p.m. The floor was filled with Humphrey supporters. Hundreds of McCarthy supporters were trapped in the tear gas–drenched McCarthy storefront office downtown. Mayor Daley's police and security guards inside the hall were mirroring the increased police aggressiveness outside the hall. A thuggish Daley ward enforcer was seated in the press gallery.

Daley's men stopped New York McCarthy delegate Alex Rosenberg for not having credentials. "They were trying to tear them off my neck so they could arrest me for not having credentials," said Rosenberg. Paul O'Dwyer jumped into the ruckus to help his fellow New York delegate. O'Dwyer was a pacifist candidate for Senate whose older brother was a former mayor of New York City. CBS reporter Mike Wallace knew O'Dwyer. Wallace and his camera crew approached and with his first question, Mike Wallace took a punch in the jaw.

Eugene McCarthy and Hubert Humphrey had their names placed in nomination early in the evening. Largely lost in the noise of the night was the historic moment of Channing Phillips's name being placed in nomination. He was the leader of the District of Columbia delegation that had been pledged to Bobby Kennedy. Channing Phillips was the first African American name placed in nomination at a Democratic convention.

The first African American mayor of a major American city, Carl Stokes, was a Humphrey delegate from Ohio. Viewers watching at home in Cleveland saw their mayor begin his seconding speech for Humphrey's nomination when suddenly the TV screen was filled with coverage of the riots. Delegates crowded around TV sets in the Amphitheatre corridors.

The Democratic Party's plan for Wednesday night was for America to listen to glowing speeches about the leading Democratic presidential hopefuls and then watch the triumphant nominee go over the top on a routine first ballot and claim the nomination. Instead, America was watching the worst night of rioting yet.

Carl Albert recognized Colorado's request to speak. A delegate asked the chair to order Mayor Daley to suspend "his police-state tactics." Albert angrily ruled the request out of order. Mayor Daley's scowl was permanent now.

Allard Lowenstein was recognized. He called for adjourning the convention. "People's rights are being abused on the streets, maced and beaten unconscious."

Frank Mankiewicz, a Kennedy delegate for McGovern, told the chair that Chicago was now flowing with blood.

Carl Albert tried to keep the nominating process going. He gave the podium to Connecticut senator Abraham Ribicoff to place George McGovern's name in nomination. Senator Ribicoff began with his prepared remarks. He said, "The basic problem that we face here tonight is an indivisible peace—

peace abroad and peace at home." That was a line Tom Hayden could have written. Ribicoff seemed to have the hall's attention, but nothing about George McGovern could get a rise out of the delegates one way or another. "George McGovern," he continued, "understood from the very depths of his being that napalm, and gas, and 500,000 Americans in the swamps of Vietnam was not the answer to the people of Vietnam or the people of the United States. George McGovern, ladies and gentlemen, had another solution for Vietnam. I served with him in the Kennedy Administration. And there, George was in charge for President Kennedy of the Food for Peace program. And George's concept for underdeveloped countries is food; his concept is shelter, education, health, opportunity, and to bring a sense of brotherhood to submerged billions of people, wherever they may be."

Senator Ribicoff was a Kennedy man for McGovern. He mentioned Jack and Bobby Kennedy and echoed Bobby on domestic policy: "George McGovern is not satisfied that ten million Americans go to bed hungry every night!"

There were some speechwriter flourishes about "a new wind" coming "out of the prairies of South Dakota." And then Senator Abraham Ribicoff, one of the most dignified and polished members of the Senate, a man never known for rhetorical excess, shocked the convention, thrilling some and enraging others, with the most awful, memorable moment at a convention podium in the previous history of conventions. He departed from his prepared text to say: "Mr. Chairman, I have a speech here. As I look at the confusion in this hall, and watch on television the turmoil and violence that is competing with this great convention for the attention of the American people, there is something else in my heart tonight—that's not the speech I prepared to give. The youth of America rallied to the standards of men like George McGovern like they did to the standards of John F. Kennedy and Robert Kennedy. And with George McGovern as President of the United States we wouldn't have to have Gestapo tactics in the streets of Chicago!

Ribicoff's speech was being treated like most nominating speeches. Delegates were ignoring it and filling the hall with the noise of their own voices talking and yelling to one another. So it took a second before they realized what they had just heard. "Gestapo tactics"?! A huge roar filled the hall. Daley men all over the hall created deafening boos. Antiwar delegates cheered. No one was silent. Mayor Daley jumped to his feet with the entire Illinois delegation shouting their boos. "You bet. You bet," Ribicoff said directly to the Illinois delegation to assure them that they'd heard him correctly and he meant every word. Daley shouted directly to Ribicoff words the microphone couldn't pick up: "Fuck you, you Jew son of a bitch! You lousy motherfucker, go home!" You didn't have to be a professional lip reader to pick up what Daley was saying, but soon enough professional lip readers were clarifying that for the public. Ribicoff was close enough to hear what Daley was saying. Ribicoff looked down at him, showing no fear, and said, "How hard it is . . . How hard it is to accept the truth, when we know the problems facing our nation."

Richard Daley wasn't the only one to indelibly stain himself that night. The mood in the Buckley-versus-Vidal debate on ABC that night matched Chicago's mood. It was their most vicious encounter yet.

Gore Vidal was wearing his eyeglasses because his eyes were tearing up from tear gas that seeped into ABC's makeshift studio inside the Amphitheatre. William Buckley was still in pain from a collarbone fracture he'd suffered before the Republican convention.

Howard K. Smith asked them to comment on "the security that we have seen all week at this convention and the events tonight on the streets beyond this convention hall."

Vidal said, "It's like living under a Soviet regime here. . . . You've seen the roughing up . . . the police have seriously injured twenty-one newsmen." He quoted Chicago's most famous columnist, Mike Royko, saying, "The biggest threat to law and order in the last week has been the Chicago Police Department."

Buckley did not defend the Chicago police. He did

the opposite by equating them to politicians: "The point is that policemen violate their obligations just the way politicians do."

Buckley had this advice for the TV audience: "Don't do what's happening here in Chicago tonight, which is to infer from individual and despicable acts of violence, a case for implicit totalitarianism in the American system."

Buckley complained of being kept awake last night until 5:00 a.m. by all the noise in the streets. He was horrified that fourteen floors above the street he could hear the "utter obscenities directed at the President of the United States, at the mayor of this city."

Vidal then delivered a message from Norman Mailer to Buckley. Vidal reported, "He said, 'You tell Buckley to come out here. He might be very interested to see how his beloved police are behaving.'"

In defense of the protesters, Vidal told Buckley, "They came here for free assembly. They came here to demonstrate against the Vietnam War, which you happen to love. I'm sorry for that. They have not been allowed to hold a meeting in Soldier Field which they should have had, could have had, would have had a peaceful demonstration. Instead, the police fired [up] by Mayor Daley and by a lot of jingoes around here have been roughing up everybody from the press to the delegates to the kids out there, and you want to sit here and talk about all that law and order."

Howard K. Smith sent them toward the final explosion by asking about news film they'd just seen: "Mr. Vidal, wasn't it a provocative act to try to raise the Vietcong flag in the park, in the film we just saw? Wouldn't that invite—raising a Nazi flag in World War II would have had similar consequences?"

Vidal: "You must realize what some of the political issues are here."

Buckley: "You are so naïve."

Vidal: "There are many people in the United States [who] happen to believe that the United States' policy is wrong in Vietnam and the Vietcong are correct in wanting to organize their country in their own way politically. This happens to be pretty much the opinion of Western Europe and many other parts of the world. If it is a novelty in Chicago that is too bad. I assume that the point of American democracy is you can express any point of view you want—"

Buckley tried to interrupt, and Vidal said, "Shut up a minute."

Buckley: "No I won't. Some people are pro-Nazi and the answer is that they were well-treated by people who ostracized them, and I am for ostracizing people who egg on other people to shoot

American Marines and American soldiers. I know you don't care."

Vidal: "As far as I am concerned, the only pro- or crypto-Nazi I can think of is yourself, failing that, I would only say that we can't have . . ."

"Let's stop calling names," said Howard K. Smith.

"Now listen, you queer," barked Buckley, "stop calling me a crypto-Nazi or I'll sock you in your goddamn face and you'll stay plastered."

Vidal: "Oh, Bill . . ."

Smith: "Gentlemen! Let's not call names . . ."

Buckley: "Let Myra Breckinridge go back to his pornography and stop making any allusions of Nazism. . . ."

Smith: "I beg you . . ."

Howard K. Smith's begging was too late to save William F. Buckley Jr. from the worst version of himself.

Gore Vidal never pretended to be something he wasn't. He never hid his homosexuality, but in those days, he didn't talk about it publicly. America was still decades away from TV comedies with openly gay characters. Americans weren't wondering is he or isn't he about famous actors. It was inconceivable that Rock Hudson was gay until he died of AIDS in

1985. Flamboyant celebrities like Liberace were not even suspected of being gay by most of their fans.

Buckley calling Vidal a queer was offensive to all sides. The prudes in the audience considered such talk pornographic. The sophisticates saw it as gay bashing, although that phrase hadn't been coined yet. Buckley's antigay outburst got worse, much, much worse, with age. In each of the remaining four decades of his life, as the gay rights movement grew and matured, Buckley's homophobic attack on Vidal became all the more outrageous and unforgettable. Buckley knew that. He never stopped regretting what he'd said to Vidal and he never stopped hating him. For Vidal, the hatred was mutual.

That night, Gore Vidal knew he'd got the better of William Buckley in the exchange, and he was enough of a visionary to see how badly Buckley's gay bashing would age. Over the years, Vidal never missed an opportunity to keep the memory of that moment alive. As they were leaving the studio, Vidal said to Buckley, "Well, I guess we gave them their money's worth tonight."

RICHARD NIXON AND BOB HALDEMAN were watching the convention coverage in Key Biscayne, Florida. They were at the home of one of Nixon's closest confidants, Bebe Rebozo, the Florida banker and investor. Rebozo's contacts and funding

sources ranged from the reclusive billionaire Howard Hughes to organized crime figures. Nixon and
Haldeman were more or less gaping in disbelief at
the TV screen. They knew what this meant for the
Democratic Party.

"My God," Haldeman said. "This is really going to
be bad. They're on both sides of a losing game."

It was about 7:00 p.m. when word of the events
on the street began reaching Hubert Humphrey. He
was entertaining the loyal Pennsylvania delegation
in his suite at the Hilton. They were calling room
service for food, and the crowd was getting ready to
watch the nomination on TV.

Then came a strange smell. It was faint, but the
World War II veterans in the room recognized it.

Tear gas?

Yes, tear gas. Through the Hilton air-conditioning
vents wafted traces of tear gas from Grant Park.

Humphrey ignored the tear gas. He withdrew
from the crowd, ate dinner with his staff, worked on
his acceptance speech, took a shower, had a massage,
and changed into a starched white shirt and freshly
pressed suit. Around 8:00 p.m. some staffers suggested he look out the window, but at that time there
was a brief lull in the action and Humphrey didn't
see anything very serious going on.

As San Francisco mayor Joseph Alioto nominated
him, Humphrey watched on TV. Then came Mayor
Carl Stokes with his speech seconding Humphrey's

nomination. But as soon as Stokes appeared, he disappeared, and rioting filled the screen. The biggest moment of Humphrey's career was shattered. Humphrey couldn't believe the TV networks were preempting his nominating speeches. Photographers came in to get shots of the candidate watching the nominating process. Humphrey lit up for them, but after they left he simply stared at coverage of the rioting. The staff got quiet.

"I'm going to be president someday," Humphrey yelled at the TV and the networks delivering these images. "I'm going to appoint the FCC. We're going to look into all this!" The networks were stealing his moment.

At 10:00 p.m., Hubert Humphrey gave a press conference in his suite.

Was he unhappy about the situation in the street?

Yes, of course, Humphrey told the press. These protesters didn't represent the people of Chicago, he said, "They've been brought in from all over the country."

It occurred to some reporters that conventions were supposed to bring in people from all over the country. Humphrey was reflexively resorting to the most canned whistle-stop language politicians use everywhere they go: praise for the fundamental goodness of the local people, as if that had anything to do with what America was watching tonight. Luckily for Humphrey no one was paying attention to what he was saying.

Two flights below Humphrey's suite at the Hilton, on the fifteenth floor, Gene McCarthy's operational center was a different scene. The volunteers had indeed established a first-aid clinic, and now the suite was overrun with people being given amateur medical treatment. Heads and bodies were bandaged with torn-up bedsheets. McCarthy walked in. He went from bed to bed, cot to cot, like a military officer visiting a field hospital. He asked how the wounded were holding up.

McCarthy called a staffer at the Amphitheatre. He told the staffer to withdraw his name from nomination. It was too late. McCarthy had been watching the rioting from his window instead of the convention coverage on TV. He didn't realize his name had already been placed in nomination. The balloting was now under way.

Finally, the TV coverage switched back to the convention for the balloting. Hubert Humphrey watched intently and marked each uptick on a pad with an exaggerated flourish of enthusiasm. He watched himself go over the top at 11:47 p.m., with the Pennsylvania delegation's votes.

He worked up a whoop.

Then, as if to prove he meant the whoop, he said, cueing the photographers, "I feel like really jumping." He got up and literally jumped up and down.

At the Amphitheatre, the final delegate tally was Humphrey 1,760¼, McCarthy 601, McGovern 146½.

Channing Phillips won 67½ votes. Teddy Kennedy got 12¾.

It was midnight in the hall when one of Daley's delegates moved to make the nomination unanimous. "No! No! No!" shouted the insurgents, but Carl Albert declared the motion carried anyway, and Al Lowenstein and Richard Goodwin, handing out candles, led McCarthy delegates into the street for a funereal vigil.

Eugene McCarthy left the first-aid suite and went down to the hotel ballroom to give a press conference. He told reporters that he had just called Humphrey to congratulate him.

The next day, McCarthy entered the ballroom to cheers from the "Clean for Gene" kids, many of whom had started with the campaign in New Hampshire. The **New York Times** called this speech McCarthy's "farewell address" to his campaign. McCarthy was emotional. He said, "I may be visibly moved. I have been very careful not to be visibly moved throughout my campaign. If you people keep on this way, I may, as we say, 'lose my cool.'"

McCarthy told his team, "We have not lost the fight on the issue." They had mobilized the country's opposition to the war. He predicted correctly that the changes they fought for would make the nominating process more democratic in 1972.

That afternoon, McCarthy left the Hilton and headed across the street to Grant Park. The Secret

Service tried to talk him out of it. If rioting broke out when McCarthy was in the park, they couldn't protect him and, the Secret Service pointed out, McCarthy would risk being blamed for causing the riot. McCarthy chose to go; the Secret Service insisted that Abigail stay behind. She watched from the hotel window as McCarthy moved on through the National Guard line and into the park.

With police lines surrounding Grant Park, protesters sat in groups and talked, some weeping, some stunned, some trying to rally for more action. They sang, they chanted. Speakers were scheduled to address them—Norman Mailer, Robert Lowell, Julian Bond, and some antiwar delegates from the hall.

Delegates urged the protesters not to abandon the system. Tom Hayden told the demonstrators they were "a vanguard of people who are experienced in fighting for their survival under military conditions." David Dellinger called the day a tragic victory. Rennie Davis, still recovering from his injuries, had some advice: "Don't vote," he said, "build a National Liberation Front for America."

Then Eugene McCarthy appeared.

McCarthy made his way to the microphone, where he was introduced by the most famous black comedian in the country, Dick Gregory, who was now spending more time on political activism than comedy.

McCarthy began by saying, "It was easier to get into here than it was to get into the Democratic Convention." The crowd roared their approval. Then he said, "I'm happy to be here to address the government of the people in exile." And the roar of approval filled the air again.

He lost most of the crowd when he told them that he and his supporters would continue to work within the political process.

"No!" roared the crowd.

"Yes!" said McCarthy.

He knew what he had to say now to keep faith with his young supporters and to prove to this crowd that he was not just another establishment politician. He said, "I will not endorse either of them." He got another big cheer.

McCarthy might have liked to have had more time to think about endorsing Humphrey, but there in Grant Park with the vanquished army of what he was calling "the government of the people in exile," it seemed perfectly clear to him that he could never endorse Humphrey.

McCarthy, of course, quoted poetry—a line from Robert Lowell, who was present. Then, with the smell of tear gas in the air, in a park named for the general who had won the Civil War and that had now become the battlefield for a movement to stop a war, Eugene McCarthy said, "When I began, I promised that instead of riots and protests, we'd have dancing in the streets. I still hope we are on the way to opening up the spirit of hope and happiness."

THIRTY

THE PERFECT CRIME

The last night of the Democratic convention was like an extra inning in a game that was already lost. No one cared. The country was still reeling from Wednesday night. So was Chicago.

There was violence on the last night, but nothing like Wednesday night. Dick Gregory led a march to the Amphitheatre that brought out the tear gas and got Gregory arrested. Hubert Humphrey's nomination acceptance speech went off without a hitch and was as boring and long as the worst convention speeches always are. He tried to speak about the horrors of Wednesday night, but he didn't know how and his speechwriters didn't help much. After the routine opening line accepting the nomination, Humphrey said, "One cannot help but reflect the deep sadness that we feel over the troubles and the violence which have erupted, regrettably and tragically, in the streets of this great city, and for the personal injuries which have occurred. Surely we have now learned the lesson that violence breeds counterviolence and it cannot be condoned, whatever the source. I know that every delegate to this convention shares tonight my sorrow and my distress over these incidents."

America knew that the mayor they saw the night before calling Senator Abe Ribicoff a "Jew son of a bitch" was not sharing the sorrow and distress that the antiwar delegates felt. Humphrey couldn't find anything even slightly credible to say that wouldn't get him in trouble with Richard Daley or the McCarthy Democrats, so he ended up saying what fearful politicians always do: nothing anyone could remember.

After mentioning JFK's assassination, he devoted a few lines to surveying the glories of the Johnson presidency, strangely skipping civil rights and ending with a sentiment that no one in the hall or watching on TV felt: "And tonight, to you, Mr. President, I say thank you. Thank you Mr. President."

Humphrey delivered a line on Vietnam that only his speechwriters could follow: "Let those who believe that our cause in Vietnam has been right, or those who believe that it has been wrong, agree here and now, **agree here and now,** that neither vindication nor repudiation will bring peace or be worthy of this country!" His Vietnam policy came down to this: "I will do everything within my power, within

the limits of my capacity and ability to aid the negotiations and to bring a prompt end to this war!"

THE CANDIDATE IS SUPPOSED to get a bump
in the polls after the convention. By the time the
Democrats were leaving Chicago, the question was
how much of a polling bump the Democratic convention would give the Republican candidate.

Nixon enjoyed such an overwhelming postconvention lead in the polls against Humphrey that many
in both parties were presuming a big Republican
win. Nixon was ahead by fifteen points and it was
already September. If the Democrats had scheduled
their convention in July, they would now have an
extra month to recover from it. But the convention
was scheduled years in advance for an incumbent
president who only needed a short sprint from convention to easy victory in November.

Nixon could have run a classic front-runner campaign of playing it safe were it not for George Wallace.
The riots in Chicago were everything Wallace could
have hoped for. He surged to 20 percent in the polls
as his predictions of a civil war started to look real to
his supporters. Humphrey slid down to 28 percent in
the polls. Nixon had to do something about Wallace
or risk falling short of the 270 electoral votes needed
to win the presidency. If no candidate reached 270,

the House of Representatives would decide the winner and, despite the chaos of Chicago, the Democrats still had a lock on the House. If Wallace threw the election to the House, Hubert Humphrey would be the next president.

In September, Wallace led a march through Chicago with an escort of Alabama state troopers. The march crossed the city limits and stopped in the adjoining town of Cicero. Supporters' signs said "Law and Order." Some said "Law and Wallace." Protesters flanking the march chanted, "Wallace is a pig."

Everyone in Illinois understood why Wallace marched just across the Chicago border to Cicero to give his speech. Cicero was an all-white town that wanted to stay that way. In 1951, Governor Adlai Stevenson had to call out the National Guard when a rioting mob of thousands burned an apartment building that the black family of a Chicago bus driver had just moved into. The black family moved out. Racism won, and Cicero seemed very proud of that. The Cicero crowd loved every word of George Wallace's speech.

A protester standing on the edge of the Cicero rally held up a McCarthy sign and a poster saying "Don't Let Wallace Make This a Police State." A middle-aged woman yelled, "Shoot 'em, kill 'em!" at the protester and slapped him to the cheers of the crowd. Another yelled, "You nigger-loving homosexual!"

"Hey, you Hebe bastard!" yelled a Wallace supporter at a reporter taking notes. "You Jew bastard!"

NBC News reporter Douglas Kiker observed, while covering the Wallace campaign, "It was as if somewhere, sometime a while back, George Wallace had been awakened by a white, blinding vision: they all hate black people, all of them. They're all afraid, all of them. Great God! That's it! They're all Southern! The whole United States is Southern! Anybody who travels with Wallace these days on his presidential campaign finds it hard to resist arriving at the same conclusion."

Wallace voters who agreed to be interviewed sounded like Trump voters in 2016. Most of them denied race had anything to do with their choice of candidate. They said they supported Wallace because he told it like it was and wasn't afraid to speak his mind.

Wallace was more Nixon's problem than Humphrey's. Wallace was attracting the most conservative voters, all of whom would otherwise be going to Nixon. A smaller part of Wallace's support included union workers who would normally be with the Democrats but were worried about law and order. The challenge for Nixon was in how to compete with Wallace without risking the support of Strom Thurmond and the Southern Republicans.

"I don't talk about race or segregation anymore,"

Wallace told reporters in September. "We're talking about law and order and local control of schools, things like that." Nixon, with Strom Thurmond's coaching, had assured all of the Southern delegations at the Republican convention that he would not support federal intrusion in school integration. Humphrey was even saying that Nixon had made an overt deal for the nomination with Strom Thurmond and the segregationists. Nixon told his people he would not try to "out-Wallace Wallace." Nixon decided to avoid states where Wallace was strongest—Alabama, Mississippi, Louisiana—and concentrate on states that could deliver an electoral college win—Florida, North Carolina, South Carolina, and Virginia. In those Southern states, Nixon's pitch would be that a vote for Wallace was a wasted vote that could only hand the election to Humphrey. Nixon wasn't worried about the big crowds turning out to see Wallace in Boston, New York, and other Northern cities. Wallace had no chance of winning electoral votes in those states. Nixon knew he couldn't win those states, either.

The West looked strong for Nixon. An Arizona Republican said Nixon couldn't lose there unless he "committed rape in public on the statehouse stairs in Phoenix." Maine and Vermont looked good, too. Nixon saw his most important battleground states as Pennsylvania, Ohio, Illinois, Texas, and California. Kevin Phillips was much more optimistic than Nixon. He believed he saw a sea change deep in the polling data and opinion surveys on issues that heavily favored Republicans. The Republican candidate had lost forty-four states only four years earlier, and now Phillips thought the Republican might win forty-six states. Kevin Phillips saw only Massachusetts and Rhode Island going for Humphrey, while Alabama and Mississippi would go for Wallace. Everything else was Nixon country. Nixon would always say, "I don't believe it" when Phillips predicted he would win New York.

Kevin Phillips was prescient about the coming Republican wave, but he wouldn't find the right candidate until 1980 to ride that wave of antitax, antigovernment, antiabortion, pro–law-and-order feeling to the White House. Those feelings Phillips was noticing in opinion surveys were only beginning to stir in 1968. They had not yet solidified into a voting bloc.

John Mitchell's hyperdisciplined management of the Nixon campaign became the newest model of the professionalization of campaigns. The Nixon campaign had its offices on Park Avenue, where Maurice Stans easily raised tens of millions of dollars via well-managed fund-raising networks. Alan Greenspan ran domestic-policy research and Herb Klein did communications, constantly in touch with the volunteer operations that Richard Kleindienst ran out of Washington. Overseeing it all was Mitchell, with Len Garment at his side.

No presidential campaign had ever been run with such modern corporate sophistication. Division heads came in every morning to report to Mitchell. One day a week, Republican National Committee people flew up from Washington to report and advise. Two hundred people were on staff in New York managing ninety advance people constantly moving throughout the country, smoothing the way for personal appearances by Nixon, Agnew, and various star speakers supporting them. It couldn't have been more different from the frantic Nixon campaign of 1960. No fifty-state exhausting travel schedule this time. With Nixon's travel limited to the battleground states, he remained well rested, calm, and upbeat. John Ehrlichman made sure Nixon's traveling press was comfortable, too. The chartered press plane named after Nixon's daughter Tricia had first-class accommodations and the press secretary, Ron Ziegler, made sure reporters felt cared for and had easy access to the candidate's staff.

The candidate's plane was named after Nixon's other daughter, Julie. Bob Haldeman had everything on **Julie** under tight control. He sat right outside the door of Nixon's private compartment, gatekeeping for the candidate and managing Nixon's rest time. Pat Buchanan and Bill Safire flew with Nixon. The technology for telephones on planes was in its infancy, but **Julie** had seven phones, a teletype machine, and a copier. The Nixon campaign was ready for rapid response even in the air.

On the ground, the New Nixon drew his biggest crowd in Chicago. It was as if all the silent supporters of the Chicago police came out for their "law and order" candidate. Nixon also attracted huge audiences in San Francisco and Houston. Nixon spoke of unity and recovery, not just for Republicans but for Democrats and independents, too. Where Wallace drew battle lines, Nixon preached unity, except for "those who indulge in violence." Nixon said he was running for the people whom he started calling the "forgotten Americans." In Nixon's speeches, the "forgotten Americans" were laborers and managers, white people and black people, hardworking people who were troubled by what they were seeing but never took to the streets with their shouted lists of demands. Later Nixon called them the "silent majority," a term that wasn't used again until Donald Trump echoed it in the 2016 campaign.

Nixon avoided specific policy positions to the point where he was reported to have a "secret plan to end the war." Many voters and much of the press believed Nixon actually said those words: "secret plan to end the war." It was actually a UPI reporter who summarized Nixon's Vietnam policy with those words after covering Nixon speeches. Many other reporters subsequently made the mistake of attributing the words to Nixon. The Nixon campaign didn't fight with the press over the misquote because the underlying message was that Nixon had a plan to end the war. That false quote became the most memorable quote of the Nixon campaign. To this day highly knowledgeable political analysts refer to Nixon's saying he had a secret plan to end the war.

What did sound like policy in Nixon speeches was his constant criticism of the Johnson-Humphrey administration, but Nixon's alternative policies were not clear. He was offering new leadership in the urgent context of a national crisis and, according to the polls, that was enough. So while the reporters flying on the **Tricia** had plenty of access to staff, there was never anything of substance to ask the staff about. Following Roger Ailes's strategy for the primaries, interviews with the candidate himself were offered mainly to friendly, sometimes fawning local TV reporters. The campaign also used an Ailes innovation they called the Nixon format. Buying time on local TV, Nixon would appear with a panel and a moderator, chosen and paid for by the campaign. Nixon could lean back, cross his legs, field softball questions, and ramble on about college football. Through September, the Nixon campaign encountered nothing but smooth sailing, except for the George Wallace problem.

Wallace's rising poll numbers caught the media's

attention. More reporters started attending Wallace rallies. There were more reports of violence between Wallace supporters and protesters. In Cleveland, the police clubbed protesters. As these news reports gained critical mass late in September, the Wallace campaign looked like a mini replay of Chicago all the time. Most of the weary public wanted to forget Chicago. The Wallace campaign wouldn't let them.

Choosing a vice presidential running mate is the only genuinely presidential decision a presidential candidate has to make. Like most real presidential decisions, it is a multiple choice question with very few possible answers. Spiro Agnew was an unusual choice because he was not known nationally and wasn't on anyone's short list except Nixon's. Hubert Humphrey's choice was completely unsurprising: Maine's Senator Edmund Muskie. Senator Muskie was on everyone's short list. He was a former governor in his tenth year in the Senate. As with most vice presidential candidates, there wasn't much Muskie could do to help Humphrey, but he certainly couldn't hurt him. Muskie had no policy disagreements with Humphrey. Muskie was the safe choice, a respected senator accustomed to dealing with the national news media. George Wallace did not make the safe choice.

A third-party candidate usually doesn't have any good choices for a running mate. Respected governors and senators aren't available to third parties. Wallace would have preferred to run alone, but some states' ballots required him to have a running mate. The decision that Wallace didn't want to make turned out to be the most important one of his campaign. Wallace's running mate changed everything.

In an effort to strengthen his credentials on foreign policy, defense policy, and the Vietnam War, Wallace persuaded retired air force major general Curtis LeMay to join him on the ticket and introduced him as his running mate on October 3 in a ballroom at the Hilton in Pittsburgh.

General Curtis LeMay was known to some in the news media but unknown to most voters. He commanded a bomber division in World War II and always flew the lead bomber himself in combat. Under President Eisenhower, he was the commander of the Strategic Air Command and a firm believer in bombs. His nickname was "Bombs Away LeMay." During the Cuban missile crisis, General LeMay urged JFK to bomb the Soviet nuclear missile sites in Cuba. He said that the United States should tell North Vietnam to stop their attacks in the South, "or we're going to bomb them back into the Stone Age." It took only seven minutes for Curtis LeMay to bomb the Wallace campaign back to the Stone Age.

The Wallace staff prepared LeMay for questions about nuclear weapons. They explained how to sidestep reporters' questions and stay focused on the campaign's message. He didn't listen. The first question for LeMay came from **Los Angeles Times** reporter Jack Nelson: "What would be your policy in the employment of nuclear weapons?"

"Well, we seem to have a phobia about nuclear weapons," said LeMay. "I don't believe the world will end if we explode a nuclear weapon." LeMay used the rats at nuclear test sites as evidence of life after a nuclear blast: "The rats are supposed to be vaporized inside the firewall but the rats out there are bigger, fatter and healthier than they ever were before."

Wallace interrupted and tried to steer LeMay away from nuclear weapons. It didn't work. LeMay said, "It doesn't make much difference to me if I have to go to war and get killed in the jungle of Vietnam with a rusty knife or get killed with a nuclear weapon. Matter of fact, if I had the choice, I'd lean toward the nuclear weapon."

Wallace kept interrupting and LeMay kept talking about nuclear weapons: "I don't want to explode one unless we have to. As a matter of fact, I don't want to stick the rusty knife into anybody's belly until I have to either." Wallace interrupted again to say that he and LeMay didn't want to use nuclear weapons. LeMay said, "If I found it necessary, I would use anything we could dream up, anything that we could dream up, including nuclear weapons if it was necessary."

And that was the end of the Wallace for president campaign.

Wallace and his men pulled LeMay off the stage,

knowing that the general's comments would be the lead on the network news shows that night and on the front page of every newspaper tomorrow. It turned out that even Wallace supporters didn't want to have to consider the choice of being killed by a rusty knife in the jungle of Vietnam or by a nuclear bomb. They found nothing reassuring about the body weight of rats at nuclear test sites. Curtis LeMay became a laughingstock and the Wallace-LeMay ticket plunged in the polls immediately.

THE ONLY GOOD THING about the Humphrey campaign was Lawrence O'Brien. He was a longtime Kennedy man from western Massachusetts, a veteran of JFK's Senate campaigns and the presidential campaign. He was in Dallas on the last day of the Kennedy presidency and flew back to Washington with Mrs. Kennedy and LBJ on Air Force One. Larry O'Brien was with Bobby's presidential campaign until the end and then agreed to take over Humphrey's campaign. He took no salary for running the Humphrey campaign because the campaign had no money.

The Humphrey campaign had every problem a campaign could have, from no money to not enough professional staff to no message, but the biggest problem was the candidate. A better candidate could have attracted more money. Humphrey could have been a better candidate if only he could have figured out what to say.

In his first big postconvention speech, in Minnesota, Humphrey defended Mayor Daley's police and called the Chicago protesters' rioting premeditated. The next day in New York he went on TV and said that he didn't condone police brutality and that some of the Chicago police might have overreacted. In Philadelphia, when reporters asked him about Vietnam, Humphrey said that with or without progress in the Paris negotiations, "we could start to remove some of the American forces in early 1969 or late 1968." Secretary of State Dean Rusk instantly denied that possibility, and President Johnson told the American Legion that no one could predict when the troops might start coming home. Asked by reporters in Houston to explain his apparent disagreement with the administration, Humphrey triumphantly pointed to a headline in the **Houston Post** about a marine regiment returning from Vietnam. That story was not about troop reduction in Vietnam. Each of those returning marines was being replaced on the battlefield with another marine. In Denver, Humphrey told students that the peace plank was so close to his own position that he "could have" run on it. Then, reminded by reporters that the peace plank called for an unconditional end to the bombing, Humphrey disagreed with the peace plank.

Everywhere Humphrey went, he faced the wrath

of antiwar protesters. He couldn't shake the imagery of Chicago. Since Chicago, the protesters' hatred of "the Hump" seemed limitless. Nixon encountered fewer protesters because he campaigned in more conservative areas. Humphrey drew more protesters because he was part of the administration currently waging the war in Vietnam and because he seemed a bit more persuadable than Nixon. Humphrey needed McCarthy's voters, and they were telling Humphrey there was only one way to get them. In fact, they were shouting it at Humphrey: "Peace now!"

In Boston, Humphrey held a rally with Ted Kennedy. Every time Humphrey tried to speak, the chants would go up: "Sellout! Sellout! Sellout!" "Bullshit! Bullshit! Bullshit!" Humphrey started yelling back at the protesters—"Cut it out!" He looked weak.

"We're broke, Hubert." That's what Larry O'Brien told Humphrey when Humphrey complained of not seeing any Humphrey lawn signs and bumper stickers on the road. Democratic Party donors who had gone all out for McCarthy and Kennedy had nothing left for Humphrey. Besides, Humphrey looked like a bad bet. O'Brien knew they had to give donors something to bet on. Humphrey needed to take a clear position on Vietnam.

Humphrey had a particularly bad day campaigning in Seattle. Protesters with bullhorns kept shouting "Fascist!" and "Dump the Hump!" Humphrey sat up late in his hotel room and decided there was only one way to get his campaign on track. The next day he flew to Salt Lake City and met with campaign staff and advisers. The subject was Vietnam.

In the Salt Lake meeting, Humphrey listened to all the reasons he was boxed in—LBJ, the Paris peace talks, the fact that what Humphrey would have to say to get McCarthy's endorsement would lose Johnson's endorsement. Humphrey had heard it all before. He knew what everyone was going to say before they said it. Finally, Humphrey cut them all off. He kept everyone up until 5:00 a.m., dictating the main points he wanted to make in a Vietnam speech. Humphrey was going to break with LBJ and call for an unconditional bombing halt.

The next day, George Ball, former LBJ ambassador to the United Nations, offered some surprising help. Ball delivered a secret message from Averell Harriman, chief negotiator in the Paris talks. Humphrey feared Harriman's reaction to anything Humphrey would say about Vietnam. Ball reported that Harriman secretly wanted an unconditional bombing halt and would not object if Humphrey took that position. Harriman hoped to nudge LBJ through Humphrey.

Humphrey and his team finished writing the speech on September 30, and O'Brien came up with $100,000 for a national TV broadcast from Salt Lake

City. This would be the Democratic candidate's first nationally broadcast speech since winning the nomination.

Right before air time, Humphrey called Johnson and read him the most important lines. Sounding somewhat apologetic, Humphrey said there was nothing in the speech that would interfere with the Paris peace talks. Johnson complained about the speech's not mentioning all three of the conditions for a bombing halt and, quoting what Humphrey had read him, asked, "Negotiate in good faith with whom?" Humphrey tried to explain, but Johnson only said, "Mmm, all right, okay . . . Thank you, Hubert."

Forty-five minutes before Humphrey's call, Nixon had called the president. Enough of Humphrey's speech had leaked that Nixon wanted to know whether Humphrey was, in effect, announcing a change in Johnson's policy. LBJ assured Nixon that Humphrey was on his own. Then Johnson suggested a line of attack for Nixon to use against Humphrey's call for a bombing halt: any bombing halt would cost American lives.

To a national television audience that night, Humphrey announced: "As President, I would be willing to stop the bombing of North Vietnam as an acceptable risk for peace, because I believe that it could lead to success in the negotiations and a shorter war. This would be the best protection for our troops."

Then, for anyone who thought he was being too soft on North Vietnam, Humphrey added, "If the Government of North Vietnam were to show bad faith, I would reserve the right to resume the bombing."

At the last minute, the Democratic Party decided to include a fund-raising request at the end of the Humphrey broadcast. Small checks came flooding in. By the end of the week, there was a total of $250,000. By October 10, the campaign had a million dollars—nothing compared to what Maurice Stans was raising for Nixon, but a sign that the speech had worked.

Some antiwar Democrats came Humphrey's way after the speech. Some McCarthy groups announced their support for Humphrey. Allard Lowenstein finally endorsed him. The ADA, Humphrey's old political home, had been ignoring him; now it came back to him, as did several members of Congress. John Connally had been otherwise engaged when Humphrey had come to Texas in September; now the governor was campaigning actively for the nominee. Even old friend Abe Ribicoff, who had drawn Mayor Daley's anti-Semitic fury in Chicago, came out for Humphrey. Paul O'Dwyer, the pacifist New York Senate candidate, endorsed Humphrey, saying, "My decision to endorse the Humphrey-Muskie ticket would not have come without a change in the Vietnam policy for which these men have stood in public."

Humphrey's new Vietnam position lowered protest turnout at his campaign rallies. Most important, Humphrey started moving up in the polls.

Humphrey's running mate, Ed Muskie, was sent on the attack against Nixon. Muskie's job was to revive Nixon's "Tricky Dick" image. A Humphrey campaign ad played the Republican slogan "Nixon's the One" with the question "Which Nixon is the one?" Humphrey TV ads carried the tagline "Trust Humphrey." As Muskie became more prominent and more popular, the tagline said "Humphrey-Muskie: There is no alternative."

Curtis LeMay's disastrous debut as a vice presidential candidate put a new focus on the nominees for vice president, to the delight of the Democrats. Muskie was by far the most popular VP candidate in polls. One TV ad began with the sound of a man laughing. The camera pulled back to reveal not the man but what was making him laugh. It was a TV screen with only the words "Agnew for Vice-President?" The laughing continued as the screen cut to these words: "This would be funny if it weren't so serious. . . . Paid for by Citizens for Humphrey-Muskie."

Frank Sinatra appeared in a Humphrey campaign ad saying Humphrey was "a man who promised he would stop the bombing in Vietnam as an acceptable risk for peace. He's a man who promised that he would bring peace and order to our streets. He's a man who said that every American child had a right to a full education." Sinatra spent half of the ad soliciting contributions for Humphrey. "He needs money," said Sinatra as the campaign's P.O. box address appeared on the screen. "Send in your contributions large or small." The screen filled with the words that an announcer spoke: "Humphrey-Muskie: Two you can trust." Agnew had no such prominence in Nixon ads.

Humphrey worked hard to regain the traditional Democratic constituency of union voters who had switched to Wallace. Labor had always been Humphrey's base. With the help of union leadership, Humphrey delivered the message that Wallace's record on labor in Alabama was abysmal. The support Wallace enjoyed in the North was collapsing.

As Wallace went down in the polls, Humphrey went up. By mid-October, Hubert Humphrey had drawn within five points of Richard Nixon, a possible tie within the margin of error of the polls. Pennsylvania, Michigan, and New York were back in play.

Nixon and his team could see they had reason to worry. Nixon had bet everything on taking no specific positions on anything. Humphrey actually did have positions, it turned out, real ones, lots of them, reflected in his party's and his own record on labor and civil rights. Now he even had a position on Vietnam that was clearer than Nixon's. It was Nixon's turn to regroup.

In the first week of October, Nixon flew to Bebe Rebozo's home in Key Biscayne and held a three-day staff meeting to try to get the campaign back on track. Most of the problems were simple enough to address. The press had begun demanding policy details. So they would give them details in ten radio broadcasts on serious issues, coordinated with live-audience TV appearances, plus two books—one whipped up in only six days—titled **Nixon Speaks Out** and **Nixon on the Issues**.

The debate problem had to be solved without a debate. Front-runners have nothing to win in a debate and everything to lose. Humphrey was finally getting traction on his demand for a debate. Nixon had been saying he didn't want to elevate the Wallace campaign by having a debate that would have to include Wallace. Humphrey kept saying Nixon was afraid to debate. The Nixon campaign solution was to do more Roger Ailes–produced TV shows called **The Nixon Answer**, in which Nixon took questions from a panel of citizens with a studio audience applauding every answer. The shows were produced and broadcast in battleground states.

The most vexing problem was Spiro Agnew. Pat Buchanan had been traveling with the running mate. His report to Nixon was not good. Agnew's speeches were colorless and his improvisations were memorably inappropriate. Agnew was adding fuel to the Humphrey-Muskie ad that was nothing but the sound of laughter at the idea of Agnew in the White House.

"If you've seen one slum you've seen them all," Agnew said. He called a Japanese reporter a "fat Jap." He called Hubert Humphrey "squishy soft on Communism," which was so absurdly untrue that it refreshed memories of "Tricky Dick" that the New Nixon had worked so hard to erase. Agnew was giving the Democrats someone to attack. The decision at Key Biscayne was to put Agnew on a tighter leash and use him more sparingly.

With Humphrey closing the gap in the polls, Nixon needed to start pulling in Wallace voters. Humphrey was picking up the union voters who were fleeing Wallace, but too many of the most conservative voters who should be Nixon's were sticking with Wallace. Nixon couldn't clearly appeal to the racism of those voters without losing support in the North. The best message the Nixon campaign could deliver to Wallace voters was that a vote for Wallace was really a vote for Humphrey.

The Nixon campaign did not feel threatened by Humphrey's fund-raising surge. The Nixon campaign was still spending twice as much on TV and newspaper ads and four times as much on radio ads. The change in the Humphrey campaign that the Nixon campaign had to deal with was Humphrey's new independent position on Vietnam. Humphrey's move up in the polls after his Vietnam speech made

Nixon all the more certain that the worst thing that could happen to his campaign was any movement toward peace in Vietnam. Any other candidate would consider the situation in Vietnam and the peace talks in Paris to be beyond his control. Not Richard Nixon.

A week after Humphrey's Vietnam speech, Nixon made a major speech in Washington and reversed himself on Vietnam. Instead of saying he would never say anything to jeopardize the Paris peace talks, he did exactly that. Nixon said that after the election, "We might be able to do much more than we can do now." That statement was aimed directly at Paris. But what did it mean? Was Nixon trying to tell the North Vietnamese that he would be more flexible in peace talks than LBJ? Was Nixon trying to tell the South Vietnamese that he would get them a better deal than LBJ? Was he sending a message to the North and South to hang on and wait for Nixon to take over the Paris peace talks? The only way for either side to "hang on" was to agree to nothing in Paris and keep the war going. Of course, that would mean the continued loss of life of American soldiers. That is exactly what Richard Nixon decided was necessary for him to win the presidency.

After giving that speech, Nixon called the president. It was, as usual, a friendly sounding call. Nixon wanted to keep this communication line open. For his part, Johnson was eager to give Nixon the strong impression that the president expected nothing big to happen in the peace talks, not before election day anyway. Johnson said any movement in Paris was unlikely.

In fact, Johnson was excited and tense about a new prospect for peace that could cement his legacy in Vietnam as a success: peace with honor. The secret breakthrough in Paris was an out-of-the-blue, off-the-record communication from Hanoi's diplomats' floating the notion that they might accept the presence of South Vietnam's government in the peace talks. The Russians confirmed the North's message, saying that if the United States stopped bombing, South Vietnam would be accepted in the talks. North Vietnam was secretly agreeing to LBJ's most important condition for ending the bombing as well as strongly implying that the North would also accept a demilitarized zone and an end to attacks on South Vietnam. It would just have to appear to the world as if the United States stopped bombing before those conditions were agreed to. Publicly, LBJ would appear to be adopting the new Humphrey position. The end of America's disastrous war in Vietnam was in sight.

Johnson moved slowly and carefully. He needed to know that President Thieu of South Vietnam would agree to join the peace talks. President Thieu did agree. LBJ needed assurances from Harriman and his negotiators in Paris that the North's negotiators knew that if the North violated the DMZ or resumed attacks on the South, U.S. bombing would start up again. Harriman reported back that the North got the message.

Johnson followed the White House custom of briefing the presidential candidates on important foreign policy issues. The candidate conferences calls included all three candidates: Nixon, Humphrey, and Wallace. On these calls, LBJ didn't give any hint of the sudden progress toward peace.

Johnson was hopeful and agonized at the same time. If he took this chance and stopped the bombing unilaterally, the North Vietnamese might betray his trust and violate his secret conditions. It never crossed his mind that the South Vietnamese might betray his trust. If Johnson didn't take this chance, he might lose his best opportunity to leave a legacy of peace with honor in Vietnam. For once, the generals and all of LBJ's advisers agreed that given the overtures by Hanoi and the Kremlin, given Thieu's willingness to negotiate, and given the coming winter weather that made bombing ineffective, there would be no downside to halting the bombing and beginning talks with all parties at the table.

Nixon's friend Senator Everett Dirksen called the president to tell him that Nixon was upset that he was hearing leaks that Johnson was pushing for developments in the Paris peace talks as a ploy to get

Humphrey elected. The leaks made Johnson even more cautious.

On October 25, with just eleven days until the election, Nixon told reporters that he had learned that an unconditional bombing halt was under consideration in the White House and that some were saying President Johnson was playing party politics with the peace talks. "This," said Nixon, "I do not believe." This was the perfect combination of the Old and New Nixon. He passed along a rumor about the president to hurt Humphrey, then washed his hands of the rumor in the next sentence. Nixon knew he was risking his secret telephone relationship with Johnson. LBJ could see that the relationship was reaching its limit. Two days later, in a speech at the Waldorf-Astoria in New York, Johnson went fully negative on Nixon, reaching back to blame Nixon and Eisenhower for losing Cuba to communism. The secret alliance of Nixon and Johnson on Vietnam policy was over.

On October 28, eight days before the election, Johnson finally agreed with his advisers that the bombing halt was his best move. The day after that, the Russians recommitted themselves to helping to bring North Vietnam to the negotiating table. Then at 2:30 a.m. on October 30, Johnson met with General Abrams, who had secretly flown from Vietnam just for this meeting. Abrams advised the president to order the bombing halt. At 5:00 a.m. on that same day, Johnson decided to do it. Diplomats had said President Thieu could get a South Vietnamese negotiating team to Paris right away. Johnson planned to go on TV the next night to announce the news to the American people. Talks could begin within three days. An end to the war in Vietnam was in sight.

A few hours after he made his decision and scheduled the speech, Johnson received some disturbing news. The veteran Democratic foreign policy strategist Alexander Sachs had an unimpeachable source saying that Nixon's campaign manager, John Mitchell, was trying to scuttle the peace talks. Johnson didn't know John Mitchell. He didn't know what to make of this.

Then Dean Rusk called. President Thieu had just balked. The South Vietnamese president was suddenly saying that three days weren't enough to get a delegation to Paris. Because Thieu had said earlier that one day would be plenty of time, Johnson sat up straight.

The president looked again at the message from Alexander Sachs and what Sachs's source said about John Mitchell. Things started making horrible sense. Johnson went into a frenzy of activity trying to keep the peace process on track, beginning with finding out what Nixon was up to.

The CIA and the NSA had listening devices in the South Vietnamese embassy in Washington and in

President Thieu's office in Saigon. Johnson started reading those surveillance reports and quickly saw the outline of what the Nixon campaign was up to. Johnson knew Anna Chennault. It instantly made sense to him that Nixon would use her to communicate with President Thieu. The surveillance showed that she was serving as go-between from the Nixon campaign to Ambassador Diem to President Thieu. By the afternoon of October 30, Johnson had drawn a reasonably accurate picture of what was happening.

The president called the FBI and put Anna Chennault under surveillance. He ordered the South Vietnamese embassy to be put under additional surveillance. The president wanted to know everyone who came and went. Johnson sent direct word to Saigon that if it came out that President Thieu had avoided his best chance for peace, the American people would never support further warfare on his behalf. Johnson also passed the word to President Thieu that trusting Nixon about anything was a mistake.

The FBI reported that Anna Chennault had spent half an hour with Ambassador Diem at the embassy.

The next day, Johnson called Senator Dirksen and gave him fragments of what he knew. LBJ wanted to give Dirksen just enough to scare Nixon. Johnson hoped that once Dirksen told Nixon what the president knew, Nixon would back off and stop interfering with the peace talks. Johnson specifically mentioned Anna Chennault's involvement to Dirksen and suggested that the Nixon campaign would be destroyed if any news like this got out. Johnson refrained from accusing Nixon personally. He put it to Dirksen that some of Nixon's people had gone way too far, and they'd better bottle up Anna Chennault if they knew what was good for them.

The president mentioned only the political danger that Nixon was risking with this interference with the peace talks. He didn't mention the criminal risk. Since 1799, it has been a federal crime to intervene "without authority of the United States to try to influence the measures or conduct of any foreign government . . . in relation to any disputes or controversies with the United States."

Next, Johnson held his regular briefing conference call with the three presidential candidates. Johnson wanted to use the call to scare Nixon. The president wanted Nixon to imagine what might happen if he revealed what he knew. In the call, the president informed the candidates that he would be going on TV that night to announce a permanent bombing halt and an immediate start to negotiations in Paris with all parties at the table. Johnson then complained that there had been some partisan interference with his negotiations. He said some people had started to tell the South Vietnamese to wait for a new political party to take power in Washington. Johnson thought that this was enough for Nixon to figure out how much of his plans had been discovered by Johnson.

After the conference call, LBJ called Humphrey and told him that there was now a strong chance for peace, and it was Nixon's people who were telling both North and South Vietnam to wait until after the election. He told Humphrey he knew what Nixon was doing, but he couldn't prove it yet. Johnson presumed he had done enough to scare Nixon and could now get President Thieu moving forward again. Peace in Vietnam and the LBJ legacy might still be ensured.

The final piece of the electoral puzzle that Hubert Humphrey had to solve was his former friend Eugene McCarthy. After the convention, McCarthy vacationed in France and stayed quiet. McCarthy might have been able to remain quiet if Nixon held an insurmountable lead, but as Humphrey edged ever closer to Nixon in the polls, pressure built every day of October for McCarthy to endorse Humphrey and save the country from Nixon. To endorse Humphrey, McCarthy would have to break the promise he'd made not to endorse anyone in his last public speech in Grant Park with the smell of tear gas in the air.

The thought of Richard Nixon as president was enough to compel most prominent McCarthy supporters to endorse Humphrey. Humphrey's Vietnam speech brought more McCarthy supporters his way. By late October, Gene McCarthy was the only holdout.

None of McCarthy's colleagues in the Senate could persuade him to endorse Humphrey. None of McCarthy's and Humphrey's mutual friends and supporters in Minnesota could persuade McCarthy to endorse Humphrey. The most powerful voice in pressuring McCarthy to endorse was a New Yorker who had never been involved in McCarthy's political life.

A. Philip Randolph was a labor organizer and civil rights leader who first proposed a march on Washington in 1941. When it finally happened in 1963, made immortal by Martin Luther King Jr.'s "I have a dream" speech, A. Philip Randolph was one of its leaders. The next year, President Johnson awarded him the Presidential Medal of Freedom. On Friday, October 25, 1968, twelve days before the election, A. Philip Randolph bought a full-page ad in the **New York Times** written for an audience of one.

Times readers who saw the ad that day also saw a front-page picture of George Wallace and Curtis LeMay at a rally they'd held in Madison Square Garden the night before. The **Times** reported that three thousand police officers surrounded the garden and that Wallace's speech "sent part of his 16,000 listeners home shouting 'White power.'"

"An Appeal from Black Americans" was the top

line of Randolph's ad. The next line, in larger print than any headline in the **Times**, said "Do not turn your back, Senator McCarthy."

The ad was a letter to McCarthy signed by thirty-one prominent black Americans, such as Aretha Franklin, Sammy Davis Jr., Jackie Robinson, the psychologist Kenneth B. Clark, Channing Phillips, and Martin Luther King's father, Martin Luther King Sr.

It was a perfectly written letter that left McCarthy no way out: "The 1968 election will be a moral test for American democracy. Upon the outcome depends the destiny of millions of black Americans and the future shape of American society. . . . Do you believe that Richard Nixon, who owes his nomination to Strom Thurmond, will resist the pressures of the Wallace movement? . . . You spent ten months and millions of dollars trying to alter American policies in Vietnam. But long after this war is over, we will still be grappling with the question of whether America shall be two nations—one white and one black, one rich and one poor. . . . The growing hate in the land **must** trouble you as it troubles us. The desperation of the poor **must** move you as it moves us. The threat of an American apartheid **must** repel you as it repels us. You must know, as we do, that the election of Richard Nixon or George Wallace will produce a new era of social neglect, at best, and repression at worst. Can you honestly believe that the election of Hubert Humphrey will have the same consequences? **You cannot believe this**. Why, then, do you withhold your support from him? . . . We do not appeal to you for Hubert Humphrey or for the future of your own movement. We appeal to you on behalf of black Americans who have a life-and-death stake in the outcome of the 1968 election and who believe that you can affect that outcome. Your responsibility is a heavy one. The consequences of your decision in the next few days will reverberate through American life and politics for a generation, and these consequences could rest most heavily on the backs of black Americans. At this late hour, therefore, we appeal to you with all the force and urgency we command, to give your active help to Hubert Humphrey. Our whole world does depend on it."

Gene McCarthy was not going to be able to tell A. Philip Randolph and the cosigners of the letter that he couldn't endorse Humphrey because he'd made a promise to the kids in Grant Park who had been battered by the Chicago police. A. Philip Randolph's cause came first, long before the antiwar protesters took to the streets. He grew up in a home in the South where his mother and father each had guns in case they had to fight off lynch mobs. Gene McCarthy knew there was only one answer to A. Philip Randolph's letter.

On October 29, exactly one week before election day, Gene McCarthy finally endorsed Hubert Humphrey. McCarthy did not try to hide their differences. He said that Humphrey's position on the war "falls far short of what I think it should be." McCarthy downplayed the importance of his endorsement: "Most Americans today, I think, are quite capable of making their own decision." Then he said, "To those, however, who may be waiting for my decision, I wish to announce that on November 5 I intend to vote for Vice President Hubert Humphrey and recommend that those who have waited for this statement of my position do the same." He said there were two reasons for his endorsement: "Hubert Humphrey has shown a better understanding of our domestic needs" and would be better at "reducing military tensions in the world."

Gene McCarthy had something to prove. He needed his young followers to know that the first presidential candidate they supported was not just another politician who was endorsing his party's nominee in order to ensure his own future within the party. There was only one way to do that: "In order to make it clear that this endorsement is in no way intended to reinstate me in the good graces of the Democratic party leaders, nor in any way to suggest my having forgotten or condoned the things that happened both before Chicago and at Chicago, I announce at this time that I will not be a candidate of my party for re-election to the Senate from the state of Minnesota in 1970. Nor will I seek the Presidential nomination of the Democratic party in 1972."

And so, eleven months after announcing his campaign for president, Eugene McCarthy announced the end of his political career.

The next day McCarthy phrased his endorsement as only he could: "I'm voting for Humphrey and I think you should suffer with me."

On Halloween night, October 31, the president interrupted regular television programming and made a surprise announcement: "Good evening, my fellow Americans. I speak to you this evening about very important developments in our search for peace in Vietnam. We have been engaged in discussions with the North Vietnamese in Paris since last May. . . . Last Sunday evening, and throughout Monday, we began to get confirmation of the essential understanding that we had been seeking with the North Vietnamese on the critical issues between us for some time. I spent most of all day Tuesday reviewing every single detail of this matter with our field commander, General Abrams, whom I had ordered home, and who arrived here at the White House at 2:30 in the morning and went into immediate conference with the President and the appropriate members of his Cabinet. We received General Abrams' judgment and we heard his recommendations at some length. Now, as a result of all of these developments, I have now ordered that all air, naval, and artillery bombardment of North Vietnam cease as of 8:00 a.m., Washington time, Friday morning. I have reached this decision on the basis of the developments in the Paris talks. . . . The Joint Chiefs of Staff, all military men, have assured me—and General Abrams very firmly asserted to me on Tuesday in that early, 2:30 a.m. meeting—that in their military judgment this action should be taken now, and this action would not result in any increase in American casualties. . . . We have reached the stage where productive talks can begin. We have made clear to the other side that such talks cannot continue if they take military advantage of them. . . . We could be misled, and we are prepared for such a contingency. We pray God it does not occur. . . . I do not know who will be inaugurated as the 37th President of the United States next January. But I do know that I shall do all that I can in the next few months to try to lighten his burdens as the contributions of the Presidents who preceded me have greatly lightened mine. I shall do everything in my power to move us toward the peace that the new President—as well as this President and, I believe, every other American—so deeply and urgently desires. Thank you for listening. Good night and God bless all of you."

Immediately after the president's speech, Nixon and Agnew began a rally in Madison Square Garden with nineteen thousand supporters. Tickets to the rally were free. Young voters with long hair who had valid tickets were turned away on the assumption that they were potential hecklers and protesters. The

Nixon campaign paid for the rally to be carried live on ABC. Nixon told the crowd that it would not be appropriate for him or his running mate to comment on the latest developments in the delicate peace talks in Paris. "Neither he nor I will destroy the chance of peace," said Nixon.

During the rally, John Mitchell called Anna Chennault at home. The next day in Saigon, President Thieu, speaking to a joint session of the National Assembly, betrayed the man who was keeping him alive: Lyndon Johnson.

Lyndon Johnson had destroyed his presidency and his political career and sent over 36,000 Americans to their deaths in Vietnam in order to keep Thieu alive and in power. Within twenty-four hours of Johnson's announcement of his historic breakthrough for peace, President Thieu betrayed him and completely pulled out of his agreement to join the peace talks. Thieu said South Vietnam would not join talks that included the Vietcong. He was willing to negotiate only government to government with North Vietnam. "We will only talk to them," he said. Thieu knew this was an impossible demand.

The news so shocked the White House that the only reaction the press could report at first was "No comment." On the same day that Thieu broke with LBJ, Anna Chennault again called Ambassador Diem at the South Vietnamese embassy in Washington. The FBI was listening to the call. The FBI report said Chennault told the ambassador that "she had received a message from her boss . . . to give personally to the ambassador. She said the message was . . . 'Hold on. We are gonna win . . . Please tell your boss to hold on.'" The report was sent to the president.

Lyndon Johnson had over the last four years unwittingly empowered the president of South Vietnam to have more power over the American presidential election than the president of the United States. Johnson thought he was delivering the election's decisive October surprise on the last day of October, but three days before the election the final surprise was delivered by the man the world thought was Johnson's puppet, Nguyen Van Thieu.

LBJ's announcement of the bombing halt followed by peace talks now looked like little more than a last-minute attempt to tip the election for Humphrey. Nixon confidently and politely tried to add to the president's embarrassment. "In view of recent reports," he said, "prospects for peace are not as bright as they were even a few days ago." With the election only three days away, the president was publicly humiliated and he didn't know what to do.

Johnson called Everett Dirksen. He explained to Senator Dirksen exactly what President Thieu had agreed to. He said General Abrams "reached an explicit agreement with Thieu that the gap between the bombing and the talks would be two or three days." Johnson strongly hinted that Anna Chennault interfered without actually mentioning her name. He said the message she delivered was "just hold on until after the election." Johnson didn't specify how he knew this. He simply said, "We're pretty well informed on both ends." He left it to Dirksen to conclude that the CIA and FBI were on the case with wiretaps and surveillance.

"Now I'm reading their hand, Everett," said Johnson. "I don't want to get this in the campaign."

"That's right," said Dirksen.

"And they oughtn't to be doing this," said Johnson. "This is treason."

"I know."

Having convinced Senator Dirksen that he had information that could destroy Nixon and convict him of a crime, the president made one more attempt to save the peace talks.

"I know who's doing this," said Johnson. "I think it would shock America if a principal candidate was playing with a source like this on a matter this important."

"Yeah."

"They ought to know that we know what they're doing. I know who they're talking to and I know what they're saying."

"Yeah."

"Well, now, what do you think we ought to do about it?" asked Johnson.

"Well," said Dirksen, "I better get in touch with him, I think, and tell him about it."

"I think you better tell him that his people are saying to these folks that they oughtn't to go through with this meeting."

"Yeah."

"And I think they're making a very serious mistake."

"Yeah."

"And you're the only one I'm going to say it to."

"Yeah."

"I know this, that they're contacting a foreign power in the middle of a war."

"That's a mistake," said Dirksen.

"And it's a damn bad mistake."

"Oh, it is."

"You're the only man that I have enough confidence in to tell them," said Johnson. "But you better tell them they better quit playing with it."

"I'll try to get a hold of them tonight," said Dirksen.

"They ought to stop this business about trying to keep the conference from taking place."

"Exactly."

"Well, you just tell them that their people are messing around in this thing and if they don't want it on the front pages, they better quit it," said Johnson. "And they ought to tell their people that are contacting these embassies to go on with the conference."

"Right," said Dirksen.

"Okay," said Johnson.

"I agree."

"Bye."

And so, through a Republican senator he trusted, the Democratic president was reaching out to a Republican presidential candidate who he thought was capable of treason in the hope that the candidate would go against his own interests and save the president's peace talks and help the Democratic candidate for president. This moment was the darkest presidential secret of a very dark year.

The next day Nixon called Johnson.

"Mr. President, this is Dick Nixon."

"Yes, Dick."

"I just want you to know that I got a report from Everett Dirksen with regard to your call and I, uh, just went on **Meet the Press** and I, uh, I said that, uh, on **Meet the Press** that I had given you my personal assurance that I would do everything possible to cooperate both before the election and, if elected, after the election. And if you felt, or the Secretary of State felt that anything would be useful that I could do, that I would do it. That I felt Saigon should come to the conference table. That I would, if you felt it was necessary, go there, go to Paris, anything you wanted. I just wanted you to know that I feel very, very strongly about this and any rumblings around about somebody trying to sabotage the Saigon government's attitude they certainly have no, absolutely no credibility as far as I'm concerned."

"I'm very happy to hear that, Dick, because that is taking place."

Johnson then spent several minutes complaining about things Nixon aides had been saying in newspaper articles about the stalled peace talks. When Johnson circled back to the Nixon campaign's interference in the peace talks, he repeatedly let Nixon himself off the hook.

"I didn't say it was with your knowledge," said Johnson. "I hope it wasn't."

"My God," said Nixon, "I would never do anything to encourage Hanoi, I mean Saigon not to come to the table."

"Well, I think if you take that position, you're on very, very sound ground."

Nixon told the president he supported everything he was doing in the peace process: "And if we can get it done now, fine, that's what we ought to do. Just the quicker, the better and the hell with the political credit. Believe me, that's the way I feel about it."

"Well, that's fine, Dick," said Johnson. "The important thing is for your people not to tell the South Vietnamese—if they'll tell them just what you tell me, why, it will be best for all concerned."

Johnson never used the word **treason** with Nixon. He assumed Dirksen had told Nixon that Johnson thought Nixon's back-channel communication to

President Thieu was treason. Johnson thought his conversations with Dirksen and Nixon should be enough to scare Nixon. He was wrong. When Nixon hung up the phone, he thought the call went much easier than expected and he and his team burst into relieved laughter.

Johnson didn't know what to do next. President Thieu was not going to suddenly reverse his position. The president's only option with two days left before the election was to go through with the threat he delivered to Dirksen and leak this bombshell story to the press and create those headlines he described to Dirksen about a presidential candidate betraying his country and causing more American casualties in Vietnam. That wouldn't be as easy as Johnson made it sound to Dirksen.

National Security Adviser Walt Rostow urged Johnson to expose the whole story and "destroy" Nixon. Then the president conferred with Secretary of State Dean Rusk and Secretary of Defense Clark Clifford. They pointed out that making this story public would expose some highly sensitive American intelligence-gathering techniques in Washington and Saigon. They were very worried about having to reveal that the best evidence was picked up on a wiretap of an embassy in Washington. They had important wiretaps at embassies all over town that would be compromised. And the Anna Chennault phone call was not a smoking gun. She never said the word **Nixon**. They were sure that Richard Nixon could and would deny that the phone call had anything to do with him. They all knew Anna Chennault and expected her to hang tough for Nixon and deny that she was talking about Nixon. And then there was the good of the country.

"Some elements of this story are so shocking in their nature," Clifford said, "that I'm wondering whether it would be good for the country to disclose the story, and then possibly have a certain individual elected. It could cast his whole administration under such doubt that it might be inimical to our country's interests."

Johnson worried that the story might eventually leak sometime in the future and what would people say about "our knowing of it and our being charged with hushing it or something?"

"I don't believe that would bother me," said Clifford. Rusk agreed.

The impeachment of a newly elected president did not fit their definition of "good for the country." Impeachment of a president under any circumstances was inconceivable to them. Impeachment was something that happened once a hundred years ago for minor reasons that the Senate dismissed when they heard the impeachment case against President Andrew Johnson in 1868. That impeachment was considered a historical oddity that occurred in the turbulence of the post–Civil War era. The duties and burdens and powers of the presidency had grown exponentially since then. So had the awe for the office. In the nuclear age, the awe for the office and the man continued to increase to the point where the job title had changed to leader of the free world, a description that has never been true and never been doubted by voters, the press, or people working in the White House. By 1968, impeaching the leader of the free world for anything was unthinkable, especially to wise men like Clark Clifford and Dean Rusk. They both knew that if LBJ revealed what Nixon had done and Nixon got elected anyway, impeachment would become a real option, and in their minds, that would not be good for the country. Having a president who publicly got away with what voters would see as treason would not be good for the country, either. Nixon knew from personal experience that inside the White House there was no difference between what was good for the country and what was good for the presidency. Nixon could easily guess what Clark Clifford and Dean Rusk would advise the president to do about the treason he described to them.

One definition of the perfect crime is a crime the authorities are afraid to prosecute. Richard Nixon knew he had committed the worst crime in American political history—a crime that arguably cost more than twenty thousand American soldiers their lives by extending the war. And he also knew it was the perfect crime. Richard Nixon knew what Lyndon Johnson, Clark Clifford, and Dean Rusk would decide to do when faced with no good choice. Nothing. For the good of the country.

Years later, pieces of the story leaked, as LBJ had anticipated. It became known as the Chennault affair. Anna Chennault denied that she was trying to influence the South Vietnamese. The real smoking gun showing Nixon's direct involvement was revealed in 2017 by John A. Farrell in a **New York Times** article and in his biography of Nixon. In researching his book, Jack Farrell read Bob Haldeman's handwritten notes of the 1968 campaign. Haldeman's notes of Nixon's direct verbal orders to him quote Nixon saying, "Keep Anna Chennault working on SVN [South Vietnam]." As the prospect of a bombing halt and peace talks loomed, Haldeman quotes Nixon asking, "Any other way to monkey wrench it? Anything RN [Richard Nixon] can do." Haldeman's notes also reveal the reaction inside the Nixon campaign when LBJ discovered the Chennault affair. In these notes, Haldeman uses Chennault's nickname "Dragon Lady," abbreviated to D. Lady: "LBJ called Dirksen—says he knows Repubs through D. Lady are keeping SVN in present position if this proves true—and persists—he will go to nation & blast Reps & RN. Dirksen very concerned."

Nine years later, when asked about the Chennault affair in an interview, Nixon denied "having any contact with the South Vietnamese." He said, "I couldn't have done that in conscience."

The night before the election, each campaign purchased two hours of national television time to make their final pitch to the voters in telethons with the candidates taking voters' questions by phone. The two-hour telethons were broadcast live twice, first to the East Coast, then to the West Coast, so the candidates actually did four hours of live television on the last night of the campaign. Humphrey's telethon was on ABC. Nixon's was on CBS. The campaigns were hoping viewers would stick with their telethon or at least switch back and forth. Humphrey got an audience of about fourteen million people. Nixon got fifteen million.

Roger Ailes produced Nixon's telethon. He had Nixon sitting comfortably in a swivel chair with sportscaster Bud Wilkinson asking questions phoned into the show. That format invited the suspicion that the questions might not really be from the audience. Humphrey had a stool that he frequently left to move around the studio. He was much more animated than Nixon. Humphrey took phone calls directly from the viewers. Humphrey was joined on stage by Ed Muskie, but Spiro Agnew did not appear with Nixon.

The campaigns made sure the candidates faced the hard issues first so they would be forgotten after two hours of TV. Nixon handled the issue of Spiro Agnew's qualifications early in the show and Humphrey talked about Vietnam early and moved on.

Nixon's telethon played it safe, as front-runners always do. All he had to do was hang on to his tiny lead in the polls for one more day. Humphrey's telethon was livelier. Humphrey was the candidate with the momentum and he looked like it. And the Humphrey telethon had a surprise caller. Gene McCarthy called not with a question, but with his blessing. McCarthy repeated his endorsement in an election where everyone now knew every vote would matter.

The final Gallup poll before election day showed Nixon at 43 percent, Humphrey at 42 percent, and Wallace at 15 percent.

"One more day." That's what Humphrey people kept saying on election day. They wished they had one more day of campaigning. They studied the polling momentum showing how long it took for Humphrey to go up in the polls and they figured they needed one more day to move up one more percentage point. The country went to bed on election night with votes still being counted and the election too close to call.

It all came down to Illinois. Again. At dawn on Wednesday morning, when the TV networks reported that Chicago votes had not been counted, Pat Nixon excused herself, went into a bathroom, and threw up. But the Republicans had a plan for Illinois this time. Richard Daley's game had always been to release the Chicago vote counts after the rest of the state reported its results. That way, according to legend, Daley knew exactly how many votes he had to deliver. This time Republican precincts outside of Chicago withheld their results while the Nixon campaign publicly demanded that Daley release the Chicago results. Daley ran out of excuses for withholding the votes Wednesday morning. He released the votes without knowing exactly how many Humphrey needed to win. Chicago's votes were not enough to give the state to Humphrey after the Republican votes came in. Illinois's 26 electoral votes put Nixon over the top in the electoral college.

Another Richard Nixon presidential election was decided by less than 1 percent of the vote. This time Nixon was on the winning side of that gap. Nixon won 43.4 percent of the vote. Humphrey won 42.7 percent. Wallace won 13.5. Humphrey was the second sitting vice president in history to lose a presidential election. Nixon was the first.

At 11:30 a.m., Nixon spoke to his weary supporters in the ballroom of the elegant Waldorf-Astoria Hotel in midtown Manhattan. He said: "I, as you probably have heard, have received a very gracious message from the Vice President congratulating me for winning the election. I have also had a telephone conversation with him, and I thought I might share with you and also our television audience some of the thoughts that I expressed to him in that telephone conversation. I congratulated him for his gallant and courageous fight against great odds. I admire a fighter, and he proved himself to be one. He never gave up and he gave us a good fight. I also told him that as he finished this campaign that I know exactly how he felt. **I know exactly how he felt.** I know how it feels to lose a close one. Having lost a close one eight years ago and having won a close one this year, I can say this—winning's a lot more fun."

Nixon did not mention the central issue of the campaign in his victory speech: the Vietnam War, the life or death issue that drove the campaign and brought Humphrey within 1 percent of victory. Instead Nixon offered this description of what he said he would like to achieve in the White House: "One final thought that I would like to leave with regard to the character of the new Administration. I saw many signs in this campaign. Some of them were not friendly and some were very friendly. But the one that touched me the most was one that I saw in Deshler, Ohio, at the end of a long day of whistle-stopping, a little town, I suppose five times the population was there in the dusk, almost impossible to see—but a teenager held up a sign, 'Bring Us Together.' And that will be the great objective of this Administration at the outset, to bring the American people together. This will be an open Administration, open to new ideas, open to men and women of both parties, open to the critics as well as those who support us. We want to bridge the generation gap. We want to bridge the gap between the races. We want to bring America together. And I am confident that this task is one that we can undertake and one in which we will be successful."

President Richard Nixon did not bring America together. His inauguration was the first one in history to attract protesters. Eight thousand antiwar protesters came to Washington on Inauguration Day in 1969. Four years later, Nixon won a landslide reelection victory over Senator George McGovern, who ran as an antiwar Democratic nominee with the Vietnam War still raging. Nixon's second inauguration drew a hundred thousand protesters to Washington. The next inauguration protest was in 2017, when Donald Trump's inauguration was followed by at least half a million protesters in Washington and millions more in all fifty states and around the world.

Throughout his presidency, Nixon remained obsessed with what the records of the Johnson administration might reveal about the Chennault affair and who had those records. In 1971, when Bob Haldeman reported the rumor that the left-leaning Brookings Institute might have a stash of Johnson administration records of the Chennault affair, President Nixon said, "Goddamn it, go in and get those files. Blow the safe and get it." That caper was planned on Nixon's order, then canceled at the last minute. Another break-in was carried out at Larry O'Brien's office in the Watergate office building. That break-in led to the unraveling of a web of criminal conduct in the Nixon administration, and seventeen months after Nixon's second inauguration, when the House Judiciary Committee voted in favor of impeachment, Richard Nixon addressed the nation from the Oval Office at 9:01 p.m. on August 8, 1974, and said something no president before or since has said: "I shall resign the Presidency at noon tomorrow."

Vice President Gerald Ford was sworn in as president at noon the next day in the East Room of the White House by Chief Justice Warren Burger. President Ford said, "My fellow Americans, our long national nightmare is over." Spiro Agnew had resigned the vice presidency the year before after reaching a plea agreement with federal prosecutors on corruption and tax evasion charges from his years as governor.

Before he left the White House that day, Richard Nixon made his final remarks to the White House staff. He had no teleprompter and no notes. It was raw Nixon, the Nixon America saw in what appeared to be his last press conference in 1962, when he said, "You don't have Nixon to kick around anymore." Most of Nixon's speech, which was carried live by all the networks, was boilerplate stuff about the importance of government service, but every line was dramatic because the situation was so surreal—a president quitting. He didn't talk about himself, but he did wander into a remembrance of his father and mother. He told their stories from the heart, but they seemed to be his way of saying, "You people have never understood how difficult my climb up the ladder has been."

After praising government service, Nixon said, "There are many fine careers." Then after an emotional pause, he said, "I remember my old man. I think that they would have called him sort of a little man, common man. He didn't consider himself that way. You know what he was? He was a streetcar motorman first, and then he was a farmer, and then he had a lemon ranch. It was the poorest lemon ranch in California, I can assure you. He sold it before they found oil on it." The White House audience laughed along with Nixon at that bit of bad luck. He continued, "And then he was a grocer. But he was a great man, because he did his job, and every job counts up to the hilt, regardless of what happens."

Nixon took a breath after his father's story, then, sounding even more emotional, he said, "Nobody will ever write a book, probably, about my mother. Well, I guess all of you would say this about your mother—my mother was a saint." His eyes watered when he said the word **saint**. He took a breath and continued: "And I think of her, two boys dying of tuberculosis, nursing four others in order that she could take care of my older brother for three years in Arizona, and seeing each of them die, and when they died, it was like one of her own. Yes, she will have no books written about her. But she was a saint."

His eyes watered again. The TV cameras cut to people in the audience crying.

Nixon composed himself, reverted to more thanks to all the people who came to see his last words in the White House, and he was gone.

Exactly one month later, President Ford signed a pardon granting "a full, free, and absolute pardon unto Richard Nixon for all offenses against the United States which he, Richard Nixon, has committed or may have committed or taken part in during the period from January 20, 1969 through August 9, 1974."

Nixon knew that, under the law, acceptance of a pardon is an admission of guilt. Less than ten minutes after Ford issued the pardon, Nixon accepted. Nixon staff released a written statement saying "I have been informed that President Ford has granted me a full and absolute pardon for any charges which may be brought against me for actions taken during the time I was the President of the United States. In accepting this pardon, I hope that his compassionate act will contribute to lifting the burden of Watergate from our country."

For the rest of his life President Ford carried in his

wallet a quote from a 1915 Supreme Court decision saying a pardon "carries an imputation of guilt and acceptance of a confession of it."

The last line of Nixon's statement accepting the pardon said, "That the way I tried to deal with Watergate was the wrong way is a burden I shall bear for every day of the life that is left to me."

Every day of the life that was left to him, Richard Nixon also had to bear the burden of the knowledge that his pardon did not protect him from anything he did before the presidency, and that what he did to win the presidency was his greatest crime.

EPILOGUE

The Republicans

Richard Nixon made John Mitchell the sixty-seventh attorney general of the United States and the first one convicted of a crime. Mitchell served nineteen months of a four-year sentence for the Watergate conspiracy. The second attorney general convicted of a crime was Mitchell's successor, Richard Kleindienst, who served only a month for not testifying truthfully to a Senate committee.

Bob Haldeman became Nixon's White House chief of staff. He was convicted of conspiracy, obstruction of justice, and perjury. Haldeman served eighteen months in prison. John Ehrlichman, chief domestic policy adviser to the president, was convicted of the same charges and also served eighteen months in prison. John Dean was Nixon's White House counsel. As the top lawyer in the White House, Dean was deeply involved in the cover-up of the Watergate conspiracy. He delivered the most memorable quote in the Senate investigation when he testified that he told Nixon "there was a cancer growing on the presidency." John Dean cooperated with the investigators and testified for the prosecution in some of the Watergate trials. He served only four months in custody on a military base in Maryland.

Maurice Stans became Nixon's secretary of commerce. Investigators tried and failed to trace the cash used to pay the Watergate burglars to Stans's fundraising activities for the Nixon campaign. Stans was indicted for perjury and obstruction of justice. He was acquitted. Then he pleaded guilty to lesser charges of violating campaign finance laws and paid a fine of $5,000.

In the Watergate investigation, forty-eight Nixon administration officials were found guilty of crimes. The seven charged with the burglary of Larry O'Brien's office at the Watergate complex were not government employees. The Watergate burglars were all found guilty and served sentences from two months to four years.

WHEN VICE PRESIDENT GERALD FORD became president in 1974, he chose Nelson Rockefeller as his vice president. In the presidential campaign of 1976 against Jimmy Carter and Walter Mondale, Gerald Ford decided he needed a more conservative running mate and chose Senator Bob Dole of Kansas. Vice President Rockefeller watched the 1976 campaign from the sidelines as President Ford never found a satisfactory answer for voters to the question that would nag him for the rest of his life: Why did he pardon Richard Nixon?

In 1981, Gerald Ford told Henry Kissinger, "Sometimes I wish I had never pardoned that son of a bitch."

IN 1976, RONALD REAGAN ran for the Republican presidential nomination against President Ford and lost. In 1980, Reagan ran as the Republican nominee against President Jimmy Carter's reelection and won. He was reelected in 1984. Ronald Reagan's winning campaign slogan in 1980 was "Make America Great Again." Donald Trump chose those exact words as his winning slogan thirty-six years later.

JOHN LINDSAY LEFT THE Republican Party in 1969 and won reelection as mayor of New York City running as an independent. In 1971, Mayor Lindsay became a registered Democrat. In 1972, he ran for president as a Democrat. Lindsay dropped out of the race after the Wisconsin primary and endorsed antiwar candidate George McGovern. Lindsay's political career ended after his second term as mayor. The political category John Lindsay occupied in 1968—liberal Republican—no longer exists.

ROGER AILES CONTINUED WORKING on campaigns, including Ronald Reagan's presidential campaigns. In 1996, Rupert Murdoch hired Ailes to create the Fox News channel as a Republican-supporting cable news network. By 2003, Fox News had the largest audience of all the cable news networks. Roger Ailes befriended Donald Trump long before he ran for president. Ailes delivered consistently positive coverage of the Trump campaign on Fox News. In July 2016, during the Republican National Convention, Fox News fired Roger Ailes after the network reached a $20 million settlement with a female employee who charged Ailes with sexual harassment. Multiple accusations of sexual harassment were settled for tens of millions of dollars during Roger Ailes's twenty years of running Fox News.

PAT BUCHANAN SERVED AS a speechwriter and special assistant to the president in the Nixon White House. He was director of communications in the Reagan White House. When Reagan's vice president, George H. W. Bush, succeeded Reagan in the presidency, Buchanan worried that Bush was too willing to compromise with the Democrats controlling Congress. In 1992, Buchanan followed the Gene McCarthy model and challenged the incumbent president of his own party in the New Hampshire primary. Attacking President Bush from the right, Buchanan got 38 percent of the vote in New Hampshire, which, like McCarthy's New Hampshire second-place finish, was treated as a win in the media. President Bush easily beat Buchanan in the primaries, but Buchanan showed the surprising strength of the right wing of the Republican Party's intense opposition to illegal immigration and international trade agreements. Pat Buchanan's slogan was "America First."

Buchanan knew that the slogan "America First" was created by a group trying to keep the United States out of World War II. In the beginning, the America First Committee attracted pacifists, as well as Democrats and Republicans. But it soon became closely associated with well-known anti-Semites who had no sympathy for the plight of Jews in Nazi Germany. Pat Buchanan didn't mind the overtone of anti-Semitism in his "America First" slogan. He was accused of anti-Semitism many times over the course of his career. He often seemed to go out of his way to invite the charge. When President Barack Obama nominated Elena Kagan to the Supreme Court, Buchanan said, "If Kagan is confirmed, Jews, who represent less than two percent of the U.S. population, will have thirty-three percent of the Supreme Court seats."

Buchanan may have grown comfortable with anti-Semitic remarks during the years he spent with his political mentor, Richard Nixon. White House audiotapes revealed Nixon to be a relentless anti-Semite. He called Henry Kissinger "my Jew boy," sometimes to his face. When he was thinking about firing Leonard Garment from the White House staff, Nixon yelled, "God damn his Jewish soul!" Once, when considering possible appointees, Nixon said, "No Jews. We are adamant when I say no Jews." Nixon knew a secret taping system was recording every word when he said, "Most Jews are disloyal," and "Generally speaking, you can't trust the bastards. They turn on you. Am I wrong or right?"

Nixon did not find fault only with Jews. When Barack Obama was twelve years old, the tapes caught Nixon, saying that black people wouldn't be able to run a government for at least a hundred years, maybe a thousand. "The Irish can't drink," said Nixon, whom Kissinger had to block from taking phone calls from foreign leaders at night because the president was drunk. "The Italians, of course," said Nixon, "those people 'course don't have their heads screwed on tight."

Pat Buchanan ran for president in 2000 as a third-party candidate. Because of a flaw in the design of the Florida ballot in Palm Beach County, it was easy to make the mistake of voting for Buchanan when the voter tried to vote for the Democrat Al Gore.

With liberal Palm Beach County's large Jewish population, Buchanan could have realistically expected
to get a few hundred votes there, 400 tops. He got
3,407 votes. Al Gore lost the state to George W. Bush
by 537 votes, which gave Bush the electoral college
win. Buchanan got more votes in liberal Palm Beach
County than he did in any other county, including
Florida's most conservative counties. Buchanan himself admitted that it was probably a mistake. "When
I took one look at that ballot on Election Night," said
Buchanan, "it's very easy for me to see how someone
could have voted for me in the belief they voted for
Al Gore."

After Pat Buchanan endorsed Donald Trump
for president in 2016, Trump began adding to his
speeches the slogan "America First." When Donald
Trump won on a Buchanan platform, Pat Buchanan
said, "The ideas made it, but I didn't."

Vietnam

The year after Richard Nixon resigned the presidency, Nguyen Van Thieu resigned the presidency of
South Vietnam on April 21, 1975. He immediately
flew to Taiwan. After a short period in London, he
spent the rest of his life at the outer edge of suburban Boston in the town of Foxboro, Massachusetts.
He lived a quiet life in Foxboro, stayed out of the

limelight, and was occasionally seen walking his dog around the Neponset Reservoir by the few people who knew who he was. He died in 2001 at the age of seventy-six.

The Nixon administration spent five years negotiating the withdrawal of U.S. forces from Vietnam. During those five years, Nixon expanded the war into Cambodia and Laos and ordered a Christmas bombing of Hanoi that was the heaviest bombing of the war. Nixon's erratic war tactics and National Security Adviser Henry Kissinger's conduct of the Paris peace talks accomplished nothing that LBJ couldn't have accomplished at any time during the war. Two years after the United States signed the 1973 Agreement on Ending the War and Restoring Peace in Vietnam, the war ended in complete victory for North Vietnam.

The most powerful new antiwar voice to emerge during the Nixon administration was decorated navy veteran John Kerry, who saw combat in Vietnam. He became a leader of Vietnam Veterans Against the War. He was a patrician-sounding Yale man who volunteered for combat when most of his classmates were doing whatever it took to avoid military service. The Nixon administration feared Kerry because he brought an eloquence and credibility to the antiwar movement that no other long-haired twenty-eight-year-old could. On April 22, 1971, dressed in his old military fatigues and wearing a chest full of medals, Kerry sat in the witness seat at the Senate Foreign Relations Committee, the same seat he would occupy forty-two years later in his confirmation hearing for secretary of state after serving as chairman of the committee. At that first appearance at the committee, in 1971, there wasn't a senator who saw him who wouldn't bet that John Kerry was going to be one of them someday. He delivered the most memorable Senate testimony of the entire Vietnam War period. John Kerry has never been more riveting a speaker than he was the first time he spoke in that Senate hearing room. His opening statement was interrupted by applause and followed by applause and tears. Chairman William Fulbright only mildly discouraged the applause. It looked as if the chairman wished he could applaud too. Kerry told the senators what was happening in the war at a level of detail they had never heard. He described a recent meeting of Vietnam veterans: "They told the stories of times that they had personally raped, cut off ears, cut off heads, taped wires from portable telephones to human genitals and turned up the power, cut off limbs, blown up bodies, randomly shot at civilians, razed villages in the fashion reminiscent of Genghis Khan, shot cattle and dogs for fun, poisoned food stocks, and generally ravaged the countryside of South Vietnam in addition to the normal ravage of war and the normal and very particular ravaging which is done by the applied bombing power of this country."

John Kerry said that what was happening in Vietnam was a civil war that in no way threatened the United States. "Each day to facilitate the process by which the United States washes her hands of Vietnam, someone has to give up his life so that the United States doesn't have to admit something that the entire world already knows, so that we can't say that we've made a mistake. Someone has to die so that President Nixon won't be, and these are his words, 'the first President to lose a war.'

"And we are asking Americans to think about that because how do you ask a man to be the last man to die in Vietnam? How do you ask a man to be the last man to die for a mistake?" No more powerful question about Vietnam was ever asked in Washington. The answer came four years later as the North Vietnamese closed in on Saigon.

On April 29, 1975, eight days after President Thieu fled the country, two U.S. Marines were killed in a rocket attack. Charles McMahon was eleven days away from his twenty-second birthday. Darwin Lee Judge was nineteen years old. They were both one day away from leaving Vietnam when they became the answer to John Kerry's question. They were the last two men to die for a mistake. President Ford had given a speech six days earlier declaring an end to the

Vietnam War, but no one told that rocket that killed Charles McMahon and Darwin Lee Judge. The day after marines McMahon and Judge were killed, the last American helicopter left Saigon at 5:27 a.m. on April 30, 1975. North Vietnam immediately took complete control of South Vietnam. America had been fighting for nothing in Vietnam every day of the Nixon administration. During the Nixon years, 21,195 Americans were killed in Vietnam, bringing the total to 58,315.

Twenty years later, in 1995, the United States and Vietnam established full diplomatic relations. They established full trade relations in 2001. Glossy American travel magazines feature alluring photo spreads of Vietnam's beaches and lists of the best restaurants in Saigon and Hanoi. Close to half a million American tourists visit Vietnam every year—almost the troop strength the United States had in Vietnam in 1968. Those American tourists are welcomed by a country where at least 1.3 million of their soldiers and citizens in the North and South were killed in a war that was prolonged and made more lethal by two American presidents who were determined not to be the first American president to lose a war. And so America lost a war, but the president did not admit it.

During what they both knew were Richard Nixon's final days in the White House, Henry Kissinger told the president, "History will treat you well."

"It depends on who writes the history," said Nixon.

The Democrats

Hubert Humphrey called Lyndon Johnson the morning after the election and apologized for losing.

"Well, I'm sorry I let you down a little," said Humphrey.

"No, you didn't. No, you didn't," said Johnson. "It's a lot of other folks, but not you. It was our own people in the party that created all the problems, all the conditions, and stirred up all the divisiveness, and now they're blaming everybody else."

"Yep."

"But you came out of it in mighty good shape, and I just wish it could have been a few hundred more," said Johnson.

"That's right, well, if we could've just done a little better, but we're not going to cry. Nothing you can do about it."

Two years later, Humphrey ran for his old job of senator. With Gene McCarthy not running for re-election, Minnesota had an open Senate seat. Humphrey won and two years later ran for president again in 1972. The delegate selection process had changed dramatically since 1968. It had become much more open and democratic. The inside game of hunting delegates was not as important as the primaries. The architect of many of those changes, Senator George McGovern, running as an antiwar candidate, crushed

Humphrey in the primaries and won the 1972 Democratic nomination for president. Humphrey served in the Senate until his death from cancer at age sixty-six in January 1978. His wife, Muriel, was appointed to serve the rest of the year in the Senate until Minnesota could elect a new senator.

One of the last phone calls Hubert Humphrey made was to Richard Nixon. He invited him to his funeral.

The first time Richard Nixon set foot in Washington after resigning the presidency was to attend Hubert Humphrey's memorial service in the Capitol Rotunda. The Senate chaplain read the "Peace Prayer of Saint Francis," which contained a line about being pardoned that provoked the television coverage to cut to a close-up of Richard Nixon.

> O divine Master, grant that I may not so much seek
> to be consoled as to console,
> to be understood as to understand,
> to be loved as to love.
> For it is in giving that we receive,
> it is in pardoning that we are pardoned,
> and it is in dying that we are born to eternal life.
> Amen.

ED MUSKIE WAS THE front-runner in the polls when the race for the 1972 Democratic presidential nomination began, but George McGovern did much better than expected in the early primaries and soon was running ahead of Muskie. Ed Muskie continued to serve in the Senate until 1980, when he became secretary of state for the last year of the Carter administration.

GEORGE WALLACE RAN FOR president as a Democrat in 1972. Wallace never had a chance in the Democratic field dominated by George McGovern. Wallace's campaign ended in an assassination attempt in Maryland that left him paralyzed from the waist down. The gunman said the shooting was not politically motivated. He was only seeking fame. In the late 1970s, Wallace claimed he was a born-again Christian and apologized for his segregationist past. About blocking the entrance to the University of Alabama, he said, "I was wrong. Those days are over and they ought to be over." George Wallace was elected to his final term as governor in 1982 and appointed a record number of African Americans to government positions in Alabama.

TED KENNEDY SPENT THE rest of his life in the United States Senate. His forty-seven years in office made him the third longest-serving senator in history. When he ran for president in 1980, he did what he advised Bobby not to do—he ran against a Democratic incumbent president. When he surrendered to Jimmy Carter in an emotional speech at the Democratic convention, his last line was "the dream shall never die."

ALLARD LOWENSTEIN WON A Long Island congressional seat on election night in 1968. Two years later, he was defeated in his reelection campaign. He ran for Congress three more times from different New York districts and lost. During his 1974 campaign, he became friendly with William F. Buckley Jr., who surprised everyone by endorsing Al Lowenstein. In 1977, President Carter appointed Lowenstein the United States representative to the United Nations Commission on Human Rights. On March 14, 1980, a man suffering from paranoid delusions entered Lowenstein's Manhattan office and shot and killed him. William F. Buckley Jr. and Ted Kennedy delivered eulogies at Al Lowenstein's funeral.

SEVEN MONTHS AFTER THE Democratic convention, Tom Hayden was charged by federal prosecutors with conspiracy to cross state lines to incite riots at the convention. Hayden's codefendants were Dave Dellinger, Rennie Davis, Abbie Hoffman,

Jerry Rubin, Bobby Seale, Lee Weiner, and John
Froines. They immediately became known as the
Chicago Eight. Some of the charged coconspira-
tors had never met. Bobby Seale showed up for the
arraignment without a lawyer. When he saw Dave
Dellinger, thirty years older than the other codefendants, he asked him for his business card, assuming
his alleged coconspirator was a lawyer. The trial was
a spectacle unlike anything ever seen in an American courtroom. When Abbie Hoffman was asked
his name and address on the witness stand, he said,
"Abbie Hoffman, Woodstock Nation." The trial was
a zany Yippie happening and deadly serious at the
same time. The nation was riveted to the coverage
and the characters, including the cranky, impatient
seventy-four-year-old federal judge, Julius Hoffman,
who failed to control the proceedings. When Bobby
Seale continued to interrupt, the judge had U.S.
marshals remove him from the courtroom. Ten minutes later, he was carried back in, chained to his chair
and gagged. Judge Hoffman was oblivious to the
imagery—seen only in drawings because no cameras
were allowed in the courtroom—of a black man in
chains and gagged. Bobby Seale in chains instantly
became the image of American justice around the
world. Eventually, Judge Hoffman separated Bobby
Seale's case and the trial headlines were about the
Chicago Seven. They were all convicted. The con-
victions were overturned on appeal.

Three months before the Chicago Eight were charged by the Nixon Justice Department run by Attorney General John Mitchell, the violence at the Democratic convention was described as a "police riot" by the National Commission on the Causes and Prevention of Violence. The commission was created by President Johnson five days after the assassination of Bobby Kennedy. The thirteen-member presidential commission was a mostly white male group, a cross section of the establishment, and included a university president, the archbishop of New York, two judges, and senators and congressmen of both parties, including LBJ's friend Hale Boggs of Louisiana. It was not a liberal group. They concluded that the rioting that the Chicago Eight were charged with conspiring to incite was the fault of the police.

The commission's report said: "During the week of the Democratic National Convention, the Chicago police were the targets of mounting provocation by both word and act. It took the form of obscene epithets, and of rocks, sticks, bathroom tiles, and even human feces hurled at police by demonstrators. Some of these acts had been planned; others were spontaneous or were themselves provoked by police action. Furthermore, the police had been put on edge by widely published threats of attempts to disrupt both the city and the Convention. That was the nature of the provocation. The nature of the response was unrestrained and indiscriminate police violence on many occasions, particularly at night. That violence was made all the more shocking by the fact that it was often inflicted upon persons who had broken no law, disobeyed no order, made no threat. . . . Newsmen and photographers were singled out for assault, and their equipment deliberately damaged. Fundamental police training was ignored; and officers, when on the scene, were often unable to control their men. As one police officer put it: 'What happened didn't have anything to do with police work.'"

In 1976, Tom Hayden ran for the United States Senate in California, where he finished a close second in the Democratic primary. In 1982, he won a seat in the California Assembly running as a Democrat. He served in the Assembly for ten years and was then elected to the California Senate, where he served eight years. During his political career, Tom Hayden was a delegate at the Democratic National Convention six times. He endorsed Barack Obama for president in the 2008 Democratic primaries. In 2016, he was an early supporter of Democratic Socialist Bernie Sanders in the Democratic primaries. As the establishment candidate, Hillary Clinton, closed in on the nomination with a massive lead in superdelegates not chosen by primary elections, Tom Hayden switched his support to Clinton before he cast his vote in the California primary. In an April essay in the **Nation**, he tried to be the peacemaker between the insurgent Sanders wing of the Democratic

Party and the establishment Clinton wing. In a more positive endorsement of Clinton than anything Gene McCarthy said about Hubert Humphrey in 1968, Tom Hayden wrote, "I'm worried that terrible friction is brewing between the two Democratic camps left in this primary. Democrats all have to unite to win the White House and the Supreme Court this year." Tom Hayden didn't live to see who won the White House. He died after a long illness on October 23, 2016, at the age of seventy-six.

ONE YEAR AFTER THE 1968 Democratic National Convention, Eugene and Abigail McCarthy separated. Their daughter Mary became a professor at Yale Law School and died of cancer in 1990 at age forty-one.

Abigail's career as an author and essayist blossomed after her separation from Gene. Still, she said, "I wouldn't have chosen to get separated myself." The separation liberated Abigail professionally. "I've grown and become free in a way I never was before," she said, "but I'm not recommending it." Long, loving marriages never have simple explanations for why they come apart, why they survive so many bumps in the road before going off it. Abigail once said, "I have never been sure in my own mind whether it was the strain of political life or the very particular strains of the 1968 campaign or just the 1960s. I really probably think all those things entered into it. Although I would never undo 1968, I believed in it as much as Gene did."

Abigail McCarthy died five years before Gene in 2001 in her Washington home at age eighty-five. Abigail and Gene never divorced.

EUGENE McCARTHY'S LIFE PEAKED at age fifty-two in 1968. After separating from Abigail in 1969, he had a relationship with CBS correspondent Marya McLaughlin, who became the network's first female on-camera reporter in 1965. They remained a couple until she died in 1998. The obituary notice posted by her family included a long list of her surviving relatives, including grandnieces and grandnephews. The last name on the list was Eugene McCarthy, who was identified as a "close friend." Her CBS News obituary did not mention McCarthy. They never publicly acknowledged their relationship.

Gene McCarthy kept his promise about not running for reelection to the Senate in 1970. He moved to a farmhouse seventy miles west of Washington in the Blue Ridge Mountains. In 1972, McCarthy couldn't resist running for the presidency again even though he seemed only to be going through the motions, as he did in 1968 after Bobby Kennedy's assassination. Ed Muskie was the front-runner in 1972, eventually overtaken by George McGovern. McCarthy was never a factor. His best showing in the primaries was his 36 percent to Muskie's 62 percent in Illinois. In 1976, McCarthy ran for president as an independent. The campaign was essentially a comfortably paced lecture tour in opposition to the two-party system. He won less than 1 percent of the vote in November.

Most politicians are more frustrated by the way their own party disappoints them than the way the other party opposes them. They expect opposition from the opposing party. That's the way it's supposed to be. Dealing with that opposition is a full-time job, and they expect to have the support of their own party in that eternal struggle. But when their own party turns against them, disagrees with them, or just goes off in another direction, they feel unsupported by their party and sometimes betrayed. That's why Lyndon Johnson's best relationship with a presidential candidate through most of 1968 was with Richard Nixon. And it's why the low point in Gene McCarthy's respect for a Democratic president was during the Jimmy Carter years. McCarthy saw Carter as standing for nothing. He said Carter was one of the many modern, bland presidential candidates who ran for "Governor of the United States." Because McCarthy was out of serious politics during the Carter administration and Abigail wasn't around, there was nothing to contain his harshest negative impulses. His anti-Carter rhetoric eventually knew no bounds. In 1980, he actually called Jimmy Carter "the worst president we ever had." With the Nixon resignation and pardon only six years old, no one other than a few Nixon devotees could take McCarthy's statement seriously. When McCarthy endorsed Ronald Reagan over Jimmy Carter in 1980, he may well have brought zero McCarthy voters with him. By then, McCarthy was regarded as a pure contrarian by the people who were still paying attention.

There is a Yeats verse that Gene McCarthy recited in 1968 that explained something about why he was running for president:

> Nor law, nor duty bade me fight,
> Not public men, nor cheering crowds,
> A lonely impulse of delight
> Drove to this tumult in the clouds.

That lonely impulse of delight drove Gene McCarthy in many directions over the years, none stranger than his interlude as a Reagan Democrat.

In the second year of the Reagan presidency, McCarthy returned to the Democratic Party to run for Senate again in Minnesota. He won only 24 percent of the vote in the Democratic primary. He ran his last quixotic presidential campaign in 1992 as a Democrat, at age seventy-six. That was the first presidential campaign that I saw up close. The McCarthy campaign in New Hampshire, as far as I could tell, was limited to the candidate's sitting in the lobby of the Sheraton Wayfarer sometimes alone, sometimes affably chatting with some of the older reporters who recognized him. The winner of the Democratic presidential nomination that year, Bill Clinton, was a former junior staffer on the Senate Foreign Relations Committee when Gene McCarthy made his first decision to run for president, the decision that changed history.

McCarthy published a book of his poetry in 1997 titled **Cool Reflections: Poetry for the Who, What, When, Where and especially Why of it all**.

Eugene McCarthy opposed the last American war of his lifetime. "This is a faith based war," McCarthy said of President George W. Bush's invasion of Iraq in 2003. "It's not a kind of war you can win." The eighty-seven-year-old McCarthy sounded like the man who addressed "the government of the people in exile" in Grant Park thirty-five years earlier: "The Bush administration is sort of like an intruder. He doesn't care whether what he does is legal or traditional or not. He just goes ahead and does it."

Eugene McCarthy died on December 10, 2005, at age eighty-nine. That night, Ted Kennedy issued this statement: "Gene's name will forever be linked with our family. In spite of the rivalry with Bobby in the 1968 campaign, I admired Gene enormously for his courage in challenging a war America never should have fought. His life speaks volumes to us today as we face a similar critical time for our country."

Bill Clinton delivered Eugene McCarthy's eulogy at the National Cathedral. He told a story of needing to borrow a pair of black shoes for a formal event in the summer of 1970 in Washington. A friend got his big-footed neighbor, Gene McCarthy, to lend the shoes. Clinton, then twenty-four years old, remembered having a pleasant chat with McCarthy, then in his last year in the Senate. In his eulogy, President Clinton said, "I still think a lot about those shoes and how one way or another every national Democrat since 1968 has had to walk in them."

There are many what-ifs about the 1968 presidential campaign that could have changed the outcome. What if President Thieu had not broken his promise to LBJ to send a delegation to the Paris peace talks? What if Hubert Humphrey had had one more day to campaign? What if Humphrey's campaign had not been outspent two to one in TV advertising? What if there had been no rioting during the Democratic convention? In an election decided by less than 1 percent of the vote, any one of those things could have made the difference. What if Nelson Rockefeller had called Spiro Agnew to tell him he'd decided not to run for president? What if Rockefeller had committed to a serious campaign early and stuck with it? What if Ronald Reagan did that? What if Richard

Nixon hadn't appeared on **The Mike Douglas Show** and never met Roger Ailes?

Less than 1 percent . . .

What if Bobby Kennedy had left the stage on the other side of the room and walked away from his assassin instead of toward him on that last night of his life in Los Angeles? What if presidential candidates had received Secret Service protection before Bobby Kennedy was assassinated? What if Martin Luther King Jr. had not stepped out onto the balcony of the Lorraine Motel? What if rioting had not broken out all over the country after the King assassination? What if Lyndon Johnson had not dropped out of the campaign? What if Bobby Kennedy had not run? What if Gene McCarthy did throw his support to Ted Kennedy at the convention? Who would have been the Democratic nominee?

The biggest what-if of all is what if Eugene McCarthy had not run? What if Nicholas Katzenbach had not provoked Senator McCarthy with his testimony about the president's unlimited power to wage war in Southeast Asia without a declaration of war? What if Al Lowenstein had not urged McCarthy to run?

If Gene McCarthy hadn't run, Bobby Kennedy would not have run and would not have been assassinated on the night of the California primary. President Johnson would have run for reelection. Election night would have come down to Johnson versus

Nixon. No matter what the outcome, Bobby Kennedy surely would have run for president as the antiwar candidate in 1972. And then . . . and then . . . and then . . .

But Gene McCarthy did run. He made the bravest decision of any candidate in 1968, a decision that changed his party, changed the campaign, changed the antiwar movement into an important faction of the Democratic Party, and changed the course of history.

The most important thing Gene McCarthy did in 1968 was save lives. We have no idea when the Vietnam War would have ended if Gene McCarthy hadn't made ending the war a presidential campaign issue in 1968. The war ended seven years after McCarthy ran. If the first antiwar presidential candidate did not run until 1972, would the war have ended seven years later, in 1979? We don't know.

The peace movement won. The peace movement drove U.S. forces out of Vietnam, not the North Vietnamese army. American politics responds slowly to protest, so it took several years for the peace movement to win. Richard Nixon and Henry Kissinger complained for the rest of their lives that they were not able to achieve peace with honor in Vietnam because congressional support for the war kept dropping. That is a complaint about democracy. More and more members of Congress turned against the war because the peace movement—their voters—

forced them to turn against the war. The Nixon-Ford administration would not have declared an end to the war in 1975 if the peace movement hadn't forced them to. The last man to die for a mistake would not have been killed in Vietnam on April 29, 1975. Would that man have been killed in 1976? In '77, '78, '79? How many more would have died?

The millions of women and men who were active in the peace movement saved lives by forcing the war to end sooner than it would have if they hadn't taken to the streets in protest, something most of them had never done before for anything.

Martin Luther King Jr. saved lives by raising his singular voice against the war. Bobby Kennedy saved lives by adding his antiwar voice to the growing chorus when it was still a politically risky choice. Al Lowenstein, Tom Hayden, John Kerry, and other leaders of the antiwar movement saved lives. Abigail McCarthy and her daughter Mary saved lives. There are thousands of Americans who owe their lives to the people who forced the United States to get out of Vietnam on April 30, 1975.

I received a draft notice in December 1972. I was in college. Two weeks later, I had to report for my physical exam at an army facility in South Boston. The place was filled with young men standing in line for their physicals. Some had doctors' letters that they hoped would disqualify them. Others were going to pretend to be gay or mentally ill to get disqualified. I

passed the physical and went home to wait for my induction notice to arrive in the mail telling me exactly
when to report for duty. Then about a week before
my induction notice was supposed to arrive, President Nixon ended the draft, on January 27, 1973.

If Gene McCarthy had not run for president in
1968, the draft would not have ended in 1973. None
of the young men I saw at the induction center that
day were killed in Vietnam because the political pressure of the antiwar movement forced Nixon to end
the draft. Many of the young men I saw at the induction center went on to have children and grandchildren who don't know that they owe their lives to
the people who stopped the draft and the war. There
are thousands of families living in Vietnam today
who wouldn't be there if the war had continued for
another year or two or three.

The last word about Gene McCarthy should always be that no one did more to stop the killing in
Vietnam than Senator Eugene McCarthy.

> "If I have to run for president to do it, I'm
> going to do it."
>
> SENATOR EUGENE MCCARTHY,
> AUGUST 17, 1967

ACKNOWLEDGMENTS

My first gratitude is to the Sisters of Saint Joseph at Saint Brendan's School in Dorchester for teaching me how to read and write.

This book began as a recurring conversation with Suzanne Gluck, my literary agent at WME, who had been trying to pull a second book out of me for years. When I started rambling about 1968, she went quiet. When I stopped, Suzanne convinced me there was a book there. She then convinced Penguin Press president Ann Godoff to hear me out. Ann and Penguin Press publisher Scott Moyers immediately became eager and tireless supporters of this book.

The problem was time. I had been thinking about writing another book for decades, but I was always engaged in something too time consuming to allow me to write a book on the side. Now I was writing a couple of thousand words a day for a nightly TV show. I needed help. William Hogeland signed on to mastermind the research that allowed me to spend most of my time writing. Christina Arvanities took control of my schedule and managed to carve out hours for book writing during the day and then deliver me to MSNBC just in time to write a script for my 10:00 p.m. show. Christina turned my handwritten pages into a typed manuscript and plugged holes in the research as we discovered them. When I was concentrating on the book, my executive producer Greg Kordick and the show's staff heroically managed all the last-minute show preparation by always figuring out before I did what we were going to need. John Nichols, Melissa Ryerson, Steve Lewis, Joanne Denyeau, Sterling Brown, Joy Fowlin, John Yuro, Maura Daly, Jill Lazzaro, Ariana Pekary, Patty Gaffney, Lisa Feierman, Kyle Griffin, Peter Cosma, Adrienne Carr, Beryl Holness, Adam Hemmert, Aisha Elkheshin, Noel Gutierrez-Morfin, and our interns kept the show going, sometimes with minimal input from me. Scott Moyers brilliantly edited the manuscript, which I, of course, delivered after the deadline, putting maximum stress on Scott and the Penguin Press team, which they bore with grace and forbearance.

To everyone mentioned here, my gratitude is everlasting.

NOTES

Seizing the Moment

1 Richard Nixon was in a makeup chair: The account of the first Ailes-Nixon meeting is drawn from Perlstein, **Nixonland**, 233–5, and McGinnis, chapter 5.

1 "I can shave within 30 seconds": Schroeder, 2–4.

1 The day after the debate: "Was Nixon Sabotaged by TV Makeup Artists?"

1 "My God, they've embalmed him": Ling, 82.

3 "We're going to build this whole campaign": Perlstein, **Nixonland**, 235.

10 "It is a tragic irony": "Remarks by Attorney General Robert F. Kennedy Before the National Congress of American Indians."

Chapter One: Declaring War

19 Fulbright was Clinton's hero: "President Eulogizes Former Mentor—William Fulbright."

20 Katzenbach stepped into history: Katzenbach, 113–5.

21 Chairman Fulbright pressed: The exchange quoted here is drawn from the hearing transcript in Hirschfield, **Power of the Presidency,** 153–61. For Katzenbach's thinking, see Katzenbach, 227–9.

22 Gulf of Tonkin incident: Ellsberg, chapter 1. For LBJ's speech to the nation, see "Lyndon Johnson: Report on the Gulf of Tonkin Incident."

28 American ground troops: "The Vietnam War: Military Statistics."

30 McCarthy rose from his seat: For McCarthy's walkout and quoted remarks, see Sandbrook, 162, based on oral history taken from Carl Marcy, and on Ned Kenworthy's memory as quoted by Stout, 70; also see Rising, 56–7. Kenworthy's story the next day covered Katzenbach's war-powers testimony, not McCarthy's statements.

Chapter Two: "Why Isn't He a Priest?"

33 "Dump Johnson": For the progress of the movement, see chapter 5.

34 He was Lyndon's guy: For McCarthy's relationship to LBJ, see chapter 3.

35 **"The escalation came from the enemy":** Sandbrook, 126.

35 **so aloof that he didn't show up:** For McCarthy in the Senate, see chapter 3.

36 **Gene McCarthy had an abiding belief:** The ensuing account of McCarthy's early life and education and the nature of his family and town are drawn from Sandbrook, chapter 1, and Rising, 2–4.

38 **"Why isn't he a priest?":** Abigail McCarthy, 30–2. The account of Gene's and Abigail's courtship and engagement, Gene's brief effort to become a priest, and their early marriage and travels are drawn from Abigail McCarthy, 40–102.

40 **McCarthy began dabbling:** Sandbrook, chapter 3, offers much detail on the history of the ADA and the postwar reform movement, as well on as McCarthy's role.

41 **"I'll run myself if I have to":** Sandbrook, 47.

41 **Abigail was caught off guard:** Abigail McCarthy, 147–51.

42 **took up the cause of militant anticommunism:** Sandbrook, 42–7, details a multitude of issues in postwar liberal anticommunism, with specific attention to McCarthy, Humphrey, and the Minnesota ADA.

43 **Humphrey made a rafters-shaking speech:** "Hubert Humphrey 1948 Civil Rights Speech."

43 **Thurmond was relentless:** "Strom Thurmond, Foe of Integration, Dies at 100."

44 **his own idiosyncratic way:** Sandbrook, 42–3.

44 **the liberal coalition began splintering:** Ibid., 47.

45 **"loved the business from the start":** Ibid.

Chapter Three: Sleepy Hollow

46 **McCarthy was swept to victory:** Sandbrook, 86–7.

46 **new boss was Lyndon Johnson:** Dallek, **Lone Star Rising,** chapters 6–9, details LBJ's rise in the House; chapters 10–12 cover his Senate career before majority leadership.

49 **Texas radio station KTBC:** Ibid., 247–51.

50 **"Landslide Lyndon":** The account of manipulations in the runoff primary is drawn largely from Daniel; also see Dallek, **Lone Star Rising,** 327–42.

51 **the prestigious Senate Finance Committee:** Sandbrook, 94–6; Abigail McCarthy, 261–3.

52 **"To try and embellish it":** Nistler, "JFK and Eugene McCarthy."

53 **"I'm a better man than John Kennedy":** Sandbrook, 102.

53 **"I'm twice as liberal as Humphrey":** Ibid., 99. McCarthy wrote to Time denying having made the comment.

54 **"I say to you the political prophets":** Eugene McCarthy, **Parting Shots from My Brittle Bow,** 11–4.

54 **given permission:** Sandbrook, 104.

55 **Sleepy Hollow:** Ibid., 106–10, details the listlessness of McCarthy's career during the JFK years.

56 **auditions for a running mate:** The ensuing drama between LBJ, Humphrey, and McCarthy is drawn from Sandbrook, 111–6, and Abigail McCarthy, 264–76.

58 **they were each questioned alone:** Questions and answers excerpted from the **Meet the Press** transcript.

60 **She sounded out Lindy Boggs:** Abigail McCarthy, 267; and for the Stevenson discussion, 272.

60 **"Sadistic son of a bitch":** Sandbrook, 116.

61 **Abigail made a move of her own:** Abigail McCarthy, 272–3.

Chapter Four:
"A Hard and Harsh Moral Judgment"

64 **the case of Loving v. Virginia:** "Loving v. Virginia (1967)."

65 **spoke against the war in Vietnam:** King, "Beyond Vietnam: A Time to Break Silence."

66 **made opposition to the war its centerpiece:** Rising, 46–7.

66 **Gene McCarthy's evolution on Vietnam:** Stages in McCarthy's development discussed here are drawn from Sandbrook, chapters 7 and 8; also see Rising, 55–9.

67 **Mary McCarthy:** Abigail McCarthy, 286; "Mary

McCarthy; Daughter of Ex.-Sen. Eugene McCarthy."

68 **sending the president an open letter:** Sandbrook, 134–5.

69 **Clergy and Laymen Concerned About Vietnam (CALCAV):** Ibid., 146–9, covering the protest and the confrontation in McCarthy's office and reviewing divisions among Catholics regarding the war.

72 **"a hard and harsh moral judgment":** Ibid., 148–9, and Rising, 55, give slightly different versions of McCarthy's remarks.

72 **played down the significance of the speech:** Compare the **New York Times'** take in "2,000 Clerics Ask 3-Day Peace Fast" with the detailed, dramatic coverage of McCarthy's challenge to LBJ in the **Des Moines Register**'s "Urges a 'Harsh Judgment' on U.S. Policy in Vietnam."

73 **"I go to bed every night":** "The President's News Conference, February 2, 1967."

Chapter Five: Dump Johnson

74 **Allard Lowenstein:** Discussion of Lowenstein's life and work is informed by his major biographers Chafe and Cummings. Chafe, though clear-eyed, is admiring of its subject's importance to the fight to save American political liberalism in the 1960s and '70s; Chafe plays up CIA support for the National Student Association (NSA) and alleges that Lowenstein later served as a CIA agent, thus presenting Lowenstein's idealism and effectiveness as compromised. (Cummings's evidence has been challenged by other Lowenstein supporters: www.nybooks.com/articles/1986/01/30/allard -lowenstein-an-exchange/.) There is no question about Lowenstein's anticommunist liberalism, his intensity by the mid-1960s about ending American military involvement in Southeast Asia, and his importance to the antiwar insurgency within the Democratic Party in the 1968 election.

75 **his friend Donald Rumsfeld:** Mann.

76 **"I'm going to be spending the rest of the year":** Newfield, 177.

76 **Working with Curtis Gans:** "Curtis Gans, Political Analyst and 'Dump Johnson' Organizer, Dies at 77"; "Curtis Gans, 77, Is Dead; Worked to Defeat President Johnson." On Gans's role in the Dump Johnson movement, see White, 84, and Chester, Hodgson, and Page, 62.

77 **rift developing between liberalism and radicalism:** On the origins of the National Student Association: Chafe, 92–110. For Lowenstein as reformer, not a radical, see Newfield, 178. For the dispute between Lowenstein and Harris and Lowenstein's eventual success, see Chafe, 251, and Rising, 53 (Cummings, 231–2, presents Lowenstein's position as "watered down").

78 **"Well, somebody's going to get hurt":** Chafe, 252.

79 **ADA had no use for any talk of dumping:** Ibid., 265; Perlstein, **Nixonland**, 218–9; Chester, Hodgson, and Page, 60–2.

81 **"Hubert, that's shit":** Perlstein, **Nixonland**, 218.

81 **questioning Lowenstein's political judgment:** Chafe, 264.

81 **Dump Johnson had caught fire:** Chester, Hodgson, and Page, 62–4; Perlstein, **Nixonland**, 219–20. For Lowenstein's efforts and tactics, see Chafe, 267–70.

Chapter Six: The General

84 **"I spoke at a few campuses":** Newfield, 176.

85 **"I voted for him in 1964":** Ibid., 176–7.

88 **"Kennedy was the first national politician":** Schlesinger, 756.

88 **Their only question was when:** Chester, Hodgson, and Page (112) note that RFK seemed a virtual lock for the 1972 nomination.

88 **they watched Bobby change:** Ibid., 109–11, and Perlstein, **Nixonland**, 220.

89 **Bobby grew up weak and klutzy:** The account of RFK's childhood is drawn largely from Thomas, **Robert Kennedy,** chapters 1–2; Schlesinger, 3–73; and Goodwin, chapter 31.

89 **"the runt":** Thomas, **Robert Kennedy,** 30; Tye, xi.

90 **Joseph Patrick Kennedy Sr.:** For much detail on the famously overbearing patriarch, see Good-

win, **The Fitzgeralds and the Kennedys,** chapters 16–34. Thomas, **Robert Kennedy,** 32–4, distills the rough parenting style; Hamilton, 210–14, captures unsavory aspects of the political man.

91 **with the nickname "Black Robert":** Thomas, **Robert Kennedy,** 32.

92 **"He is going to be the President of the United States":** Thomas, **Robert Kennedy,** 48.

92 **sparring partner to the champ:** Ibid., 30.

93 **"Me being my usual moody self":** Ibid., 44.

94 **Operation Aphrodite:** Hamilton, 659–61, recounts the mission and its failure.

96 **best-known Senate committee lawyer:** For much detail on the phases of RFK's bumpy progress toward a national profile on the rackets committees, see Thomas, **Robert Kennedy,** 64–89.

97 **Bobby spat fighting words:** Ibid., 83.

98 **"The Kennedy boys":** Ibid., 85.

99 **display of defiance:** It is Thomas's insight (**Robert Kennedy,** 75), citing Goodwin, **The Fitzgeralds and the Kennedys,** that in this moment of reaction to his father, RFK began to come into his own.

100 **Jack Kennedy's 1960 presidential campaign:** RFK's growing importance to JFK is covered by Thomas, **Robert Kennedy,** chapter 4.

102 **"You'll get yours":** Thomas, **Robert Kennedy,** 97.

102 **make him the running mate:** Ibid., 97–9.

103 **"Let's grab our balls and go":** Ibid., 110.

Chapter Seven:
"We Will Never Be Young Again"

104 **"The President has been shot":** The account of the afternoon, evening, and first days after JFK's assassination, with RFK's suspicions, new responsibilities, and despair, and his developing conflict with LBJ, is drawn largely from Thomas, **Robert Kennedy,** 276–80.

105 **Cronkite announced that news:** "JFK Assassination: Cronkite Informs a Shocked Nation."

107 **"One of your guys did it":** Thomas, **Robert Kennedy,** 277.

108 **"We will never be young again":** Moynihan, 70.

109 **It was Bobby who on Jackie's behalf:** Thomas, **Robert Kennedy,** 280–2, reviews the funeral, RFK's new role as a family support, and the graveside visit.

110 **Bobby almost always referred to LBJ:** Tye, 301. Also see Thomas, **Robert Kennedy,** 291.

110 **"the little shitass":** Thomas, **Robert Kennedy,** 115.

111 **"You've got to do something":** Ibid., 281.

111 **"President Kennedy isn't the president":** Ibid., 290.

112 **a surprise attack from Bobby:** LBJ's obsession with RFK is detailed in Goodwin, **Lyndon Johnson and the American Dream,** 199–202, and Thomas, **Robert Kennedy,** 295.

112 **As he came to the podium:** Thomas, **Robert Kennedy,** 295.

113 **She had read the speech in draft:** Ibid., 296.

114 **secret efforts:** Ensuing accounts of RFK's multitude of clandestine and other efforts during the JFK administration are drawn from ibid., chapters 5–9, which also discusses the Kennedy ethos of "deniability" (144–5).

115 **James Meredith:** The University of Mississippi battle is detailed in ibid., 195–203.

116 **Bobby felt compelled:** Ibid., 128–32, covering RFK's conflicted efforts on behalf of the Freedom Riders.

117 **"You know, I have to tell you":** Ibid., 244–5, on the meeting; for Baldwin's remarks, see the Kenneth Clark oral history in **Notable New Yorkers**.

117 **Bobby gave Hoover:** Thomas, **Robert Kennedy**, 159–71, details the tense relationship between the Kennedys and Hoover.

117 **overthrow Castro:** Ibid., 153–9, covers assassination attempts on Castro, the relationship with mobsters, and the use of Maheu as a cutout.

118 **William Parker:** Ibid., 142; "Chief Parker's Time Is Past."

119 **He tried to ignore the commission:** Thomas, Robert Kennedy, 284.

Chapter Eight: Old Politics

122 **a wild feeling of expectancy:** Newfield, 169–70, and Thomas, **Robert Kennedy**, 344.

122 **"Viva, Kennedy!":** Newfield, 169.

122　**the Bedford-Stuyvesant neighborhood:** Ibid., 90–2.

122　**the farmworkers' cause:** "Robert Kennedy Took On Kern County Sheriff."

124　**"I can't hear a word he's saying":** Newfield, 170.

124　**"I don't even know":** Ibid., 56.

124　**the press had picked up with gusto:** Chester, Hodgson, and Page, 106–7.

124　**Mailer had a new vision:** Mailer, **Miami and the Siege of Chicago,** 91. Newfield, 164, describes a meeting between RFK and Mailer.

125　**Mudd asked him to explain:** Newfield, 35.

125　**The Kennedy Senate staff trended young:** Ibid., 52–4, discusses the younger staffers, including Walinsky and Greenfield.

126　**"Lyndon Johnson is a lame duck president":** Ibid., 171.

126　**Frank Mankiewicz:** "Longtime Democratic Operative Dies"; Newfield, 55.

126　**"anything that hurts him":** Newfield, 55.

127　**"To hell with '68":** Ibid., 344.

127　**Some older advisers in the Kennedy camp:** Chester, Hodgson, and Page, 111–13, review the arguments of the old-guard JFK men.

128　**Richard Daley . . . expressed no interest:** White, 185.

129　**he met in Paris with a French diplomat:** Dallek, **Flawed Giant,** 447–8, covers the ensuing conflict between RFK and LBJ.

130　**"I'll destroy you":** Ibid., 447.

131 **"How can we possibly survive"**: Schlesinger, 777.

131 **On March 2, 1967, RFK gave a speech**: Ibid., 770–1, reviews the drafting process.

132 **"He's through with domestic problems"**: Thomas, **Robert Kennedy**, 349.

132 *To Seek a Newer World*: The title is drawn from Tennyson's "Ulysses."

133 **Huckleberry Capone**: Thomas, **Robert Kennedy**, 347.

133 **on a plane, in August 1967**: For the development of Lowenstein's and RFK's relationship, see Chafe, 270. For the plane conversation, see Newfield, 184, and Chester, Hodgson, and Page, 62–3.

134 **"If you want to run, we'll let you"**: Thomas, **Robert Kennedy**, 349.

135 **"That's a matter for the people of California"**: Chester, Hodgson, and Page, 63.

135 **the annual national ADA board meeting**: Ibid., 64.

135 **Richard Goodwin had arrived**: Ibid., 64–5, presents Goodwin's idea that LBJ was too much of a coward to run against RFK.

136 **impromptu freewheeling debate**: The discussion is reported by Chafe, 270–1; Perlstein, **Nixonland**, 222–3; Newfield, 270–1.

136 **The most strident advocates**: Perlstein, **Nixonland**, 222.

136 **a transformed man**: Newfield, 18, lists some of RFK's new intellectual and artistic interests;

Thomas, **Robert Kennedy,** explores the issue of transformation, 345–7, with specific mention of the RFK-Ginsberg encounter.

136 **He wore bright green pants:** Perlstein, **Nixonland,** 222, emphasizing RFK's attire and languor at the meeting.

138 **"You're a historian, Arthur":** Ibid.

139 **"You understand, of course":** Chafe, 271.

Chapter Nine: "A Decent Interval"

140 **Al Lowenstein had a backup list:** Chester, Hodgson, and Page, 65–7, review Lowenstein's tireless efforts with the candidates mentioned here; also see Chafe, 267–71.

142 **George McGovern suggested Lee Metcalf and Eugene McCarthy:** Chester, Hodgson, and Page, 67.

143 **Curtis Gans began talking to Mary:** Chafe, 271.

143 **In August 1967, Gerry Hill:** Chester, Hodgson, and Page, 67.

144 **For McCarthy there was only one candidate:** White, 85.

145 **On October 20, breakfast was served:** The meeting between Lowenstein, Gans, and McCarthy is described by Chester, Hodgson, and Page, 67, and White, 85.

146 **"How do you think we'd do in Wisconsin?":**

White, 85, presents that question as the tipping point.

146 **Abigail McCarthy was not:** Abigail McCarthy, 292–3, on her misgivings.

147 **antiwar protestors converged:** Hunt, 67–9, details Dellinger's forming MOBE and the alliance with Rubin.

149 **"Yippies":** For a thorough exploration of the Yippies, see Farber, chapter 1.

150 **marching to the Pentagon:** For the day of protest, the march to the Pentagon, the "levitation," and the violence and arrests, see Mailer, **Armies of the Night.**

151 **Abigail found Mary's friends:** Abigail McCarthy, 286–7.

152 **"I know that somebody has to":** Ibid., 294.

152 **"I think I may do it":** Schlesinger, 826.

153 **"What day would you suggest?":** Witcover, **85 Days,** 34.

153 **"You're kidding":** Ibid.

154 **McCarthy called Martin Luther King Jr.:** Abigail McCarthy, 299–300.

154 **Abigail and Coretta had become close:** Ibid., 383–4.

155 **"only a possibility":** Sandbrook, 168.

155 **One intermediary was Mary McGrory:** Abigail McCarthy, 305–6.

155 **"Well, tell him that if I run":** Ibid., 305.

156 **"I'm not worried":** For the non-event meet-

ing, see Schlesinger, 883, and Abigail McCarthy, 305–6.

156 **McCarthy heard from two men:** Sandbrook, 168–9.

157 **"I am concerned that the administration":** Ibid., 173, sets the scene. For McCarthy's speech, see "Press Conference of Senator Eugene J. McCarthy, Senate Caucus Room, Washington, D.C., November 30, 1967."

Chapter Ten: Peace with Honor

159 **All of Lyndon Johnson's advisers:** Dallek, **Flawed Giant,** 525–6.

159 **"The Bobby problem":** Tye, 301, and Goodwin, **Lyndon Johnson and the American Dream,** 200.

160 **Jack Kennedy had struck Johnson:** For LBJ's views of the Kennedy brothers, see Goodwin, **Lyndon Johnson and the American Dream,** 201.

160 **Robert Kennedy the reborn dove:** See ibid., 253, on LBJ's resentment of RFK's turnabout on the war.

161 **"Hey, Hey, LBJ":** "Hey! Hey! LBJ."

161 **Johnson had created a cabinet task force:** Dallek, **Flawed Giant,** 487–9.

164 **"Withdrawal":** Ibid., 483–99, explaining the policy as a form of escalation and noting (501) that LBJ had no belief that peace was at hand.

165 **"stalemate":** Ibid., 443, 470.

165 **right-wing critics did not understand:** Ibid., 444.

166 **"We are winning":** Ibid., 496; and for Westmoreland's and others' reluctance to emphasize bad news, 497–98.

167 **As McNamara's confidence collapsed:** Ibid., 495.

168 **"cannot be bombed to the negotiating table":** Congressional Record, 25,388. For LBJ's reaction, see Dallek, **Flawed Giant,** 478.

169 **"Tell me how I can hit them in the nuts, Bob!":** Schlesinger, 823.

169 **"whereas in 1965, the enemy was winning":** Schmitz, 69.

169 **"I hope they do try something":** Sorley, 177.

169 **the intelligence came as excellent news:** Dallek, **Flawed Giant,** 502.

Chapter Eleven: Peter the Hermit

171 **Four days after McCarthy announced his candidacy:** The account of Lowenstein-McCarthy tension at the CCD kickoff is drawn from Chester, Hodgson, and Page, 76; White, 85–8; and Chafe, 279, with Gary Hart's impressions.

174 **McCarthy remained diffident:** The immediate stalling of the campaign is covered by White, 92–3; Chafe, 281; and Sandbrook, 175–6.

175 **now they didn't like each other:** Chafe, 281.

175 **Blair Clark:** White, 92; "Journalist, Democratic Activist Blair Clark Dies."

176 **Mary McGrory convinced Clark:** Abigail McCarthy, 307.

176 **Blair Clark went to Washington:** White, 93.

176 **He went young:** Ibid., covering the early staffers mentioned here.

177 **the candidate found fund-raising distasteful:** Chester, Hodgson, and Page, 82.

177 **When he arrived to make a speech:** Sandbrook, 176.

178 **"like Peter the Hermit":** Ibid.

178 **The radical magazine *Ramparts*:** Chester, Hodgson, and Page, 83.

178 **he was making Johnson look good:** Ibid.

179 **the candidate was "vain and lazy":** Newfield, quoted by Chafe, 281.

179 **General Westmoreland had plenty of intelligence:** Sorley, 52, emphasizes the general's business-school background and focus on technocratic efficiency.

179 **"the best we have":** "Notes of Meeting (239)."

179 **"undertake an intensified countrywide effort":** Oberdorfer, 138.

180 **Westmoreland publicly reported:** Schmitz, 56, calling the numbers "optimistic."

180 **"The Viet Cong has been defeated":** Ibid., 58.

180 **Westmoreland had 331,000 U.S. Army troops:** Willbanks, 7.

181 **That meant running in New Hampshire:** The account of moving McCarthy toward entering the primary relies on Chester, Hodgson, and Page, 83–7; and White, 94.

181 **almost reason enough for McCarthy not to:** Chester, Hodgson, and Page, 83.

183 **"No, I don't think so":** Ibid., 84.

183 **Studds and Hoeh briefed Blair Clark:** For the full memo, see ibid., 85–6.

183 **Clark joined McCarthy on the train:** White, 94.

184 **The North Vietnamese military buildup continued:** The account of the Tet Offensive focuses on incidents in the first phase. For the full complexity of Tet, see Schmitz.

185 **attacks . . . near remote borders:** Schmitz, 90–1.

185 **Blair Clark called Studds and Hoeh:** Chester, Hodgson, and Page, 87.

Chapter Twelve: "Clean for Gene"

188 **they offered candidates cards to play:** Chester, Hodgson, and Page, 80–1.

188 **1,312 was the magic number:** Ibid.

191 **exactly $400 in the bank:** Ibid., 88.

191 **the papers declined to run big stories:** Ibid., 87–8.

191 **rented a former electrical-supply warehouse:** Ibid., 88.

191 **the Attic Group:** Abigail McCarthy, 310–2.

191 **no one in Washington wanted to rent space:** Ibid., 309, with a description of the campaign headquarters.

192 **she didn't know who he was:** Ibid., 322–4, for the disorganization of the national campaign office, the efficiency of the Attic Group, and Hersh's giving McGerr her own pamphlet.

193 **Abigail packed up the kids for a ski weekend:** Ibid., 324–5.

194 **On January 30, thirty-five battalions of Vietcong:** Schmitz, chapter 3, covers the attacks and responses.

194 **increased support for intensifying warfare:** Dallek, Flawed Giant, 505, on the "rally effect."

195 **"The greatest source of Communist propaganda":** "Notes of Meeting (39)."

195 **"if you need more troops, ask for them":** Dallek, Flawed Giant, 507.

195 **In the first week of February:** See "Nguyen Ngoc Loan, 67, Dies; Executed Viet Cong Prisoner."

197 **Too many kids, said Gans:** Chester, Hodgson, and Page, 90, for tension between the national office and the New Hampshire organizers.

197 **Sy Hersh got along okay with the Concord office:** Ibid., 91, for tension between Hersh and Eller.

197 **"the man who's been helping the Senator":** Ibid.

197 **Her brother Stephen Quigley:** Abigail McCarthy, 334.

197 **There were four big players:** Chester, Hodgson, and Page, 91.

198 **Rumors flew:** Abigail McCarthy, 334–6, on early concerns about Stein.

199 **Lyndon Johnson slept almost not at all:** Dallek, Flawed Giant, 557.

199 **Tet sent thousands of kids unexpectedly flooding:** Chester, Hodgson, and Page, 92–3.

199 **Johnson promised to send 10,500:** See Dallek, Flawed Giant, 507–8, with the Joint Chiefs' 206,000 troop request. White, 98, underscores the impact of that news on the young.

200 **the largest number of campaign volunteers:** White, 97–9, details the organizational creativity of the students' efforts.

201 **"My campaign may not be organized at the top":** Rising, 67.

201 **They made Gene McCarthy come alive:** Chester, Hodgson, and Page, 95–6.

201 **He did not call the war immoral:** Ibid., 96.

202 **"New Hampshire can bring America back to its senses":** Ibid., 92.

202 **The Democratic machine in New Hampshire:** Ibid., 94–5, on the pledge card as a "gift" to McCarthy.

203 **"It's all these kids":** Ibid., 97.

204 **it would be a disgrace:** Ibid., 99.

204 **"the Communists in Vietnam are watching":** Ibid., 98, with McIntyre's remarks.

204 *Euphoric:* Abigail McCarthy, 351.

205 **"I think New Hampshire is the only place":** "Remarks at a Dinner of the Veterans of Foreign Wars."

205 **On election day, March 12:** Chester, Hodgson, and Page, 99–100, cover the snow, the machine's excuses, and the scene at the Wayfarer.

206 **"Chicago!":** Abigail McCarthy, 353.

207 **"People have remarked":** Chester, Hodgson, and Page, 100.

Chapter Thirteen: The New Nixon

209 **Nixon grew up just south of Whittier:** General information on Nixon's childhood, education, and marriage is drawn from Farrell, chapters 1 and 2, and Thomas, **Being Nixon**, chapters 1 and 2.

211 **He willfully and repeatedly confused:** Thomas, **Being Nixon**, 35–6.

211 **Nixon tripped him up:** Ibid., 45–55.

212 **"the Pink Lady":** Ibid., 59–60; Perlstein, **Nixonland**, 34–5; Farrell, chapter 8.

212 **She called him "Tricky Dick":** Thomas, **Being Nixon**, 60.

212 **"I personally believe":** Helen Gahagan Douglas Project, 168.

213 **"secret political fund":** Wills, chapter 5, details "the Checkers speech" and the politics surrounding it.

214 **"Well, General, you know how it is":** Farrell, 189.

214 **"the most demeaning experience":** Matson, 154.

218 **Nixon feared a sore loser image:** Farrell, 298.

218 **"Now that all the members of the press":** "Richard M. Nixon: 1962 California GOP Concession Speech."

220 **met with the ever imperious Governor Rockefeller:** This account of the making of the Fifth Avenue Treaty relies on Smith, 344–6.

222 **Now rich enough:** Perlstein, **Nixonland,** 65–6, and Chester, Hodgson, and Page, 239–40, cover the change in Nixon's fortunes.

223 **the star bond lawyer John Mitchell:** Thomas, **Being Nixon,** 152–3, and White, 52–3.

223 **Leonard Garment:** White, 52, and Chester, Hodgson, and Page, 256. Frank captures Garment's fascination with Nixon, as does Perlstein, **Nixonland,** 86–7.

223 **20 percent anti-Semitic:** Frank.

225 **Goldwater framed his opposition:** In "William F. Buckley: Bush Will Be Judged on 'Failed' Iraq War," Buckley tells Judy Woodruff that on Rehnquist's advice, Goldwater made a constitutionalist argument against the civil rights bill.

226 **Nixon was convinced:** Chester, Hodgson, and Page, 253, and Perlstein, **Nixonland,** 62.

226 **To establish a center:** Perlstein, **Nixonland,** 62–4, details the spinning, including reference to the Oregon call center and the meeting with the Michigan governors.

227 **the ugliest Republican convention in memory:**

Perlstein, **Before the Storm**, 396–417, describes the convention's frenzies.

228 **Meanwhile, Bob Haldeman waited:** Perlstein, Nixonland, 63.

228 **Nixon spoke on Goldwater's behalf:** Ibid., 64.

228 **"extremism in the defense of liberty is no vice":** Perlstein, **Before the Storm**, 416.

228 **Eisenhower and Nixon met with Goldwater:** White, 37.

229 **"The center must lead":** Perlstein, Nixonland, 65.

229 **"Are you out of your fucking mind, Garment?":** Thomas, **Being Nixon**, 153.

230 **Nixon placed all management in Mitchell's hands:** Ibid.

230 **The strategy in 1966:** Perlstein, Nixonland, 138–40, lays out the approach, with LBJ as its target.

233 **William Safire:** Ibid., 84–5.

234 **Patrick Buchanan:** Thomas, **Being Nixon**, 143. For Sons of Confederate Volunteers, see Buchanan, "Why Do the Neocons Hate Dixie So?"

234 **"one of the most divisive":** Widely quoted, see, e.g., "Speechwriter Warns Nixon Not to Visit Martin Luther King's Widow; Calls King 'Divisive' and 'a Fraud.'"

234 **Alan Greenspan:** Thomas, **Being Nixon**, 143. For the Rand connection, see Greenspan, as quoted in "Rand's Influence on Alan Greenspan."

235 **"Jews have troubled the world":** "Nixon Think Tank Stalls over Anti-Semitic Letters."

235 **he knew the war was working for him:** The account of the struggle over the Manila conference relies on Perlstein, **Nixonland**, 154–62, and Witcover, **Resurrection of Richard Nixon**, 170. Also see White, 58.

238 **"He made a temporary stand":** "Transcript of the President's News Conference on Foreign and Domestic Matters"; also quoted by Witcover, **Resurrection of Richard Nixon**, 164.

238 **"He hit us!":** Perlstein, **Nixonland**, 161.

238 **"broken the bipartisan line on Vietnam policy":** Ibid., 162.

238 **"I respect you":** Ibid., 163.

239 **Nixon knew he needed more political experience:** White, 57.

239 **Maurice Stans:** Chester, Hodgson, and Page, 254–5.

239 **Kevin Phillips:** Perlstein, **Nixonland**, 277; Thomas, **Being Nixon**, 162.

239 **Bob Haldeman:** Thomas, **Being Nixon**, 154.

240 **John Ehrlichman:** Ibid., 154–5.

241 **"This is not my last press conference":** Most sources on Nixon's career report the joke while differing on exact wording.

Chapter Fourteen: "Nixon's the One"

243 **Nixon didn't announce in New Hampshire:** Perlstein, **Nixonland**, 232–3, describes the tactical smoothness of the primary campaign.

243 **"You can't handshake your way out":** Ibid., 233.

243 **Working with Ailes:** Ibid., 234–5, distilling the Ailes TV-spot strategy. White, 154–6, emphasizes Haldeman's background and involvement.

245 **George Romney:** Background on Romney's childhood, marriage, family, and business life and pre-1968 political career is drawn from Harris.

248 **Freedom Day in Michigan:** For Romney's involvement with the civil rights movement, see Blum and Harvey.

248 **"My name is George Romney":** Harris.

249 **data-driven approach:** Ibid.

249 **Nelson Rockefeller:** General biographical material on Rockefeller relies on Smith, parts 1–4.

250 **The real scandal for the press:** Ibid., 406–9, details political issues in Rockefeller's remarriage.

251 **Fred Trump:** For Trump's innovations in benefitting from FHA loans, see Blair, 168–9, 170–2, and 185–6. For his racially discriminatory rental practices, see " 'No Vacancies' for Blacks: How Donald Trump Got His Start, and Was First Accused of Bias."

253 **Rockefeller gave Romney:** White, 44–5, and Smith, 496–7, for Kissinger's and Rockefeller's deal with Javits.

254 **Romney was in a quandary over the war:** The account of Romney's efforts to arrive at a position on the war relies on White, 65–6.

255 **The worst day of the Romney campaign:** Ibid.,

66–8, detailing the "brainwashing" incident and Romney's failure to manage it.

256 **Kissinger exited:** Smith, 497. For Bailey's and McNamara's remarks, and the **Detroit News'** call for withdrawal, see White, 68–9.

257 **In October, the National Governors Association Conference:** For White's version, see White, 69. For Smith's, see Smith, 498.

257 **He demanded his New Hampshire supporters:** Smith, 498.

258 **"The way to stop crime":** White, 64, on reporters' amusement.

259 **"The country was asking for a straight arrow":** "Mrs. Romney Had a Hunch of Pullout."

Chapter Fifteen: "Abigail Said No"

261 **Bobby Kennedy called Gene McCarthy:** Newfield, 218.

261 **Lyndon Johnson's reaction:** White, 127–9; Chester, Hodgson, and Page, 137; Goodwin, **Lyndon Johnson and the American Dream,** 336–8.

262 **Nothing could persuade him to stop worrying:** Schlesinger, 834.

262 **"Bobby Kennedy: Hawk, Dove, or Chicken?":** Chester, Hodgson, and Page, 116.

263 **"artful dodging":** Ibid., 115–6, with the **Profiles in Courage** crack.

263 **he would lose his soul:** Newfield, 195–6.

263 **Ethel Kennedy cut the piece out:** Thomas, Robert Kennedy, 252.

263 **a "Run Bobby Run" banner:** Ibid., 352.

263 **Bobby received on the same day:** Newfield, 199.

263 **"I have told friends and supporters":** Ibid., 204.

264 **"I'm an unforeseen circumstance!":** Thomas, Robert Kennedy, 356.

264 **"Do you understand?":** Newfield, 204.

264 **told Bobby he quit:** Thomas, Robert Kennedy, 356.

264 **It looked to Dolan:** Chester, Hodgson, and Page, 117, cover the projections for California and Wisconsin.

265 **"Half a million American soldiers":** Excerpted from Newfield, 205.

265 **Bobby sent Dolan and another staffer:** Chester, Hodgson, and Page, 119.

266 **"Are we," Kennedy asked the Senate:** Schlesinger, 844.

266 **Bobby called Teddy Kennedy from California:** Chester, Hodgson, and Page, 119, with Teddy's failure to call McCarthy and Goodwin's ambivalence.

267 **"Tell him to support me":** Schlesinger, 848.

267 **On the evening of March 12:** For RFK's team and his team on the evening of the New Hampshire primary, see ibid., 848–9; Chester, Hodgson, and Page, 119 (with specific reference to the UJA dinner); and Newfield, 218.

268 **"You never should have trusted the traditional politicians":** Newfield, 218.

269 **"I think I can get the nomination":** White, 102–3, with Gene's euphoria and the martini.

269 **"I am actively assessing the possibility":** Newfield, 218–9, covers RFK's morning, remarks to the press, and meeting with McCarthy.

270 **"The happy man was put away":** White, 103, covering McCarthy's landing and reception of RFK's entry into the race.

272 **"We mustn't give up":** Abigail McCarthy, 368–9, describes Clark's arrival and words of encouragement.

272 **"That Bobby: he's something, isn't he?":** Schlesinger, 887.

272 **a team meeting late that afternoon:** For the evening and its aftermath, see ibid., 850–1, and Newfield, 219–20.

273 **"What the hell's the point":** Chester, Hodgson, and Page, 124. Schlesinger, 850, has "I don't know what we are meeting about."

273 **"Bobby's therapy":** Newfield, 220.

273 **Bobby looked distracted:** Schlesinger, 851.

273 **Bobby seemed relieved:** Witcover, 85 Days, 73.

273 **The next morning Bobby and Sorenson:** The ensuing account of the "peace commission" relies mainly on Chester, Hodgson, and Page, 119–24. All others, including Witcover, Newfield, and White, differ on exactly how the plan finally dissolved.

274 **huge office overlooking the Potomac:** Witcover, 85 Days, 76.

275 **Sorensen and Bobby lunched with George McGovern:** Newfield, 222.

275 **Sorensen found himself drafting:** White, 192.

275 **The Saturday announcement was tactical:** Witcover, **85 Days**, 76, makes this point as well.

276 **Richard Goodwin and Blair Clark were meeting:** White, 192.

276 **"You'd better get the caucus room":** For the flight to New York, see Newfield, 233–35.

276 **"Not to run":** Excerpted from Newfield, 224–5.

277 **Bobby started making calls:** Ibid., 225–6.

277 **"You can keep me off your calendar":** Ibid., 225.

277 **a chartered plane was leaving Washington:** For the proposed deal, see White, 192. For the passengers, see Abigail McCarthy, 368.

278 **The plane landed in Green Bay:** For the ensuing movements of all players, and the conversation between McCarthy and Teddy Kennedy later in this chapter, see Abigail McCarthy, 368–75, and Witcover, **85 Days**, 85–6.

278 **Back at Hickory Hill:** For the scene at Hickory Hill and tensions among the RFK team during the drafting session, see White, 193–4; Newfield, 226–8; and Schlesinger, 854–5.

281 **"They're all coming from Washington":** All ensuing dialogue in the hotel is drawn from Abigail McCarthy, 368–75. Witcover, **85 Days**, 86, reports a differing version, based on Kennedy's claim, at odds with most other sources on logis-

tics, that McCarthy had not only been alerted to the visit but had also sent a staff plane to Chicago to bring Kennedy to Green Bay.

283 **"Should I put into my statement":** Newfield, 227, with Lowenstein's response.

284 **"Ted, that doesn't make any sense":** Ibid.

284 **Walinsky groaned aloud:** Witcover, **85 Days,** 85.

287 **Schlesinger found himself awakened:** Schlesinger, 856, sets Teddy Kennedy's return at 6:00 a.m. and reports that the whole RFK team had gone to sleep at Hickory Hill about 1:30 a.m. Chester, Hodgson, and Page, 125, say that only the Camelot men stayed over, getting an "inside track" on the speech, and the younger staffers returned at 7:00 a.m. Newfield, 227, says that Schlesinger fell asleep about 2:00 a.m. while working on the draft and that Teddy woke him up at 5:00 a.m.; Sorenson then finished the speech. Witcover, **85 Days,** 85, says that Schlesinger, too, had gone home, leaving the speech to the others.

288 **"Abigail said no":** Teddy Kennedy's remarks are reported by Schlesinger, 856.

288 **Bobby was wandering around aimlessly:** Ibid., 856–7, for the breakfast scene, with all dialogue.

288 **the Senate Caucus Room was packed:** Witcover, **85 Days,** 86–9, describes the scene and emphasizes the speech's denying a personal vendetta against LBJ. Chester, Hodgson, and Page, 125–6, capture the family-party aspect of the event.

289 **a roar of supporters' cheers:** Chester, Hodgson,

and Page describe the reporter's question as causing an "uproar."

290 **"Do you know what I think will happen to Bobby?":** Schlesinger, 857.

Chapter Sixteen:
The Poor People's Campaign

291 **"to dislocate the functioning of a city":** King, 5.

292 **Economic Bill of Rights:** "Economic and Social Bill of Rights."

292 **George Meany would not endorse:** Hentoff, 1–2.

293 **Stokely Carmichael was sitting in the front row:** Branch, 604.

294 **"Very frankly":** "The Promised Land (1967–1968)."

294 **"as we labor there two or three months":** Ibid.

294 **"In order for nonviolence to work":** "Stokely Carmichael: Passive Boycotts."

294 **his old friend the Reverend James Lawson:** Branch, 718.

294 **a major strike:** For sanitation workers' conditions in Memphis and the deaths of Cole and Walker, see Branch, 684–5.

295 **"I am a man":** Chester, Hodgson, and Page, 13. The galvanizing force of the strike and the city government's reaction are detailed in Branch, 697–701.

296 **thought Memphis was a sideshow:** Ibid., 718.

297 **"war on sleep":** "Interview with Andrew Young, Part 1."

297 **decided to fly:** Branch, 718.

298 **"politics of fear":** Tom Turnipseed, "The Last Word with Lawrence O'Donnell," January 7, 2016.

299 **"Niggers hate whites":** Frady, 16 (Frady always renders the offensive word "nigguh").

300 **Wallace's twin-engine plane came to a stop:** Ibid., 1–7, tells the story of the New Hampshire arrival and the speech in Concord, as well as the ruckus at Dartmouth discussed later in this chapter.

301 **"If one of these two national parties":** Ibid., 5.

301 **Wallace aimed his presidential campaign:** Ibid., 16, outlines Wallace's long-standing rhetorical focus on "the common folks."

301 **"all we'd have to do right now":** Ibid., 11.

302 **Wallace began his political life:** The story of Wallace's beginnings in politics, development as a national segregationist, and 1964 campaign is distilled from rich detail in Carter, chapters 3–7, and Frady, parts 3 and 4.

302 **"no son of a bitch":** Carter, 95, and Frady, using slightly different phrasing, 131.

303 **"The President wants us to surrender":** "Alabama Governor George Wallace, Public Statement of May 8, 1963."

303 **"When you and I start marching":** For the violence in Cincinnati and Wallace's reaction, see Lesher, 270.

304 **Wallace's strategy for a third-party run:** Lesher, 387–9, and Chester, Hodgson, and Page, 284–6.

305 **"I don't even believe in Irish marrying Germans":** Facts, 469–74, with reference as well to the other Wallace organizers and supporters mentioned here.

305 *Meet the Press* **in April 1967:** Lesher, 389–90.

Chapter Seventeen:
"Something Bad Is Going to Come of This"

309 **"We've seen some terrible forces unleashed":** Thomas, **Being Nixon**, 157, gives the scene, based on Ehrlichman's memories.

310 **hoping for a draft-Rockefeller movement:** The story of Rockefeller's first moves toward running is drawn from Norton, 512–6; Chester, Hodgson, and Page, 216–23; and Perlstein, **Nixonland**, 244–5.

310 **"You'd better ask a psychiatrist":** Chester, Hodgson, and Page, 102.

312 **"We can win":** Norton, 515.

313 **Robert Kennedy grabbing hand after hand:** Ibid.

313 **grabbed the version of the statement:** Ibid., 516.

314 **"He has the same figures as we have":** Ibid., 517–8, with the poll results.

317 **Reagan began his political life as a Democrat:** Evans, chapter 1, details Reagan's early New Deal liberalism.

317 **Nixon as president . . . would be as bad:** Morris, 292–3, citing a privately held letter with no date given; Edwards, 392, gives the date as December 12, 1952.

318 *General Electric Theater*: For sample shows, including **The Virginian**, starring William Holden, as quoted in the text, see **General Electric Theater**.

319 **Top Hollywood stars knew and liked Reagan:** Evans, 57–8, clarifies Reagan's personal role in making the show a success.

320 **Lemuel Ricketts Boulware:** Boulware's decisive influence on Reagan is Evans's overarching thesis. For Boulware's innovations at G.E., see Evans, chapter 3.

320 **crisscrossing the country to visit GE plants:** Ibid. details the process by which Boulware's political-messaging speeches were at first integrated with the plant tours and then superseded them. For Reagan's development as simultaneously a conservative and a speechmaker, see ibid., 65–7.

321 **"can't see a fat man standing" . . . "up to man's age-old dream":** While these lines are documented only in Reagan's famous 1964 "A Time for Choosing," also known as "The Speech," see ibid., 66, noting that early versions of "The Speech" show the direct influence of Boulware's vision.

322 **collective bargaining and government regulation hampered:** Ibid., 55.

323 **GE published four major periodicals:** For publications, classes, book groups, political content, etc., see ibid., 50–5.

324 **He was a quick study:** Ibid., 75–6, shows how G.E.'s right-wing reading matter was designed for quick absorption and memorization, and notes that Reagan's mind was habitually filled with abundant fact.

324 **mashed-potato circuit:** Ibid., 83.

325 **Tennessee Valley Authority:** Morris, 313–4, tells the story, citing Reagan's 1965 autobiography and an interview with Reagan's agent Arthur Park.

325 **The waiver exclusively permitted:** "Reagan Was Subject of Screen Inquiry."

326 **Reagan accused JFK and Arthur Schlesinger:** Morris, 320.

327 **"No nation in history":** Reagan, "A Time for Choosing."

328 **"Oh, Christ, Ronnie!":** Smith, 498.

Chapter Eighteen:
"Stand Up and Be Counted"

330 **the president's planned big speech:** The progress of the speech is closely traced in White, 124–39.

331 **writing resignation letters:** Goodwin, **Lyndon Johnson and the American Dream**, 339.

331 **seemed to energize Johnson:** Ibid., 338.

332 **"Make no mistake about it":** Dallek, **Flawed Giant**, 510.

332 **becoming more belligerent:** See White, 124–39.

332 **they were nearly unanimous:** Dallek, **Flawed Giant**, 511–2, and White, 126–30, trace the development of LBJ's top staff and veteran policy consultants on Vietnam.

333 **As the plans for Chicago developed:** Perlstein, **Nixonland**, 289–92, distills the tensions and differences discussed here, with reference to Hayden, Davis, Dellinger, Hoffman, Rubin, and others; Farber, chapters 1–4, offers rich detail on the same subject.

334 **"a police state and a people's movement":** Perlstein, **Nixonland**, 292.

334 **"the Democrats can't hold a convention":** Ibid.

335 **"Perhaps a small minority":** "Tom Hayden, 1960s Radical, Dead at 76."

335 **several trips to North Vietnam:** Hayden and Lynd, chapter 1.

336 **"A modern revolutionary group":** Bowers, Ochs, Jensen, and Schulz, 28. Perlstein, **Nixonland**, 290, also notes the similarity of Ailes-Nixon and Rubin-Hoffman in embracing television.

337 **"It's nonsense":** Rubin, 83.

337 **"They all wear suits and ties":** Farber, 215.

337 **"We will burn Chicago":** Perlstein, **Nixonland**, 291.

338 **"psychedelic longhaired mutant-jissomed":** Farber, 54.

338 **8½-by-11-inch poster:** "Yippie: Chicago, August 25–30."

339 **Hayden scorned McCarthy:** Rising, 61.

339 **like rooting for the New York Mets:** Farber, 39.

339 **they had actually met:** Newfield, 134–6, relates the RFK-Hayden conversation.

340 **"We expected concentration camps":** Farber, 39.

340 **"participation mystique":** Ibid., 39–40.

340 **convened to coordinate their plans:** Rising, 73, describes the disunity of the meeting.

341 **"We all live the dream":** Rubin, "Can We Survive Bobby?"

Chapter Nineteen:
"It's Not Important What Happens to Me"

342 **"I got an A in economics":** The McCarthy remarks quoted here are drawn from Sandbrook, 192.

343 **On March 24, a Gallup poll:** Perlstein, Nixonland, 247.

343 **Richard Goodwin was secretly planning:** Chafe, 288, and Witcover, 85 Days, 118.

343 **Al Lowenstein felt he couldn't:** Chafe, 286–9, details Lowenstein's efforts to forge unity between the two antiwar camps.

344 **he found himself under suspicion:** Ibid., 289.

345 **the McCarthy campaign was flying high:** White, 140–1.

345 **Wisconsin organization ran itself better:** Abigail McCarthy, 357–60.

346 **"one of those electric guitar 'musical' groups":** Perlstein, Nixonland, 247.

346 **he found it listless:** Chester, Hodgson, and Page, 8, and White, 122, 131.

346 **working on the Vietnam speech:** See White, 124–39.

346 **McCarthy appeared at a rally:** Eugene McCarthy, Year of the People, 98.

347 **after landing in Memphis:** The discussion of King's arrival, the mood at the Masonic Temple, and King's speech there relies on Branch, 718–20.

350 **Bobby traveled all over the country:** Clarke, 51–67, provides much detail on the RFK trips of March and early April, noting that in this context RFK loosened his connections to the JFK legacy and emerged as a national candidate in his own right. White, 200–3, captures the excitement of crowds.

350 **He was heckled and razzed:** Witcover, 85 Days, 101.

350 **"Where were you in New Hampshire?":** Newfield, 238.

350 **"Yeah, but I'm worth waiting for":** Clarke, 53.

350 **"In the streets":** Thomas, Robert Kennedy, 363.

351 **"The answers of the New Frontier":** Clarke, 65.

351 **the elders counted and figured:** White, 204–7, details the punctilious delegate strategy, with spe-

cific reference to the role of Daley and other bosses, in contrast to the spontaneity of RFK's appearances.

352 if Bobby won an overwhelming Kennedy sweep: Solberg, 335.

352 In the blazing sun at a shopping center: Rallies in Sacramento, San Jose, and Los Angeles are described by Newfield, 239–41.

353 Bobby was closely watching polls: Witcover, 85 Days, 122–5, discusses the primary strategy.

354 the president could hear protest chants: Risen, 25.

354 The speech drafts had undergone so many changes: See White, 124–39.

354 The LBJ campaign team had been stunned: Ibid., 131.

355 LBJ found some time: Risen, 26.

355 They worked on new drafts until late: White, 136–7.

355 Johnson added some words of his own: Chester, Hodgson, and Page, 4, discuss LBJ's secret additions and his signal to Lady Bird.

355 Gene McCarthy was making a speech: For candidates' locations, see ibid., 5.

355 Richard Nixon was especially tense: Witcover, Resurrection of Richard Nixon, 274–6.

356 At McCarthy's Wisconsin campaign headquarters: The scene is reported by White, 141–5.

356 His voice was strong and clear: For the impression of regained health and vigor, see ibid., 142–3.

356 The president announced: "LBJ Will Not Seek Re-Election."

359 Goodwin leaped to his feet: White, 143.

359 "He's not running, he's not running!": Ibid., 144–5, with McCarthy's reactions to the news on TV and his reciting poetry.

360 "You're kidding": Thomas, **Robert Kennedy,** 365.

360 "I wonder if he would have done this": Ibid.

361 "He didn't deserve to be president anyway": Ibid.

361 The first call Lyndon Johnson received: Abigail McCarthy, 256, quoting LBJ.

361 "It's not important what happens to me": Ibid., 257.

Chapter Twenty:
"I've Seen the Promised Land"

362 "you'd better get ready damn quick": Solberg, 321–2, reports the scene and LBJ's remark.

363 "It's easier to satisfy Ho Chi Minh": Dallek, Flawed Giant, 538, also discussing LBJ's relief and restoration of health and credibility after the withdrawal from the race, 530–1.

365 "You are a brave and dedicated man: Thomas, **Robert Kennedy,** 365. For more on RFK's learning the news of the withdrawal and his immediate reactions, see Clarke, 72–4.

365 **Dr. King flew back and forth to Memphis:** King's busy movements in the early spring of '68 are traced nearly minute-by-minute by Branch, 683–722.

366 **"Like anybody, I would like to live a long life":** King, "I've Been to the Mountaintop."

367 **Bobby Kennedy was campaigning in Indiana:** Clarke, 88–90, describes RFK's learning the news of King's assassination and immediate reactions.

367 **"Was he shot?":** Ibid., 88.

368 **"I could take my wife and family and we could sleep":** Ibid., 90.

368 **the crowd saw Bobby step up:** Ibid., 92–4, describing the crowd's mood and RFK's reactions to staffers' input.

369 **"Ladies and gentlemen":** "Remarks on the Assassination of Martin Luther King, Jr."

371 **at the end of Bobby's speech:** Clarke, 98.

371 **The rioting lasted a week:** Perlstein, **Nixonland**, 256–62, covers protests, riots, and police violence in many cities; Risen offers a dedicated study focused especially on multiple cities, with special attention to Washington.

371 **"White America made her biggest mistake":** Risen, 92.

372 **A convoy of military trucks:** The description of military operations in Washington is drawn from ibid., chapters 9 and 11.

372 **Army Operations Center (AOC):** Ibid., 69–75, providing background on the growth of the AOC

as a force for managing domestic disturbance, with reference to "the Vance Book," SEADOC, and USAINTC.

374 **The president's top staff:** See ibid., chapters 9 and 11.

375 **More than 50,000 troops:** Statistics are drawn from White, 243–4.

375 **Abigail McCarthy was at the Atlanta airport:** Abigail McCarthy, 383–90, discusses her relationship with Coretta King and her experiences in Atlanta after the assassination.

376 **law-and-order rhetoric:** For the rise in Nixon's law-and-order rhetoric, see Chester, Hodgson, and Page, 17. For RFK's lean that way, see Witcover, **85 Days,** 146.

376 **George Wallace's poll numbers went up:** Chester, Hodgson, and Page, 293.

376 **"If I were a Negro":** Ibid., 17.

376 **Two funeral services:** "CBS News Special Report: the Funeral of Martin Luther King, Jr."

376 **Wallace was not invited, and Ronald Reagan apparently made no effort:** Chester, Hodgson, and Page, 17.

377 **"That could have been me":** Thomas, **Robert Kennedy,** 368.

Chapter Twenty-One: The Happy Warrior

378 **a memorial service for Dr. King:** Perlstein, Nixonland, 263.

378 **Mark Rudd had been planning:** Zimmerman, 177–81.

378 **"If we really want to honor":** Ibid., 177.

379 **"We will destroy at times":** Rudd, 56–7.

379 **Tom Hayden was in the thick of it:** Perlstein, Nixonland, 266.

379 **In Hamilton Hall:** Ibid., 263–4, detailing the takeover.

381 **"We can do better in Vietnam":** Chester, Hodgson, and Page, 166.

381 **"lawlessness and violence":** Witcover, **85 Days,** 146, noting RFK's playing down leftist rhetoric in Indiana.

381 **"seize the universities of this country":** Perlstein, **Nixonland,** 265–6, details Nixon's anti-crime rhetoric and quotes the six-thousand-word Nixon position paper "Toward Freedom from Fear" on rising crime statistics and liberalism's failure to deal with them.

382 **"a "great tragedy that began":** Ibid., 257.

382 **Wallace's poll numbers just kept rising:** See Chester, Hodgson, and Page, 293, with the Gallup poll of May 7.

383 **"Whatever became of Hubert?":** Lehrer, also quoted by Solberg, 277.

384 **Humphrey felt trapped:** Solberg, 272–84, details LBJ's freeze-out, beginning with Humphrey's Vietnam memo, and presents Humphrey's subservient role as chief promoter of the war; for

Humphrey's evident conversion to LBJ's way of thinking, see Solberg, 292–300.

386 the vice president announced: Ibid., 332.

386 Walter Mondale: Hatfield gives a thorough yet deft overview of Mondale's career.

388 What followed was a very long speech: Humphrey, "Remarks Declaring Candidacy for the Democratic Presidential Nomination."

Chapter Twenty-Two: Don't Lose

393 George Smathers: "George A. Smathers, 93; Former Florida Senator"; "LBJ Calls on Congress to Enact Voting Rights Bill, March 15, 1965."

395 The Kennedys launched the Indiana campaign: Solberg, 335. The story of RFK's Indiana campaign is drawn from "How Bobby Kennedy Won the '68 Indiana Primary."

399 Nelson Rockefeller stepped up to a microphone: Details of Rockefeller's reentry are drawn from " 'Choice' Offered by Rockefeller as He Joins Race."

401 "Let me talk to Happy": Smith, 528, recounts the Rockefeller-LBJ meeting.

402 The Tinker team pitched Rocky: For much detail on the Rockefeller ad campaigns, polling strategy, and conflicts between the admen and the political professionals, see Chester, Hodgson, and Page, 383–90.

404 **Rockefeller actually won the primary:** White, 271.

404 **The Kennedy victory was so big in Nebraska:** "Nebraska Gives 53% to Kennedy."

405 **he had to compete in Oregon:** For Oregon's unusual filing rules, see "Oregon Holds Last Primary for President."

406 **McCarthy went on the attack:** Perlstein, *Nixonland*, 271.

406 **"to hold his breath":** Rising, 77, also telling the Portland Zoo story.

406 **McCarthy could endorse him:** Chester, Hodgson, and Page, 301, with Hill's "playing footsie" remark.

407 **had accepted money from the Humphrey campaign:** Sandbrook, 204–5.

407 **at the Cow Palace in San Francisco:** For McCarthy's speech, see Rising, 77; "McCarthy Jibes at Both Rivals"; and "McCarthy Calls Rivals Ill-Equipped to Avoid Future Vietnams." Chester, Hodgson, and Page, 301–4, emphasize the novel critique of JFK-era policy.

409 **"You can say that Bobby spoiled it":** "McCarthy Would Favor Humphrey over Kennedy," also with "Bobby Was for Lyndon Johnson . . ."

409 **"If I get beaten in any primary":** Eugene McCarthy, *Year of the People*, 150.

409 **the first Kennedy in history to lose:** Rising, 78.

410 **"I congratulate Senator McCarthy":** "Kennedy Pledges to Quit If Beaten in California Bid."

Chapter Twenty-Three:
"Everything's Going to Be Okay"

412 **He moved to Bobby's left:** Sandbrook, 197; Chester, Hodgson, and Page, 344–5; Perlstein, Nixonland, 272.

416 **"It should be a time of great confidence":** Humphrey, "Remarks Declaring Candidacy for the Democratic Presidential Nomination."

417 **"After last night in Oregon":** "Kennedy Pledges to Quit If Beaten in California Bid," also with RFK's "under no circumstances."

417 **The California Kennedy campaign:** See Palermo for a deft distillation of RFK's California campaign.

418 **McCarthy had his own troupe:** Perlstein, Nixonland, 271, discusses celebrity McCarthy supporters.

418 **"If the Vice President is nominated":** Newfield, 275.

419 **McCarthy and Kennedy appeared together:** Ibid., 277.

419 **"an electronic tennis game":** "Perhaps an Earnest Hunt for Pertinence Would Be More Helpful Than Debates."

421 **Al Lowenstein, continued to dream:** Perlstein, Nixonland, 270.

422 **Juan Romero:** Background on and quotations from Romero are drawn from "The Busboy Who Cradled a Dying RFK Has Finally Stepped Out of the Past."

423 **Roosevelt Grier:** For Grier's memories, see "Rosey Grier on the Kennedy Assassination," and Pilkington. For Grier's role in protecting Ethel Kennedy, see Kaiser, chapter one.

424 **"What I think is":** Excerpts are taken from "June 5, 1968: RFK's California Victory Speech."

425 **"I saw Kennedy lurch":** Hamill.

Chapter Twenty-Four: Stop Nixon

429 **The funeral was at St. Patrick's:** Newfield, 303–4, and Thomas, **Robert Kennedy,** 392–4.

429 **"My brother need not be idealized":** Kennedy, "Address at the Public Memorial Service for Robert F. Kennedy."

430 **McCarthy had the most trouble adjusting:** Abigail McCarthy, 406–8.

430 **McCarthy met with Humphrey:** Sandbrook, 205.

431 **two Nelson Rockefellers:** The account of Rockefeller's belated rush toward the convention is drawn from White, 272–5, and Smith, 529–36.

432 **"Thass right, man, thass right!":** White, 273.

432 **Rockefeller was met by an excited crowd:** Mailer, **Miami and the Siege of Chicago,** 19–24.

433 **Miami Beach had no factories:** The description of Miami Beach in 1968 is drawn from Chester, Hodgson, and Page, 429–31; White, 275–7; and Mailer, **Miami and the Siege of Chicago,** 11–15.

434 **The Chamber of Commerce had been working hard:** Chester, Hodgson, and Page, 431.

434 **The police department intended:** Ibid., 431–2, reviews the police and other security organizations' precautions.

436 **Even boring:** White emphasizes the deliberate sense of placidity and tedium, 282–3, e.g., and contrasts the mood to that of untelevised conventions of the past.

437 **gavel-to-gavel coverage:** Perlstein, **Nixonland**, 304, notes that only CBS and NBC could afford complete coverage.

439 **he had been campaigning:** The ensuing account of the Greeneville Group's strategy and Reagan's role in appealing to Southern conservatives relies on Chester, Hodgson, and Page, 437–48.

442 **Nixon had been getting worried:** Ibid., 446–8, for Nixon's relationship to the Southern bosses and Strom Thurmond.

442 **"Well, where is he?":** Ibid., 447.

444 **"Never let up on the Communists":** Thomas, **Being Nixon**, 159, covers the car ride; Perlstein, **Nixonland**, 299, documents the Nixon-Thurmond agreements.

444 **"I love Reagan":** Chester, Hodgson, and Page, 448.

445 **Reagan had kept saying he wasn't running:** Ibid., 442.

445 **startled Governor John Volpe:** Ibid., 443.

445 **Reagan dropped in on eight state delegations:**
     See ibid., 448–9, for Reagan's July maneuvers, em-
     phasizing the term "drop in"; and 449–50 for his
     arrivals in and departures from Chicago.

446 NIXON OVERTAKES HUMPHREY AND MᴄCARTHY:
     Ibid., 392, details Rockefeller's thinking regarding
     polling; White, 278–9, explains the Rockefeller-
     Reagan "erosion" strategy.

Chapter Twenty-Five: "Great Television"

449 **The front-runner arrived in Miami Beach:**
     Mailer, **Miami and the Siege of Chicago**, 40–1,
     and Chester, Hodgson, and Page, 456.

450 **Invincible and inevitable:** Nixon's assets and
     advantages and the style of the convention cam-
     paign are detailed in Chester, Hodgson, and Page,
     455–6. White, 280–2, provides details on the
     modern, technical efficiency at Nixon headquar-
     ters.

452 **a group of Southern delegations:** Chester,
     Hodgson, and Page, 457–9, describes the South-
     ern delegates' worries and Mitchell's efforts to
     mollify them.

453 **Reagan was making the rounds:** Ibid., 449–50,
     457–9, covers Reagan's maneuvers on Monday
     and Monday night.

453 **"It's very difficult to disagree":** Ibid., 449.

454 **"Gosh, I was surprised!":** Ibid., 450.

454 **Mitchell's team was always a step ahead:** Ibid.,

455–6, describes the size and the tactical superiority of Nixon's floor team.

455 **couldn't have been more bland:** Both White, 383–4, and Perlstein, **Nixonland**, 297, underscore the dullness of the mood on Monday night.

455 **huddled pockets of Southern delegates:** Chester, Hodgson, and Page, 458, point to the real Monday-night action.

456 **Strom Thurmond was with Nixon and Mitchell:** The meeting and its panicky mood are described in ibid., 459–61, with specific reference to the Southern delegations' concerns about both "guidelines" and the running-mate pick.

456 **Nixon met with the Southerners:** Ibid., 461–5. Perlstein, **Nixonland**, 299–300, calls the substance of Nixon's promises "Dixiecrat."

458 **"The dam will break!":** Chester, Hodgson, and Page, 466.

459 **Spiro Agnew:** Agnew's background is drawn largely from Witcover, **White Knight**, chapters 2 and 3.

459 **"I have difficulty imagining myself":** Ibid., 149.

460 **Ted Agnew adored Rocky:** Ibid., chapter 9, closely follows the course of Agnew's promotion of Rockefeller as discussed here.

462 **"That's pretty definite":** Ibid., 188.

464 **"Has anybody told Agnew?":** Ibid., 198, reports Hinman's and Abraham's conversation.

464 **Nixon had already started calling:** Ibid., chapter 10, follows Agnew's developing support of Nixon.

464 **"Very seriously":** Ibid., 207.

465 **placing Nixon's name in nomination:** Ibid., 222, dates the request to mid-July.

465 **"vigorously" endorsing Nixon:** Ibid., 223–4.

465 **The Florida delegation:** Chester, Hodgson, and Page, 467–9, relates the struggle over the Florida delegation and states that most of the women in the delegation were "crazy for Reagan."

466 **"get Strom's ass over here":** Ibid., 468.

467 **The Nixon plan had been to pressure Alabama:** Ibid., 469–70, details the Alabama strategy and the decision to favor California instead.

468 **where could they hunt?:** Ibid., 470–2, on the Nixon team's last-ditch delegate hunting, with Romney's refusal and Case's battle.

471 **the band played "Dixie":** Mailer, **Miami and the Siege of Chicago**, 66–7.

472 **intense ten-minute nightly debates:** For an overview of the circumstances of the debates, see Buckley and Vidal, **Buckley vs. Vidal**, Introduction.

474 **"Tonight the key question":** Excerpts quoted from Buckley and Vidal, **Buckley vs. Vidal**, Debate 3, August 5, 1968.

476 **"Great television":** "The Buckley vs. Vidal Debates: The Original Knock-down, Drag-out TV."

477 **Reagan people found new hope:** Chester, Hodgson, and Page, 473–4; Perlstein, **Nixonland**, 301, with the Oberdorfer story.

478 **the roll-call vote began:** Chester, Hodgson, and Page, 474.

478 **Rockefeller watched:** White, 289–90.

Chapter Twenty-Six:
The Last Liberal Standing

480 **Richard Nixon was in his penthouse:** White, 292, and Witcover, **Resurrection of Richard Nixon,** 347.

480 **The final score:** Chester, Hodgson, and Page, 475, calling the tally "the final scorecard." Perlstein, **Nixonland,** 301, notes the comparative narrowness of victory.

481 **"Ronnie didn't do as well":** White, 290, reports the Nixon-Rockefeller call.

481 **Ronald Reagan left his trailer:** Perlstein, **Nixonland,** 302, and Mailer, **Miami and the Siege of Chicago,** 70.

482 **"I won the nomination":** Mailer, **Miami and the Siege of Chicago,** 69–70.

482 **John Lindsay:** Background on Lindsay is drawn from Cannato, chapter 1; Roberts, chapter 3; and Pileggi. Lindsay's operation and strategy at Miami Beach are detailed in Chester, Hodgson, and Page, 493–4.

484 **Lindsay sent Nixon a note:** White, 293n3.

484 **the vice presidential nomination:** For the late-night penthouse meetings, see Chester, Hodg-

son, and Page, 485–8; White, 292–3; and Witcover, **White Knight**, 225–6. For the morning meeting, see Chester, Hodgson, and Page, 488–9; White, 293–4; and Witcover, **White Knight**, 227. For the final meeting, see Chester, Hodgson, and Page, 489–90; White, 294–5; and Witcover, **White Knight**, 227–8.

487 **his numbers went down:** Perlstein, **Nixonland**, 302, and Witcover, **Resurrection of Richard Nixon**, 351.

487 **Nixon already knew:** Witcover, **Resurrection of Richard Nixon**, 349–50.

488 **"We seem to have come down":** Chester, Hodgson, and Page, 489.

488 **"put in a call to Ted Agnew":** Ibid., 490.

488 **which one he would prefer:** Ibid., 489–90.

489 **"some kind of disease":** "The Unlikely No. 2."

489 **"Are you sitting down?":** Witcover, **White Knight**, 229, with the Agnews' travel plans and Nixon's subsequent press conference.

490 **"a darn good man":** Ibid., 231.

491 **"the South did have veto power":** Chester, Hodgson, and Page, 482.

491 **last-ditch rebellion:** The ensuing account of the dump-Agnew effort is drawn from ibid., 493–5; Pileggi, 44; and Cannato, 382–5.

493 **"How many votes do you have?":** Chester, Hodgson, and Page, 495.

493 **Brownell put the situation to Lindsay:** Pileggi, 44, is the sole source for the scene in the trailer.

495 **One of the most remarkable effects:** The exchange is excerpted from Buckley and Vidal, **Buckley vs. Vidal,** Debate 6, Thursday, August 8, 1968.

495 **riots broke out across the bay:** Mailer, **Miami and the Serge of Chicago,** 81.

Chapter Twenty-Seven: The Peace Plank

497 **The Stevens was the biggest hotel:** Information on the Stevens and its transformation to the Hilton is drawn from Allegrini, chapters 5 and 6.

498 **McCarthy arrived in Chicago:** White, 315.

500 **he sometimes felt like a charlatan:** For McCarthy's depression, self-doubt, and crisis, see Abigail McCarthy, 407, and Sandbrook, 230–1.

500 **there was no work to get back to:** For the RFK assassination as a source of McCarthy's rudderlessness, see Sandbrook, 203–7.

501 **Clark . . . was fired four times:** Ibid., 206, covers the firings.

502 **"just going through the motions":** "Interview with Senator Eugene McCarthy, 1968 Democratic Party Contender."

502 **McCarthy canceled three scheduled meetings:** Sandbrook, 207.

502 **Gene and Abigail were barely speaking:** Ibid., 206, discusses the strained state of the marriage and rumors of Gene's affair.

502 **Abigail's absence from the campaign:** Abigail McCarthy, 406–10, and Sandbrook, 206.

503 **"What was different":** White, xxi.

504 **Coalition for an Open Convention (COC):** Chafe, 300, 305 (referring to the organization as the National Coalition for an Open Convention); Cummings, 372–5, detailing Lowenstein's tension with both the radicals and McCarthy himself; Farber, 100, on the radicals' negative attitudes toward COC. For McCarthy's efforts to manage the influx of students, see White, 314–5, and Farber, 110.

504 **Mayor Richard Daley:** The account of Daley's background and attitudes is drawn from Chester, Hodgson, and Page, 503–12; Farber, 119; Royko; and Cohen and Taylor.

505 **demanding women be given the right to vote:** Cohen and Taylor, 22.

505 **"I didn't raise my son to be a policeman":** Royko, 45.

507 **"They have vilified me":** Chester, Hodgson, and Page, 504.

507 **"Write what he means":** "Chicago Journal; Syntax Is a Loser in Mayoral Race."

507 **"shoot to kill":** "Shoot to Kill, Shoot to Maim."

507 **Crossing Richard Daley was unthinkable:** Farber, 115, detailing the bases of Daley's clout.

508 **MOBE began reaching out in June:** For Davis's and Hayden's efforts and Daley's and the city's responses, see ibid., 101–2, 150–1.

508 **"See you in Chicago":** Ibid., 105.

508 **"Nobody is going to take over this city":** Ibid., 122.

509 **Everywhere Hubert Humphrey went:** Solberg, 342–3.

509 **his position seemed painfully and unfairly precarious:** Chester, Hodgson, and Page, 568.

509 **Johnson's tone was not reassuring:** Solberg, 339, and White, 379.

510 **LBJ was micromanaging:** Solberg, 357; Chester, Hodgson, and Page, 543–4; White, 317–8.

510 **Johnson slighted Humphrey:** White, 325.

510 **Mayor Daley was no more excited:** Ibid., 328.

511 **He barely commented on the urban riots:** Solberg, 342.

512 **The debate in the Rules Committee:** The account of maneuvers in and around the Rules Committee is drawn largely from White, 319–20, seeing the Humphrey strategy as largely successful; and Chester, Hodgson, and Page, 557–9, more skeptically reviewing the interplay among Humphrey, Connally, Goodwin, and McCarthy, and presenting the Humphrey campaign as flailing.

514 **The Credentials Committee had to decide:** Discussion of battles in the Credentials Committee is drawn largely from Chester, Hodgson, and Page, 544–56, for Joseph Rauh's strategy, the conflict over seating the Georgia delegation, and the compromise imposed by Chairman Hughes; White, 320–1, for a concise overall view; and Richardson,

157–8, for the Maddox-Bond dispute. All sources make reference to the legacy of the Mississippi Freedom Delegation's experiences at the '64 convention.

515 **regulars could accept a Nixon win:** Chester, Hodgson, and Page, 544–8, 550.

515 **"I implore you not to be so stupid.":** Ibid., 547.

515 **a single man was empowered:** White, 320.

515 **"You mean this is how the system works?":** Chester, Hodgson, and Page, 549.

516 **"I said all along the system doesn't work":** Ibid.

516 **"Achieve panic":** Ibid., 551.

516 **"You've got to stop those kids":** Ibid.

516 **Sam Brown and Curtis Gans led:** Ibid., 552–3, with reference as well to Mixner's remark.

516 **Geoffrey Cowan:** White, 320.

517 **Rauh's strategy:** Background on Rauh is drawn from "Joseph Rauh Jr., Groundbreaking Civil Liberties Lawyer, Dies at 81."

520 **"When Strom Thurmond escorted Richard Nixon":** "Remarks, Vice President Hubert H. Humphrey."

521 **"aren't worth the gunpowder that's needed to blow them up":** Stricherz, 84. For Rauh's conflicts with younger McCarthy supporters, see Chester, Hodgson, and Page, 554.

522 **Julian Bond:** Richardson, 157–8. Chester, Hodgson, and Page, 555–6, discusses the positive impression Bond made and Hughes's tactics in imposing the compromise.

524 **the Platform Committee:** The account of the peace plank and its fate in the committee is largely drawn from Chester, Hodgson, and Page, 524–37, and White, 321–6.

525 **Johnson had three conditions:** LBJ's positions and maneuvering regarding the Paris peace process are covered by Dallek, **Flawed Giant**, 536–43.

526 **a peace plank would help:** For Gilligan's and the peace-plank coalition's meetings and tactics, see Chester, Hodgson, and Page, 525–8.

527 **"It would be like throwing a child":** Ibid., 526.

527 **Humphrey would have to arrive:** Humphrey's flailings over his Vietnam position and LBJ's manipulations are detailed by Solberg, 348–51.

528 **"I'll have to show it to the President":** Ibid., 348.

528 **the president met with Richard Nixon:** Hughes, 11–14, details the July 26 meeting; also see Dallek, **Flawed Giant**, 571. Also see the full transcript in U.S. Department of State Archive, **Foreign Relations of the United States, 1964–1968, Volume VI, Vietnam, January–August 1968,** Document 310.

530 **Johnson believed he was on the verge:** Solberg, 349–50.

531 **Richard Nixon was keeping his own secret:** The account of the Chennault affair in this and the next chapter is drawn from the scrupulous reporting and analysis of Hughes, 1–67, as supported with new and even more fully incontro-

vertible evidence in Farrell, 343n, with reference to H. R. Haldeman's contemporaneous notes.

531 **secret meeting:** Sources differ on when and where the meeting took place: Chennault remembered a snowy day; Diem remembered Friday, July 12 (scholars generally credit his accuracy); Chennault placed the meeting at Nixon's apartment; Diem placed it at Nixon's campaign headquarters.

534 **Johnson called him with congratulations:** Hughes, 15–17.

534 **Nixon and Agnew arrived on August 7:** Ibid., 17; also see the transcript in "Notes of Meeting (327)."

535 **Johnson summoned Humphrey:** Solberg, 349–50, covers the August 8 meeting and quotes Kearns as "saddened."

536 **McGovern announced his candidacy:** "Senator McGovern Ready to Run Against Humphrey."

536 **"the goals for which Robert Kennedy gave his life":** "McGovern Opens Presidential Bid with Peace Plea," with the ensuing quotations on RFK's legacy, the applause of RFK supporters, and the endorsements by top RFK men.

537 **McCarthy people saw McGovern as a shill:** for tensions between the McGovern and the McCarthy campaigns, see Sandbrook, 228; Chester, Hodgson, and Bowles, 560–62; and "A New Way to Scuttle Eugene McCarthy."

538 **"He indicated that he would be satisfied":**

"Senator McGovern Ready to Run Against Humphrey."

538 **Humphrey went off script:** Chester, Hodgson, and Page, 529–30, also describing the RFK team's reaction.

538 **Hale Boggs told . . . David Ginsburg:** Solberg, 351.

539 **establishment support for the peace plank:** Chester, Hodgson, and Page, 530.

539 **"You can take this down":** Hughes, 17–8, reports the August 20 Johnson-Nixon conversation.

539 **the president had been too slow:** Dallek, **Flawed Giant,** 542.

540 **"not a major crisis":** Chester, Hodgson, and Page, 532, also with reference to McCarthy's later clarification.

540 **"Ken, I expected all the other fools":** Ibid., 560.

540 **The Platform Committee moved to Chicago:** Ibid., 532–7, details the machinations described here by which LBJ and Boggs rendered the peace plank a minority position.

Chapter Twenty-Eight:
"The Whole World's Watching"

544 **reconsidering his decision:** LBJ's reasons for a possible reversal, as related here, are drawn from Dallek, **Flawed Giant,** 569–72, and Goodwin, **Lyndon Johnson and the American Dream,** 350–1.

544 **"Nixon can be beaten":** Goodwin, Lyndon Johnson and the American Dream, 351.

544 **"I'm for a draft":** Dallek, Flawed Giant, 572.

545 **the situation on Chicago's streets:** Farber, 160–5, details mutual escalation between the city and the protest organizers, with numbers of armed officers and threats and preparations by organizers.

545 **"The North Vietnamese are shedding blood":** Davis, 79, citing an FBI memorandum.

546 **headquartered in Lincoln Park:** Farber, 166–7, describes the scene in the park and the "Seed" offices.

546 **"chicks who can type":** Ibid., 166.

546 **the park would be officially closed:** Davis, 49.

547 **The officers shot him three times:** Farber, 165.

547 **nominate a pig:** Ibid., 165–8, relating the event and reactions. Also see Rubin, "Inside the Great Pigasus Plot."

547 **MOBE . . . occupied an office downtown:** For MOBE's thinking, see Farber, 166–7, 168–9.

548 **more than 5,000 National Guardsmen:** Ibid., 169–70, for numbers and movements of troops.

549 **The strategic question of the day:** Ibid., 172.

549 **Allen Ginsberg arrived:** Ibid., 173, and "Testimony of Allen Ginsberg."

549 **"The park isn't worth dying for":** Farber, 173–4, with arguments among the leaders.

549 **"do what is necessary":** Ibid., 174.

549 **When darkness fell:** Ibid., 174–5, for the evacuation of the park on Saturday night.

550 **the protesters walked on sidewalks:** Ibid., 175–7, for the Sunday march and rally at Grant Park.

551 **"We had the power":** Ibid., 177.

551 **The music festival:** The account of the music festival and the evening confrontation in Lincoln Park on Sunday is drawn from ibid., 177–83, and "Testimony of Allen Ginsberg."

553 **troops from Fort Hood:** White, 328.

553 **a seating chart:** For both the seating and the microphones, see Chester, Hodgson, and Page, 541–2, and Mailer, **Miami and the Siege of Chicago,** 115.

553 **Ted Kennedy had publicly announced:** The account of the draft-Ted movement's acceleration and its ultimate fate relies on Chester, Hodgson, and Page, 564–76, and White, 330–2.

553 **"I pick up a fallen standard":** "Kennedy Attacks Vietnam Policy; Asks End of Hate."

556 **"we might do it together":** Chester, Hodgson, and Page, 571.

557 **floor fight erupted over the unit rule:** White, 329.

557 **the Credentials Committee's turn:** Ibid., 332–4.

558 **Albert finally gaveled the first session:** Ibid., 329.

558 **McCarthy asked Dick Goodwin yet again:** Chester, Hodgson, and Page, 572–5, covers the cli-

max and denouement of the McCarthy-Kennedy negotiation. Also see White, 332.

559 "I can't make it": Chester, Hodgson, and Page, 572, based on Goodwin's memory, and with "I don't think I can make it," based on that of the journalist Peter Maas.

559 "I never could have done it for Bobby": White, 332.

560 No one in the Kennedy camp trusted Gene McCarthy: For varying interpretations of McCarthy's motivations and the failure of the negotiations, see Chester, Hodgson, and Page, 575–6, and White, 332.

562 The CBS report: Chester, Hodgson, and Page, 574.

562 finally resolve all the credentials fights: Richardson, 159, not closely distinguishing between the events of Monday and Tuesday evenings.

563 Dan Rather . . . was shoved to the floor: White, 333, and "The Democratic National Convention, 1968" (excerpt).

563 Albert turned to the Platform Committee's report: White, 335, covers the conflict on the floor and the postponement. For the role of the Wisconsin delegation in leading resistance and the maneuvers of Albert, Daley, and Bailey, see "Democrats Delay Fight on the Vietnam Plank; Kennedy Rejects Draft."

564 "held for the delegates": "Democrats Delay Fight on the Vietnam Plank; Kennedy Rejects Draft," with the observation that "the galleries were visibly less than half-full, and most of the uproar was coming from the floor."

565 **rioting in Lincoln Park had become ritualized:** For Tuesday night in Lincoln Park, see Farber, 191–2.

565 **"The whole world's watching":** Ibid., 187.

565 **"perhaps they refused to obey":** Ibid., 188.

566 **"pick up a crowbar":** Ibid., 190.

566 **Tuesday night in Grant Park:** Ibid., 192–4.

566 **"by any means necessary":** Ibid., 192.

566 **Lyndon Johnson had told reporters:** "The President's News Conference Held on His 60th Birthday at Austin, Texas, August 27, 1968."

566 **his future slipped away on TV:** Dallek, **Flawed Giant**, 573, covers the decision not to attend.

Chapter Twenty-Nine:
"The Government of the People in Exile"

569 **a mimeographed list:** Chester, Hodgson, and Page, 579–80, covers the peace-plank proceedings, with the list, Zablocki's remarks, the arguments pro and con, and the vote tally.

570 **"would substitute beards for brains":** Ibid., 580.

570 **They were distraught:** For the floor protests, see ibid., 581, and Mailer, **Miami and the Siege of Chicago**, 164–5.

572 **MOBE had the permit:** The account of Wednesday afternoon's permitted rally's developing into

the police riot of Wednesday evening is drawn from Mailer, **Miami and the Siege of Chicago**, 165–78; Farber, 195–203; White, 344–52; and Chester, Hodgson, and Page, 582–3.

572 **Thirty police formed a wedge:** Chester, Hodgson, and Page, 582.

572 **flipped down their face shields:** Mailer, **Miami and the Siege of Chicago**, 167.

573 **telling the crowd to remain calm:** Ibid., 166, with the targeted attack on Davis. Also see Farber, 196.

573 **"Go in, fella":** Chester, Hodgson, and Page, 582.

573 **Dave Dellinger, always the pacifist:** Farber, 196.

573 **"if blood is going to flow":** Ibid., 196–7.

573 **the National Guard was moving into the park:** Ibid., 197–8.

574 **Allen Ginsberg now addressed the crowd:** Mailer, **Miami and the Siege of Chicago**, 167.

574 **Despite every police tactic:** Ibid., 167–8, with descriptions of the park's layout.

574 **three mule-drawn wagons:** Ibid., 168, with "Join us!"; Farber, 199.

575 **police had formed a line:** For the climactic "battle of Michigan Avenue," see Farber, 199–202; Mailer, **Miami and the Siege of Chicago**, 168–72; Chester, Hodgson, and Page, 582–3; White, 346–51.

575 **"What's holding us up":** White, 347.

575 **"Fuck you, LBJ!":** White, 348, and Farber, 199.

575 **Gene McCarthy was on the twenty-third floor:** White, 351–2, covers McCarthy's view and reactions.

575 **police officers suddenly charged:** Ibid., 348–9; Mailer, **Miami and the Siege of Chicago,** 168–9; Farber, 200–1 (with "Kill! Kill! Kill!").

576 **"If I go down I claim them":** White, 352.

576 **up against the plate-glass window:** Mailer, **Miami and the Siege of Chicago,** 170–1, quoting Jack Newfield.

577 **"This is just the beginning":** Ibid., 171, quoting Newfield.

577 **"The Democrats are finished":** White, 348.

577 **"The whole world is watching!":** Ibid., 349.

577 **began to watch at about 9:30 p.m.:** Farber, 210; Chester, Hodgson, and Page, 583; White, 350.

578 **mirroring the increased police aggressiveness:** Chester, Hodgson, and Page, 581, detailing control measures in the hall.

578 **"They were trying to tear them":** "A Time to Remember: Turmoil of Chicago."

578 **Paul O'Dwyer jumped into the ruckus:** Chester, Hodgson, and Page, 583, with Wallace getting hit.

578 **Channing Phillips's:** Ibid., 585.

579 **suddenly the TV screen was filled:** White, 352–3.

579 **"his police-state tactics":** Chester, Hodgson, and Page, 584.

579 **"People's rights are being abused":** White, 353.

579 **Chicago was now flowing with blood:** Ibid., 353.

579 **"The basic problem that we face":** Ribicoff, "Speech Nominating George McGovern for the U.S. Presidency."

581 **it took a second:** Mailer, **Miami and the Siege of Chicago,** 180–1, offers the most graphic description of the moment.

581 **"Fuck you, you Jew son of a bitch!":** Mailer, **Miami and the Siege of Chicago,** 180, and Chester, Hodgson, and Page, 584–5, report the general purport of Daley's remark without quoting it (Mailer: "telling Ribicoff to go have carnal relations with himself"); the latter notes that "millions of lip-reading television viewers" saw Daley use "an expression he was said never to use." Perlstein, 327, **Nixonland,** gives the wording as rendered here. Royko, 189, does also, while giving Daley supporters' denials and suggesting, contra Chester, Hodgson, and Page, that only one lip-reader came up with the quotation.

582 **Buckley-versus-Vidal debate:** Excerpts quoted from Buckley and Vidal, **Buckley vs. Vidal,** Debate 10, August 28, 1968, with "I guess we gave them their money's worth" in the editor's note.

587 **"My God," Haldeman said:** White, 374.

587 **events on the street began reaching Hubert Humphrey:** Ibid., 339–44 and 352–6, tracks Humphrey's movement's on Wednesday. Also see Chester, Hodgson, and Page, 584–85.

588 **"I'm going to be president someday":** White, 353.

588 **"they've been brought in":** Chester, Hodgson, and Page, 585.

589 **Gene McCarthy's operational center:** Ibid.,

with McCarthy's effort to withdraw his name from nomination, and White, 359–60.

589 **"I feel like really jumping":** White, 353–4, reporting the artificiality of Humphrey's joy; Chester, Hodgson, and Page, 585, report the whoop.

589 **final delegate tally:** Chester, Hodgson, and Page, 585.

590 **"No! No! No!":** Ibid., 586, with the candlelight march and McCarthy's press conference.

590 **"I may be visibly moved":** For the speech at the Hilton, see "Eugene McCarthy, Who Galvanized a Generation of War Opponents, Dies"; "McCarthy Pledges Drive Will Go On.

590 **"McCarthy left the Hilton:** "McCarthy Pledges Drive Will Go On."

591 **With police lines surrounding Grant Park:** Farber, 202, describes the overnight and Thursday scenes in the park.

591 **McCarthy made his way to the microphone:** For McCarthy's Grant Park speech and interaction with the crowd, see "McCarthy Pledges Drive Will Go On," and Chester, Hodgson, and Page, 588–9.

Chapter Thirty: The Perfect Crime

593 **Dick Gregory led a march:** Farber, 204.

593 **"One cannot help but reflect":** "Humphrey's 1968 DNC Acceptance Speech."

595 **Nixon was ahead by fifteen points:** White, 385,

and Chester, Hodgson, and Page, 610, on presumptions of a sweep.

595 **were it not for George Wallace:** White, 387.

596 **Wallace led a march through Chicago:** Ibid., 406–8.

596 **The Cicero crowd:** For the 1951 riots, see "The Time Bomb That Exploded in Cicero: Segregated Housing's Inevitable Dividend."

596 **"Shoot 'em, kill 'em!":** White, 408, with the other invective quoted here.

597 **"It was as if somewhere, sometime":** Carter, 344.

597 **because he told it like it was:** White, 425.

597 **"I don't talk about race or segregation":** Chester, Hodgson, and Page, 622.

598 **not try to "out-Wallace Wallace":** White, 385, with the Nixon electoral strategy outlined here; also see Chester, Hodgson, and Page, 620–1.

598 **"committed rape in public":** White, 385.

599 **Kevin Phillips saw only Massachusetts:** Chester, Hodgson, and Page, 621.

599 **Mitchell's hyperdisciplined management:** White, 381–4, details the campaign's efficiencies and amenities, with attention to Haldeman's role.

601 **On the ground, the New Nixon:** Ibid., 378–80, covers Nixon's speeches, crowds, and rhetoric.

601 **"those who indulge in violence":** Ibid., 379.

601 **"forgotten Americans":** Ibid.

601 **Nixon avoided specific policy positions:** Ibid., 386–8. For "the secret plan," see Safire.

602 **Following Roger Ailes's strategy:** Chester, Hodgson, and Page, 687–8, with "the Nixon format."

604 **retired air force major general Curtis LeMay:** Background on LeMay is drawn from ibid., 694–6, and "George Wallace: Settin' the Woods on Fire."

604 **"bomb them back into the Stone Age":** Chester, Hodgson, and Page, 695.

605 **"we seem to have a phobia":** Ibid., 699, and "George Wallace: Settin' the Woods on Fire."

605 **"It doesn't make much difference to me":** For this and LeMay's other extended quotations, see "George Wallace: Settin' the Woods on Fire."

606 **Lawrence O'Brien:** For O'Brien as Humphrey's manager, see Chester, Hodgson, and Page, 632–3; White, 394–7; Solberg, 377–8.

607 **Humphrey defended Mayor Daley's police:** For the flailing and reversals in Humphrey's speeches, see White, 390–1, with Johnson's and Rusk's contradictions. Also see Chester, Hodgson, and Page, 633–4.

607 **the wrath of antiwar protesters:** White, 391–3, detailing the chanting and profanity.

608 **"We're broke, Hubert":** Perlstein, **Nixonland,** 347.

608 **bad day campaigning in Seattle:** White, 412.

609 **Salt Lake meeting:** For the speechwriting process, see ibid., 413–5, and Chester, Hodgson, and Page, 643–8, with major differences. Chester, Hodgson, and Page dates Ball's influence on the process to an earlier point than the Salt Lake meeting and says that Ball had left by the time the speech was drafted and could only be contacted by phone; White places Ball's arrival in Salt Lake City on September 30, the day after the late-night drafting session. For the DNC funding, see White, 414.

610 Humphrey called Johnson: Hughes, 21–2, reports the conversation based on recordings that contradict Humphrey's later assertion, followed also by White, that he'd given Johnson some advance warning; that the president made no overt objections and accepted, grudgingly, Humphrey's independence; and that Humphrey admitted Harriman's input.

610 Nixon had called the president: Hughes, 20–1.

610 "I would be willing to stop the bombing": Chester, Hodgson, and Page, 649.

611 antiwar Democrats came Humphrey's way: White, 415–6, details the financial upswing and the endorsements.

611 "My decision to endorse": New York Times, November 3, 1968.

612 Ed Muskie, was sent on the attack: White, 418–9. For the ads, see "1968: Nixon vs. Humphrey vs. Wallace."

612 "a man who promised": "1968: Nixon vs. Humphrey vs. Wallace."

613 With the help of union leadership: White, 426.

614 Nixon flew to Bebe Rebozo's home: Ibid., 432–5, detailing the substance and results of the Key West meeting.

615 "If you've seen one slum": Ibid., 433, with Agnew's other remarks quoted here.

616 "We might be able to do much more": Hughes, 25.

616 Nixon called the president: Ibid., 26.

617 The secret breakthrough in Paris: The first news of a breakthrough coincided almost exactly with Nixon's Vietnam speech and the follow-up phone call. See ibid., 26–33, detailing the sudden behind-the-scenes progress and LBJ's cautious, conflicted pursuit of resolution. White, 440–2, covers the same ground, lacking some of Hughes's White House information but with close attention to foreign diplomacy.

618 briefing the presidential candidates: Hughes, 30.

618 Everett Dirksen called the president: Ibid., 32–3.

619 "This," said Nixon, "I do not believe": Ibid., 33.

619 went fully negative on Nixon: Ibid., 33–4.

619 Johnson finally agreed with his advisers: Ibid., 35–7, with the Russian recommitment and Abrams meeting.

620 some disturbing news: Ibid., 4–8, detailing the Sachs allegation about Mitchell, the Rusk call about Thieu, and LBJ's pursuit of what became known as "the Chennault affair."

621 The president called the FBI: Ibid., 38–9, with the wiretaps and Chennault's movements.

621 Johnson called Senator Dirksen: Ibid., 39–40.

622 his regular briefing conference call: Ibid.,

40–3, with LBJ's subsequent private call with Humphrey.

625 **"Do not turn your back"**: "An Appeal from Black Americans."

627 **"falls far short"**: "McCarthy Backs Humphrey Race."

628 **"I'm voting for Humphrey"**: Wills, 445.

628 **"I speak to you this evening"**: "Text of President Johnson's Broadcast to the Nation Announcing a Bombing Halt."

630 **"Neither he nor I will destroy"**: Hughes, 43.

630 **John Mitchell called Anna Chennault**: Chennault, 190–1.

630 **"We will only talk to them"**: "Thieu Says Saigon Cannot Join Paris Talks Under Present Plan."

631 **"her boss"**: Hughes, 46.

631 **"In view of recent reports"**: Ibid.

631 **"reached an explicit agreement with Thieu"**: "Lyndon Johnson and Everett Dirksen on 2 November 1968."

634 **"Mr. President, this is Dick Nixon"**: "Lyndon Johnson and Richard Nixon on 3 November 1968."

636 **Rostow urged Johnson to expose**: Farrell, 344.

637 **"Some elements of this story"**: Hughes, 54–5, with the exchange among LBJ, Rusk, and Clifford.

639 **"Keep Anna Chennault working"**: Farrell, 343.

639 **"Any other way to monkey wrench it?"**: Ibid., 344.

639 **"LBJ called Dirksen"**: Ibid., n. 643.

640 **"any contact with the South Vietnamese":** Hughes, 167–8.

640 **Roger Ailes produced Nixon's telethon:** Brownell, 191.

640 **Humphrey's telethon:** Ibid., 189–90.

641 **It all came down to Illinois:** Chester, Hodgson, and Page, 759–62, cover the state-by-state electoral issues, with attention to Illinois.

642 **decided by less than 1 percent:** White, 462, with vote tallies.

642 **"I, as you probably have heard, have received":** "President-Elect Richard Nixon Declares Victory in 1968."

644 **"Goddamn it, go in and get those files":** Hughes, 2.

646 **"There are many fine careers":** "President Nixon Farewell to Staff."

648 **pardon "carries an imputation of guilt":** "For Ford, Pardon Decision Was Always Clear-Cut."

Epilogue

649 **John Mitchell:** "John N. Mitchell Dies at 75; Major Figure in Watergate."

649 **Richard Kleindienst:** "Richard G. Kleindienst, Figure in Watergate Era, Dies at 76."

651 **"Sometimes I wish":** "Martinis, Steak and History."

651 **"Make America Great Again":** "How Don-

ald Trump Came Up with 'Make America Great Again.'"

651 **John Lindsay:** "John V. Lindsay, Mayor and Maverick, Dies at 79."

652 **Roger Ailes:** Greenburg. Also see "More Trouble at Fox News: Ailes Faces New Sexual Claims and O'Reilly Loses Two Advertisers."

652 **Pat Buchanan:** "Biography."

653 **"America First":** For Buchanan's adoption of the slogan, see Buchanan, "A Crossroads in Our Country's History." For its anti-Semitic 1930s overtones, see Calamur.

653 **"If Kagan is confirmed":** Buchanan, "Are Liberals Anti-WASP?"

654 **"my Jew boy":** Merkley, 73.

654 **"God damn his Jewish soul!":** "Nixon White House Tapes—Online," Tape 45, May 1, 1973. www.nixonlibrary.gov/forresearchers/find/tapes /tape045/045-093.mp3.

654 **"No Jews":** Reeve.

654 **"Jews are disloyal":** "New Tapes Reveal Depth of Nixon's Anti-Semitism."

654 **black people wouldn't be able:** Reeve.

654 **"The Irish can't drink":** See "In Tapes, Nixon Rails About Jews and Blacks," also with reference to Nixon's characterization of Italians.

655 **"When I took one look":** "Pat Buchanan on NBC's Today Show, Thursday, November 9, 2000."

655 **"The ideas made it":** Alberta.

655 **Nguyen Van Thieu:** "Nguyen Van Thieu, 78;

S. Vietnam's President." See Bass for Thieu's life in exile. "Nguyen Van Thieu Is Dead at 76; Last President of South Vietnam" has the sightings at the Neponset Reservoir.

657 **"They told the stories of times":** Kerry, "Statement Before the Senate Foreign Relations Committee." Discrepancies between the source's transcript and recording have been corrected here.

658 **two U.S. Marines were killed:** For Charles McMahon, see Toussaint. For Darwin Lee Judge, see "Judge, Darwin Lee."

659 **21,195 Americans were killed:** Garcia.

659 **Close to half a million American tourists:** See "International Visitors to Viet Nam in December and 12 Months of 2015."

659 **at least 1.3 million:** The figure, based on research by Guenter Lewy, widely reported, is generally viewed as conservative. For discussion of varying ranges and sources, see Valentine.

659 **"It depends on who writes the history":** Farrell, 559.

660 **Hubert Humphrey called Lyndon Johnson:** "Humphrey Calls LBJ After Losing to Nixon: Nov. 6, 1968, 11:32 A.M."

661 **The first time Richard Nixon set foot:** "Carter Leads Tributes as Thousands Pass By Coffin in Rotunda." Also see Solberg, 456. For the prayer, see "Peace Prayer of Saint Francis."

662 **Ed Muskie:** "Edmund S. Muskie, 81, Dies; Maine Senator and a Power on the National Scene."

662 **George Wallace:** "George Wallace, Segregation Symbol, Dies at 79."

662 **"I was wrong":** Edwards, Wattenberg, and Lineberr, 76. Also see Rowan.

663 **Allard Lowenstein:** "Ex-Rep. Lowenstein Killed by a Gunman; Antiwar Leader Shot at Law Office." Chafe covers the murder and the killer's background (449–59) and discusses the Buckley relationship (345–6).

663 **Tom Hayden was charged by federal prosecutors:** For the Chicago Eight and Chicago Seven trials, see Bingham, chapter 8. Also see "The Chicago Eight Trial: Excerpts from the Trial Transcript."

664 **asked him for his business card:** Bingham, 135.

664 **"Abbie Hoffman, Woodstock Nation":** Ibid., 138.

665 **"During the week of the Democratic National Convention":** Walker, 1, also quoted by Bingham, 137n.

666 **Tom Hayden ran for the United States Senate:** For Hayden's career after the summer of 1968, see "Tom Hayden, 1960s Radical, Dead at 76" and "Tom Hayden, Civil Rights and Antiwar Activist Turned Lawmaker, Dies at 76."

667 **"I'm worried that terrible friction":** Hayden.

667 **Eugene and Abigail McCarthy separated:** Abigail McCarthy, 435.

667 **Their daughter Mary:** "Mary McCarthy; Daughter of Ex.-Sen. Eugene McCarthy."

667 **"I wouldn't have chosen":** "Abigail McCarthy Dies at 85."

667 **"I have never been sure":** "Abigail McCarthy: Writer Aided Husband's Political Career."

668 **Eugene McCarthy's life peaked:** The account of McCarthy's life, campaigns, and relationships after 1968 relies on Sandbrook, chapters 11 and 12, with discussion of the McLaughlin relationship, 229–30.

668 **"close friend":** "Paid Notice: Deaths, McLaughlin, Marya."

669 **comfortably paced lecture tour:** Sandbrook, 270–1.

669 **who ran for "Governor of the United States":** "Eugene J. McCarthy, Senate Dove Who Jolted '68 Presidential Race, Dies at 89."

670 **"the worst president":** Hitchens.

671 **"This is a faith based war":** Sandbrook, 291.

671 **"The Bush administration":** "Eugene McCarthy (1916–2005): The Legacy of the Former Senator and Anti-War Presidential Candidate."

671 **"Gene's name will forever be linked":** "Eugene J. McCarthy, Senate Dove Who Jolted '68 Presidential Race, Dies at 89."

672 **"I still think a lot":** "Senator McCarthy Memorial Service."

BIBLIOGRAPHY

"Abigail McCarthy Dies at 85." **Washington Post,** February 3, 2001. www.washingtonpost.com/archive /local/2001/02/03/abigail-McCarthy-dies-at-85 /12869c80-e2b2-4d49-ba07-77f7a6143928.

"Abigail McCarthy: Writer Aided Husband's Political Career." **Los Angeles Times,** February 4, 2001. articles.latimes.com/2001/feb/04/local/me-21042.

"Alabama Governor George Wallace, Public Statement of May 8, 1963." **New York Times,** May 9, 1963.

Alberta, Tim. "The Ideas Made It, But I Didn't." **Politico,** May–June 2017. www.politico.com /magazine/story/2017/04/22/pat-buchanan-trump -president-history-profile-215042.

Allegrini, Robert V. **Chicago's Grand Hotels: The Palmer House, The Drake, and The Hilton Chicago**. Charleston, SC: Arcadia Publishing, 2005.

"An Appeal from Black Americans." **New York Times,** October 25, 1968.

Bass, Thomas A. "The Lives They Lived: Nguyen Van Thieu, B. 1924; Exile on Newberry Street." **New York Times Magazine,** December 30, 2001. www .nytimes.com/2001/12/30/magazine/the-lives-they -lived-nguyen-van-thieu-b-1924-exile-on-newberry -street.html.

Bingham, Clara. **Witness to the Revolution**. New York: Random House, 2016.

"Biography." Patrick J. Buchanan Official Website. buchanan.org/blog/biography.

Blair, Gwenda. **The Trumps: Three Generations of Builders and a Presidential Candidate**. New York: Simon & Schuster, 2001.

Blum, Edward J., and Paul Harvey. "How (George) Romney Championed Civil Rights and Challenged His Church." **Atlantic,** August 13, 2012. www .theatlantic.com/national/archive/2012/08/how -george-romney-championed-civil-rights-and -challenged-his-church/261073/.

Bowers, John W., Donovan J. Ochs, Richard J. Jensen, and David P. Schulz. **The Rhetoric of Agitation and Control**. Long Grove, IL: Waveland Press, 2009.

Branch, Taylor. **At Canaan's Edge: America in the King Years, 1965–68**. New York: Simon & Schuster, 2006.

Brownell, Kathryn Cramer. **Showbiz Politics: Hollywood in American Political Life**. Chapel Hill: University of North Carolina Press, 2014.

Buchanan, Patrick. "A Crossroads in Our Country's History." 4President. www.4president.org/speeches /buchanan1992announcement.htm.

———. "Are Liberals Anti-WASP?" **WorldNetDaily**, May 13, 2010. www.wnd.com/2010/05/153417/.

———. "Why Do the Neocons Hate Dixie So?" **The American Cause,** November 26, 2003. www .theamericancause.org/pathatedixie.htm.

Buckley, William F., and Gore Vidal. **Buckley vs. Vidal: The Historic 1968 ABC News Debates.** Memphis, TN: Devault-Graves Digital Editions, 2015.

"The Buckley vs. Vidal Debates: The Original Knock-down, Drag-out TV." **Washington Post,** August 5, 2015. www.washingtonpost.com/lifestyle/style/the -buckley-vs-vidal-debates-the-original-knock-down -drag-out-tv/2015/08/05/a8fac4e6-3a21-11e5-9c2d -ed991d848c48_story.html.

"The Busboy Who Cradled a Dying RFK Has Finally Stepped Out of the Past." **Los Angeles Times,** August 29, 2015. www.latimes.com/local/california /la-me-0830-lopez-romero-20150829-column.html.

Calamur, Krishnadev. "A Short History of 'America First.'" **Atlantic,** January 21, 2017. www.theatlantic .com/politics/archive/2017/01/trump-america-first /514037/.

Cannato, Vincent J. **The Ungovernable City: John Lindsay and His Struggle to Save New York.** New York: Basic Books, 2001.

"Carter Leads Tributes as Thousands Pass by Coffin in Rotunda." **New York Times,** January 15, 1978.

"CBS News Special Report: The Funeral of Martin Luther King, Jr." Paley Center. www .paleycenter.org/collection/item/?q=charles+kuralt &p=9&item=T81:0796.

Chafe, William H. **Never Stop Running: Allard Lowenstein and the Struggle to Save American Liberalism.** Princeton, NJ: Princeton University Press, 1998.

Chennault, Anna. **The Education of Anna.** New York: Times Books, 1980.

Chester, Lewis, Godfrey Hodgson, and Bruce Page. **An American Melodrama: The Presidential Campaign of 1968.** New York: Viking Press, 1969.

"The Chicago Eight Trial: Excerpts from the Trial Transcript." Famous Trials. famous-trials.com /chicago8/1335-chi7-trial.

"Chicago Journal: Syntax Is a Loser in Mayoral Race." **New York Times,** February 21, 1989. www .nytimes.com/1989/02/21/us/chicago-journal-syntax -is-a-loser-in-mayoral-race.html.

"Chief Parker's Time Is Past." **Los Angeles Times,** April, 19, 2009. articles.latimes.com/2009/apr/19 /opinion/ed-parker19.

"'Choice' Offered by Rockefeller as He Joins Race." **New York Times,** April 30, 1968.

Clarke, Thurston. **The Last Campaign.** New York: Henry Holt, 2008.

Cohen, Adam, and Elizabeth Taylor. **American Pharaoh: Richard J. Daley: His Battle for Chicago and the Nation.** New York: Little, Brown, 2000.

Congressional Record: Proceedings and Debates of the United States Congress, Volume 113, Part 19. U.S. Government Printing Office, 1967.

Cummings, Richard. **The Pied Piper: Allard K. Lowenstein and the Liberal Dream**. New York: Grove Press, 1985.

"Curtis Gans, 77, Is Dead; Worked to Defeat President Johnson." **New York Times,** March 16, 2015. www .nytimes.com/2015/03/17/us/curtis-gans-77-is-dead -worked-to-depose-president-johnson.html.

"Curtis Gans, Political Analyst and 'Dump Johnson' Organizer, Dies at 77." **Washington Post,** March 16, 2015.

Dallek, Robert. **Flawed Giant: Lyndon Johnson and His Times, 1961–1973**. New York: Oxford University Press, 1999.

———. **Lone Star Rising: Lyndon Johnson and His Times, 1908–1960**. New York: Oxford University Press, 1991.

Daniel, Josiah. "Case Changed History and Defined 'Lawyering.'" **Texas Lawbook**, July 26, 2012. www.velaw.com/uploadedFiles/VEsite/Resources /DefinedLawyering2012.pdf.

Davis, James Kirkpatrick. **Assault on the Left: The FBI and the Sixties Antiwar Movement**. Westport, CT: Praeger, 1997.

"The Democratic National Convention, 1968" (excerpt). CBS News. YouTube video, 1:37. Posted April 30, 2016. www.youtube.com/watch?v=UxXoj NYtf04.

"Democrats Delay Fight on the Vietnam Plank; Kennedy Rejects Draft." **New York Times,** August 28, 1968.

"Economic and Social Bill of Rights." King Center, February 6, 1968. www.thekingcenter.org/archive /document/economic-and-social-bill-rights.

"Edmund S. Muskie, 81, Dies; Maine Senator and a Power on the National Scene." **New York Times,** March 27, 1996. www.nytimes.com/1996/03/27 /us/edmund-s-muskie-81-dies-maine-senator-and-a -power-on-the-national-scene.html.

Edwards, Anne. **The Reagans: Portrait of a Marriage**. New York: St. Martin's Press, 2003.

Edwards, George C., Martin P. Wattenberg, and Robert P. Lineberry. **Government in America: People, Politics and Policy** (Brief Study Edition). Hoboken, NJ: Pearson Education, 2004.

Ellsberg, Daniel. **Secrets: A Memoir of Vietnam and the Pentagon Papers**. New York: Penguin Books, 2002.

"Eugene J. McCarthy, Senate Dove Who Jolted '68 Presidential Race, Dies at 89." **New York Times,** December 12, 2005. www.nytimes.com/2005/12/12 /obituaries/us/eugene-j-McCarthy-senate-dove-who -jolted-68-presidential-race.html.

"Eugene McCarthy, Who Galvanized a Generation of War Opponents, Dies." Minnesota Public Radio, December 10, 2005. news.minnesota.publicradio.org /features/2005/06/15_olsond_geneMcCarthy/.

"Eugene McCarthy (1916–2005): The Legacy of the Former Senator and Anti-War Presidential Candidate." Democracy Now, January 18, 2006. www.democracynow.org/2006/1/18/eugene _McCarthy_1916_2005_the_legacy.

Evans, Thomas W. **The Education of Ronald Reagan: The General Electric Years and the Untold Story of His Conversion to Conservatism**. New York: Columbia University Press, Studies in Contemporary American History, 2008.

"Excerpted Watergate-Related Conversations." Richard Nixon Presidential Library and Museum. www .nixonlibrary.gov/forresearchers/find/tapes/excerpts /watergate.php.

"Ex-Rep. Lowenstein Killed by a Gunman; Antiwar Leader Shot at Law Office." **New York Times,** March 15, 1980.

Facts, Volumes 18–22. Anti-Defamation League of B'nai B'rith, 1968.

Farber, David. **Chicago '68**. Chicago, IL: University of Chicago Press, 1988.

Farrell, John A. **Richard Nixon: The Life**. New York: Doubleday, 2017.

"For Ford, Pardon Decision Was Always Clear-Cut." **New York Times,** December 29, 2006. www.nytimes .com/2006/12/29/washington/29pardon.html.

"48 Are Involved: Aides Won't Say How Serious President Is on Clemency Move." **New York Times,** September 11, 1974.

Frank, Jeffrey. "When Leonard Garment Met Richard Nixon." **New Yorker,** July 18, 2013. www.newyorker .com/news/news-desk/when-leonard-garment-met -richard-nixon.

Frady, Marshall. **Wallace: The Classic Portrait of Alabama Governor George Wallace.** New York: Random House, 1996.

Garcia, Manuel, Jr. **Fifty-Year Look Back, 1963–2013;** Part II: **1968–2013.** Swans Commentary. www .swans.com/library/art19/mgarci76.html.

General Electric Theater. Times Past Old Time Radio. otrarchive.blogspot.com/2010/07/general-electric -theater.html.

"George A. Smathers, 93; Former Florida Senator." **Washington Post,** January 21, 2007. www .washingtonpost.com/wp-dyn/content/article/2007 /01/20/AR2007012000767.html.

"George Wallace, Segregation Symbol, Dies at 79." **New York Times,** September 14, 1998. www.nytimes .com/1998/09/14/us/george-wallace-segregation -symbol-dies-at-79.html.

"George Wallace: Settin' the Woods on Fire." **American Experience,** April 23, 2000.

Goodwin, Doris Kearns. **The Fitzgeralds and the Kennedys.** New York: Simon & Schuster, 1987.

————. **Lyndon Johnson and the American Dream.** St. Martin's Griffin, 1991.

Greenberg, David. "How Roger Ailes Created Modern Conservatism." **Politico,** July 20, 2016. www.politico

.com/magazine/story/2016/07/roger-ailes-fox-donald
-trump-2016-conservatism-214076.

"H. R. Haldeman, Nixon Aide Who Had Central
Role in Watergate, Is Dead at 67." **New York Times,**
November 13, 1993. www.nytimes.com/1993/11/13
/obituaries/h-r-haldeman-nixon-aide-who-had-central
-role-in-watergate-is-dead-at-67.html.

Hamill, Pete. "Two Minutes to Midnight." **Village
Voice,** June 13, 1968.

Hamilton, Nigel. **JFK: Reckless Youth.** New York:
Random House, 1992.

Harris, George T. **Romney's Way: A Man and an
Idea.** New Orleans, LA: Garrett County Digital,
2012.

Hatfield, Mark O. "Walter F. Mondale." Senate
Historical Office. www.senate.gov/artandhistory
/history/resources/pdf/walter_mondale.pdf.

Hayden, Tom. "I Used to Support Bernie, but Then I
Changed My Mind." **Nation,** April 12, 2016.

———, and Staughton Lynd. **The Other Side.** New
York: New American Library, 1967.

Helen Gahagan Douglas Project, Volume IV. Regional
Oral History Office, University of California.
archive.org/stream/helengahaganpro04dougrich
/helengahaganpro04dougrich_djvu.txt.

Hentoff, Nat. "A Craving for Equal Justice:
Rescuing Martin Luther King Jr." www.eisen
howerfoundation.org/docs/VillageVoice_Rescuing
MartinLutherKingJr.pdf.

"Hey! Hey! LBJ." Vietnam War Song Project. YouTube video, 2:14. Posted June 26, 2012. www.youtube.com/watch?v=J_krQH_zZqE.

Hirschfield, Robert S., ed. **The Power of the Presidency: Concepts and Controversy.** New York: Aldine Transaction, 2012.

Hitchens, Christopher. "Peanut Envy." **Slate,** May 21, 2007. www.slate.com/articles/news_and_politics/fighting_words/2007/05/peanut_envy.html.

"How Bobby Kennedy Won the '68 Indiana Primary." **Newsweek,** May 19, 1968. www.newsweek.com/how-bobby-kennedy-won-68-indiana-primary-207076.

"How Donald Trump Came Up with 'Make America Great Again.'" **Washington Post,** January 18, 2017. www.washingtonpost.com/politics/how-donald-trump-came-up-with-make-america-great-again/2017/01/17/fb6acf5e-dbf7-11e6-ad42-f3375f271c9c_story.html.

"Hubert Humphrey 1948 Civil Rights Speech." American Speeches. YouTube video, 9:51. Posted January 25, 2009. www.youtube.com/watch?v=8nwIdIUVFm4.

Hughes, Ken. **Chasing Shadows**. Charlottesville: University of Virginia Press, 2014.

"Humphrey Calls LBJ After Losing to Nixon: Nov. 6, 1968, 11:32 A.M." Miller Center. YouTube video, 3:46. Posted on November 7, 2012. www.youtube.com/watch?v=YttmffiWyjA.

Humphrey, Hubert H. "Remarks Declaring Candidacy for the Democratic Presidential Nomination."

April 27, 1968. American Presidency Project. www
.presidency.ucsb.edu/ws/?pid=77814.

"Humphrey's 1968 DNC Acceptance Speech."
YouTube video, 37:02. Posted February 12, 2012.
www.youtube.com/watch?v=HJ-659b76h4.

Hunt, Andrew E. **David Dellinger: The Life and
Times of a Nonviolent Revolutionary.** New York:
New York University Press, 2006.

"In Tapes, Nixon Rails About Jews and Blacks." **New
York Times,** December 10, 2010. www.nytimes.com
/2010/12/11/us/politics/11nixon.html.

"International Visitors to Viet Nam in December
and 12 Months of 2015." Viet Nam National
Administration of Tourism. vietnamtourism.gov.vn
/english/index.php/items/9968.

"Interview with Andrew Young, Part 1." Coursera.
www.coursera.org/learn/nonviolence/lecture/JjiQc
/interview-with-andrew-young-part-1.

"Interview with Senator Eugene McCarthy, 1968
Democratic Party Contender." National Security
Archive, Episode 13, "Make Love, Not War."
nsarchive.gwu.edu/coldwar/interviews/episode-13
/McCarthy1.html.

"JFK Assassination: Cronkite Informs a Shocked
Nation." **CBS News Sunday Morning**. YouTube
video, 1:50. Posted November 17, 2013. www
.youtube.com/watch?v=6PXORQE5-CY.

"John D. Ehrlichman, Nixon Aide Jailed for Watergate,
Dies at 73." **New York Times,** February 16,
1999. www.nytimes.com/1999/02/16/us/john-d

-ehrlichman-nixon-aide-jailed-for-watergate-dies-at
-73.html.

"John Dean, Who Worked for Nixon, Sizes Up
Trump." **New York Times,** April 13, 2017. www
.nytimes.com/2017/04/13/style/john-dean-richard-
-nixon-watergate-donald-trump.html.

"John N. Mitchell Dies at 75; Major Figure in
Watergate." **New York Times,** November 10, 1988.
www.nytimes.com/1988/11/10/obituaries/john-n
-mitchell-dies-at-75-major-figure-in-watergate.html.

"John V. Lindsay, Mayor and Maverick, Dies at
79." **New York Times,** December 21, 2000. www
.nytimes.com/2000/12/21/nyregion/john-v-lindsay
-mayor-and-maverick-dies-at-79.html.

"Joseph Rauh Jr., Groundbreaking Civil Liberties Lawyer,
Dies at 81." **New York Times,** September 5, 1992.
www.nytimes.com/1992/09/05/us/joseph-rauh-jr
-groundbreaking-civil-liberties-lawyer-dies-at-81.html.

"Journalist, Democratic Activist Blair Clark Dies."
Washington Post, June 8, 2000.

"Judge, Darwin Lee." P.O.W. Network. www
.pownetwork.org/bios/j/j052.htm.

"June 5, 1968: RFK's California Victory Speech." ABC
News. abcnews.go.com/Archives/video/rfk-california
-victory-speech-assassination-10118429.

Kaiser, Robert Blair. **R.F.K. Must Die!** New York:
Overlook Press, 2008.

Katzenbach, Nicholas. **Some of It Was Fun.** New
York: W. W. Norton, 2008.

Kennedy, Edward M. "Address at the Public Memorial Service for Robert F. Kennedy." June 8, 1968. American Rhetoric. www.americanrhetoric.com /speeches/ekennedytributetorfk.html.

"Kennedy Attacks Vietnam Policy; Asks End of Hate." **New York Times**, August 22, 1968.

"Kennedy Pledges to Quit if Beaten in California Bid." **New York Times**, May 30, 1968.

Kennedy, Robert F. "Remarks on the Assassination of Martin Luther King, Jr." April 4, 1968. American Rhetoric. www.americanrhetoric.com/speeches /rfkonmlkdeath.html.

———. **To Seek a Newer World**. Garden City, NY: Doubleday, 1968.

"Kenneth Clark, Oral History" (Session 9), p. 391, **Notable New Yorkers**. www.columbia.edu/cu/lweb /digital/collections/nny///clarkk/transcripts/clarkk _1_9_391.html.

Kerry, John. "Statement Before the Senate Foreign Relations Committee." April 22, 1971. American Rhetoric. www.americanrhetoric.com/speeches/john kerrysenateforeignrelationsvietnamwar.htm.

King, Martin Luther, Jr. "Beyond Vietnam: A Time to Break Silence." April 4, 1967. YouTube video, 56:48. Posted January 15, 2011. www.youtube.com /watch?v=OC1Ru2p8OfU.

———. **The Crisis in America's Cities**. August 15, 1967. King Center. www.thekingcenter.org/archive /document/crisis-americas-cities.

———. "I've Been to the Mountaintop." April 3, 1968. American Rhetoric. www.americanrhetoric .com/speeches/mlkivebeentothemountaintop.htm.

"The Last Word with Lawrence O'Donnell," January 7, 2016 (transcript). www.msnbc.com/transcripts/the -last-word/2016-01-07.

"LBJ Calls on Congress to Enact Voting Rights Bill, March 15, 1965." Politico, March 15, 2011. www.politico.com/story/2011/03/lbj -calls-on-congress-to-enact-voting-rights-bill-march -15-1965-051248.

"LBJ Will Not Seek Re-Election." ABC News. abcnews .go.com/Archives/video/march-31-1968-lbj-seek -election-9626199.

Lehrer, Tom. "Whatever Became of Hubert?" Metrolyics. www.metrolyrics.com/whatever -became-of-hubert-lyrics-tom-lehrer.html.

Lesher, Stephan. George Wallace: American Populist. Cambridge, MA: Perseus Publishing, 1994.

Ling, Peter J. John F. Kennedy. London: Routledge, 2013.

"Longtime Democratic Operative Dies." Politico, October 24, 2014. www.politico.com/story/2014/10 /frank-mankiewicz-dies-112168.

"Loving v. Virginia (1967)," No. 395. caselaw.findlaw .com/us-supreme-court/388/1.html.

"Lyndon Johnson: Report on the Gulf of Tonkin Incident." Miller Center. YouTube video, 5:55. Posted June 13, 2008. www.youtube.com/watch?v=Dx8 -ffiYyzA.

"Lyndon Johnson and Everett Dirksen on 2 November 1968." Presidential Recordings, Digital Edition. Miller Center. prde.upress.virginia.edu/conversations /4006123.

"Lyndon Johnson and Richard Nixon on 3 November 1968." Presidential Recordings, Digital Edition. Miller Center. prde.upress.virginia.edu/conversations /4006126.

Mailer, Norman. **The Armies of the Night: History as a Novel, the Novel as History.** New York: Plume, 1995.

———. **Miami and the Siege of Chicago: An Informal History of the Republican and Democratic Conventions of 1968.** New York: Random House, 2016.

Mann, James. "Close-Up: Young Rumsfeld." **Atlantic,** November 2003. www.theatlantic.com/magazine /archive/2003/11/close-up-young-rumsfeld/302824/.

"Martinis, Steak and History." **Washington Post,** October 7, 2007. www.washingtonpost.com/wp-dyn /content/article/2007/10/04/AR2007100402081.html.

"Mary McCarthy; Daughter of Ex.-Sen. Eugene McCarthy." **Los Angeles Times,** August 1, 1990. articles.latimes.com/1990-08-01/news/mn-1556_1 _eugene-McCarthy.

Mattson, Kevin. **Just Plain Dick: Richard Nixon's Checkers Speech and the "Rocking, Socking" Election of 1952.** New York: Bloomsbury, 2012.

"Maurice Stans Dies at 90; Led Nixon Commerce Dept." **New York Times,** April 15, 1998. www

.nytimes.com/1998/04/15/us/maurice-stans-dies-at
-90-led-nixon-commerce-dept.html.

McCarthy, Abigail. **Private Faces, Public Faces**. New York: Curtis Books, 1972.

McCarthy, Eugene. **Parting Shots from My Brittle Bow: Reflections on American Politics and Life**. Golden, CO: Fulcrum Publishing, 2004.

———. **The Year of the People**. Garden City, NY: Doubleday, 1969.

"McCarthy Backs Humphrey Race." **New York Times**, October 30, 1968.

"McCarthy Calls Rivals Ill-Equipped to Avoid Future Vietnams." **New York Times**, May 24, 1968.

"McCarthy Jibes at Both Rivals." **New York Times**, May 23, 1968.

"McCarthy Pledges Drive Will Go On." **New York Times**, August 30, 1968.

"McCarthy Would Favor Humphrey over Kennedy." **New York Times**, May 22, 1968.

McGinnis, Joseph. **The Selling of the President**. New York: Trident Press,1969.

"McGovern Opens Presidential Bid with Peace Plea." **New York Times**, August 11, 1968.

"**Meet the Press**: America's Press Conference of the Air." Vol. 8, no. 30, August 23, 1964. www2.mnhs .org/library/findaids/00442/pdfa/00442-01342.pdf.

Merkley, Paul Charles. **American Presidents, Religion, and Israel: The Heirs of Cyrus**. Westport, CT: Greenwood Publishing Group, 2004.

Miller Center, University of Virginia. "The Secret White House Tapes." millercenter.org/the-presidency /secret-white-house-tapes.

"More Trouble at Fox News: Ailes Faces New Sexual Claims and O'Reilly Loses Two Advertisers." **New York Times,** April 3, 2017. www.nytimes.com /2017/04/03/business/media/fox-news-roger-ailes -harassment-suit.html.

Morris, Edmund. **Dutch: A Memoir of Ronald Reagan.** New York: Modern Library, 1999.

Moynihan, Daniel Patrick. **Moynihan: A Portrait in Letters of an American Visionary.** New York: Public Affairs, 2010.

"Mrs. Romney Had a Hunch of Pullout." **Holland Evening Sentinel** (UPI), February 29, 1968.

"Nebraska Gives 53% to Kennedy." **New York Times,** May 15, 1968.

Newfield, Jack. **RFK: A Memoir.** New York: Nation Books, 2003.

"New Tapes Reveal Depth of Nixon's Anti-Semitism." **Washington Post,** October 6, 1999. www .washingtonpost.com/wp-srv/politics/daily/oct99 /nixon6.htm.

"A New Way to Scuttle Eugene McCarthy." **Eugene Register-Guard,** August 12, 1968.

"Nguyen Ngoc Loan, 67, Dies; Executed Viet Cong Prisoner." **New York Times,** July 16, 1998. www .nytimes.com/1998/07/16/world/nguyen-ngoc -loan-67-dies-executed-viet-cong-prisoner.html.

"Nguyen Van Thieu, 78; S. Vietnam's President." **Los Angeles Times,** October 1, 2001. articles.latimes .com/2001/oct/01/local/me-52050.

"Nguyen Van Thieu Is Dead at 76; Last President of South Vietnam." **New York Times,** October 1, 2001. www.nytimes.com/2001/10/01/us/nguyen-van-thieu -is-dead-at-76-last-president-of-south-vietnam.html.

"1968: Nixon vs. Humphrey vs. Wallace." Living Room Candidate: Presidential Campaign Commercials 1952–2016. Museum of the Moving Image. www.livingroomcandidate.org/commercials /1968.

Nistler, Mike. "JFK and Eugene McCarthy." Newspaper Archive of Tri-County News, November 20, 2013. tricountynews.mn/newsx/local -history/34811-jfk-and-eugene-McCarthy.

"Nixon Think Tank Stalls over Anti-Semitic Letters." **Los Angeles Times,** April 15, 1997. articles.latimes .com/1997-04-15/news/mn-48906_1_nixon-center.

Nixon White House Tapes—Online. Richard Nixon Presidential Library and Museum. www.nixonlibrary .gov/virtuallibrary/tapeexcerpts/index.php.

"Notes of Meeting (39)." **Foreign Relations of the United States, 1964–1968,** Volume VI, **Vietnam, January–August 1968**. history.state.gov /historicaldocuments/frus1964-68v06/d39.

"Notes of Meeting (239)." **Foreign Relations of the United States, 1964–1968,** Volume V, **Vietnam, 1967**. history.state.gov/historicaldocuments/frus1964 -68v05/d239.

"Notes of Meeting (327)." **Foreign Relations of the United States, 1964–1968, Volume VI, Vietnam, January–August 1968.** history.state.gov /historicaldocuments/frus1964-68v06/d327.

" 'No Vacancies' for Blacks: How Donald Trump Got His Start, and Was First Accused of Bias." **New York Times,** August 27, 2016. www.nytimes.com/2016/08 /28/us/politics/donald-trump-housing-race.html.

Oberdorfer, Don. **Tet! The Turning Point in the Vietnam War.** New York: Doubleday, 1971.

"Oregon Holds Last Primary for President." **Chicago Tribune,** March 10, 1968. archives.chicagotribune .com/1968/03/10/page/14/article/oregon-holds-last -primary-for-president.

"Paid Notice: Deaths, McLaughlin, Marya." **New York Times,** September 16, 1998. www.nytimes.com/1998 /09/16/classified/paid-notice-deaths-mclaughlin -marya.html.

Palermo, Joseph A. "Here's What RFK Did in California in 1968." **Huffington Post,** January 10, 2008. www.huffingtonpost.com/joseph-a-palermo /heres-what-rfk-did-in-cal_b_80931.html.

"Pat Buchanan on NBC's **Today Show,** Thursday, November 9, 2000." American Presidency Project. www.presidency.ucsb.edu/showflorida2000 .php?fileid=buchanan11-09.

Patrick J. Buchanan Official Website. buchanan.org /blog/.

"Peace Prayer of Saint Francis." Loyola Press: A Jesuit Ministry. www.loyolapress.com/our-catholic-faith

/prayer/traditional-catholic-prayers/saints-prayers
/peace-prayer-of-saint-francis.

"Perhaps an Earnest Hunt for Pertinence Would Be
More Helpful Than Debates." **New York Times,**
June 3, 1968.

Perlstein, Rick. **Before the Storm: Barry Goldwater
and the Unmaking of the American Consensus.**
New York: Nation Books, 2009.

———. **Nixonland: The Rise of a President and the
Fracturing of America.** New York: Scribner, 2008.

Pileggi, Nicholas. "Inside Lindsay's Head." **New York
Magazine,** January 4, 1971.

Pilkington, Ed. "The Night Bobby Died." **Guardian,**
January 12, 2007. www.theguardian.com/film/2007
/jan/13/features.weekend.

"President-Elect Richard Nixon Declares Victory in
1968." Richard Nixon Foundation. YouTube video,
13:15. Posted August 14, 2012. www.youtube.com
/watch?v=v3xT-lSIC7A.

"President Eulogizes Former Mentor—William
Fulbright." **Los Angeles Times**, February 18, 1995.
articles.latimes.com/1995-02-18/news/mn-33379_1_j
-william-fulbright.

"President Nixon Farewell to Staff." C-Span, August 9,
1974. www.c-span.org/video/?320754-1/president
-nixon-farewell-staff.

"The President's News Conference, February 2, 1967."
American Presidency Project. www.presidency.ucsb
.edu/ws/?pid=28383.

"The President's News Conference Held on His
    60th Birthday at Austin, Texas, August 27, 1968."
    American Presidency Project. www.presidency.ucsb
    .edu/ws/index.php?pid=29094.
"Press Conference of Senator Eugene J. McCar-
    thy, Senate Caucus Room, Washington, D.C.,
    November 30, 1967." 4President.org. www.4president
    .org/speeches/McCarthy1968announcement.htm.
"The Promised Land (1967–1968)," transcript.
    "Eyes on the Prize: America's Civil Rights
    Movement, 1954–1985." www.pbs.org/wgbh//amex
    /eyesontheprize/about/pt_204.html.
"Rand's Influence on Alan Greenspan." Objectivism
    Reference Center. www.noblesoul.com/orc/bio
    /turbulence.html.
Reagan, Ronald. "A Time for Choosing." October 27,
    1964. Reagan Foundation. YouTube video,
    29:32. Posted April 2, 2009. www.youtube.com
    /watch?v=qXBswFfh6AY.
"Reagan Was a Subject of '60s Screen Inquiry." New
    York Times, September 21, 1986. www.nytimes.com
    /1986/09/21/us/reagan-was-a-subject-of-60-s-screen
    -inquiry.html.
Reeve, Elspeth. "Some Newly Uncovered Nixon
    Comments on the Subjects of Jews and Black
    People." Atlantic, August 21, 2013. www.theatlantic
    .com/politics/archive/2013/08/some-new
    -comments-richard-nixon-subject-jews-and-blacks
    /311870/.

Relyea, Harold C., and L. Elaine Halchin. **Informing Congress: The Role of the Executive Branch in Times of War.** New York: Novinka Books, 2003.

"Remarks, Vice President Hubert H. Humphrey," August 19, 1968. www2.mnhs.org/library/findaids /00442/pdfa/00442-02683.pdf.

"Remarks at a Dinner of the Veterans of Foreign Wars." American Presidency Project. www.presidency .ucsb.edu/ws/?pid=28730.

"Remarks by Attorney General Robert F. Kennedy Before the National Congress of American Indians." Department of Justice. Speeches of Attorney General Robert F. Kennedy. www.justice.gov/sites/default /files/ag/legacy/2011/01/20/09-13-1963.pdf.

Ribicoff, Abraham. "Speech Nominating George McGovern for the U.S. Presidency." August 28, 1968. American Rhetoric. www.americanrhetoric .com/speeches/abrahamribicoff1968dnc.htm.

"Richard G. Kleindienst, Figure in Watergate Era, Dies at 76." **New York Times,** February 4, 2000. www.nytimes.com/2000/02/04/us/richard -g-kleindienst-figure-in-watergate-era-dies-at-76 .html.

"Richard M. Nixon: 1962 California GOP Concession Speech." American Rhetoric. www.americanrhetoric .com/mp3clips/politicalspeeches/richardnixonconcess ion3242343432.mp3.

Richardson, James. **Willie Brown: A Biography.** Berkeley: University of California Press, 1996.

Risen, Clay. **A Nation on Fire: America in the Wake of the King Assassination**. Hoboken, NJ: John Wiley, 2009.

Rising, George. **Clean for Gene: Eugene McCarthy's 1968 Presidential Campaign**. Westport, CT: Praeger, 1997.

"Robert Kennedy Took On Kern County Sheriff." UFW. YouTube video, 1:34. Posted August 18, 2015. www.youtube.com/watch?v=G66myWragTg.

Roberts, Sam, ed. **America's Mayor: John V. Lindsay and the Reinvention of New York**. New York: Museum of the City of New York/Columbia University Press, 2010.

"Rosey Grier on the Kennedy Assassination." Pioneers of Television. www.pbs.org/wnet/pioneers -of-television/video/rosey-grier-on-the-kennedy -assassination/.

Rowan, Carl T. "The Rehabilitation of George Wallace." **Washington Post,** September 5, 1991. www.washingtonpost.com/wp-srv/politics/daily /sept98/wallace090591.htm.

Royko, Mike. **Boss: Richard J. Daley of Chicago.** New York: E. P. Dutton, 1971.

Rubin, Jerry. **Do It: Scenarios of the Revolution.** New York: Simon & Schuster, 1970.

———. "Can We Survive Bobby?" **Berkeley Barb,** March 29–April 4, 1968. voices.revealdigital.com/cgi -bin/independentvoices?a=d&d=BFBJFGD196803 29.1.2.

————. "Inside the Great Pigasus Plot." **Ramparts,** December 1969. www.unz.org/Pub/Ramparts -1969dec-00010.

Rudd, Mark. **Underground: My Life with SDS and the Weathermen.** New York: HarperCollins, 2010.

Sandbrook, Dominic. **Eugene McCarthy and the Rise and Fall of Postwar American Liberalism.** New York: Anchor Books, 2004.

Safire, William. "Secret Plan: Don't Be Agog at Demagoguing." **New York Times Magazine,** May 21, 2000. partners.nytimes.com/library /magazine/home/20000521mag-onlanguage.html.

Schlesinger, Arthur, Jr. **Robert Kennedy and His Times.** Boston: Houghton Mifflin, 1978.

Schmitz, David. **The Tet Offensive: Politics, War, and Public Opinion.** Lanham, MD: Rowman & Littlefield, 2005.

Schroeder, Alan. **Presidential Debates: Risky Business on the Campaign Trail.** New York: Columbia University Press, 2016.

"Senator McCarthy Memorial Service." C-Span, January 14, 2006. www.c-span.org/video/?190739-1 /senator-McCarthy-memorial-service.

"Senator McGovern Ready to Run Against Humphrey." **New York Times,** August 10, 1968.

"Shoot to Kill, Shoot to Maim." **Chicago Reader,** April 4, 2002. www.chicagoreader.com/chicago /shoot-to-kill---shoot-to-maim/Content?oid= 908163.

Smith, Richard Norton. **On His Own Terms: A Life of Nelson Rockefeller**. New York: Random House, 2014.

Solberg, Carl. **Hubert Humphrey: A Biography**. St. Paul, MN: Borealis Books, 1984.

Sorley, Lewis. **Westmoreland: The General Who Lost Vietnam**. Boston: Houghton Mifflin Harcourt, 2011.

"Speechwriter Warns Nixon Not to Visit Martin Luther King's Widow; Calls King 'Divisive' and 'a Fraud.'" History Commons. www.historycommons.org/context.jsp?item=a0469kingbuchanan.

"Stokely Carmichael: Passive Boycotts." Black Talk Radio. YouTube video, 1:48. Posted April 23, 2012. www.youtube.com/watch?v=Q_QbWDoJBvk.

Stout, Richard. **People: The Story of the Grass-Roots Movement That Found Eugene McCarthy**. New York: Harper & Row, 1970.

Stricherz, Mark. **Why the Democrats Are Blue: Secular Liberalism and the Decline of the People's Party**. New York: Encounter Books, 2007.

"Strom Thurmond, Foe of Integration, Dies at 100." **New York Times**, June 27, 2003. www.nytimes.com/2003/06/27/us/strom-thurmond-foe-of-integration-dies-at-100.html.

"Testimony of Allen Ginsberg," December 12, 1969. In "The Chicago Eight Trial: Excerpts from the Trial Transcript," famous-trials.com/chicago8/1324-ginsberg.

"Text of President Johnson's Broadcast to the Nation Announcing a Bombing Halt," transcript. **New York Times,** November 1, 1968. www.nytimes.com/books /98/04/12/specials/johnson-bombhalt.html.

"Thieu Says Saigon Cannot Join Paris Talks Under Present Plan." **New York Times,** November 2, 1968.

Thomas, Evan. **Being Nixon: A Man Divided.** New York: Random House, 2015.

———. **Robert Kennedy: His Life.** New York: Simon and Schuster, 2000.

"The Time Bomb That Exploded in Cicero: Segregated Housing's Inevitable Dividend." **Commentary,** November 1, 1951. www .commentarymagazine.com/articles/the-time -bomb-that-exploded-in-cicerosegregated-housings -inevitable-dividend/.

"A Time to Remember: Turmoil of Chicago." **New York Daily News,** August 25, 1996.

"Tom Hayden, 1960s Radical, Dead at 76." **New American,** October 24, 2016. www .thenewamerican.com/index.php?option=com _k2&view=item&id=24467:tom-hayden-1960s -radical-dead-at-76&Itemid=627.

"Tom Hayden, Civil Rights and Antiwar Activist Turned Lawmaker, Dies at 76." **New York Times,** October 24, 2016. www.nytimes.com/2016/10/25/us /tom-hayden-dead.html.

Toussaint, Kristin. "Remembering the Last Marine to Die in Vietnam, 40 Years After the Fall of Saigon." Boston.com, April 30, 2015. www.boston.com

/news/local-news/2015/04/30/remembering-the
-last-marine-to-die-in-vietnam-40-years-after-the
-fall-of-saigon.

"Transcript of the President's News Conference on
Foreign and Domestic Matters." **New York Times,**
November 5, 1966.

"2,000 Clerics Ask 3-Day Peace Fast." **New York
Times,** February 1, 1967.

Tye, Larry. **Bobby Kennedy: The Making of a Liberal
Icon.** New York: Random House, 2016.

"The Unlikely No. 2." **Time,** August 16, 1968.

"Urges a 'Harsh Judgment' on U.S. Policy in Vietnam."
Des Moines Register, February 2, 1967.

U.S. Department of State Archive. **Foreign Relations
of the United States, 1964–1968,** Volume VI,
Vietnam, January–August 1968. 2001-2009.state
.gov/r/pa/ho/frus/johnsonlb/vi/14376.htm.

Valentine, Tom. "How Many People Died in the
Vietnam War?" Vietnam War, April 11, 2014.
thevietnamwar.info/how-many-people-died-in-the
-vietnam-war/.

"The Vietnam War: Military Statistics." Gilder Lehrman
Institute. www.gilderlehrman.org/history-by-era
/seventies/resources/vietnam-war-military-statistics.

Vietnam War Song Project. rateyourmusic.com/list
/JBrummer/vietnam-war-song-project-1/.

Walker, Daniel. **Rights in Conflict: The Violent
Confrontation of Demonstrators and Police in the
Parks and Streets of Chicago During the Week of
the Democratic National Convention of 1968; A**

Report Submitted to the National Commission on the Causes and Prevention of Violence. New York: Bantam Books, 1968.

"Was Nixon Sabotaged by TV Makeup Artists?" Chicago Daily News, September 27, 1960.

White, Theodore. The Making of the President 1968. New York: HarperCollins, 2010.

Willbanks, James H. The Tet Offensive: A Concise History. New York: Columbia University Press, 2007.

"William Buckley vs. Gore Vidal." YouTube video, 1:10. Posted August 15, 2007. www.youtube.com /watch?v YymnxoQnf8.

"William F. Buckley: Bush Will Be Judged on 'Failed' Iraq War." Truthdig, posted March 31, 2016. www .truthdig.com/eartotheground/item/20060401 _william_f_buckley_bush_will_be_judged_on _failed_iraq_war.

Wills, Garry. Nixon Agonistes: The Crisis of the Self-Made Man. Boston: Houghton Mifflin, 1969.

Witcover, Jules. 85 Days: The Last Campaign of Robert Kennedy. New York: William Morrow, 1989.

———. The Resurrection of Richard Nixon. New York: G. P. Putnam's Sons, 1970.

———. White Knight: The Rise of Spiro Agnew. New York: Random House, 1972.

"Yippie: Chicago, August 25–30." cf.collectorsweekly .com/uploads/2012/03/yippppp.jpg.

Zimmerman, Robert. Genesis: The Story of Apollo 8. New York: Dell, 1999.

INDEX